James Baird McClure

Garfield

From the Log Cabin to the White House and the Worlds Eurologies

James Baird McClure

Garfield
From the Log Cabin to the White House and the Worlds Eurologies

ISBN/EAN: 9783337128821

Printed in Europe, USA, Canada, Australia, Japan

Cover: Foto ©ninafisch / pixelio.de

More available books at **www.hansebooks.com**

GEN. JAMES A. GARFIELD.

GEN. GARFIELD'S FORMER RESIDENCE AT HIRAM, OHIO.

MRS. JAMES A. GARFIELD.

MARY.   JAMES.   HARRY.   IRWIN.   ABRAM
GENERAL GARFIELD'S CHILDREN.

Entered according to Act of Congress, in the year 1881, by
J. B. McClure & R. S. Rhodes,
In the Office of the Librarian of Congress, at Washington.

Preface.

A new interest now attaches to every incident, and story, and everything that entered into and made up the great life of the immortal Garfield. This volume presents, in an exceedingly interesting manner, all the essential points in the life of the martyred President, including that seemingly saddest of all events, his assassination, over which, it is said, three hundred millions of people mourned. Near the close of the volume will be found the final funeral service on the great "Memorial Day," an event unparralleled in the history of man.

J. B. McCLURE.

Chicago, Oct. 10, 1881.

A

	Page
Anecdote of Gen. Garfield at Murfreesboro, Illustrating a Noble Trait of His Character..................................	130
Anecdote of Garfield's Early Life—His Greatness Anticipated by a Woman in Connection with a Laughable Incident..	35
An Interesting Reminiscence—Garfield and Arthur both School Teachers, in the Same Room at North Pownal, Vermont..	33
An Interesting Story in Connection with the Sick-room—Gen. Garfield as a Reader.................................	41
An Interesting Reminiscence of Garfield's Youth—A Letter He Wrote Twenty-three Years Ago that Helped to Make a College President, and that President Now Reads It to His Students...	119
A Pen Picture of Garfield...................................	34
A Splendid Record—Summary of Garfield's Labors—The Rewards of Industry...................................	49
A Trying Ordeal—In the Hands of the Doctors—Melting Down an "Ague Cake" with Calomel!—How the Crucible (Young Garfield) Endured It—He is Saved by a Kind Mother..	21
Arthur's Letter of Acceptance...............................	153

B

Boyhood of Gen. Garfield—The Farmer Boy on the Towpath—A Tough Time—Good Health and Indomitable Energy Triumphant.................................... 18

C

Chester A. Arthur—Sketch of His Life..................... 150

Col. Garfield's First Great Battle—He Defeats Humphrey Marshall and Wins a Brigadier-Generalship............. 58

Comparative Statement of Ballots........................ 93

Closing Scenes in Garfield's War Record—Why He Left the Army... 66

D

Dignity of American Citizenship—Garfield's Speech in Washington, June 16, 1880..................................... 132

Dying Words of Gen. Garfield's Father—He Leaves His Four Children in Care of His Wife............................ 115

E

Enthusiasm on Fire—Making the Nomination of Gen. Garfield Unanimous at the Chicago Republican Convention—Speeches of Messrs. Conkling, Logan, Beaver, Hale, Pleasants, and Harrison........................... 98

F

First Vote for Garfield in the Chicago Convention—The Man Who Gave It Voted for Zachary Taylor and Abraham Lincoln Under Like Circumstances...................... 107

Full Details of Garfield's Pound Gap Expedition—Strategy and Victory—Battle of Pittsburg Landing, etc........... 59

CONTENTS.

G

Garfield at College—He Graduates with High Honors—His Personal Appearance at This Period that of a Newly Imported Dutchman....................................	27
Garfield a Home—His Residence in Mentor—His Family and His Mother...	42
Garfield in War—How He Volunteered to Put Down the Rebellion, and was Promoted—Interesting Incidents on the Field of Battle.......................................	53
Garfield Nomination Joke....................................	111
Garfield on the Democracy—Extract from One of His Old Speeches—His Walk in the Democratic Graveyard......	73
Garfield "Photographed" by "Gath"—A Remarkably Interesting Pen Picture of the Great Man—His Physical, Social, Moral, and Intellectual Powers..................	46
Garfield's Celebrated Speech at the Andersonville Reunion Held at Toledo, Ohio, Oct. 3, 1879—How the General Looks "Without Gloves!"...............................	78
Garfield's Extra Session Speech—Turning on the Light..	128
Garfield's First Ride on the Cars—First Visit to Columbus—First School, Etc.—Interesting Reminiscences...........	126
Garfield's Great Speech at Columbus, Acknowledging His Election as United States Senator.......................	83
Garfield's Life in Hiram Sketched by President Hinsdale, of Hiram College—An Interesting History.................	116
Garfield's School Days—He Attends a High School—Takes His Frying-pan Along—The Old, Old Story of What Grit Will Do..	25
Garfield's Speech at the Wisconsin Republican Reunion—Outlining the Condition of the Country................	76
Gen. Garfield as a Wood-Chopper—He Contracts to Put Up Twenty-five Cords—His Visit to Cleveland Harbor, and Laughable Interview with "The Captain"..........	19
Gen. Garfield's Letter of Acceptance.......................	142

CONTENTS.

Gen. Garfield En Route for Home After His Nomination for President—From Illinois to Ohio—Incidents and Welcomes by the Way	102
Gen. Garfield is Called to the Halls of Congress from the Fields of War—How it was Done—Early Experience of the Farmer Boy on the Floor	69
Gen. Garfield on the Floor of the Great Chicago Convention—Full Text of His Eloquent Speech Nominating John Sherman for President—Delivered June 5, 1880	87
Gen. Garfield's First Important Speech After His Nomination—It is Delivered to the Students of Hiram College on "Commencement Day"—An Interesting Address	44
Gen. Garfield's Marriage—A Happy Home—What the General Says of His Wife	31
Gen. Garfield's Proclamation to the Citizens of Sandy Valley	62
Gen. Garfield's Speech Before the Hiram College Reunion Association—The Commencement Day of 1880 Long to be Remembered	123

H

Heroic Conduct of Gen. Garfield on the Field of Chickamauga—Driving Back Longstreet's Columns and Saving Gen. Thomas	63
How the News of Garfield's Nomination was Received at Hiram College—Ringing the Old Bell	107

I

Increasing Fame of the College President—His Election to the State Senate, and What He Did	32

CONTENTS.

O

Off the Tow-path—Why Young Garfield Abandoned the Canal—A Providential Escape that Set Him to Thinking and Sent Him Home................................ 22

P

Professor Garfield in the Hiram Eclectic Institute—He Becomes President of the Institution—How He Became a Preacher....................................... 29

President Hinsdale's Stories and Tribute to Gen. Garfield, the Man who was in Hiram College Before Him—The Canal and Wood-Chopping Incidents—How He Made Success Possible, and Why He Succeeded.............. 36

S

Seventeen years a Member of Congress—Garfield's Great Work in the Halls of Legislation—A Triumphant Leader 71

Summary of Ballots in the National Republican Convention—Nominating Garfield for President............. 97

T

The Break to Garfield—Thirty-fourth Ballot.............. 94
The Canal Story, Told by Garfield's Employer............. 134
The Way Garfield Got His Military Education............. 140
The General and Fugitive Slave......................... 141
The Habits and Methods of Garfield..................... 138
"The Members from New York".......................... 133
The Turning Point in Garfield's Life.................... 135
The Thirty-fifth Ballot................................ 95
The Thirty-sixth and Last Ballot—Garfield Nominated.... 96
The Full Particulars of the Assassination 166
The Story of Col. Rockwell 174
The Suffering President—Incidents on the Sick Bed....... 178
The Medical Record.................................... 180
The Run to Long Branch................................ 181
The Engineer's Story.................................. 185
The Last Days' Bulletin............................... 188
The Death Bed Scene................................... 189

CONTENTS.

The Autopsy	191
The Mother and Her Dead Son	193
The Services in the Francklyn Cottage	196
The Body in State in the Capitol Rotunda at Washington	198
Services at the Vault in Cleveland	200
"The End," by J. G. Holland	209
The World Wide Sympathy	210
Affecting Incidents	211
The Birth Place of Gen. Garfield—How it Looked on the Great Memorial Day	213
The Assassination of President Lincoln	219
The Maxims of Garfield	226

What Foreign-Born Citizens say of the Convention	108
Who is General Garfield	113
Who Have been Assassinated Among Public Men During the Last 30 Years	216

Classification.

HOME LIFE	17
WAR RECORD	53
SPEECHES	69
GARFIELD'S NOMINATION	91
MISCELLANEOUS	113
ASSASSINATION, DEATH AND BURIAL	166

"The man who wants to serve his country must put himself in the line of its leading thought, and that is the restoration of business, trade, commerce, industry, sound political economy, hard money, and the honest payment of all obligations, and the man who can add anything in the direction of accomplishing any of these purposes is a public benefactor."—(*Garfield in Congress, Dec. 10, 1878.*)

STORIES AND SKETCHES
—OF—
General Garfield.

HOME LIFE.

Boyhood of Gen. Garfield—The Farmer Boy—On the Tow-path—A Tough Time—Good Health and Indomitable Energy Triumphant.

General James Abram Garfield, the farmer boy, canal boatman, carpenter, school teacher, college professor, preacher, soldier, congressman, the popular candidate of the Republican party for Presidential honors, was born in the township of Orange, Cuyahoga County, Ohio, fifteen miles from Cleveland, on the 19th of November, 1831. His father, Abraham Garfield, was born in Otsego County, New York, and was of a family that had resided in Massachusetts for several generations. His mother, Eliza Ballou, niece of the Rev. Hosea Ballou, the noted Universalist clergyman, was born in Cheshire County, New Hampshire. The General is, therefore, of New England stock.

James Abram was the youngest of four children. The father died in 1833, leaving the family dependent upon a small farm and the exertions of the mother. There was nothing about the elder Garfield to distinguish him from the other plodding farmers of the rather sterile township of Orange. No one could discern any qualities in him, which, transmitted to the next generation, might help to make a statesman, unless it was industry; but his wife, who is still living at an advanced age, was always fond of reading when she could get leisure from her hard household duties, and was a thoroughly capable woman, of strong will, stern principles, and more than average force of character.

Of the children, no one besides James has made the slightest mark in the world. The older brother is a farmer in Michigan, and the two sisters are farmers' wives.

The General had a tough time of it when a boy. He toiled hard on the farm early and late in summer, and worked at the carpenter's bench in winter. The best of it was he liked work. There was not a lazy hair on his head.

He had an absorbing ambition to get an education, and the only road opened to this end seemed that of manual labor. Ready money was hard to get in those days.

The Ohio Canal ran not far from where he lived, and, finding that the boatmen got their pay in cash, and earned better wages than he could at farming or carpentry, he hired out as a driver on the tow-path, and soon got up to the dignity of holding the helm of a boat. Then he determined to ship as a sailor on the lakes, but an attack of fever and ague interfered with his plans.

He was ill three months, and when he recovered he decided to go to a school called Geauga seminary, in an adjoining county. His mother had saved a small sum of money, which she gave him, together with a few cooking utensils and a sack of provisions. He hired a small room and cooked his own food to make his expenses as light as possible. He paid his own way after that, never calling on his mother for any more assistance.

By working at the carpenter's bench mornings and evenings and vacation times, and teaching country schools during the winter he managed to attend the seminary during the spring and fall terms, and to save a little money toward going to college. He had excellent heath, a robust frame, and a capital memory, and the attempt to combine mental and physical work, which has broken down many farmer boys ambitions to get an education, did not hurt him.

Gen. Garfield as a Wood-Chopper—He Contracts to Put Up Twenty-five Cords
—His Visit to Cleveland Harbor, and Laughable
Interview with the "The Captain."

The friends and early companions of the General relate wonderful stories of his precocity, telling how he could read at 3 years, and possessed remarkable capacity for committing to memory what he had read, so that at the age when boys usually learn their letters he was somewhat advanced in literature. During all the years of boyhood he simply worked and attended school, and grew strong and hearty, until, at the age of sixteen, he was fully capable of doing a strong man's work on the farm. In the spring of this year he went to the Township of Newburg, now in the limits of Cleveland, to chop cordwood.

He took a job of putting up twenty-five cords, and manfully did he set himself in his solitude to his task. To the north of him, as he worked, was the lake in slaty blue. There, in miniature, was the ocean of which he had so long dreamed. Everything had to be won by little. The ocean was a great way off. He could not early reach it. He would begin his life of a sailor on the lake, and then seek a wider range upon the "ocean blue." The work of wood-chopping was vigorously prosecuted, and time flew with great rapidity.

He felt that the pay for wood-chopping was hardly sufficient for a start, and so he hired out to a Mr. Treat, during the haying and harvesting season, but he still dreamed on. When this job was finished he went home to his mother and announced his intentions. She knew well that it was useless to oppose him, now that he had really set his heart upon it, and so, in the midst of prayer and God-blessings, he departed.

He visited the harbor in Cleveland. Here he found a single vessel about to depart for a trip up the lakes. In all his dreams he had never seen a Captain except as a sort of mixture of angel and dashing military officer in blue coat and brass buttons. He went on board this vessel and inquired for the Captain. He was told, with a smile, by one of the men, that the Captain would come up from the hold in a few minutes. He had not long to wait. Presently a drunken wretch, brutal in every feature, came up, swearing at every step.

"There is the Captain," said one of the men.

The country lad stepped forward and modestly asked if a hand was wanted.

Turning upon the youth, the brute poured a volley of pent-up curses and oaths, and made no other answer.

The poor awkward boy was for a moment amazed, and then, turning away, walked about to recover himself. He was by no means cured of his longing for the sea; he had too strong a will for that, and this had taken too strong a hold upon him. Revolving the matter in his mind, he came to the conclusion that he had failed because he lacked some initiatory process. As the lake was to the ocean, so should the canal be to the lake; he would apply at the canal and gain some training there.

Young Garfield Tries the Canal—Thirteen Duckings on the First Trip, and one Fight—The First Victory.

Notwithstanding his poor success with "the Captain," young Garfield determined to persevere, and the very first canal-boat he visited wanted a driver, and he got the place. The General avers that, by actual count, he fell into the canal thirteen times on the first trip. Knowing nothing of the art of swimming, he came very near drowning. He worked faithfully and well, however, and at the end of his first round trip he was promoted from driver to bowsman.

On his first trip to Beaver, in this new capacity, he had his first fight. He was standing on the deck, with the setting pole against his shoulder. Some feet away stood Dave, a great, good-natured boatman, and a firm friend of the young General. The boat gave a lurch, the pole slipped from the youth's shoulder, and flew in the direction of Dave.

"Look out, Dave!" called Garfield; but the pole was there first, and struck Dave a severe blow in the ribs.

Garfield expressed his sorrow, but it was of no use. Dave turned upon the luckless boy with curses, and threatened to thrash him. Garfield knew he was innocent even of carelessness.

The threat of a flogging from a heavy man of 35 roused the hot Garfield blood. Dave rushed upon him with his head down, like an enraged bull. As he came on, Garfield sprang one side and dealt him a powerful blow just back of and under the left ear. Dave went to the bottom of the boat with his head between two beams, and his now heated foe went after him, seized him by the throat, and lifted the same clenched hand for another blow.

"Pound the blamed fool to death, Jim," called the appreciative Captain. "If he haint no more sense to get mad at accidents he orto die;" and, as the youth hesitated, "Why don't you strike? Blame me, if I'll interfere."

He could not; the man was down, helpless in his power. Dave expressed regret at his rage. Garfield gave him his hand, and they were better friends than ever.

The victory gave the young man much prestige among the canal men. The idea that a boy could thrash Dave was something that the roughs could not understand.

Off the Tow-Path.—Why Young Garfield Abandoned the Canal.—A Providential Escape that Set Him to Thinking and Sent Him Home.

The General says that two causes were instrumental in causing him finally to abandon the canal. One was his mother, and the other was the ague cake in his side.

He had worked but a short time when he began to feel the ague in his system, and finally it assumed a very serious form.

His many falls into the water, and the thorough wetting which followed increased his disease, and finally one especially heavy fall led him to reason quite fully over the matter. It was night, and in the darkness he grasped for something to draw himself out of the water. As luck would have it he chanced to reach the dragrope of the boat. Hand over hand he grasped the rope, and finally he drew himself up.

He thought of his mother, and how he had left her with the intention of going upon the lake, and how she still believed he was there.

The next day's warm sun dried his clothes, but he was sicker than ever with the chills, and he determined upon reaching Cleveland to go and visit his mother and lay off long enough to get well.

It was after dark when he approached the home of the widow and orphans. Coming quietly near he heard her voice in prayer within. He bowed and listened as the fervent prayer went on. He heard her pray for him.

When the voice ceased he softly raised the latch and entered. Her prayer was answered. Not till that solemn time did he know that his going away had crushed her.

A Trying Ordeal—In the Hands of the Doctors—Melting Down an "Ague Cake" with Calomel!—How the Crucible (Young Garfield) Endured It—He is Saved by a Kind Mother.

After the terrible ducking and narrow escape that closed the labors of young Garfield on the canal, he was at once prostrated with the "ague cake," as the hardness of the left side is popularly called. One of the old school M.D.'s salivated him, and for several awful months he lay on the bed with a board so adjusted as to conduct the flow of saliva from his mouth while the cake was dissolving under the influence of calomel, as the doctor said!

Nothing but the indissoluble constitution given him by his father carried him through. However it fared with that obdurate cake, his passion for the sea survived, and he intended to return to the canal. The wise, sagacious love of the mother won. She took counsel of other helps. During the dreary months with tender watchfulness she cared for him. She trusted in his noble nature; she trusted in good faith that, although he constantly talked of carrying out his old plans, he would abandon them.

Not for years did he know the agony these words cost her. She merely said, in her sweet, quiet way:

"James, you're sick. If you return to the canal, I fear you will be taken down again. I have been thinking it over. It seems to me you had better go to school this spring, and then, with a term in the fall, you may be able to teach in the winter. If you can teach winters and want to go on the canal or lake summers, you will have employment the year round."

Wise woman that she was, in his broken condition it did not seem a bad plan. While he revolved it, she went on:

"Your money is now all gone, but your brother Thomas and I will be able to raise $17 for you to start to school on, and you can perhaps get along, after that is gone, upon your own resources."

He took the advice and the money,—the only fund ever contributed by others to him either in fitting or passing through college,—and went to The Geauga, a seminary at Chester.

In speaking of this longing for the sea, the General said, half regretfully:

"But even now, at times, the old feeling, (the longing for the sea) comes back," and, walking across the room, he turned, with a flashing eye: "I tell you I would rather now command a fleet in a great naval battle than to do anything else on this earth. The sight of a ship often fills me with a strong fascination, and when upon the water, and my fellow-landsmen are in the agonies of sea-sickness, I am as tranquil as when walking the land in the serenest weather."

And so the mother conquered. When a thirst for knowledge was once engendered in the youth, the mother stood in no danger of losing him. But during all those years of education, there were obstacles of great magnitude to be overcome, poverty to be struggled against, and victories to be won.

Garfield's School Days—He Attends a High School—Takes His Frying-pan Along—The Old Old Story of What Grit Will Do.

Up to the time of young Garfield's canal experience he seemed to have cherished little ambition for anything beyond the prospects offered by the laborious life he had entered. But it happened that one of the winter schools was taught by a promising young man named Samuel Bates. He had attended a high school in an adjacent township, known as the "Geauga Seminary," and with the proselyting spirit common to young men in the backwoods, who were beginning to taste the pleasures of education, he was very anxious to take back several new students with him.

Garfield listened to Mr. Bates, and was tempted. He had intended to become a sailor on the lakes, but he was yet too ill to carry out this plan, and so he finally resolved to attend the high school one term, and postpone sailing till the next fall.

That resolution made a scholar, a Major General, a Senator-elect, and a Presidential candidate out of him, instead of a sailor before the mast on a Lake Erie schooner. The boy never dreamed of what the man would be.

Early in March, 1849, young Garfield reached Chester (the site of the Geauga Seminary) in company with his cousin and another young man from his village. They carried with them frying-pans and dishes as well as their few school books. They rented a room in an old, unpainted frame house near the academy, and went to work. Garfield bought the second Algebra he had ever seen, and began to study it. English Grammar, Natural Philosophy, and Arithmetic were the list of his studies.

His mother had scraped together a little sum of money to aid him at the start, which she gave him with her blessing when he left his humble home. After that he never had a dollar in his life that he did not earn. As soon as he began to feel at home in his classes he sought among the carpenters of the village for employment at his trade.

He worked mornings, evenings, and Saturdays, and thus earned enough to pay his way. When the summer vacation came he had a longer interval for work; and so when the fall term opened he had enough money laid up to pay his tuition and give him a start again.

By the end of the fall term Garfield had made such progress that a lad of 18 thought he was able to teach a district school. Then the future seemed easy to him. The fruits of the winter's teaching were enough, with his economical management to pay the expenses of the spring and fall terms at the academy. Whatever he could make at his morning and evening work at his carpenter's trade would go to swell another fund, the need of which he had begun to feel.

For the backwoods lad, village carpenter, tow-path canal hand, would-be sailor, had now resolved to enter college. "It is a great point gained," he said years afterwards, "when, in our hurrying times, a young man makes up his mind to devote several years to the accomplishment of definite work." It was so now in his own case. With a definite purpose before him he began to save all his earnings, and to shape all his exertions to the one end.

Through the summer vacation of 1850 he worked at his trade, helping to build houses within a stone's throw of the academy. During the next session of the academy he was able to abandon boarding himself, having found a boarding house where he found the necessaries of life for $1 per week.

The next winter he taught again, and in the spring removed to Hiram to attend the "Institute" over which he was afterward to preside. So he continued teaching a term each winter, attending school through spring and fall, and keeping up with his classes by private study during the time he was absent. Before he had left Hiram Institute he was the finest Latin and Greek scholar that the school had ever seen—and at this day he reads and writes the language fluently.

At last, by the summer of 1854, the carpenter and towpath boy had gone as far as the high school and academies of his native region could carry him. He was now nearly 23 years old. The struggling, hard-working boy had developed into a self-reliant man.

He was the neighborhood wonder for scholarship, and a general favorite for the hearty, genial ways that had never deserted him. He had been brought up in "the Church of the Disciples," as it loved to call itself, of which Alexander Campbell was the great light. At an early age he had followed the example of his parents in connecting himself with this church. His life corresponded with his profession. Everybody believed in and trusted him.

He had saved from his school-teaching and carpenter work about half enough money to carry him through the two years in which he thought he could finish the ordinary college course.

Garfield at College—He Graduates with High Honors—His Personal Appearance at this Period that of a " Newly-Imported Dutchman."

When he was 23 years of age young Garfield concluded he had got about all there was to be had in the obscure cross-roads academy. He calculated that he had saved about half enough money to get through college, provided he could begin, as he hoped, with the Junior year. He was growing old, and he determined that he must go to college that fall.

How to procure the rest of the needed money was a mystery; but at last his good character, and the good will this brought him, solved the question.

He was in vigorous lusty health, and a life insurance policy was easily obtained. This he assigned to a gentleman who thereupon loaned him what money was needed, knowing that if he lived he would pay it, and if he died the policy would secure it.

Pecuniary difficulties thus disposed of, he was ready to start. But where? He had originally intended to attend Bethany College, the institution sustained by the church of which he was a member, and presided over by Alexander Campbell, the man above all others whom he had been taught to admire and revere. But as study and experience had enlarged his vision, he had come to see that there were better institutions outside the limits of his peculiar sect.

So in the fall of 1854 the pupil of Geauga Seminary and the Hiram Institute applied for admission at the venerable doors of Williams College. He knew no graduate of the college and no student attending it; and of the President he only knew that he had published a volume of lectures which he liked, and that he had written a kindly word to him when he spoke of coming.

The Western carpenter and village school-teacher received many a shock in the new sphere he had now entered. On every hand he was made to feel the social superiority of his fellow-students. Their ways were free from the awkward habits of the untrained laboring youth. Their speech was free from the uncouth phrases of the provincial circles in which he moved. Their toilets made the handiwork of his village tailor sadly shabby. Their free-handed expenditures contrasted strikingly with his enforced parsimony. To some tough-fibred hearts these would have been only petty annoyances. To the warm, social, generous mind of young Garfield they seem, from more than one indication of his college life that we can gather, to have been a source of positive anguish.

But he bore bravely up, maintained the advance standing in the junior class to which he had been admitted on his arrival, and at the end of his two years' course (in 1856) bore off the metaphysical honor of his class—reckoned at Williams among the highest within the gift of the institution to her graduating members.

But now, on his return to his home, the young man who had gone so far East as to old Williams, and had come back decorated with her honors, was thought good for anything.

A daguerreotype of him taken about this time represents a rather awkward youth, with a shock of light hair standing straight up from a big forehead, and a frank, thoughtful face, of a very marked German type. There is not, however, a drop of German blood in the Garfield family, but this picture would be taken for some Fritz or Carl just over from the Fatherland.

Proffessor Garfield in the Hiram Eclectic Institute.—He Becomes President of the Institution.—How He Became a Preacher.

Before he went to college Garfield had connected himself with the Disciples, a sect having a numerous membership in Eastern and Southern Ohio, West Virginia, and Kentucky, where its founder, Alexander Campbell, had traveled and preached.

The principal peculiarities of the denomination are their refusal to formulate their beliefs into a creed, the independence of each congregation, the hospitality and fraternal feeling of the members, and the lack of a regular ministry.

When Garfield returned to Ohio it was natural that he should soon gravitate to the struggling little school of the young sect at Hiram, Portage county, near his boyhood's home.

Here he was straightway made tutor of Latin and Greek in the Hiram Eclectic Institute, in which only two years before he had been a pupil, and so he began to work for money to pay his debts. So high a position did he take, and so popular did he become, that the next year he was made President of the institute, a position which he continued to hold until his entrance into political life, but a little before the outbreak of the war.

Two years of teaching (during which time he married) left him even with the world. Through the school year of 1858-9 he even began to save a little money. At the same time he commenced the study of law.

Hiram is a lonesome country village, three miles from a railroad, built upon a high hill, overlooking twenty miles of cheese-making country to the southward. It contains fifty or sixty houses clustered around the green, in the center of which stands the homely red-brick college structure. Plain living and high thinking was the order of things at Hiram College in those days. The teachers were poor, the pupils were poor, and the institution was poor, but there was a great deal of hard, faithful study done, and many ambitious plans formed.

The young President taught, lectured, and preached, and all the time studied as diligently as any acolyte in the temple of knowledge. He frequently spoke on Sundays in the churches of the towns in the vicinity to create an interest in the college.

Among the Disciples any one can preach who has a mind to, no ordination being required. From these Sunday discourses came the story that Garfield at one time was a minister. He never considered himself as such, and never had any intention of finding a career in the pulpit. His ambition, if he had any outside of the school, lay in the direction of law and politics.

Gen. Garfield's Marriage—A Happy Home—What the General says of his Wife.

During his professorship at Hiram, Garfield married Miss Lucretia Rudolph, daughter of a farmer in the neighborhood, whose acquaintance he had made while at the academy, where she was also a pupil.

She was a quiet, thoughtful girl, of singularly sweet and refined disposition, fond of study and reading, possessing a warm heart and a mind with the capacity of steady growth.

The marriage was a love affair on both sides, and has been a thoroughly happy one. Much of Gen. Garfield's subsequent success in life may be attributed to the never-failing sympathy and intellectual companionship of his wife and the stimulus of a loving home circle. The young couple bought a neat little cottage fronting on the college campus, and began their wedded life poor and in debt, but with brave hearts.

Speaking of his wife recently, Mr. Garfield said:

I have been wonderfully blessed in the discretion of my wife. She is one of the coolest and best-balanced women I ever saw. She is unstampedable. There has not been one solitary instance of my public career where I suffered in the smallest degree for any remark she ever made. It would have been perfectly natural for a woman often to say something that could be misinterpreted; but without any design, and with the intelligence and coolness of her character, she has never made the slightest mistake that I ever heard of. With the competition that has been against me, many times such discretion has been a real blessing.

She has borne him a large family of children, two of whom—the eldest boys—are now preparing for college. Their home since their marriage has been in Hiram until three or four years ago, when they removed to Mentor, Lake County, where their residence now is.

Increasing Fame of the College President—His Election to the State Senate and What He Did.

The College President began to draw attention through wider circles than those which he had been a center as a teacher, and his oratorical powers had brought him prominently before the public. As President of the institute, it was natural that he should secure a prominent position among educated men, and his reputation grew very rapidly until, in 1859, the people of his county thought him a proper man to represent them in the State Senate. He was elected by a large majority, and took an influential part in legislation and debate.

It is generally supposed that General Garfield was once a clergyman. This is not strictly true; he frequently appeared in the pulpit of the Disciples Church, in accordance with the liberal usages of that denomination, but never entertained any idea of becoming a minister, nor did he ever take holy orders. Since his entrance into politics as a member of the Legislature he has not performed any ministerial duties, but has turned his attention more to the practice of law.

When the war broke out General Garfield was a leading member of the Ohio State Senate, and was the foremost of a small band of Republicans who thought it impolitic to adopt the constitutional amendments which had been sent by Congress to the States forbidding forever legislation on the subject of slavery. He took the lead in revising an old statute about treason, and when what was known as the "million war bill" came up, he was the most conspicuous of its advocates.

Anecdote of Garfield's Early Life—His Greatness Anticipated by a Woman in Connection with a Laughable Incident.

A reminiscence of Gen. Garfield's earlier manhood is found in the recital given by one Capt. Stiles, the present Sheriff of Ashtabula county, Ohio. In 1850, Capt. Stiles relates that Garfield taught the district school of Stiles' district, and "boarded around." Like many other school-masters of the pioneer days, Garfield's wardrobe was scanty, consisting of but one suit of jean.

One day the school-master was so unfortunate as to rend his pantaloons across the knee in an unseemly degree. He pinned up the rend as best he could, and went to the homestead of the Stiles' where he was then boarding. Good Mrs. Stiles cheerfully said to the unfortunate pedagogue:

"Oh, well, James, never mind; you go to bed early and I will put a nice patch under that tear, and darn it all up so nice that it will last all winter, and when you get to be United States Senator nobody will ask you what kind of clothes you wore when you were keeping school."

Last winter when Gen. Garfield was elected Senator from the State of Ohio Mrs. Stiles, who is still a hale old lady, sent her congratulations to him and reminded him of the *torn pantaloons;* and for her kindly congratulations she received a most touching reply from the newly-elected Senator, assuring her that the incident was fresh in his memory.

An Interesting Reminiscence—Garfield and Arthur Both School Teachers in the Same Room at North Pownal, Vt.

North Pownal, Bennington, Co., Vt., formerly known as Whipple's Corners, is situated in the southwestern corner of the State, and by the usually travelled road one passes in an hour's ride from New York through the corner of Vermont by way of North Pownal into the State of Massachusetts.

In 1851 Chester A. Arthur, fresh from Union College, came to North Pownal, and for one summer taught the village school. About two years later James A. Garfield, then a young student at Williams College, several miles distant, in order to obtain the necessary means to defray his expenses while pursuing his studies, came also to North Pownal and established a writing-school in the room formerly occupied by Mr. Arthur, and taught classes in penmanship during the long winter evenings.

Thus, from a common starting-point in early life, after the lapse of more than a quarter of a century, after years of manly toil, these distinguished men are brought into a close relationship before the nation and before the civilized world.

A Pen Picture of Garfield.

In person Gen. Garfield is six feet high, broad-shouldered and strongly built. He has an unusually large head, that seems to be three-fourths forehead, light-brown hair and beard, large, light-blue eyes, a prominent nose, and full cheeks. He dresses plainly, is fond of broad-brimmed slouch hats and stout boots, eats heartily, cares nothing for luxurious living, is thoroughly temperate in all respects save in that of brain-work, and devoted to his wife and children and very fond of his country home. Among men he is genial, approachable, companionable, and a remarkably entertaining talker.

A Pen Picture of Gen. Garfield's Wife—A Model Woman.

Mrs. Garfield is a lady of medium height, and of slight but well-knit form. She has small features, with a somewhat prominent forehead, and her black hair, crimped in front and done up in a modest coil, is slightly tinged with gray. A pair of black eyes, and a mouth about which there plays a sweetly bewitching smile, are the most attractive features of a thoroughly expressive face. In dress she is quite as plain as the present mistress of the White House, whom she resembles in several respects. Her manners are graceful and winning in the extreme. Though she is noted for her modest, retiring ways and her thorough domesticity more than for any other distinguishing characteristic, her educational accomplishments are many and varied. In all the public life of her distinguished companion she has been his constant helpmeet and adviser. She is a quick observer, an intelligent listener, but undemonstrative in the extreme. When the General was at Chickamauga, and everybody at Hiram was painfully anxious to get the latest news from the field of battle, she sat quiet and patient in what is now Professor Hinsdale's cosy library, and was able to control the inmost emotions that swayed her breast. How she received the news of the General's nomination at Chicago will probably never be fully known, but everybody here is sure that she was as undemonstrative as when waiting for news from Chickamaugua.

President Hinsdale's Stories and Tribute to Gen. Garfield, the Man Who was in Hiram College Before Him—The Canal and Wood-Chopping Incidents—How He Made Success Possible, and Why He Succeeded.

President B. A. Hinsdale, of Hiram College, on the day of Garfield's election to the United States Senate, made the following announcement to the students in the chapel:

"To-day a man will be elected to the United States Senate in Columbus who, when a boy, was once the bell-ringer in this school and afterward its President. Feeling this, we ought, in some way, to recognize this step in his history. I will to-morrow morning call your attention to some of the more notable and worthy features of Gen. Garfield's history and character."

The address which President Hinsdale delivered on the occasion is as follows:

YOUNG LADIES AND GENTLEMEN: I am not going to attempt a formal address on the life and character of Gen. Garfield. There is now no call for such an attempt, and I have made no adequate preparations for such a task. My object is far humbler: simply to hold up to your minds some points in his history, and some features in his character that young men and women may study with interest and profit.

I shall begin by destroying history, or what is commonly held to be history. The popularly accepted account of Gen. Garfield's history and character is largely fabulous. We are not to suppose that the ages of myth and legend are gone; under proper conditions such growths spring up now; and I know of no man in public life around whom they have sprung up more rankly than around the subject of my remarks.

No doubt you have seen some of the stories concerning him and his family that appear ever and anon in the newspapers; that his mother chopped cordwood; that she fought wolves with fire to keep them from devouring her children, her distinguished son being one of the group; that the circumstances of the family were the most pinching; that Garfield himself could not read at the age of 21; that he was peculiarly reckless in his early life; that, when he had become a man, he went down from the pulpit to thrash a bully who interrupted him in his sermon on the patience of Job.

These stories, and others like them, are all false and all harmful. They fail of accomplishing the very purpose for which they were professedly told—the stimulation of youth. To make the lives of the great distorted and monstrous is not to make them fruitful as lessons.

If a life be anomalous and outlandish, it is, for that reason, the poorer example. It is all in the wrong direction. It makes the impression that, in human history, there is no cause and no effect; no antecedent and no consequent; that everything is capricious and fitful; and suggests that the best thing to do is to abandon one's self to the currents of life, trusting that some beneficent gulf stream will seize you and bear you to some happy shore. No, young people, do not heed such instruction as this.

The best lives for them to study are those that are natural and symmetrical; those in which the relation between cause and effect is so close and apparent that the dullest can see it; and that preach in the plainest terms the sermon on the text: "Whatever a man soweth that shall he also reap."

Irregular and abnormal lives will do for "studies," but healthy, normal, harmonious lives should be chosen for example. And Gen. Garfield's life from the first has been eminently healthy, normal, and well-proportioned.

He was born in the woods of Orange, Cuyahoga County, in 1831. His father died when the son was a year and a half old. Abram Garfield's circumstances were those of his neighbors. Measured by our standard they were all poor; they lived on small farms, for which they, had gone in debt, hoping to clear and pay for them by their toil. Garfield dying, left his wife and four young children in the condition that any one of his neighbors would have done in like circumstances—poor. The family life before had been close and hard enough; now it became closer and harder.

Grandma Garfield, as some of us familiarly call her, was a woman of unusual energy, faith, and courage. She said the children should not be separated, but kept them together; and that the home should be maintained, as when its head was living. The battle was a hard one, and she won it. All honor to her, but let us not make her ridiculous by inventing impossible stories.

To external appearance, young Garfield's life did not differ materially from the lives of the neighbors' boys.

He chopped wood, and so did they; he mowed, and so did they; he carried butter to the store in a little pail, and so did they. Other families that had not lost their heads naturally shot ahead of the Garfields in property; but such differences counted far less then than they do now. The traits of his maturer character appeared early; studiousness, truthfulness, generosity of nature, and mental power. So far was he from being reckless, that he was almost serious, reverent and thoughtful. So far was he from being unable to read at 21 that he was a teacher in the district schools before he was 18.

He was the farthest removed from being a pugilist, though he had great physical strength and courage, coolness of mind, was left-handed withal, and was both able and disposed to defend himself and all his rights, and did so on due occasion.

His three months' service on the canal has been the source of numerous fables and morals. The morals are as false as the fables, and more misleading. All I have to say about it is: James A. Garfield has not risen to the position of a United States Senator because he "ran on a canal." Nor is it because he chopped more wood than the neighbors' boys. Many a man has run longer on the canal, and chopped more wood, and never became a Senator.

Gen. Garfield once rang the school bell when a student here. That did not make him the man he is. Convince me that it did, and I will hang up a bell in every tree in the campus, and set you all to ringing. Thomas Corwin, when a boy, drove a wagon, and became the head of the Treasury; Thomas Ewing boiled salt, and became a Senator; Henry Clay rode a horse to mill from the "Slashes," and he became the great commoner of the West. But it was not the wagon, the salt, and horse that made these men great.

These are interesting facts in the lives of these illustrious men; they show that, in our country, it has been, and still is possible for young men of ability, energy, and determined purpose to rise above a lowly condition, and win places of usefulness and honor. Poverty may be a good school; straightened circumstances may develop power and character; but the principal conditions of success are in the man, and not in his surroundings.

Garfield is the man he is because nature gave him a noble endowment of faculties that he has nobly handled. We must look within, and not without, for the secret of destiny. The thing to look at in a man's life are his aspirations, his energy, his courage, his strength of will, and not the wood he may have chopped, or the salt he may have boiled. How a man works, and not what he does, is the test of worth.

His success did not lie in his technical scholarship, or his ability as a drill-master. Teachers are plenty who much surpass him in these particulars. He had great ability to grasp a subject; to organize a body of intellectual materials; to amass facts and work out striking generalizations; and, therefore, he excelled in rhetorical exposition. An old pupil who has often heard him on the stump, once told me, "the General succeeds best when talking to the people just as he did to his class." He imparted to his pupils largeness of view, enthusiasm, and called out of them unbounded devotion to himself.

This devotion was not owing to any plan or trick, but to the qualities of the man. Mr. H. M. James of the Cleveland schools, an old Hiram scholar, speaking of the old Hiram days before Garfield went to college, once wrote me: "There began to grow up in me an admiration and love for Garfield that has never abated, and the like of which I have never known. A bow of recognition, or a simple word from him, was to me an inspiration."

Probably all were not equally susceptible, but all the boys who were long under his charge (save, perhaps, a few "sticks") would speak in the same strain. He had great power to energize young men. Gen. Garfield has carried the same qualities into public life. He has commanded success. His ability, knowledge, mastery of questions, generosity of nature, devotion to the public good, and honesty of purpose, have done the work. He has never had a political "machine." He has never forgotten the day of small things. He has never made personal enemies.

It is difficult to see how a political triumph could be more complete or more gratifying than his election to the Senate. No "bargains" no "slate," no "grocery" at Columbus. He did not even go to the Capital City. Such things are inspiring to those who think politics in a broad way. He is a man of positive convictions, freely uttered. Politically he may be called a "man-of-war;" and yet few men, or none, begrudge him his triumph. Democrats vied with Republicans the other day in Washington in snowing him under with congratulations; some of them were as anxious for his election as any Republican could be.

It is is said he will go to the Senate without an enemy on either side of the chamber. These things are honorable to all parties. They show that manhood is more than party. The Senator is honored, Ohio is honored, and so is the school in Hiram, with which he was connected so many years. The whole story abounds in interest, and I hope I have so told it as to bring out some of its best points, and to give you stimulus and cheer.

An Interesting Story in Connection with the Sick room—General Garfield as a Reader.

The methods of study which Gen. Garfield adopted in early life have never been abandoned. There are few public men who have any spare time for books; Gen. Garfield is one of the few. He always reads.

He believes in the principle that change is rest, and, to relieve himself from the tedium of Congressional business, he resorts to literature. It is said that nearly all great orators have been fine talkers.

Gen. Garfield is a remarkable conversationalist. His private talk, when the harness of politics has been laid aside, is brilliant and fascinating. He seems never to forget anything; and in quiet moments, when friends are by him, it is pleasant to hear him tell of the old days, and to dream of the future.

> He is so full of pleasant anecdote
> So rich, so gay, so poignant is his wit—
> Time vanishes before him as he speaks,
> And ruddy morning through the lattice peeps
> Ere night seems well begun.

Some years ago Gen. Garfield suffered from a temporary disorder, and was compelled to submit to a painful surgical operation. He lay here for six weeks in this tropical sun, recovering from the effects of that operation. The town was dead. It was vacation time. Not one member of either House was here. On one of these burning days a friend had occasion to call upon him. Everything was quiet and peaceful within.

"I have been reading," said Gen. Garfield, from his sick-bed, "charming, silly old Bozzy's journey to the Hebrides, over again. He is always the same kindly, lazy, genial, old man, forever saying good things—a sleek, soft-handed, soft-hearted giant of a fellow."

"I have read," he said, turning to his visitor, "since I have been lying here, struggling with this pain, eighteen volumes; and I have indexed and commonplaced them all. Pretty fair work, I take it, for six weeks of midsummer in Washington."

The sick-room bore witness to this convalescent industry. The narrative of Bozzy's journey lay beside him, and an immense atlas, supported by an elevated stand, stood near the bed, opened at the map which showed the course of Bozzy in the journey to the Hebrides. A faithful wife was tracing with a pencil the ins and outs which the genial old philosopher took on his way to these Northern islands. It was in this way that Garfield was turning to profit the leisure that the surgeon's knife had given him.

Garfield at Home—His Residence at Mentor—His Family and His Mother.

Gen. Garfield is the possessor of two homes, and his family migrates twice a year. Some ten years ago, finding how unsatisfactory life was in hotels and boarding-houses, he bought a lot of ground on the corner of Thirteenth and I streets, in Washington, D. C., and, with money borrowed of a friend, built a plain, substantial three-story house. A wing was extended afterward to make room for the fast-growing library. The money was repaid in time, and was probably saved in great part from what would otherwise have gone to landlords. The children grew up in pleasant home surroundings, and the house became a center of much simple and cordial hospitality.

Five or six years ago the little cottage at Hiram was sold, and for a time the only residence the Garfields had in his district was a summer-house he built on Little Mountain, a bold elevation in Lake County, which commands a view of thirty miles of rich farming country stretched along the shore of Lake Erie.

Three years ago he bought a farm in Mentor, in the same county, lying on both sides of the Lake Shore and Michigan Southern Railroad. Here his family spend all the time when he is free from his duties in Washington.

The farm-house is a low, old-fashioned, story-and-a-half building, but its limited accommodations have been supplemented by numerous outbuildings, one of which Gen. Garfield uses for office and library purposes.

The farm contains about 160 acres of excellent land, in a high state of cultivation, and the Congressman finds a recreation, of which he never tires, in directing the field work and making improvements in the buildings, fences, and orchards. Cleveland is only twenty-five miles away; there is a postoffice and a railway station within half a mile, and the pretty country town of Painesville is but five miles distant. One of the pleasures of summer life on the Garfield farm is a drive of two miles through the woods to the lake shore and a bath in the breakers.

Gen. Garfield has five children living, and has lost two,

who died in infancy. The two older boys, Harry and James, are now at school in New Hampshire. Mary, or Molly as everybody calls her, is a handsome, rosy-cheeked girl of about 12. The two younger boys are named Irwin and Abram.

The General's mother is still living, and has long been a member of his family. She is an intelligent, energetic old lady, with a clear head and a strong will, who keeps well posted in the news of the day, and is very proud of her son's career, though more liberal of criticism than of praise.

Gen. Garfield's First Important Speech After His Nomination — It is Delivered to the Students of Hiram College on "Commencement Day"— An Interesting Address.

Gen. Garfield returned home from his nomination in Chicago to be present "Commencement Day" at little Hiram, where he had once been professor, and afterwards president of the institution. Here Garfield met his wife for the first time since his nomination, and that, too, at the very house where their acquaintance began, within a stone's throw of the college. To the students and his college friends there assembled he spoke most grandly. After a brief reference to old associations, he added the following evidently impromptu remarks:

"FELLOW CITIZENS, OLD NEIGHBORS, AND FRIENDS OF MANY YEARS: It has always given me pleasure to come back here and look upon these faces. It has always given me new courage and new friends, for it has brought back a large share of that richness which belongs to those things out of which come the joys of life.

"While sitting here this afternoon, watching your faces

and listening to the very interesting address which has just been delivered, it has occurred to me that the least thing you have, that all men have enough of, is perhaps the thing that you care for the least, and that is your leisure—the leisure you have to think; the leisure you have to be let alone; the leisure you have to throw the plummet into your mind, and sound the depth and dive for things below; the leisure you have to walk about the towers yourself, and find how strong they are or how weak they are, to determine what needs building up; how to work, and how to know all that shall make you the final beings you are to be. Oh, these hours of building!

"If the Superior Being of the universe would look down upon the world to find the most interesting object, it would be the unfinished, unformed character of the young man or young woman. Those behind me have probably in the main settled this question. Those who have passed into middle manhood and middle womanhood are about what we shall always be, and there is but little left of interest, as their characters are all developed.

"But to your young and your yet unformed natures, no man knows the possibilities that lie before you in your hearts and intellects; and, while you are working out the possibilities with that splendid leisure that you need, you are to be most envied. I congratulate you on your leisure. I commend you to treat it as your gold, as your wealth, as your treasure, out of which you can draw all possible treasures that can be laid down when you have your natures unfolded and developed in the possibilities of the future.

"This place is too full of memories for me to trust myself to speak upon, and I will not. But I draw again to-day, as I have for a quarter of a century, life, evidence of strength, confidence, and affection from the people who gather in this place. I thank you for the permission to see you and meet you and greet you as I have done to-day."

Garfield "Photographed" by "Gath"—A Remarkably Interesting Pen-Picture of the Great Man—His Physical, Social, Moral, and Intellectual Powers.

The following exceedingly interesting description of Gen. Garfield was written by the celebrated "Gath" soon after Garfield's nomination as President:

The writer has known Gen. Garfield pretty well for thirteen years. He is a large, well-fed, hale, ruddy, brown-bearded man, weighing about 220 pounds, with Ohio German colors, blue eyes, military face, erect figure and shoulders, large back and thighs, and broad chest, and evidently bred in the country on a farm. His large mouth is full of strong teeth, his nose, chin, and brows are strongly pronounced. A large brain, with room for play of thought and long application, rises high above his clear, discerning, enjoying eyes. He sometimes suggests a country Samson,—strong beyond his knowledge, but unguarded as a school-boy.

He pays little attention to the affectation by which some men manage public opinion, and has one kind of behavior for all callers, which is the most natural behavior at hand. Strangers would think him a little cold, and mentally shy. On acquaintance he is seen to be hearty above every thing, loving the life around him, his family, his friends, his State and country. Loving sympathetic and achieving people, and with a large unprofessing sense of the brotherhood of workers in the fields of progress, it was the feeling of sympathy and the desire to impart which took him for chief; while as to the pulpit, or on the verge of it, full of all that he saw and acquired, he panted to give it forth, after it had passed through the alembic of his mind.

Endowed with a warm temperament, copious expression, large, wide-seeing faculties, and superabundant health, he could study all night and teach or lecture all day, and it was a providence that his neighbors discovered he was too much of a man to conceal in the pulpit, where his docility and reverence had almost taken him. They sent him to the State Legislature, where he was when the war broke out, and he immediately went to the field, where his courage and painstaking parts, and love of open air occupation, and perfect freedom from self-assertion, made him the delight of Rosecrans and George H. Thomas successively. He would go about any work they asked of him, was unselfish and enthusiastic, and had steady, temperate habits, and his large brain and his reverence made everything novel to him.

There is an entire absence of non-balance or worldliness in his nature. He is never indifferent, never vindictive. A base action or ingratitude or cruelty may make him sad, but does not provoke retaliation, nor alter that faith in men or Providence which is a part of his sound stomach and athletic head. Garfield is simple as a child; to the serpent's wisdom he is a stranger. Having no use nor aptitude with the weapons of coarser natures, he often avoids mere disputes, does not go to public resorts where men are familiar or vulgar, and the walk from his home in Washington to the Capitol, and an occasional dinner out, comprise his life.

The word public servant especially applies to him. He has been the drudge of his State constituents, the public, the public societies, the moral societies, and of his party and country since 1863. Aptitude for public debate and public affairs are associated with a military nature in him. He is on a broad scale a schoolmaster of the range of Gladstone, of Agassiz, of Gallatin. With as honest a heart as ever beat above the competitors of sordid ambition, Gen. Garfield has yet so little of the worldly wise in him that he is poor, and yet has been accused of dishonesty.

He has no capacity for investment, nor the rapid solution

of wealth, nor profound respect for the penny in and out of pound, and still is neither careless, improvident, nor dependent. The great consuming passion to equal richer people, and live finely, and extend his social power is as foreign to him as scheming or cheating. But he is not a suspicious nor a high mettled man, and so he is taken in sometimes, partly from his obliging, unrefusing disposition. Men who were scheming imposed upon him as upon Grant, and other men. The people of his district, who are quick to punish public venality or defection, heard him in his defense in 1873 and kept him in Congress and held up his hand, and hence he is by their unwavering support for twenty-five years candidate for President and a National character.

Since John Quincy Adams no President has had Garfield's scholarship, which is equally up to this age of wider facts. The average American, pursuing money all day long, is now presented to a man who had invariably put the business of others above his own, and worked for that alleged nondescript—the public—gratitude all his life. But he has not labored without reward. The great nomination came to-day to as pure and loving a man as ever wished well of anybody and put his shoulder to his neighbor's wheel.

Garfield's big, boyish heart is pained to-night with the weight of his obligation, affection, and responsibility. To-day, as hundreds of telegrams came from everywhere, saying kind, strong things to him—such messages as only Americans in their rapid, good impulses pour upon a lucky friend—he was with two volunteer clerks in a room opening and reading, and suddenly his two boys sent him one—little fellows at school—and as he read it he broke down, and tried to talk, but his voice choked, and he could not see for tears. The clerks began to blubber, too, and people to whom they afterward told it.

This sense of real great heart will be new to the country, and will grow if he gets the Presidency. His wife was one of his scholars in Ohio. Like him, she is of a New England family, transplanted to the West, a pure-hearted, brave, unassuming woman; the mother of seven or eight children, and, as he told me only a few weeks ago, had never, by any remark, brought him into the least trouble, while she was unstampedable by any clamor.

He is the ablest public speaker in the country, and the most serious and instructive man on the stump. His instincts, liberal and right; his courtesy, noticeable in our politics; his aims, ingenuous; and his piety comes by nature. He leads a farmer's life, all the recess of Congress working like a field-hand, and restoring his mind by resting it. If elected, he will give a tone of culture and intelligence to the Executive office it has never yet had, while he has no pedantry in his composition, and no conceit whatever.

Gen. Garfield may be worth $25,000, or a little more than Mr. Lincoln was when he took the office. His old mother, a genial lady, lives in his family, and his kindness to her on every occasion bears out the commandment of "Honor thy father and thy mother, that thy days may be long in the land."

A Splendid Record—Summary of Garfield's Labors—The Rewards of Industry.

It is astonishing how much there is in the story of Gen. Garfield's life to excite the sympathy, appeal to the pride, and call out the commendation of young men and old men who believe in the dignity of American citizenship.

In 1840, an orphan boy struggling along the prosaic dead level of life on a farm; in 1847, working steadily under the hardships and drudgery of a canal-boatman's experience; in 1849, an aspiring student, supporting himself at an academy; in 1850, a teacher in a country school, earning money to forward his ambition to become an educated man; in 1854, a stubborn student at college; in 1858, a young man struggling against the debts incurred in educating himself; in 1859, President of an educational institute and a State Senator; in 1860, influential as a man and prominent as a politician; in 1861, the Colonel of a Union regiment, and the commander of a brigade, driving forward with resistless energy into Eastern Kentucky; in 1862, a Brigadier General, and then a Major General; in 1863, occupying Giddings' seat in Congress; re-elected in 1864, 1866, 1868, 1870, 1872, 1874, 1876, and 1878, and for nearly all the time an acknowledged leader; elected United States Senator in January, 1880, and nominated President in June.

This is the ideal career of the ambitious or aspiring American boy. Here is a man who, beginning life as a poor boy, has in truth fought his way to distinction. Pure and courageous as a boy, ambitious and self-reliant as a young man, tireless and brave as a soldier, aggressive but even-tempered as a leader in Congress, Gen. Garfield has retained every friendship of his youth, held fast to every comrade of his soldier experience, and commanded the respect of all his co-laborers in Congress.

Garfield's life is the story of a young man who has succeeded through his own efforts. Having passed through all the trials common to boys and young men in this country, he has achieved the distinction which we teach, as a part of our American system, all our boys to strive for. He is from the people and of the people, a pure, kind-hearted, tolerant, broad-spirited, and distinguished man.

Such a life record is a source of pride to any man who thoroughly believes in the possibilities of the American system of education and government. It must be an element of strength to the Presidential candidate of any party, and, judged by this record, by his talent, experience, and spirit, Garfield should be a strong candidate for the Republican party.

It is a good sign when those who know a man best like him best. It is a good sign when those who have been most intimately associated with a man arise promptly and voluntarily to testify in his behalf. It is a good sign when men are attracted to another man because he is a man of heart and principle.

HIRAM COLLEGE.

WAR RECORD.

Garfield in War—How He Voluntered to put down the Rebellion, and was Promoted—Interesting Incidents on the Field of Battle.

Troops were being raised in Ohio early in 1861, and Gen. Garfield at once notified Governor Dennison of his desire to enter the service. Garfield was sent to New York by Governor Dennison to secure arms for the equipment of the Ohio troops, and upon his return was offered a Lieutenant-Coloneley in a proposed regiment, which was never organized.

In August, 1861, however, after McClellan's West Virginia campaign, Gen. Garfield was appointed Lieutenant Colonel of the Forty-Second Ohio Regiment, for which had been recruited many of his old pupils at the Hiram Institute. Gen. Garfield went diligently at work studying tactics, and after five weeks of camp life was promoted to the Coloneley of his regiment, and started for the field.

The regiment went first to Kentucky, where it reported to Gen. Buell, and Garfield was at once assigned the command of the Seventeenth Brigade, and ordered to drive the rebel forces, under Humphrey Marshall, out of Eastern Kentucky. Up to that date no active operations had been attempted west of the Blue Ridge Mountains, and Gen. Garfield found himself in command of four regiments of infantry and eight companies of cavalry, charged with the important work of driving out of his native State an officer reported to be the ablest that Kentucky had given to the rebellion.

Gen. Garfield had never seen a gun fired in action, and had no knowledge of military service except what had been gained in a few months' experience. Garfield moved rapidly up the valley, with a force numbering only 2,200, to meet an experienced officer with 5,000 well-equipped men; but Marshall retreated before him, and after a slight skirmish, Garfield found himself in possession of the enemy's camp and baggage. He pushed the pursuit, and was reinforced by about 1,000 men. The fight that followed was severe at times, but on the whole desultory, and continued three days, until the troops had become practically disabled, because of a heavy rainstorm that flooded the mountain gorges, and made so strong a current in the rivers that Garfield's supplies were unable to reach him.

The troops were almost out of rations, and the mountainous country was incapable of supporting them. Garfield went by land to the base of his supplies, and ordered a steamer to take on a cargo and move up to the relief of his troops. The Captain declared it was impossible; finally, Garfield ordered the Captain and his crew on board, stationed sentinels in the pilot-house, and, having gained a load, started up stream. The water in the usually shallow river was sixty feet deep, and the tree tops along the banks were submerged.

The little vessel trembled from stem to stern at every motion of the engines; the waters whirled her about as if she were a skiff, and the utmost speed that steam could give her was three miles an hour. When night fell, the Captain of the boat begged permission to tie up. To attempt ascending the flood in the dark he declared was madness. But Col. Garfield kept his place at the wheel. Finally, in one of the sudden bends of the river, they drove, with a full head of steam, into the bank. Every effort to back her off was in vain. Mattocks were procured, and excavations were made around the imbedded bow. Still she stuck. Garfield at last ordered a boat to be lowered to take a line across to the opposite bank. The crew protested against venturing out in the flood. The Colonel leaped into the boat and steered it over. A windlass of rails was hastily made, and with a long line the vessel was warped off, and once more was afloat.

It was Saturday when they left Sandy Creek. All through that day and night, Sunday and Sunday night, the boat pushed her way against the current, Garfield leaving the wheel but eight hours of the whole time. At nine o'clock Monday they reached camp, and Garfield could scarcely escape being borne to headquarters on the shoulders of the men.

During the months of January, February and March there were numerous encounters with mountain guerrillas, but the Union arms finally prevailed, and the bands of marauders were driven from the State.

Just on the border, however, at the rough pass across the mountains known as Pound Gap, Humphrey Marshall still held a post of observation, with a force of about 500 men. On the 14th of March, Garfield started with 500 infantry and a couple of hundred cavalry against this detachment. The distance was forty miles. The roads were at their worst, but by evening of the next day he had reached the mountain two miles north of the gap.

Next morning the cavalry were deployed up the gap road, while the infantry were led along an unfrequented path on the side of the mountain. A heavy snowstorm also helped to mask the movement. While the enemy were watching the cavalry, Garfield had led the infantry to within a quarter of a mile of their camp. Then an attack was ordered, the enemy taken by surprise, and a few volleys sent them in confusion down the side of the mountain into Virginia. Considerable quantities of stores were captured.

That night the victorious troops rested in the comfortable log huts built by the enemy, and the next morning burned them down. Six days afterward, the command was ordered to Louisville. These operations had been conducted with such energy and skill as to receive the special commendation of the Government, and Col. Garfield was given a commission as Brigadier General. The discomfiture of Humphrey Marshall was a source of special chagrin to the rebel sympathizers of Kentucky, and Garfield took rank in the popular estimation among the most promising of the volunteer Generals.

On his return to Louisville after the campaign, he found the army of the Ohio already beyond Nashville, on its way to Gen. Grant's aid at Pittsburg Landing. He hastened after it, and assumed command of the Twentieth Brigade. He reached the field on Pittsburg Landing about one o'clock on the second day of the battle, and participated in the closing scenes.

When Gen. Buell sought to prepare a new campaign, he assigned Gen. Garfield to the task of rebuilding the bridges and railroad from Corinth to Decatur. After performing the duty with great skill and energy, he found himself reduced by fever and ague, which he had contracted in the days of his tow-path service on the Ohio Canal, and went home on sick leave.

Soon after he received orders to proceed to Cumberland Gap and relieve Gen. George W. Morgan of his command; but he was too ill to leave his bed, and another officer was sent to the service.

As soon as his health would permit, he was ordered to Washington, where he was placed upon court-martial for the noted trial of Fitz John Porter.

Gen. Garfield was one of the clearest and foremost in the conviction of Porter's guilt, and had the bill to restore Porter ever been brought up in the House of Representatives, he would have made a determined opposition to its passage; but Gen. Logan finished the shameful scheme in the Senate, and Gen. Garfield never had an opportunity to deliver a speech which he had prepared with great thoroughness and care.

After the trial of Fitz John Porter, he was appointed Chief of Staff to Gen. Rosecrans, and from the day of his appointment became the intimate associate and confidential adviser of his chief. Garfield's influence had become so important in shaping campaigns that he was always consulted, and during the successful campaigns that followed Chickamauga he took an active part.

Gen. Garfield's military career did not subject him to trials of a large scale. He approved himself a good independent commander in the small operations in Sandy Valley. His campaign there opened our series of successes in the West.

As a Chief of Staff he was unrivalled. There, as elsewhere, he was ready to accept the gravest responsibilities in following his convictions. The bent of his mind was judicial, and his judgment of military matters good.

His record will stand for him a monument of courage, and his conduct at Chickamauga will never be forgotten by a nation of brave men.

Col. Garfield's First Great Battle—He Defeats Humphrey Marshall and Wins a Brigadier-Generalship.

On the 17th of December, 1861, Garfield left Camp Chase, Ohio, with his regiment (Forty-second Ohio) under orders for the Big Sandy Valley region in Eastern Kentucky. Upon arriving in Louisville he was invited by Gen. Buell to arrange his own campaign, and he accordingly prepared a plan, which was submitted to and approved by the commanding General. The next day he started for his field of operations with a command consisting of four regiments of infantry and about two hundred cavalry.

The Big Sandy was reached and followed up for some sixty miles through a rough, mountainous region, his force driving the outposts of Gen. Humphrey Marshall before them for a considerable distance.

On the 7th of January, 1862, he drove the enemy's cavalry from Paintsville, after a severe skirmish, killing and wounding twenty-five of them. At a strong point, three miles above Paintsville, Marshall had prepared to make a stand, with 4,500 infantry, 700 cavalry, and two batteries of six guns each; but, his cavalry being driven in, his courage failed, and he hastily evacuated his works and retreated up the river.

The rapid marching thus far had much exhausted Gen. Garfield's forces; still, he resolved to pursue, and, selecting 1,100 of his best troops, he continued on to Prestonburg, a distance of fifteen miles. There he found the Rebels strongly posted on the crest of a hill, at once attacked them, and maintained the battle during five hours, the enemy's cannon meanwhile playing briskly.

Although most of Garfield's troops were now under fire for the first time, their daring valor swept all before them. The Rebels were driven from every position, and, after destroying their stores, wagons, and camp equipage, they retreated in disorder to Pound Gap, in the Cumberland Mountains. This was the first brilliant achievement of the War in the West, and a most complete and humiliating defeat to the Rebels, their loss in killed and wounded amounting to two hundred and fifty, in addition to forty taken prisoners, while the Union loss was but thirty-two, all told.

It is said that at the time of this battle, Gen. Garfield had in his possession a letter written a short time before by Humphrey Marshall to his wife, but intercepted by Gen. Buell and sent to Gen. Garfield, in which Marshall stated that he had five thousand effective men in his command. This letter General Garfield refrained from showing to his officers and men until after the battle. His commission as Brigadier dated from the battle of Prestonburg.

Full details of Garfield's Pound-Gap Expedition—Strategy and Victory—Battle of Pittsburg Landing, Etc.

About the middle of March he made his famous Pound-Gap expedition, for a proper understanding of which a few words descriptive of the locality will be necessary. Pound-Gap is a zig-zag opening through the Cumberland Mountains into Virginia, leading into a tract of fertile meadow-land lying between the base of the mountains and a stream called Pound Fork, which bends around the opening of the gap, at some little distance from it, forming what is called "the Pound." These names originated in this wise: This mountain locality was for a long time the home of certain predatory Indians, from which they would make periodical forays into Virginia for plunder, and to which they would retreat as rapidly as they came, carrying with them the stolen cattle, which they would pasture in the meadow-land just mentioned. Hence, among the settlers it became known as "The Pound," and from it the gap and stream took their names. After his defeat at Prestonburg, as has been stated, Humphrey Marshall retreated with his scattered forces through the gap into Virginia. A force of 500 rebels was left to guard the pass against any sudden incursion of Gen. Garfield's force, who, to make assurance doubly sure, had built directly across the gap a formidable breastwork, completely blocking up the way, and behind which 500 men could resist the attack of as many thousand. Behind these works, and on the southwestern slope of the mountains, they had erected commodious cabins for winter quarters, where they spent their time in ease and comfort, occasionally—by way of variety, and in imitation of their Indian predecessors—descending from their stronghold into Kentucky, greatly to the damage of the stock-yards and larders of the well-to-do farmers of that vicinity, and to the fright of their wives and children.

Gen. Garfield determined to dislodge them from their position, and so put an end to their maurauding expeditions. He accordingly set out with a sufficient force, and after two days' forced march reached the base of the mountains a short distance above the gap. Of the strength of the rebels and their position he had been well informed by the spies he had sent out, who had penetrated to their very camp in the absence of the usual pickets, which were never thrown out by them, so secure did they feel in their mountain fortress. It would have been madness to enter the gap and attack them in front, and the General did not propose or attempt it. Halting at the foot of the mountains for the night, he sent his cavalry early the next morning to the mouth of the gap to menace the rebels and draw them from behind their defences. This they did, arriving at a given time and threatening an attack. The rebels jumped at the bait and at once came out to meet them, our men rapidly retreating, and the rebels following until the latter were some distance in front of their breastworks instead of behind them. Meantime, Gen. Garfield, with his infantry, had scaled the mountain-side, in the face of a blinding snow-storm, and, marching along a narrow ridge on the summit, had reached the enemy's camp in the rear of his fortifications. A vigorous attack was now made, resulting in the complete route of the rebels, many of whom were killed, wounded, or taken prisoners, and the remainder dispersed through the mountains. The General now reassembled his forces, and spen a comfortable night in the enemy's quarters, faring sumptuously on the viands there found. The next morning the cabins, sixty in number, were burned, the breastworks destroyed, and the General set out on his return to Piketon, which he reached the following night, having been absent four days, and having marched in that time about one hundred miles over a broken country. On his return he received orders from Gen. Buell, at Nashville, to report to him in person. Arriving at that place, he found that Buell had already begun his march towards Pittsburg Landing, and pushed on after him.

Overtaking the army, he was placed in command of the Twelfth Brigade, and, with his command, participated in the second day's fight at Shiloh. He was present through all the operations in front of Corinth, and, after the evacuation of that place, rebuilt, with his brigade, the bridges on the Memphis & Charleston Railroad, and erected fortifications at Stevenson. Throughout the months of July and August he was prostrated by severe sickness, and, consequently, was not in the retreat to Kentucky or the battles fought in that State. During his illness he was assigned to the command of the forces at Cumberland Gap, but could not assume it. Upon his recovery, he was ordered to Washington, and detailed as a member of the Fitz John Porter court martial, which occupied forty-five days, and in which his great abilities as a lawyer and a soldier were called forth and freely recognized. When the court adjourned he was ordered to report to Gen. Rosecrans, and by him was placed in the responsible position of Chief of Staff, though at first it had been intended to give him only the command of a division in the field.

Gen. Garfield's Proclamation to the Citizens of Sandy Valley.

On the 16th day of January, 1862, Garfield, then in command of the Union forces in Eastern Kentucky, issued the following address to the inhabitants:

"CITIZENS OF SANDY VALLEY: I have come among you to restore the honor of the Union, and to bring back the old banner which you once loved, but which, by the machinations of evil men, and by mutual misunderstanding, has been dishonored among you. To those who are in arms against the Federal Government I offer only the alternate of battle or unconditional surrender. But to those who have taken no part in this war, who are in no way aiding or abetting the enemies of this Union—even to those who hold sentiments averse to the Union, but will give no aid or comfort to its enemies—I offer the full protection of the Government, both in their persons and property.

"Let those who have been seduced away from the love of their country to follow after and aid the destroyers of our peace lay down their arms, return to their homes, bear true allegiance to the Federal Government, and they shall also enjoy like protection. The army of the Union wages no war of plunder, but comes to bring back the prosperity of peace. Let all peace-loving citizens who have fled from their homes return and resume again the pursuits of peace and industry. If citizens have suffered from any outrages by the soldiers under my command, I invite them to make known their complaints to me, and their wrongs shall be redressed and the offenders punished. I expect the friends of the Union in this valley to banish from among them all private feuds, and let a

liberal love of country direct their conduct toward those who have been so sadly estrayed and misguided, hoping that these days of turbulence may soon be ended and the days of the Republic soon return.   J. A. GARFIELD,
"Colonel Commanding Brigade."

Gen. Garfield moved his forces to Piketon, Ky., 120 miles above the mouth of the Big Sandy. Here he remained several weeks; sending out, meanwhile, expeditions in every direction wherever he could hear of a Rebel camp or band, and at length completely cleared the whole country of the enemy.

Heroic Conduct of Gen. Garfield on the Field of Chickamauga—Driving Back Longstreet's Columns and Saving Gen. Thomas.

Gen. Garfield was made a Major-General for "gallant and meritorious services at the battle of Chickamauga." What those services were may be learned from the following extract from the history of the Forty-second Ohio Infantry, page 18:

Trying vainly to check the retreat [of Rosecrans] Gen. Garfield was swept with his chief back beyond Rossville. But the Chief of Staff could not concede that defeat had been entire. He heard the roar of Thomas' guns on the left, and gained permission of Rosecrans to go around to that quarter and find the Army of the Cumberland. While the commander busied himself with preparing a refuge at Chattanooga for his routed army, his Chief of Staff went back accompanied by a staff officer and a few orderlies, to find whatever part of the army still held its ground and save what was lost. It was a perilous ride. Long before he reached Thomas one of his orderlies was killed. Almost alone he pushed on over the obstructed road, through pursuers and pursued, found the heroic Thomas encircled by fire, but still firm, told him of the disaster on the right, and explained how he could withdraw his right wing and fix it upon a new line to meet Longstreet's column. The movement was made just in time, but Thomas' line was too short. It would not reach to the base of the mountain. Longstreet saw the gap, drove his column into it, and would have struck Thomas' column fatally in the rear. In that critical moment Gen. Gordon Granger came up with Steedman's division, which moved in heavy column, threw itself upon Longstreet, and after a terrific struggle drove him back. The dead and wounded lay in heaps where these two columns met, but the army of Gen. Thomas was saved. As night closed in around the heroic Army of the Cumberland, Gens. Garfield and Granger, on foot and enveloped in smoke, directed the loading and pointing of a battery of Napoleon guns, whose flash, as they thundered after the retreating column of the assailants, was the last light that shone upon the battlefield of Chickamauga.

This ride of Garfield's was one of the gallantest acts of the war, and so recognized at the time by the Government and people. It earned Garfield the lasting friendship and regard of Gen. Thomas and all associated with him, and gave him a name as a brave soldier which no malicious scribbler can now take away.

A correspondent on the field, W. S. Furay, under date of September 21, 1863, after describing the perilous condition of the Union Army, speaks of Garfield's ride and arrival on the battlefield, as follows:

Just before the storm broke, the brave and high-souled Garfield was perceived making his way to the headquarters of Gen. Thomas. He had come to be present at the final contest, and in order to do so had ridden all the way from Chattanooga, passing through a fiery ordeal upon the road. His horse was shot under him, and his orderly was killed by his side. Still he had come through, he scarce knew how, and here he was to inspire fresh courage into the hearts of the brave soldiers, who were holding the enemy at bay, to bring them words of greeting from Gen. Rosecrans, and to inform them that the latter was reorganizing the scattered troops, and, as fast as possible, would hurry them forward to their relief.

Just upon the side of the hill, to the left, and in rear of the still smoking ruins of the house, was gathered a group whose names are destined to be historical—Thomas, Whitaker, Granger, Garfield, Steedman, Wood. Calmly they watched the progress of the tempest, speculated upon its duration and strength, and devised methods to break its fury. The future analyst will delight to dwell upon the characteristics and achievements of each member of this group, and even the historian of the present, hastening to the completion of his task, is constrained to pause a moment only to repeat their names—Whitaker, Garfield, Granger, Thomas, Steedman, Wood.

The fight around the hill now raged with terror inexperienced before, even upon this terrible day. Our soldiers were formed in two lines, and as each marched up to the crest and fired a deadly volley at the deadly foe, it fell back a little ways, the men lay down upon the ground to load their guns, and the second line advanced to take their place! They, too, in their turn retired, and then the lines kept marching back and forth, and delivering their withering volleys, till the very brain grew dizzy as it watched them. And all the time not a man wavered. Every motion was executed with as much precision as though the troops were on a holiday parade, notwithstanding the flower of the rebel army were swarming around the foot of the hill, and a score of cannon were thundering from three sides upon it.

5

But our troops are no longer satisfied with the defensive. Gen. Turchin, at the head of his brigade charged into the rebel lines, and cut his way out again, bringing with him 300 prisoners. Other portions of this brave band followed Turchin's example, until the legions of the enemy were fairly driven back to the ground they occupied previous to commencing the fight. Thus did 12,000 or 15,000 men, animated by heroic impulses, and inspired by worthy leaders, save from destruction the Army of the Cumberland. Let the Nation honor them as they deserve.

Among those killed at this battle were: Gen. W. H. Lytle; Col. Grose, commanding a brigade in Palmer's division; Col. Baldwin, commanding a brigade in Johnson's division; Major Wall, of Gen. Davis' staff; Capt. Russell, A. A. G. on Gen. Granger's staff; Col. H. C. Heg, commanding brigade in Gen. Davis' division; Capt. Tinker, of the Sixth Ohio, and Capt. Parshall, of the Thirty-fifth Ohio.

Closing Scenes in Garfield's War Record — Why He Left the Army.

In 1862, while still an officer in the army, he was elected a Representative in Congress from Ohio, from the old Giddings district. About the same time he was sent to Washington as the bearer of dispatches. He there learned for the first time of his promotion to a Major-Generalship of volunteers " for gallant and meritorious conduct at the battle of Chickamauga." He might have retained this position in the army; and the military capacity he had displayed, the high favor in which he was held by the Government, and the certainty of his assignment to important commands, seemed to augur a brilliant future. He was a poor man, too, and the Major-General's salary was more than double that of the Congressman. But, on mature reflection, he decided that the circumstances under which the people had elected him to Congress in a measure compelled him to obey their wishes. He was furthermore urged to enter Congress by the officers of the army, who looked to him for aid in procuring such military legislation as the country needed and the army required. Under the belief that the path of usefulness to the country lay in the direction in which his constituents had pointed, Gen. Garfield sacrificed what seemed to be his personal interests, ard, on the 5th of December, 1863, resigned his commission after nearly three years' service, to enter Congress.

GEN. GARFIELD'S RESIDENCE IN WASHINGTON.

SPEECHES.

Gen. Garfield is Called to the Halls of Congress from the Fields of War—How it was Done—Early Experience of the Farmer Boy on the Floor.

The Congressional District in which Garfield lived was the one long made famous by Joshua R. Giddings. The old anti-slavery champion grew careless of the arts of politics toward the end of his career, and came to look upon a nomination and a re-election as a matter of course.

His over-confidence was taken advantage of in 1858 by an ambitious lawyer named Hutchins to carry a convention against him. The friends of Giddings never forgave Hutchins, and cast about for a means of defeating him. The old man himself was comfortably quartered in his Consulate at Montreal, and did not care to make a fight to get back to Congress. So his supporters made use of the popularity of Gen. Garfield and nominated him when he was in the field without asking his consent. This was in 1862.

When he heard of the nomination Garfield reflected that it would be fifteen months before the Congress would meet to which he would be elected, and believing, as did everyone else, that the war could not possibly last a year longer, concluded to accept. I have often heard him, says a friend, express regret that he did not help fight the war through, and say that he never would have left the army to go to

Congress had he foreseen that the struggle would continue beyond the year 1863. He continued his military service up to the time Congress met.

He was elected to succeed Joshua R. Giddings, who had served for twenty years as the representative from the district composed of the large and prosperous counties in Northeastern Ohio. He resigned from the army under the belief that the path of usefulness to his country lay in the direction of Congress rather than the military service. He sacrificed what seemed to be his personal interest, and resigning his commission he entered the Thirty-eighth Congress. Before taking his seat he was promoted to Major General of volunteers.

On entering Congress, in December, 1863, Gen. Garfield was placed upon the Committee on Military Affairs with Schenck and Farnsworth, who were also fresh from the field. He took an active part in the debates of the House, and won a recognition which few new members succeed in gaining.

He was not popular among his fellow members during his first term. They thought him something of a pedant because he sometimes showed his scholarship in his speeches, and they were jealous of his prominence. His solid attainments and able social qualities enabled him to overcome this prejudice during his second term, and he became on terms of close friendship with the best men in both Houses.

His committee service during his second term was on the Ways and Means, which was quite to his taste, for it gave him an opportunity to prosecute the studies in finance and political economy which he had always felt a fondness for. He was a hard worker and a great reader in those days, going home with his arms full of books from the Congressional Library, and sitting up late of nights to read them.

It was then that he laid the foundations of the convictions on the subject of National Finance, which he has since held to firmly amid all the storms of political agitation. He was renominated in 1864, without opposition, but in 1866 Mr. Hutchins, whom he had supplanted, made an effort to defeat him. Hutchins canvassed the district thoroughly, but the convention nominated Garfield by acclamation. He has had no opposition since by his own party.

In 1872 the Liberals and Democrats united to beat him, but his majority was larger than ever. In 1874 the Greenbackers and Democrats combined and put up a popular soldier against him, but they made no impression on the result. The Ashtabula district, as it is generally called, is the most faithful to its representatives of any in the North. It has had but four members in half a century.

Seventeen Years a Member of Congress—Garfield's Great Work in the Halls of Legislation—A Triumphant Leader.

In the Fortieth Congress Gen. Garfield was Chairman of the Committee on Military Affairs. In the Forty-first he was given the Chairmanship of Banking and Currency, which he liked much better, because it was in the line of his financial studies. His next promotion was to the Chairmanship of the Appropriations Committee, which he held until the Democrats came into power in the House in 1875. His chief work on that committee was a steady and judicious reduction of the expenses of the Government. In all the political struggles in Congress he has borne a leading part, his clear, vigorous, and moderate style of argument making him one of the most effective debaters in either House.

When James G. Blaine went to the Senate in 1877 the

mantle of Republican leadership was by common consent placed upon Garfield, and he has worn it ever since.

Recently Gen. Garfield was elected to the Senate to the seat vacated by Allen G. Thurman on the 4th of March, 1881. He received the unanimous vote of the Republican caucus, an honor never given to any man of any party in the State of Ohio. Since his election he has been the recipient of many complimentary manifestations in Washington and in Ohio.

As a leader in the House he is more cautious and less dashing than Blaine, and his judicial turn of mind makes him too prone to look for two sides of a question for him to be an efficient partisan. When the issue fairly touches his convictions, however, he becomes thoroughly aroused and strikes tremendous blows. Blaine's tactics were to continually harrass the enemy by sharp-shooting surprises and picket firing. Garfield waits for an opportunity to deliver a pitched battle, and his generalship is shown to best advantage when the fight is a fair one and waged on grounds where each party thinks itself strongest. Then his solid shot of argument are exceedingly effective. On the stump Garfield is one of the very best orators in the Republican party. He has a good voice, an air of evident sincerity, great clearness and vigor of statement, and a way of knitting his arguments together so as to make a speech deepen its impression on the mind of the hearer until the climax is reached.

Of his industry and studious habits a great deal might be said, but a single illustration will have to suffice here. Once during the busiest part of a very busy session at Washington, says a friend, "I found him in his library behind a big barricade of books. This was no unusual sight, but when I glanced at the volumes I saw that they were all different editions of Horace, or books relating to that poet."

"I find I am overworked, and need recreation," said the General.

"Now, my theory is that the best way to rest the mind is not to let it be idle; but to put it at something quite outside the ordinary line of its employment. So I am resting by learning all the Congressional Library can show about Horace and the various editions and translations of his poems."

Through the contests of the Fortieth Congress with the President he was firmly on the radical side. His health was seriously impaired by his laborious discharge of public duties, and at the close of the summer session, by the advice of his physician, he sailed for Europe.

Since his first election Gen. Garfield has served consecutively in Congress, and has been the leader on the Republican side for the last five years; his speeches are among the most effective ever delivered by any man in any parliamentary body, and, while as a leader he has not been considered sufficiently aggressive, his advice has always been carefully heeded, and has been effectual in holding back the more radical of the Republicans.

Garfield on the Democracy—Extract from one of his Old Speeches—His Walk in the Democratic Graveyard.

The following is an extract from a speech delivered by Gen Garfield, August 4th, 1876, in the National House of Representatives:

Mr. Chairman: It is now time to inquire as to the fitness of this Democratic party to take control of our great nation and its vast and important interest for the next four years. I put the question to the gentleman from Mississippi (Mr. Lamar), what has the Democratic party done to merit that great trust? He tries to show in what respects it would not be dangerous. I ask him to show in what it would be safe?

I affirm, and I believe I do not misrepresent the great Democratic party, that in the last sixteen years they have not advanced one great national idea that is not to-day exploded and as dead as Julius Cæsar. And if any Democrat here will rise and name a great national doctrine his party has advanced, within that time, that is now alive and believed in, I will yield to him. (A pause.) In default of an answer, I will attempt to prove my negative.

What were the great central doctrines of the Democratic party in the Presidential struggle of 1860? The followers of Breckenridge said slavery had a right to go wherever the Constitution goes. Do you believe that to-day? And is there a man on this continent that holds that doctrine to-day? Not one. That doctrine is dead and buried. The other wing of the Democracy held that slavery might be established in the Territories if the people wanted it. Does anybody hold that doctrine to-day? Dead, absolutely dead!

Come down to 1864. Your party, under the lead of Tilden and Vallandigham, declared the experiment of war to save the Union was a failure. Do you believe that doctrine to-day? That doctrine was shot to death by the guns of Farragut at Mobile, and driven, in a tempest of fire, from the valley of the Shenandoah by Sheridan, less than a month after its birth at Chicago.

Come down to 1868. You declared the constitutional amendments revolutionary and void. Does any man on this floor say so to-day? If so, let him rise and declare it.

Do you believe in the doctrine of the Broadhead letter of 1868, that the so-called constitutional amendments should be disregarded? No; the gentleman from Mississippi accepts the results of the war! The Democratic doctrine of 1868 is dead!

I walk across that Democratic camping-ground as in a graveyard. Under my feet resound the hollow echoes of the dead. There lies slavery, a black marble column at the head of its grave, on which I read: Died in the flames of the civil war; loved in its life; lamented in its death; followed to its bier by its only mourner, the Democratic party, but dead! And here is a double grave: sacred to the memory of squatter sovereignty. Died in the campaign of 1860. On the reverse side: Socred to the memory of Dred Scott and the Breckenridge doctrine. Both dead at the hands of Abraham Lincoln! And here a monument of brimstone: Sacred to the memory of the rebellion; the war against it is a failure; *Tilden et Vallandigham fecerunt*, A. D. 1864. Dead on the field of battle; shot to death by the million guns of the Republic. The doctrine of secession; of State sovereignty, Dead. Expired in the flames of civil war, amid the blazing rafters of the confederacy, except that the modern Æneas, fleeing out of the flames of that ruin, bears on his back another Anchises of State sovereignty, and brings it here in the person of the honorable gentleman from the Appomattox district of Virginia (Mr. Tucker). All else is dead!

Now, gentlemen, are you sad, are you sorry for these deaths? Are you not glad that secession is dead? that slavery is dead? that squatter sovereignty is dead? that the doctrine of the failure of the war is dead? Then you are glad that you were outvoted in 1860, in 1864, in 1868, and in 1872. If you have tears to shed over these losses, shed them in the grave-yard, but not in this House of living men. I know that many a Southern man rejoices that these issues are dead. The gentleman from Mississippi (Mr. Lamar) has clothed his joy with eloquence.

Now, gentlemen, if you yourselves are glad that you have suffered defeat during the last sixteen years, will you not be equally glad when you suffer defeat next November? But pardon that remark; I regret it; I should use no bravado.

Now, gentlemen, come with me for a moment into the camp of the Republican party and review its career. Our central doctrine in 1860 was that slavery should never extend itself over another foot of American soil. Is that doctrine dead? It is folded away like a victorious banner; its truth is alive for evermore on this continent. In 1864 we declared that we would put down the rebellion and secession. And that doctrine lives, and will live when the second Centennial has arrived. Freedom, national, universal, and perpetual—our great constitutional amendments, are they alive or dead? Alive, thank the God that shields both liberty and union. And our national credit! saved from the assaults of Pendleton; saved from the assaults of those who struck it later, rising higher and higher at home and abroad: and only now in doubt lest its chief, its only enemy, the Democracy, should triumph in November.

Garfield's Speech at the Wisconsin Republican Re-union—Outlining the Condition of the Country.

At the Twenty-fifth Reunion of the Wisconsin Republicans, held at Madison, in July, 1879, Gen. Garfield spoke as follows:

This vast assembly must have richly enjoyed the review of the party's history presented here and celebrated here to-day, and not only a review of the past, but the hopeful promises made for the future of that great party. The Republican party, organized a quarter of a century ago, was made a necessity to carry out the pledges of the fathers that this should be a land of liberty.

There was in the early days of the Republic, a Republican party that dedicated this very territory, and all our vast territory, to freedom, that promised much for schools, that abolished imprisonment for debt, and that instituted many wise reforms. But there were many conservatives in those days, whose measures degenerated into treason; and the Republican party of to-day was but the revival of the Republican party of seventy years ago, under new and broader conditions of usefulness.

It is well to remember and honor the greatest names of the Republican party. One of these is Joshua R. Giddings, who for twenty years was freedom's champion in Congress, and, from a feeble minority of two, lived to see a Republican Speaker elected, and himself to conduct him to the chair. Another is Abraham Lincoln, the man raised up by God for a great mission. No man ever had a truer appreciation of the principles of the Declaration of Independence, that great charter which it was the mission of the Republican party to enforce.

There was a fitness in the first platform of the Wisconsin Republicans that they based themselves upon the Declaration of Independence. While the Republicans, from the first, have been true to their principles, perfecting all they promised, as proved to-day by the whole record, the Democrats, on the other hand, steadily wrong, have been forced from one bad position to another.

Can any Democrat point with pride to his party platforms of 1854, or find in them any living issue? The issues they then presented led us into war and involved us in a great National debt. Looking for the cause of that debt I say that the Democratic party caused it.

We are, as a Nation, emerging from difficulties, and the Republican party alone can probably claim that the brightest page of our country's history has been written by the true friends of freedom and progress. The Republican party has yet work to do. We are confronted to-day in Congress by nearly the same spirit that prevailed in the years just before the war.

They tell us that the National Government is but the servant of the States; that we shall not interpose, as a Nation, to guarantee an honest election in a State; that if we will interpose, they will deny appropriations. Is this less dangerous than their position in 1861? Have we no interest except in local elections, no power to guard the ballot-box and protect ourselves against outrages upon it? Why does the South make this issue? I answer: They have a solid South, and only need to carry Ohio and New York to elect the President, and they trust to carry these States by the means they best know how to use.

There are sentimentalists and optimists who may see no danger in this. There had been sentimentalists and optimists in the Republican party, but to-day all were stalwarts. President Hayes, when he came into office, was an optimist, but he saw all his hopes of conciliation frustrated and all his advances met with scorn. We all now stand together on the issue as one.

Garfield's Celebrated Speech at the Andersonville Reunion Held at Toledo, Ohio, Oct. 3, 1879—How the General Looks "Without Gloves!"

The following is the full text of Gen. Garfield's speech at the Andersonville reunion at Toledo on Oct. 3, 1879.

"My Comrades, Ladies and Gentlemen: I have addressed a great many audiences, but I never before stood in the presence of one that I felt so wholly unworthy to speak to. A man who came through the war without being shot or made prisoner is almost out of place in such an assemblage as this.

While I have listened to you this evening I have remembered the words of the distinguished Englishman, who once said, 'that he was willing to die for his country.' Now to say that a man is willing to die for his country is a good deal, but these men who sit before us have said a great deal more than that. I would like to know where the man is that would calmly step out on the platform and say: 'I am ready to starve to death for my country.' That is an enormous thing to say, but there is a harder thing than that. Find a man, if you can, who will walk out before this audience and say: 'I am willing to become an idiot for my country.' How many men could you find who would volunteer to become idiots for their country?

Now let me make this statement to you, fellow-citizens: One hundred and eighty-eight thousand such men as this were captured by the rebels who were fighting our government. One hundred and eighty-eight thousand! How many is that? They tell me there are 4,500 men and women in this building to-night! Multiply this mighty audience by forty and you will have about 188,000. Forty times this great audience were prisoners of war to the enemies of our country. And to every man of that enormous company there stood open night and day the offer: 'If you will join the rebel army, and lift up your hand against your flag, you are free.'"

A voice—"That's so."

Gen. Garfield—"'And you shall have food, and you shall have clothing, and you shall see wife, and mother, and child.'"

A voice—"We didn't ao it, though."

Gen. Garfield—"And do you know that out of that 188,000 there were less than 3,000 who accepted the offer? And of those 3,000, perhaps nine-tenths of them did it with the mental reservation that they would desert at the first hour—the first moment there was an opportunity."

Voices—"That's so."

Gen. Garfield—"But 185,000 out of the 188,000 said: 'No! not to see wife again; not to see child again; not to avoid starvation; not to avoid idiocy; not to avoid the most loathsome of deaths, will I lift this hand against my country forever.' Now, we praise the ladies for their patriotism; we praise our good citizens at home for their patriotism; we praise the gallant soldiers who fought and fell. But what were all these things compared with that yonder? I bow in reverence. I would stand with unsandaled feet in the presence of such heroism and such suffering; and I would say to you, fellow-citizens, such an assemblage as this has never yet before met on this great earth.

"Who have reunions? I will not trench upon forbidden ground, but let me say this: Nothing on the earth and under the sky can call men together for reunions except ideas that have immortal truth and immortal life in them. The animals fight. Lions and tigers fight as ferociously as did you. Wild beasts tear to the death, but they never have reunions. Why? Because wild beasts do not fight for ideas. They merely fight for blood.

All these men, and all their comrades went out inspired by two immortal ideas.

First, that liberty shall be universal in America.

And, second, that this old flag is the flag of a Nation, and not of a State; that the Nation is supreme over all people and all corporations.

Call it a State; call it a section; call it a South; call it a North; call it anything you wish, and yet, armed with the nationality that God gave us, this is a Nation against all State-sovereignty and secession whatever. It is the immortality of that truth that makes these reunions, and that makes this one. You believed it on the battle-field, you believed it in the hell of Andersonville, and you believe it to-day, thank God; and you will believe it to the last gasp."

Voices—"Yes, we will." "That's so," etc.

Gen. Garfield—"Well, now, fellow-citizens and fellow-soldiers—but I am not worthy to be your fellow in this work. I thank you for having asked me to speak to you. [Cries of 'Go on!' 'Go on!' 'Talk to us some more,' etc.]

I want to say simply that I have had one opportunity only to do you any service. I did hear a man who stood by my side in the halls of the legislation—the man that offered on the floor of Congress the resolution that any man who commanded colored troops should be treated as a pirate, and not as a soldier; as a slave-stealer, and not as a soldier—I heard that man calmly say, with his head up in the light, in the presence of this American people, that the Union soldiers were as well treated, and as kindly treated in all the Southern prisons as were the rebel soldiers in all the Northern prisons."

Voices—"Liar," "Liar!" "He was a liar."

Gen. Garfield—"I heard him declare that no kinder men ever lived than Gen. Winder and his Commander-in-Chief, Jeff Davis. [Yells of derision, hisses, etc.] And I took it upon myself to overwhelm him with the proof [a roll of applause begins], with the proof of the tortures you suffered, the wrongs done to you, were suffered and done with the knowledge of the Confederate authorities from Jefferson Davis down—[great applause, waving of hats, veterans standing in their chairs and cheering]—that it was a part of their policy to make you idiots and skeletons, and to exchange your broken and shattered bodies and dethroned minds for strong, robust, well-fed rebel prisoners.

That policy, I affirm, has never had its parallel for atrocity in the civilized world."

Voice—"That's so."

Gen. Garfield—"It was never heard of in any land since the dark ages closed upon the earth. While history lives men have memories. We can forgive and forget all other things before we can forgive and forget this.

Finally, and in conclusion, I am willing, for one—and I think I speak for thousands of others—I am willing to see all the bitterness of the late war buried in the grave of our dead. I would be willing that we should imitate the condescending, loving kindness of him who planted the green grass on the battlefields and let the fresh flowers bloom on all the graves alike. I would clasp hands with those who fought against us, make them my brethren, and forgive all the past, only on one supreme condition: that it be admitted in practice, acknowledged in theory, that the cause for which we fought, and you suffered, was and is, and forevermore will be right, eternally right." [Unbounded enthusiasm.]

Voices—"That's it," "That's so," etc.

Gen. Garfield—"That the cause for which they fought was, and forever will be, the cause of treason and wrong. [Prolonged applause.] Until that is acknowledged my hand shall never grasp any rebel's hand across any chasm, however small." [Great applause and cheers.]

Garfield's Great Speech at Columbus, Acknowledging His Election as United States Senator.

On the 14th of January, 1880, Gen. Garfield arrived in Columbus from Washington. He had that day been formally declared United States Senator from Ohio, his nomination by the Republican Legislative caucus having taken place the week before. In an informal reception which took place in the Hall of the House of Representatives during the evening, the General made the following admirable speech:

FELLOW CITIZENS: I should be a great deal more than a man, or a great deal less than a man, if I were not extremely gratified by this mark of your kindness you have shown me in recent days. I did not expect any such a meeting as this. I knew there was a greeting awaiting me, but did not expect so cordial, generous, and general a greeting without distinction of party, without distinction of interests, as I have received to-night. And you will allow me, in a moment or two, to speak of the memories this Chamber awakens.

Twenty years ago this last week I first entered this Chamber and entered upon the duties of public life, in which I have been every hour since that time in some capacity or other. I left this Chamber eighteen years ago, and I believe I have never entered it since that time. But the place is familiar, though it was peopled not with the faces that I see before me here to-night alone, but with the faces of hundreds of people that I knew here twenty years ago, a large number of whom are gone from earth.

It was here in this Chamber that the word was first brought of the firing on Fort Sumter. I remember distinctly a gentleman from Lancaster, the late Senator Schleigh—Gen. Schleigh, who died not very long ago—I remember distinctly as he came down this aisle, with all the look of agony and anxiety in his face, informing us that the guns had opened upon Sumter. I remember that one week after that time, on motion of a leading Democratic Senator, who occupied a seat not far from that position (pointing to the Democratic side of the Chamber), that we surrendered this Chamber to several companies of soldiers, who had come to Columbus to tender their services to the imperiled Government. They slept on its carpets and on these sofas, and quartered for two or three nights in this Chamber while waiting for other quarters outside of the Capitol.

All the early scenes of the War are associated with this place in my mind. Here were the musterings—here was the center, the nerve center, of anxiety and agony. Here over 80,000 Ohio citizens tendered their services in the course of three weeks to the imperiled nation. Here, where we had been fighting our political battles with sharp and severe partisanship, there disappeared, almost as if by magic, all party lines; and from both sides of the Chamber men went out to take their places on the field of battle. I can see now, as I look out over the various seats, where sat men who afterward became distinguished in the service in high rank, and nobly served their constituency and honored themselves.

We now come to this place, while so many are gone; but we meet here to-night with the war so far back in the distance that it is an almost half-forgotten memory. We meet here to-night with a nation redeemed. We meet here to-night under the flag we fought for. We meet with a glorious, a great and growing Republic, made greater and more glorious by the sacrifices through which the country has passed. And coming here as I do to-night brings the two ends of twenty years together, with all the visions of the terrible and glorious, the touching and cheerful, that have occurred during that time.

I came here to-night, fellow-citizens, to thank this General Assembly for their great act of confidence and compliment to me. I do not undervalue the office that you have tendered to me yesterday and to-day; but I say, I think, without any mental reservation, that the manner in which it was tendered to me is far higher to me, far more desirable, than the thing itself. That it has been a voluntary gift of the General Assembly of Ohio, without solicitation, tendered to me because of their confidence, is as touching and as high a tribute as one man can receive from his fellow-citizens, and in the name of all my friends, for myself, I give you my thanks.

I recognize the importance of the place to which you have elected me; and I should be base if I did not also recognize the great man whom you have elected me to succeed. I say for him, Ohio has had few larger-minded, broader-minded men in the records of our history than that of Allen G. Thurman. Differing widely from him, as I have done in politics, and do, I recognize him as a man high in character and great intellect; and I take this occasion to refer to what I have never before referred to in public: that many years ago, in the storm of party fighting, when the air was filled with all sorts of missles aimed at the character and reputation of public men, when it was even for his party interest to join the general clamor against me and my associates, Senator Thurman said in public, in the campaign, on the stump—when men are as likely to say unkind things as at any place in the world—a most generous and earnest word of defense and kindness for me which I shall never forget so long as I live. I say, moreover, that the flowers that bloom over the garden wall of party politics are the sweetess and most fragant that bloom in the gardens of this world; and where we can fairly pluck them and enjoy their fragrance, it is manly and delightful to do so.

And now, gentlemen of the General Assembly, without

distinction of party, I recognize this tribute and compliment paid to me to-night. Whatever my own course may be in the future, a large share of the inspiration of my future public life will be drawn from this occasion and these surroundings, and I shall feel anew the sense of obligation that I feel to the State of Ohio. Let me venture to point a single sentence in regard to that work. During the twenty years that I have been in public life, almost eighteen of it in the Congress of the United States, I have tried to do one thing. Whether I was mistaken or otherwise, it has been the plan of my life to follow my conviction at whatever personal cost to myself.

I have represented for many years a district in Congress; whose approbation I greatly desired; but though it may seem, perhaps, a little egotistical to say it, I yet desired still more the approbation of one person, and his name was Garfield. He is the only man that I am compelled to sleep with, and eat with, and live with, and die with; and if I could not have his approbation I should have bad companionship. And in this larger constituency which has called me to represent them now, I can only do what is true to my best self, applying the same rule.

And if I should be so unfortunate as to lose the confidence of this larger constituency, I must do what every other fair-minded man has to do—carry his political life in his hand and would take the consequences. But I must follow what seems to me to be the only safe rule of my life; and with that view of the case, and with that much personal reference, I leave that subject.

Thanking you again, fellow-citizens, members of the General Assembly, Republicans as well as Democrats—all, party men as I am—thanking you both for what you have done and for this cordial and manly greeting, I bid you **good-night.**

Gen. Garfield on the Floor of the Great Chicago Convention—Full Text of His Eloquent Speech Nominating John Sherman For President—Delivered June 5, 1880.

It was after full fifteen minutes of applause for a preceeding candidate, in an assembly of 15,000 souls, that Gen. Garfield arose and calmly addressed the Convention at Chicago as follows:

"Mr. President: I have witnessed the extraordinary scenes of this Convention with deep solicitude. No emotion touches my heart more quickly than a sentiment in honor of a great and noble character. But as I sat on these seats and witnessed these demonstrations, it seemed to me you were a human ocean in a tempest. I have seen the sea lashed into fury and tossed into a spray, and its grandeur moves the soul of the dullest man. But I remember that it is not the billows, but the calm level of the sea from which all heights and depths are measured. When the storm has passed and the hour of calm settles on the ocean, when sunshine bathes its smooth surface, then the astronomer and surveyor takes the level from which he measures all terrestrial heights and depths. Gentlemen of the Convention, your present temper may not mark the healthful pulse of the people.

"When our enthusiasm has passed, when the emotions of this hour have subsided, we shall find the calm level of public opinion, below the storm, from which the thoughts of a mighty people are to be measured, and by which their final action will be determined. Not here, in this brilliant circle, where 15,000 men and women are assembled, is the destiny of the Republic to be decreed; not here, where I see the enthusiastic faces of 756 delegates waiting to cast their votes into the urn and determine the choice of their party; but by 5,000,000 Republican firesides, where the thoughtful fathers, with wives and children about them, with the calm thoughts inspired by love of home and love of country, with the history of the past, the hopes of the future, and the knowledge of the great men who have adorned and blessed our Nation in days gone by,—there God prepares the verdict that shall determine the wisdom of our work to-night. Not in Chicago, in the heat of June, but in the sober quiet that comes between now and November, in the silence of deliberate judgment, will this great question be settled. Let us aid them to-night.

"But now, gentlemen of the Convention, what do we want? Bear with me a moment. Hear me for this cause, and, for a moment, be silent that you may hear. Twenty-five years ago this Republic was wearing a triple chain of bondage. Long familiarity with the traffic in the body and souls of men had paralyzed the consciences of a majority of our people. The baleful doctrine of State sovereignty had shocked and weakened the noblest and most beneficent powers of the National Government, and the grasping power of slavery was seizing the virgin Territories of the West and dragging them into the den of eternal bondage. At that crisis the Republican party was born. It drew its first inspiration from the fire of liberty which God has lighted in every man's heart, and which all the powers of ignorance and tyranny can never wholly extinguish. The Republican party came to deliver and save the Republic. It entered the arena when the beleaguered and assailed Territories were struggling for freedom, and drew around them the sacred circle of liberty, which the demon of slavery has never dared to cross. It made them free forever.

"Strengthened by its victory on the frontier, the young party, under the leadership of that great man, who, on this spot, twenty years ago, was made its leader, entered the National Capital and assumed the high duties of the Government. The light which shone from its banner dispelled the darkness in which slavery had enshrouded the Capitol and melted the shackles of every slave, and consumed, in the fire of liberty, every slave-pen within the shadow of the Capitol. Our National industries, by an impoverishing policy, were themselves prostrated, and the streams of revenue flowed in such feeble currents that the Treasury itself was well nigh empty. The money of the people was the wretched notes of 2,000 uncontrolled and irresponsible State bank corporations, which were filling the country with a circulation that poisoned rather than sustained the life of business.

"The Republican party changed all this. It abolished the babel of confusion and gave the country a currency as national as its flag, based upon the sacred faith of the people. It threw its protecting arm around our great industries, and they stood erect as with new life. It filled with the spirit of true nationality all the great functions of the Government. It confronted a rebellion of unexampled magnitude, with a slavery behind it, and, under God, fought the final battle of liberty until victory was won. Then, after the storms of battle, were heard the sweet, calm words of peace uttered by the conquering Nation, and saying to the conquered foe that lay prostrate at its feet : 'This is our only revenge, that you join us in lifting to the serene firmament of the Constitution, to shine like stars forever and forever, the immortal principles of truth and justice, that all men, white or black, shall be free and stand equal before the law.' Then came the questions of reconstruction, the public debt, and the public faith.

"In the settlement of these questions the Republican party has completed its twenty-five years of glorious existence, and it has sent us here to prepare it for another lustrum of duty and of victory. How shall we do this great work? We cannot do it, my friends, by assailing our Republican brethren. God forbid that I should say one word to cast a shadow upon any name on the roll of our heroes. This coming fight is our Thermopylæ. We are standing upon a narrow isthmus. If our Spartan hosts are united we can withstand all the Persians that the Xerxes of Democracy can bring against us.

Let us hold our ground this one year, for the stars in their courses fight for us in the future. The census to be taken this year will bring reinforcements and continued power. But in order to win this victory now, we want the vote of every Republican, of every Grant Republican in America, of every Blaine man and every anti-Blaine man. The vote of every follower of every candidate is needed to make our success certain; therefore, I say gentlemen and brethren, we are here to calmly counsel together, and inquire what we shall do. A voice: 'Nominate Garfield.' [Great applause.]

"We want a man whose life and opinions embody all the achievements of which I have spoken. We want a man who, standing on a mountain height, sees all the achievements of our past history, and carries in his heart the memory of all its glorious deeds, and who, looking forward, prepares to meet the labor and the dangers to come. We want one who will act in no spirit of unkindness toward those we lately met in battle. The Republican party offers to our brethren of the South the olive branch of peace, and wishes them to return to brotherhood, on this supreme condition that it shall be admitted, forever and forever more, that, in the war for the Union, we were right and they were wrong. [Cheers.] On that supreme condition we meet them as brethren, and no other. We ask them to share with us the blessings and honors of this great Republic.

"Now, gentlemen, not to weary you, I am about to present a name for your consideration—the name of a man who was the comrade, and associate, and friend of nearly all those noble dead whose faces look down upon us from these walls to-night [cheers]; a man who began his career of public service twenty-five years ago, whose first duty was courageously done in the days of peril on the plains of Kansas, when the first red drops of that bloody shower began to fall which finally swelled into the deluge of war. He bravely stood by young Kansas then, and, returning to his duty in the National Legislature, through all subsequent time his pathway has been marked by labors performed in every department of legislation.

You ask for his monuments. I point you to twenty-five years of the national statutes. Not one great beneficent statute has been placed on our statute books without his intelligent and powerful aid. He aided these men to formulate the laws that raised our great armies and carried us through the war. His hand was seen in the workmanship of those statutes that restored and brought back the unity and married calm of the States. His hand was in all that great legislation that created the war currency, and in a greater work that redeemed the promises of the government, and made the currency equal to gold. And when, at last called from the halls of legislation into a high executive office, he displayed that experience, intelligence, firmness, and poise of character which has carried us through a stormy period of three years. With one-half the public press crying 'Crucify him!' and a hostile Congress seeking to prevent success—in all this he remained unmoved until victory crowned him.

The great fiscal affairs of the notion and the great business interests of the country he has guarded and preserved, while executing the law of resumption, and effecting its object, without a jar, and against the false prophecies of one-half of the press and all the Democracy of this Continent. He has shown himself able to meet with calmness the great emergencies of the government for twenty-five years. He has trodden the perilous hights of public duty, and against all the shafts of malice has borne his breast unharmed. He has stood in the blaze of "that fierce light that beats against the throne," but its fiercest ray has found no flaw in his armor, no stain on his shield.

I do not present him as a better Republican, or as a better man than thousands of others we honor, but I present him for your deliberate consideration. I nominate John Sherman, of Ohio.

THE NOMINATION.

Comparative Statement of Ballots.

The number of ballots cast at Chicago is by no means unprecedented. In 1852 General Scott was nominated on the fifty-third, and General Pierce on the forty-ninth ballot. The ill-omened Charleston Convention in 1860 cast fifty-seven ineffectual ballots, and went to pieces without nominating anybody. No Republican Convention, however, has ever cast ss many ballots as were recorded at Chicago. Freemont was nominated on the first ballot, Lincoln on the third for his first term and on the first for his second term,

[Exposition Building, in which was held the National Republican Convention of 1880.]

Grant on the first for each term, Greeley on the sixth, and Hayes on the seventh. The first National Convention ever held in the United States nominated Henry Clay in 1831. William Wirt, Mr. Van Buren, General Harrison and Mr. Clay were subsequently nominated on the first ballot. Mr. Polk required nine, General Cass four, James Buchanan seventeen, and Horatio Seymour twenty-two ballots.

At the Chicago Convention Gen. Garfield received 399 votes on the thirty-sixth ballot. Up to the thirty-fourth, his highest number was two. The following tables show the essential points connected with Garfield's nomination:

THE BREAK TO GARFIELD—THIRTY-FOURTH BALLOT.

STATES AND TERRITORIES.	Grant.	Blaine.	Sherman.	Edmunds.	Windom.	Washburne.	Garfield.
Alabama	16	4					
Arkansas	12						
California		12					
Colorado	6						
Connecticut		3				9	
Delaware		6					
Florida	8						
Georgia	8	9	5				
Illinois	24	10				8	
Indiana	2	20	2			6	
Iowa		22					
Kansas	4	6					
Kentucky	20	1	3				
Louisiana	8	4	4				
Maine		14					
Maryland	7	2	7				
Massachusetts	4		21			1	
Michigan	1	21					
Minnesota		6			4		
Mississippi	8	4	3			1	
Missouri	29					1	
Nebraska		6					
Nevada		6					
New Hampshire		10					
New Jersey		14	2			2	
New York	50	18	2				
North Carolina	6	14					
Ohio		9	34	1			
Oregon		6					
Pennsylvania	35	22					1
Rhode Island		8					
South Carolina	11	1	2				
Tennessee	17	4	3				
Texas	13	1	1				1
Vermont				10			
Virginia	16	3	3				
West Virginia	1	8	1				
Wisconsin	2	1				1	16
Arizona		2					
Dakota	1	1					
District of Columbia	1	1					
Idaho		2					
Montana		2					
New Mexico		2					
Utah	1	1					
Washington		2					
Wyoming	1	1					
Total	312	275	107	11	4	29	18

THIRTY-FIFTH BALLOT.

STATES AND TERRITORIES.	Grant.	Blaine.	Sherman.	Edmunds.	Windom.	Washburne.	Garfield.
Alabama	16	4					
Arkansas	12						
California		12					
Colorado	6						
Connecticut		3				9	
Delaware		6					
Florida	8						
Georgia	8	9	5				
Illinois	24	10				8	
Indiana	1	2					27
Iowa		22					
Kansas	4	6					
Kentucky	20	1	3				
Louisiana	8	4	4				
Maine		14					
Maryland	7	3	2				4
Massachusetts	4		21			1	
Michigan	1	21					
Minnesota	1	6			3		
Mississippi	8	4	3				1
Missouri	29					1	
Nebraska		6					
Nevada		6					
New Hampshire		10					
New Jersey		14	2			2	
New York	50	18	2				
North Carolina	6		13				1
Ohio		9	34	1			
Oregon		6					
Pennsylvania	36	20				1	1
Rhode Island		8					
South Carolina	11	1	2	10			
Tennessee	17	4	3				
Texas	13	1	1			1	
Vermont							
Virginia	16	3	3				
West Virginia	1	8	1				
Wisconsin	2	2					16
Arizona		2					
Dakota	1	1					
District of Columbia	1	1					
Idaho		2					
Montana		2					
New Mexico		2					
Utah	1	1					
Washington		2					
Wyoming	1	1					
Totals	313	257	99	11	3	23	50

Thirty-sixth and Last Ballot—Garfield Nominated.

States and Territories.	No. of votes.	Grant.	Blaine.	Sherman.	Washburne.	Garfield.
Alabama	20	16	4			
Arkansas	12	12				
California	12		12			
Colorado	6	6				
Connecticut	12		1			11
Delaware	6		6			
Florida	8	8		3		
Georgia	22	8	10		5	1
Illinois	42	24	6			7
Indiana	30	1				29
Iowa	22					22
Kansas	10	4				6
Kentucky	24	20	1			3
Louisiana	16	8				8
Maine	14					14
Maryland	16	6				10
Massachusetts	26	4				22
Michigan	22	1				21
Minnesota	10	2				8
Mississippi	16	7				9
Missouri	30	29				1
Nebraska	6					6
Nevada	6	2	1			3
New Hampshire	10					10
New Jersey	18					18
New York	70	50				20
North Carolina	20	5				15
Ohio*	43					43
Oregon	6					6
Pennsylvania	58	37				21
Rhode Island	8					8
South Carolina	14	8				6
Tennessee	24	15	1			8
Texas	16	13				3
Vermont	10					10
Virginia	22	19				3
West Virginia	10	1				9
Wisconsin	20					20
Arizona	2					2
Dakota	2					2
District of Columbia	2					2
Idaho	2					2
Montana	2					2
New Mexico	2					2
Utah	2					2
Washington	2					2
Wyoming	2					2
Totals	755	306	42	3	5	399

*Gen. Garfield not voting.

THE NOMINATION.

SUMMARY.

BALLOT.	Grant.	Blaine.	Sherman.	Washburne.	Edmunds.	Windom.	Garfield.	Hayes.	Harrison.	McCrary.	Davis, of Texas.	Hartranft, of Pa.
1	304	284	93	30	34	10						
2	305	282	94	31	32	10	1					
3	305	282	93	31	32	10	1		1			
4	305	281	95	31	32	10	1					
5	305	281	95	31	32	10	1					
6	305	280	95	31	32	10	2					
7	305	281	94	31	32	10	2					
8	306	284	91	32	31	10	1					
9	308	282	90	32	31	10	2					
10	305	282	92	33	31	10	1	1				
11	305	281	93	32	31	10	2	1				
12	304	283	92	33	31	10	1	1				
13	305	285	89	33	31	10	1			1		
14	305	285	89	35	31	10						
15	309	281	88	36	31	10						
16	306	283	88	36	31	10						
17	303	284	90	36	31	10					1	
18	305	283	91	35	31	10						
19	305	279	96	32	31	10	1					1
20	308	276	93	35	31	10	1					1
21	305	276	96	35	31	10	1					1
22	305	275	97	35	31	10	1					1
23	304	275	97	36	31	10	2					
24	305	279	93	35	31	10	2					
25	302	281	94	35	31	10	2					
26	303	280	93	36	31	10	2					
27	306	277	93	36	31	10	2					
28	307	279	91	35	31	10	2					
29	305	278	116	35	12	7	2					
30	306	279	120	33	11	4	2					
31	308	276	118	37	11	3	1					
32	309	270	117	44	11	3	1					
33	309	276	110	44	11	4	1					
34	312	275	107	30	11	4	17					
35	313	257	99	23	11	3	50					
36	306	42	3	5			399					

Enthusiasm on Fire—Making the Nomination of Gen. Garfield Unanimous at the Chicago Republican Convention—Speeches of Messrs. Conkling, Logan, Beaver, Hale, Pleasants, and Harrison.

Immediately after Gen. Garfield had received the 399 votes of the Chicago Convention, it was the desire of the body to make his nomination unanimous. This was effected amid the greatest enthusiasm, and called forth the following brief and eloquent speeches:

SENATOR CONKLING, OF NEW YORK.

MR. CHAIRMAN—James A. Garfield, of Ohio, having received a majority of all the votes cast, I rise to move that he be unanimously presented as the nominee of this Convention. The Chair, under the rules, anticipates my motion, and being on my feet, I avail myself of the opportunity to congratulate the Republican party upon the good-natured and the well-tempered rivalry which has distinguished this animated contest. Well, gentlemen, I would speak louder, but having sat under the cool wind of these windows, I feel myself unable to. I was in the act to say, Mr. Chairman, that I trust that the zeal, the fervor, and now the unanimity seen in the Convention will be transplanted to the field of the conflict, and that all of us who have borne a part against each other will find ourselves with equal zeal bearing the banner, and with equal zeal carrying the lance of the Republican party into the ranks of the enemy.

SENATOR LOGAN, OF ILLINOIS.

MR. CHAIRMAN AND GENTLEMEN OF THE CONVENTION—We are to be congratulated that we have arrived at a conclusion in reference to presenting the name of a candidate to become the standard-bearer of the Republican party for President of the United States. In union and harmony there is strength. Whatever may have transpired in this Convention that may have momentarily marred the feelings of any one here, I hope that in our conclusion it will pass from our minds. I, sir, with the friends of, I think, one of the grandest men that ever graced the face of the earth [applause] stood ever here to fight a friendly battle in favor of his nomination. But, sir, the Convention has chosen another leader. The men who stood by Grant's banners will be seen in the front of this contest on every field. We will go forward, sir, not with tied hands, not with sealed lips, not with bridled tongues, but to speak the truth in favor of the grandest party that has ever been organized in this country, to maintain its principles, maintain its power, and to preserve its ascendancy. And sir, with the leader you have selected, my judgment is victory will perch upon our banners. I, sir, as one of the representatives from the State of Illinois, second the nomination of James A. Garfield, of Ohio, and I hope it may be made unanimous.

GEN. BEAVER, OF PENNSYLVANIA.

The State of Pennsylvania having had the honor of first naming in this Convention the gentleman who has been nominated as the standard-bearer of the Republican party in the approaching national contest, I rise, sir, to second the motion which has been made to make that nomination unanimous, and to assure this Convention and the people of this country that Pennsylvania is heartily in accord with this nomination; that she gives her full concurrence to it, and that this country may expect from her the best majority that has been given for a Presidential candidate in many years.

MR. HALE, OF MAINE.

Mr. President: In returning heartfelt thanks to the men in this convention who have aided us in the fight that we have made for the Senator from Maine, and speaking, as I know that I do, for them here, I say this most heartily:

We have not gotten the man that we came to nominate, but we have got a man in whom we have the greatest and most perfect confidence. [Cheers.] The nominee of this convention is no new or untried man, and in that respect no dark horse. When he came here representing his State in the front of that delegation, and was seen here, every man knew him before that, and because of our faith in him, and because we were in that emergency glad to help make him the candidate of the Republicans for President of the United States, because of these things I stand here to pledge the Blaine forces of this convention to earnest effort from now until the ides of November, that shall make Jas. A. Garfield the next President of the United States.

MR. W. H. PLEASANTS, OF VIRGINIA.

MR. CHAIRMAN: As New York, Illinois, and Maine, along with Pennsylvania, have spoken, I stand here probably occupying a peculiar (but most rightly so) position to that of the majority of the people of this convention. I came here, sir, from Virginia, instructed by the State Convention to vote for that peculiar and most distinguished man, the most renowned in the world, Ulysses S. Grant, and I have proved it sincere here; I have been standing upon this floor, and upon all occasions casting my vote to the last for that man. But, sir, as the convention has thought best to nominate James A. Garfield, of Ohio, for President of the Unithd States, it may not be that we can promise you Virginia, but we can promise you this, as humble men, and as men who have on all occasions shown their devotion to the Republican principles of the country; men who, as Virginia Republicans, on one occasion, gave the electoral vote of Virginia to Ulysses S. Grant; and while a division exists in the Republican party of that State, we hope in November next to return your nominee. Although it was said that we had all to receive and nothing to give, we now receive James A. Garfield, and will endeavor to give him Virginia. I, for one—and I speak for this delegation, and for every Republican in the State—second the nomination of James A. Garfield, and the motion to make the vote unanimous.

BEN HARRISON, OF INDIANA.

I am not in very good voice to address the convention. Indiana has been a little noisy within the last hour, and, though the Chairman of this delegation, I forgot myself so much as to abuse my voice. I should not have detained the convention to add any word to what has been said in a spirit of such commendable harmony over this nomination, if it had not been for the over partiality of my friends from Kentucky, with whom we have had a good deal of pleasant intercourse. They insist, sirs, as I am the only defeated candidate for the Presidency on the floor of this convention, having received one vote from some misguided friend from Pennsylvania, who, unfortunately for me, didn't have staying qualities, and dropped out on the next ballot. I want to say to the Ohio delegation that they may carry to their distinguished citizen who has received the nomination at the hands of this convention my encouraging support. I bear him no malice at all. But, Mr. Chairman, I will defer my speeches until the campaign is hot, and then, on every stump in Indiana, and wherever else my voice can help on this great Republican cause to victory I hope to be found.

Gen. Garfield En Route for Home After His Nomination for President— From Illinois to Ohio—Incidents and Welcomes by the Way.

The first emotions of surprise being past, General Garfield bore the fresh penalties of greatness with equanimity and apparently with some sense of enjoyment. From the moment his nomination became assured, he was made the recipient of such exuberant and spontaneous honors as loyal crowds in this republic delight to bestow upon their favorites. The music of brass bands announced his first appearance in the office of the hotel in Chicago, as he came from his room, clad for his journey to his Ohio home. A band and hundreds of people accompanied him to the depot, where a great crowd had gathered to wish him God-speed to his home, and hence through the campaign to the White House. When he arrived at the depot, there was great cheering and waving of hats.

General Garfield came to Cleveland in a special car, accompanied by a number of intimate personal friends, among whom were Gov. Charles Foster, of Ohio; S. T. Everett, President of the Second National Bank of Cleveland; Gen. James Barnett, an old military friend of Gen. Garfield, he having been Chief of Artillery in the armies of Rosecrans and Thomas; Col. D. G. Swaim, Judge Advocate of the United States Army, formerly Adjutant of the 42d Ohio Volunteers (Garfield's regiment); Lieutenant-Colonel L. A. Sheldon, Mayor W. H. Williams, and Capt. Charles E. Henry, all of whom were also officers of Garfield's regiment; I. F. Mack, of the *Ohio Register*, Sandusky; N. B. Sherwin, J. W. Tyler, and Major Eggleston, of Cleveland, were also with Gen. Garfield.

Once out of the din of Chicago, Gen. Garfield and his friends lighted their cigars and passed the hours in conning over the stirring events of the past week, reading congratulatory dispatches, and in a casual way discussing the political outlook. Gen. Garfield gave brief expression to his gratification at the touching incidents of the last twenty-four hours which had brought out so many evidences of the universal appreciation in which his public services are held, and mentioned feelingly the handsome compliment paid him by the House of Representatives in Washington. Gov. Foster alluded jokingly to the popular impression that he may be Gen. Garfield's successor in Senatorial honors, saying that he was already filling Garfield's shoes, having had his own stolen at the hotel in Chicago, and been compelled to accept the loan of a pair of these needful articles from the General.

At Laporte, Ind., the first stopping place of any consequence, many hundreds of people, with a brass band, had collected to salute Gen. Garfield as he passed. Gov. Foster made a brief speech introducing Gen. Garfield, when there were deafening cheers from the multitude. Col. Sheldon followed, briefly telling the story of Chicago. At South Bend the scene was repeated, but with a larger crowd, and of course louder cheering. All along the route, at the hamlets through which the train passed without stopping, and even at farm houses, people gathered and gazed and cheered in one continued outburst.

INDIANA'S WELCOME.

At Elkhart, Ind., where the train made a stop for dinner, a brass band led the way along the railroad platform to the dining room, and after dinner it headed the column on its return to the cars. At Goshen hundreds of people were waiting with a gun mounted on a log, the first discharge from which dismounted the piece; but the crowd made up in enthusiasm for this mishap.

At Ligonier the ceremonial of introduction was somewhat varied, Gen. Garfield getting ahead and introducing Gov. Charlie Foster to the crowd of an unnamed water station, where a dozen men and boys—apparently the whole male population—had gathered. Several of the latter climbed aboard the car, inquiring for the coming man. Gen. Garfield was pointed out, and bowed.

"Hallo!" shouted the delighted spokesman of the assemblage, as the train moved away, "We'll support you."

At Kendallville the ladies of the village were largely represented in the greeting crowd, several of them bearing bouquets for presentation to the man they had assembled to honor. At Waterloo and Butler, the last two stopping places in Indiana, the scenes enacted at the stations previously passed were repeated. All along the lines crowds had been growing larger proportionately to the size of the towns, and the salutations were enthusiastic.

IN OHIO.

Crossing the line into Ohio, at Edgerton the greetings, of course, suffered no diminution in point of numbers or enthusiasm, but fewer opportunities were offered for giving expression to the public feeling than in Indiana. Everywhere the people, it was reported, were wild with enthusiasm.

At Bryan an affecting incident occurred. Mr. William Letcher, an old gentleman, a cousin of Gen. Garfield, between whom and himself exist ties of tender friendship, came on the car, prepared with a brief little speech of congratulation. He was so overcome with emotion, however, that he could only ejaculate, "Cousin James," and burst into tears. A friend recalled the fact that Mr. Letcher had held Gen. Garfield when a baby in his arms at the funeral of his father.

CONGRATULATIONS.

The following are a few of the hundreds of congratulatory telegrams received by Gen. Garfield during the day:

Prof. Simom Newcombe, the astronomer at Washington,

"Thousand congratulations on the success of the office in finding the man."

J. B. Dinsmore, Captain of "The Garfield Guards, Sutton, Nebraska:" "Gen. Garfield's Guards were organized to-night, with forty-eight members. Great enthusiasm; torchlight procession and ratification meeting."

William R. Johnson and 600 others, Ann Arbor, Mich.: "The students of the University of Michigan send congratulations."

A. S. Stratton, Mayor of Madison, Lake county (Gen. Garfield's own county), Ohio: "Madison sends greetings; immense enthusiasm; cannon, bonfires, speeches, and cheers."

Frederick W. Pitkin, Chairman, and K. G. Cooper, Secretary, Denver, Col.: "At an enthusiastic ratification meeting of the Republicans of Denver, held this evening, the following resolution was unanimously adopted:

"*Resolved*, By the Republicans of Denver in mass meeting assembled, that we heartily endorse the nomination of James A. Garfield and Chester A. Arthur, and we pledge the State of Colorado for the Chicago nominations with 5,000 majority."

Thomas H. Wilson, member of the General Assembly, Youngstown, Ohio: "Youngstown ablaze. Your friends have been hoping for just such a result, although appreciating the delicacy of your situation. The party has honored and saved itself."

Eli H. Murray, an old friend of Gen. Garfield's, now Governor of Utah: "Telegrams assure me that I was right in naming you President. God bless you."

Garfield's Informal Acceptance of the Nomination—His Sense of the Responsibility.

Near midnight, in Chicago, June 9th, 1880, the Committee appointed by Senator Hoar to wait on Generals Garfield and Arthur and notify them of their nomination, found them in the club room of the Grand Pacific Hotel, and Senator Hoar, as Chairman, made an appropriate speech.

Gen. Garfield replied:

MR. CHAIRMAN AND GENTLEMEN: I assure you that the information you have officially given to me brings the sense of very grave responsibility, and especially so in view of the fact that I was a member of your body, a fact that could not have existed with propriety had I had the slightest expectation that my name would be connected with the nomination for the office. I have felt with you great solicitude concerning the situation of our party during the struggle; but, believing that you are correct in assuring me that substantial unity has been reached in the conclusion, it gives me a gratification far greater than any personal pleasure your announcement can bring.

I accept the trust committed to my hands. As to the work of our party, and as to the character of the campaign to be entered upon, I will take an early occasion to reply more fully than I can properly do to-night.

I thank you for the assurances of confidence and esteem you have presented to me, and hope we shall see our future as promising as are indications to-night.

Senator Hoar, in the same manner, presented the nomination to General Arthur, who accepted it in a brief and informal way.

How the News of Garfield's Nomination was Received at Hiram College—Ringing the Old Bell.

When the news was received at Hiram College, where Garfield had been a school boy, Professor and President, the College bell, which Garfield used to ring for his tuition, was wildly rung, and the people came running from every part of the little town built around the College Square, to gather under the old bell to clasp hands and shout their joy.

Everybody who went to school with Garfield; every pupil who remembers him as a rigid disciplinarian, but as the first and strongest on the ball ground, where he spent many hours with his scholars; every soldier who went to the war in the old Forty-Second, and all the people of this little town, who have lived here in the same houses thirty years, when as a youth he came among them, all and each loved Garfield; and as there were many representatives of each class, we can imagine the character of the occasion.

First Vote for Garfield in the Chicago Convention—The Man Who Gave it Voted for Zachary Taylor and Abraham Lincoln Under Like Circumstances.

A prominent gentleman who, in speaking of the incidents of the Chicago Convention, which nominated Gen. Garfield, said that the Pennsylvanian who cast the first and only vote which Gen. Garfield received for several ballots was Caleb N. Taylor, a delegate from the Bucks District.

This gentleman says that while in Chicago he met Mr. Taylor, who was well known to him, he having been a Representative in Congress for several terms, and a person who, though a Quaker, always took a great interest in public affairs, but was exceedingly deaf.

Mr. Taylor accosted this gentleman in one of the corridors of the Palmer House and remarked that he expected to cast the first vote for the man who would be nominated. He declined to mention his name, but added that if he watched his vote he would discover who this gentleman was.

Mr. Taylor then mentioned several instances in his experience. He stated that, in 1848, his constituents sent him to Harrisburg with instructions to vote as they had directed, but against this verdict he had cast his vote for Zachary Taylor, and for some time his was the only vote he received, and Taylor was subsequently nominated. In 1860 he was again sent to the National Convention at Chicago, with instructions how he should vote.

He again disregarded these instructions and cast his first vote for Abraham Lincoln, who was nominated. Mr. Taylor, in the late Chicago Convention, as already stated, cast his first vote for Garfield, who was also nominated.

What Prominent Foreign-Born Citizens Say of the Convention—They Declare it Positively American.

The following opinions of intelligent foreign-born citizens, respecting the Republican Convention at Chicago, which nominated Gen. Garfield for President, are exceedingly interesting, and to the point:

OPINION OF EX-LIEUT.-GOV. MULLER.

Whoever has studied the history of the ancients, and by its aid and lights has formed an idea of the imposing magnificence of the peoples' mass-meetings as they were held in the classic times of Greece and the Roman Empire for the purpose of listening to lectures, political and other matter-of-State discussions, witnessing public plays or gladiatorial contests, can find in the picture developed before my eyes in this Republican National Convention an approaching counterpart.

Ten thousand stalwart men filled the immense and splendidly-decorated hall; all seats, row upon row, and closely joined, were occupied, so that hardly a bullet could drop to the floor. All the different delegations from the thirty eight States, the eight Territories, and the District of Columbia, had their space and seats allotted to them, and the galleries were filled with the most prominent and talented men of the country.

The impression which this convention of sovereign citizens of a free land made upon the quiet observers was grand and imposing beyond all description. No showy and gold-embroidered uniforms, no diamond-stars and decorations of any order, or other such like tinsel, as are graciously bestowed by monarchs and princes upon their devoted subjects, attracted my attention, but civic and democratic simplicity in the outward appearance of all those present greeted my eyes! Reserve, self-reliance, and intelligence were beaming on the faces of all who composed this vast assembly, and the thought that these men could ever give up all their country's traditions and its free institutions as not worthy of preservation, disappeared at once from my mind.

At all events, my observations during the session of this Convention so far have quieted all my apprehensions that among the people of this country sympathies for a so-called strong or monarchical government could ever take root.

I am convinced now that everything which has manifested itself in this direction so far emanates only from those classes of our population commonly designated as "Shoddyites," who are represented in real life by blasé aristocratic swellheads.

OPINION OF HERMAN RASTER.

The conduct of the delegates and spectators in the Convention was, in one word, American; with that everything is said. No personal altercations, no twitting, no insinuations; everywhere good cheer, pleasantness, and a disposition to oblige predominated. But then came the outbursts of real or artificial enthusiasm, poured forth with such tremendous elementary strength, that would place the demoniac yells of the Comanche Indians and the howlings of the Zulu-Caffirs by far in the shade! Whoever did not witness the proceedings of the Convention on the fourth day of its session cannot even have an approaching conception of the noise and wild enthusiasm which prevailed during that day from early morn until late at night.

A stranger, unaware of the proceedings in the hall, might have been induced to believe that pandemonium had broken loose, or that all the lunatic asylums in the country had emptied their contents into the Exposition Building.

Among the delegates, although determined in their opposition and in the promotion of their choice's interests, nothing but pleasantness and affability was perceptible. During the whole time of the six days' proceedings not a word was uttered which could be tortured into a direct insult, and not a single serious dispute took place among them as well as among all this vast concourse of excited and enthusiastic men. In this respect the conduct of the Americans in their mass-meetings and gatherings cannot be enough praised and extolled,—more particularly so when we consider the behavior of the French, the Germans, Italians, and Poles on similar occasions.

Any Convention of the importance and magnitude of that which has just adjourned in Chicago, held in France, would undoubtedly have caused hundreds of personal conflicts and duels. Such a sudden readiness and submissiveness to accept an unexpected result as a finality as is exhibited by Americans after their Conventions we look for in vain among all other civilized nations.

A Garfield Nomination Joke.

An hour or so after the latest and last from the Chicago nomination, a policeman on Randolph street halted at the door of a saloon and asked the proprietor how he liked the nomination.

"I doan' care for bolitics any more," was the reply.

"Why, what's the matter? You were greatly excited yesterday."

"If I vhas den I vhas a fool. Vhen dot first pallot vhas daken I set up der peer for de Grant crowd, for I likes to shtand vhell mit der poys."

"Yes."

"Den a pig crowdt rushes in here und yells out dot Jim Plaine vhas de coming man, und I hand out der cigars, for mein poy vhants a blace in der Gustom-house oof Jim Plaine vhas Bresident."

"Yes, I see."

"Vhell, pooty soon comes mein brudder in und says I vhas a fool, for dot feller Sherman would git all der votes pooty queek. I tinks off Sherman gits it mein poy haf a blace in der Post-office sure, und I calls in der poys und dells 'em to trink to my gandidate."

"Just so."

"I feels goot vhen I goes to bedt, but early in der mornings some Aldermans come roundt here und says: 'Shake, tont pe a fool. Edmunds ish der man who vhill knock 'em all to pieces,' und I dells efery pody I vhas an Edmundts, und I pet ten dollars he vhas voted in. Dis forenoon mein poy vhas for Grant, mein brudder vhas for Sherman und I vhas for Blaine, und vhere pe dose five kegs of lager dot I hadt dis morning? Vhen I goes home mein vhrow she saidt I vhas zwei fools, und I locks up der saloon und goes to bedt."

"Well, have you heard who was nominated?"

"Nein."

"It was Garfield."

"Garfeel? Py Sheorge! I dreats avay seven kegs of lager und two poxes of cigars, und it vhas Garfeel! Wheel, dot ends me oop. If I efer haf some more to do mit boliticks, den I am as grazy as bedtbugs. Garfeel! Vhell— vhell. Vhat a fool I vhas dot I save not mein peer und make a zure blace for mein poy mit Garfeel!"

MISCELLANEOUS.

Who Is General Garfield?

The first and superficial answer is, that he is the Republican leader in the popular branch of Congress, where he has served conspicuously for seventeen years, and that he is Senator elect from the State of Ohio—two eminent stations, which, together with the Presidential nomination, distinguish him by an unexampled combination of civic honors. Reaching behind this Congressional experience, he was an enthusiastic volunteer in the Union Army. Before his military service he was for one brief term a member of the Senate of Ohio. This carries him back to the beginning of his public career, to a time when 28 years of age he was a school-teacher in a little village on the Western reserve, in the neighborhood of the hamlet where he was born.

He came of a family of yeomen. When he was left an orphan in the cradle by his father's death his mother struggled with poverty to educate him for loftier pursuits than those of his ancestors, and the boy bravely seconded her efforts. The slow and scanty savings of labor as a canal boatman and a carpenter provided him means for a liberal education, and at the mature age of 25 he was graduated from a New England college in 1856, the same year in which the Republican party set its first Presidential ticket in the field.

This is an honorable record—as characteristic as Abraham Lincoln's of the aspirations and opportunities of life in our republic; but its recital does not touch the core of our question. The mere outline of a man's experience is not a satisfactory reply to an inquiry what manner of man that experience has left him. Answering the question in this deeper sense, Gen. Garfield is a typical representative of the civilization of New England removed into the West, where it has grown greater and ranker than it flourishes at home, as a New England wild flower might if transplanted from its rocky pasture into the rich soil of the prairie.

When Sir Charles Dilke wrote a book upon America a few years ago he styled it the "Greater Britain." In the same spirit that broad reach of the Northwestern territory, which begins at the Valley of the Gennesee, and, after crossing the Western Reserve, spreads out into an area encompassing the great lakes, might well be styled the "Greater New England." The leaven of its first settlers pervades it, tempered, but not dissipated, by space and time, and from these settlers Gen. Garfield descended, bearing among his own names a Biblical patronymic, which, like Lincoln's, betokens his Puritan descent from a New England ancestry.

Applying this key to his public career, the American people can fairly interpret its past, and conjecture its future. It explains the alliance of his fortunes with the Republican party; the ardor with which he has assisted in the abolition of slavery, and in the distinctive political measures which resulted from that event; the courage with which he always has antagonized the "Ohio idea" of financial legislation; the hesitation with which he has opposed his own liberal convictions concerning economic questions to the predominant opinions of his political associates; and the scholarly tastes which have impelled him to serve upon Congressional committees on education and the census, and as a regent of the Smithsonian Institute with no less zeal than he has applied himself to the business of the committees on Military Affairs, Banking, and the Currency and Appropriations, of all of which he has been successively Chairman. It defines also the respectable simplicity of his private life.

Dying Words of Gen. Garfield's Father—He Leaves His Four Children in Care of His Wife.

Gen. Garfield's mother, a woman of wonderful intelligence and highly endowed by nature, was wedded to a man of the most generous impulses and largeness of soul, and together they sought their fortunes in the woods of Orange, Cuyahoga County, O.

To this couple were born four children, James Abram being the last. When the youngest son was only two years old, his father, over-worked and weary from the labor of saving his wheat crop from a fire which threatened its destruction, sat in a draft of wind, and contracted a violent sore throat. A quack doctor of the time applied a blister, which caused him to choke to death. Vigorous and hearty in all his frame, in his dying moments he said to his beloved wife:

"I have planted four saplings in these woods. I must now leave them to your care."

Then, taking a last look out upon his farm, and calling his oxen by name, he died.

Garfield's Life in Hiram Sketched by President Hinsdale, of Hiram College—An Interesting History.

"Garfield's life in Hiram," says President Hinsdale, "may be divided into four parts: First, student period; second, student and teacher; third, teacher, and, fourth, citizen period. I was not in Hiram when Garfield came here, but he came in 1851. His name first appears in the catalogue of that year, 'James A. Garfield, Cuyahoga county.' It appears the same way next year, but never appears again as the name of a student. In the catalogue of 1853 it appears in the list of instructors as 'Teacher in the English Department and Ancient Languages.' He began to teach when he had been here about a year, and continued to teach, at the same time carrying on his own studies, until he went to Williams College in 1854. Previous to going to Williams his name appears only once as instructor.

The student period, then, may be said to have lasted one year, and student and teacher period two years. He entered the junior class at Williams College in 1854, and graduated in 1856, dividing the highest honors with one of his classmates. He returned to Hiram in the fall of 1856, where he had just been elected a teacher of ancient languages and literature. He occupied this position one year, until, on retirement of Mr. A. S. Hayden, he became the head of the institution. The school was then called the Western Reserve Eclectic Institute, and did not become Hiram College until 1865, so that Garfield was never President of Hiram College, as has been stated, but was Principal of the Institute, in active duty, from June, 1857, to September, 1861. When he became the head of the institution he was 26 years old.

The teacher period of his life then covers four years. He entered the army in August, 1861, taking bodily his classes in history, Latin, etc., with him into the field. At this time his active connection with the institution ceased; but so reluctant was the Board of Trustees to part with his name that he continued nominally a Principal until 1864. In the catalogue of the two following years his name appears as 'Advising Principal,' and first as a member of the Board of Trustees in 1865.

"In the fall of 1862, at 31 years of age, he was elected to Congress, but continued in the army until he took his seat in December of the year following. While in the army, he bought this house, which I now own, which is the only piece of property Garfield ever owned in Hiram. His home continued to be here until he moved to Mentor in 1877, so that the citizen period of his life may be said to reach from 1863 to 1877.

"I came to Hiram at the opening of the winter term of 1853–4. I arrived in the evening, and saw nobody until next day. That day I went with father to Mr. Hayden, then Principal, and in the parlor of the house I first saw Garfield.

"In stature he was what he is now, only not so well rounded up. His head was covered with an immense shock of tow-colored hair, which has since darkened. He was but 22 years old, and had a decidedly veally appearance. George Pow, of Mahoning County came in, and the conversation turned upon a recent contest of Pow with B U. Watkins on the rightfulness of Christians going to war. Pow had affirmed this rightfulness under certain circumstances, and, as I came in, young Garfield said: 'So, Brother Pow, you took the gunpowder side, did you?' These are the first words I remember to have ever heard Garfield speak.

"That winter I was a member of one of Garfield's classes —a class in arithmetic of 105 members, which he handled with admirable power. The impression which he made upon me then is the same which he made upon everybody then and after. I cannot describe him better than to read a passage from my history of the Delphic Society. Garfield, I should say, was then a member of the Philomathian Society, and delivered before it that winter a course of lectures on history. But here is the passage:

"'An old Hiram student, in a private letter, speaks of the Philomathians as 'wonderful men,' mentions those he thought 'master spirits,' and adds: 'Then began to grow up in me an admiration and love for Garfield that has never abated, and the like of which I have never known. A bow of recognition or a single word from him was to me an inspiration. The exact parallel or my own experiences, Garfield, you have taught me more than any other man, living or dead; and when I recall these early days, when I remember that James and I were not the last of the boys, proud as I am of your record as a soldier and a statesman, I can hardly forgive you for abandoning the academy for the field and the forum.'

"When I read the above passage," continued Hinsdale, laying the book down, "before a brilliant audience in the chapel four years ago, the cheers with which it was received showed that it struck a chord in all hearts.

"My real acquaintance with Garfield did not begin until the fall of 1856, when he returned from Williams College. He then found me out, drew near to me, and entered into all my troubles and difficulties pertaining to questions of the future. In a greater or less degree this was true of his relations to his pupils generally. There are hundreds of these men and women scattered over the world to-day who cannot find language strong enough to express their feeling in contemplating Garfield as their old instructor, adviser and friend. Since 1856 my relations with him have been as close and confidential as they could be with any man, and much closer and more confidential than they have been with any other man. I think that it would be impossible for me to know anybody better than I know him, and I know that he possesses all the great elements of character in an extraordinary degree.

"His interest in humanity has always been as broad as humanity itself, while his lively interest in young men and women, especially if they were struggling in narrow circumstances to obtain an education, is a characteristic known as widely over the world as the footsteps of Hiram boys and girls have wandered.

"The help that he furnished hundreds in the way of suggestions, teaching, encouragement, inspiration, and stimulus, was most valuable. I have repeatedly said that, as regards myself, I am more indebted to him for all that I am and for what I have done in the intellectual field than to any other man that ever lived.

"His power over students was not so much that of a drill-master or disciplinarian as that of one who was able to inspire and energize young people by his own intellectual and moral force."

An Interesting Reminiscence of Garfield's Youth—A Letter He Wrote 23 Years ago that Helped to Make a College President, and that President Now Reads it to His Students.

President Hinsdale said, at the recent Commencement at Hiram College (June, 1880), that in the fall of 1856 he left the Eclectic Institute, now Hiram College, in distress of mind growing out of his own life-questions. He had passed his 19th birthday, and the question of the future weighed heavily upon his mind. That winter he taught district-school. He had already won a friend in Mr. Garfield, then 25 years old, and just out of Williams College. Garfield was then teaching in Hiram as Professor of Ancient Languages. In his distress of mind Hinsdale wrote Garfield a letter, in which he fully opened up his mind. In reply he received a letter, which gave him great help, that illustrated some of the points in the morning's lecture. This letter, which he had religiously preserved, might give help to some of the young men before him. Besides, there was peculiar propriety in his reading it, on account of what had taken place the day before in the City of Chicago. He then proceeded to read from the original—yellow with age, and worn with repeated foldings and unfoldings—the following beautiful letter:

"HIRAM, Jan. 15, 1857.—MY DEAR BROTHER BURKE: I was made glad a few days since by the receipt of your letter. It was a very acceptable New Year's present, and I take great pleasure in responding. You have given a vivid picture of a community in which intelligence and morality have been neglected, and I am glad you are disseminating the light. Certainly men must have some knowledge in order to do right. God first said, 'Let there be light;' afterward he said, 'It is very good!'

"I am glad to hear of your success in teaching, but I approach with much more interest the consideration of the question you have proposed. Brother mine, it is not a question to be discussed in the spirit of debate, but to be thought over and prayed over as a question 'out of which are the issues of life.' You will agree with me that every one must decide and direct his own course in life, and the only service friends can afford is to give us the data from which we must draw our own conclusion and decide our course. Allow me, then, to sit beside you and look over the field of life and see what are its aspects.

"I am not one of those who advise everyone to undertake the work of a liberal education. Indeed, I believe that in two-thirds of the cases such advice would be unwise. The great body of the people will be, and ought to be (intelligent), farmers and mechanics; and in many respects they pass the most independent and happy lives. But God has endowed some of His children with desires and capabilities for a more extended field of labor and influence, and so every life should be shaped according to 'what the man hath.' Now, in reference to yourself, I *know* you have capabilities for occupying positions of high and important trust in the scenes of active life, and I am sure you will not call it flattery in me nor egotism in yourself to say so. Tell me, Burke, do you not feel a spirit stirring within you that longs to *know*, to *do*, and to *dare*; to hold converse with the great world of thought, and hold before you some high and noble object to which the vigor of your mind and the strength of your arm may be given? Do you not have longings like these, which you breathe to no one, and which you feel must be heeded, or you will pass through life unsatisfied and regretful? I am sure you have them, and they will forever cling round your heart till you obey their mandate. They are the voices of that nature, which God has given you, and which, when obeyed, will bless you and your fellow-men.

"Now, all this might be true, and yet it might be your duty not to follow that course. If your duty to your father or your mother demands that you take another, I shall rejoice to see you take that other course. The path of duty is where we all ought to walk, be that where it may. But I sincerely hope that you will not, without an earnest struggle, give up a course of liberal study. Suppose you could not begin your study again till after your majority,— it will not be too late then, but you will gain in many respects. You will have more maturity of mind to appreciate whatever you may study. You may say you will be too old to begin the cource. But how could you better spend the earlier days of life? We should not measure life by the days and moments we pass on earth.

"'The life is measured by the soul's advance—
The enlargement of its powers—the expanded field
Where it ranges, till it burns and glows
With heavenly joy, with high and heavenly hope.'

"It need be no discouragement that you will be obliged to hew your own way and pay your own charges. You can go to school two terms of every year, and pay your own way.

"I know this, for I did so when teachers' wages were much lower than they are now. It is a great truth that 'Where there is a will, there is a way.' It may be that by-and-by your father would assist you. It may be that even now he could let you commence on your resources, so that you could begin immediately. Of this you know, and I do not. I need not tell you how glad I should be to assist you in your work; but, if you cannot come to Hiram while I am here, I shall still hope to hear that you are determined to go on as soon as the time will permit. Will you not write me your thoughts on this whole subject, and tell me your prospects? We are having a very good time in the school this winter. Give my love to Roldon and Louisa, and believe me always your friend and brother.

"J. A. GARFIELD.

"P. S.—Miss Booth and Mr. Rhodes send their love to you. Henry James was here and made me a good visit a few days ago. He and I have talked of going to see you this winter. I fear we cannot do it. How far is it from here? Burke, was it prophetic that my last word to you ended on the picture of the Capitol of Congress?

"J. A. G."

The letter was written on Congress note paper, and the sheet was entirely filled, so that the last few words were written crosswise; and, as is said by the General, his last word came across the little picture at the upper left-hand corner of the sheet. Whether the General means to ask in regard to the prophetic significance in his own case, or that of Hinsdale, is not known; but it certainly came true in his own case.

Gen. Garfield's Speech Before the Hiram College Reunion Association—The Commencement Day of 1880 Long to be Remembered.

On this happy occasion, President Hinsdale introduced Gen. Garfield as follows: It is with a good deal of satisfaction and pride that I now introduce to you one into whose face most all of you have looked hundreds of times, a fellow student with some of you, and a co-worker in the institution with others, a teacher of a larger number, a man who for years has been near and dear to us, and whose presence here to-day has lifted what otherwise would have been a comparatively humble though a very pleasant and enjoyable occasion to the rank and dignity of a national matter—Gen. Garfield.

Gen. Garfield arose and said:

LADIES AND GENTLEMEN: I said that there were two chapters in the history of this Institute. You have heard the one relating to the founders. They were all pioneers of this Western Reserve, or nearly all; they were all men of knowledge and great force of character; nearly all not men of means, but they planted this little institution. In 1850 it was a cornfield, with a solid, plain brick building in the centre of it, and that was all. Almost all the rest has been done by the institution itself. That is the second chapter.

Without a dollar of endowment, without a powerful friend anywhere, but with a corps of teachers who were told to go on to the ground and see what they could make out of it, to find their own pay out of the little tuition that they could receive. They invited students of their own spirit to come on the ground and see what they could make out of it, and the response has been that many have come, and the chief part of the respondents I see in the faces around and before me to-day. It was a simple question of sinking or swimming for themselves. And I know that we are all inclined to be a little clannish over our own. We have, perhaps, a right to be, but I do not know of any place, I do not know of any institution that has accomplished more with so little means as has this school on Hiram Hill.

I know of no place where the doctrine of self-help has a fuller development, by necessity as well as finally by choice, as here on this hill. The doctrine of self-help and of force has the chief place among these men and women around here. As I said a great many years ago about that, the act of Hiram was to throw its young men and women overboard and let them try it for themselves, and all those men able to get ashore got ashore, and I think we have few cases of drowning anywhere.

Now, I look over these faces and I mark the several geological changes remarked by Mr. Atwater so well in his address; but in the few cases of change of geological fact there is, I find, no fossils. Some are dead and glorified in our memories, but those who are not are alive—I think all.

The teachers and the studens of this school built it up in every sense. They made the cornfield into Hiram Campus. Those fine groves you see across the road they planted. I well remember the day when they turned out into the woods to find beautiful maples, and brought them in; when they raised a little purse to purchase evergreen; when each young man, for himself one, and perhaps a second for some young lady, if he was in love, planted two trees on the campus and then named them after himself. There are several here to-day who remember Bolen. Bolen planted there a tree, and Bolen has planted a tree that has a lustre—Bolen was shot through the heart at Winchester.

There are many here that can go and find the tree that you have named after yourself. They are great, strong trees to-day, and your names, like your trees, are, I hope, growing still.

I believe outside of or beyond the physical features of the place, that there was a stronger pressure of work to the square inch in the boilers that run this establishment than any other that I know of, and, as has been so well said, that has told all the while with these young men and women. The struggle, wherever the uncouth and untutored farmer boys—a farmer, of course—that came here to try themselves and find what kind of people they were. They came here to go on a voyage of discovery. Your discovery was yourselves, in many cases. I hope the discovery was a fortune, and the friendships then formed out of that have bound this group of people longer and farther than most any other I have known in life. They are scattered all over the United States, in every field of activity, and if I had time to name them, the sun would go down before I had finished.

I believe the rules of this institution limits us to time— I think it is said five minutes. I may have overgone it already. We have so many already that we want to hear from, we will all volunteer. We expect now to wrestle awhile with the work before us. Some of these boys remember the time when I had an exercise that I remember with pleasure. I called a young lad out in a class and said, in two minutes you are to speak to the best of your ability on the following subject (naming it), and give the subject and let him wrestle with it. I was trying a theory, and I believe that wrestling was a good thing. I will not vary the performance save in this. I will call you and restrict you to five minutes, and let you select your theme about the old days of Hiram.

Now, we have a grave judge in this audience, who wandered away from Hiram into the Forty-Second Regiment into the South, and, after the victory, stayed there. I will call now, not as a volunteer man, but as a drafted man —Judge Clark of Mississippi.

Garfield's First Ride on the Cars—First Visit to Columbus—First School, Etc.—Interesting Reminiscences.

It was the good fortune of the writer of this to spend the first two weeks of the notable campaign of 1877 with Gen. Garfield. It was almost evident to the best-informed political calculator that the Republicans must be defeated that year. Fate was against them, and whatever herculean efforts might be made could only be in vain. The excuse was this and that, but the fact was a conglomeration of adverse circumstances which no one could successfully contend against.

The campaign was opened on a bright day in early autumn, under the beautiful elms and maples of that delightful old university town of Athens. Hon. Stanley Matthews, recently elected United States Senator, Judge West, candidate for Governor, and Gen. Garfield, together with several lesser lights in the party, were present and made speeches. It was an occasion full of importance, and was carefully reported in the daily press of the entire country.

The meeting was held on Saturday afternoon, and the General found it necessary to remain in the town over Sunday. After taking a stroll about the town during the forenoon, and reading his usual amount from some popular volume, the General, later in the day, in the presence of Capt. C. E. Henry and myself, said:

"Many interesting reminiscences which it is very difficult for me to express have run through my mind during the past twenty-four hours. While speaking from the stand in the college campus, yesterday, I could not refrain from casting my eyes up to a certain window in the main building which opens into a room where I spent a night, some twenty-five years ago, in the company of my cousin Ellis Ballou, who was a student here.

"I had come all the way from our home in Cuyahoga county with my mother. It had been an eventful journey to me.

"I had rode for the first time on the cars."

"I had been for the first time to the capital, and been shown with my mother through the halls of the State House.

"Hon. Gamaliel Kent was the Representative from Geauga county, and he showed us about. From there we come on to Athens, in the immediate vicinity of which town resided my mother's relatives.

"That winter I taught my first school in a log house in this vicinity..

"I dug the coal which was burned during the winter from the bank in the rear of the house, and worked for, I think, $10 per month. It was an eventful winter for me. I had some scholars who had been reported as somewhat hard, but I think that I succeeded reasonably well in keeping order."

"Was this before or after your canal experience?"

"It was after that, some time. I had given up all idea of a life on the canal at that time, but I did expect to go on the sea even then."

At this early period the books which the young General mostly read were tales of the sea. These were the only stories that could be easily obtained.

The General says that he most vividly remembers the "Pirate's Own Book," and the impression which it made lived with him for years. He dreamed of an impossible career on the ocean.

The great statesman was a good reader at 3 years old, and was remarkable for the faculty which he exhibited for retaining almost verbatim the contents of the volumes which he perused. It is reported by the good people of the vicinity, who were boys with the General, that he often annoyed teachers of somewhat limited education by the numberless questions which he asked them.

Garfield's Extra Session Speech—Turning on the Light.

General Garfield, at the extra session of Congress in 1879, turned a flood of the fierce light of history upon the disgraceful record of the Democratic party, and then made clear that their attitude at that time in threatening to stop the supplies of the Government unless their schemes looking to the removal of the safeguards that surround the ballot-box were permitted was as unpatriotic and pestiferous as their attitude during the war. It was in the course of this great effort that he spoke the following words, which indicate the intense patriotic earnestness and the frank fearlessness of the man:

I desire to ask the forbearance of the gentlemen on the other side for remarks I dislike to make, for they will bear witness that I have in many ways shown my desire that the wounds of the war should be healed, and that the grass that God plants over the graves of our dead may signalize the return of the Spring of friendship and peace between all parts of the country. But I am compelled by the necessity of the situation to refer for a moment to a chapter of history.

The last act of the Democratic domination in this house, eighteen years ago, was stirring and dramatic, but it was heroic and whole-souled. Then the Democratic party said: "If you elect your man as President of the United States we will shoot your Union to death."

And the people of this country, not willing to be coerced, but believing they had a right to vote for Abraham Lincoln if they chose, did elect him lawfully as President, and then your leaders, in control of the majority of the other wing of this Capitol, did the heroic thing of withdrawing from their seats, and your Representatives withdrew from their seats and flung down to us the gage of mortal battle. We called it rebellion, but we admitted that it was honorable, that it was courageous, and that it was noble to give us the fell gage of battle, and fight it out in the open field.

That conflict, and what followed, we all know too well; and to-day, after eighteen years, the book of your domination is opened where you turned down your leaves in 1860, and you are signalizing your return to power by reading the second chapter (not this time an heroic one) that declares that if we do not let you dash a statute out of the book you will not shoot the Union to death as in the first chapter—but starve it to death by refusing the necessary appropriations.

You, gentlemen, have it in your power to kill it by this movement. You have it in your power, by withholding these two bills, to smite the nerve centers of our Constitution to the stillness of death; and you have declared your purpose to do it if you cannot break down the elements

9

of free consent that, up to this time, have always ruled in the Government.

It is unnecessary to say that the sentences quoted were burned into the memories of the Democracy. In the light of Garfield's unsparing but candid arraignment they were forced to see along with the rest of the people that their party, according to the measure of its opportunity, was as much a foe to the safety and prosperity of the American Union as the Democracy of the war.

Anecdote of Gen. Garfield at Murfreesboro, Illustrating a Noble Trait of His Character.

The following reminiscence throws additional light on noble character of Garfield:

Gareschi, Rosecrans's Chief of Staff, was killed the first day of the fight at Murfreesboro. A solid shot left his body headless. Old Rosey, as he was familiarly and affectionately called by the boys, who was at Garashee's side when the fatal shot took effect, glanced at the faithful officer's corpse, and exclaiming "poor fellow," called out: "Scatter, gentlemen, scatter."

The order was obeyed by staff and orderlies with more than alacrity, as the enemy had us in blank range of a well-manned battery, the shot flying thick and fast, without any apparent respect of persons. A few days after, says Thomas Daughberty, who tells this story, I do not remember how many, but it was after we had got into quarters in the town of Murfreesboro, Garfield joined us, to take the dead man, Gareschi's place as Chief of Staff.

We boys thought he was a perfect success, and as an illustration of his kindness of heart, a virtue not often practiced by army officers in the field, toward subordinates at least, I give you this little story:

One night, very late, tne boys being rolled in their blankets on the hall floor asleep, and I at my post, sitting in a chair at the Commanding General's door, awaiting orders to be taken to their destination by my then sleeping comrades; the light but a tallow candle stuck in a sardine box; I, with chair tilted against the wall, had fallen asleep too, when Gen. Garfield, the new Chief of Staff, emerged from the headquarter-room quickly. Not noticing my extended limbs, he tripped over them and dropped to hands and knees on the floor. As he was no light weight, even then the fall was not easy.

Affrighted, I jumped to my feet, stood at attention, and, as the General arose, saluted, expecting nothing else than to be cuffed, and probably kicked, too, from one end of the hall to the other. But, to my astonishment, he kindly and quietly said: "Excuse me, Sergeant." I not only excused him, but, with all our little command, to whom the incident was told, revered him.

The First Garfield Club—Organized by the Students at Williamstown, Mass

Every ballot at the Chicago Convention was announced immediately to a large and expectant crowd at Williams College (Gen. Garfield is a graduate of Williams College) as fast as received. When the news came that a son of Williams College was nominated, the crowd went wild.

The students, headed by a man carrying the American flag, marched to the President's house, where Dr. Chadbourn made a speech. A mass meeting was then held by the students in Alumni Hall, and a grand ratification meeting was appointed. A brass band was engaged, together with prominent speakers of Berkshire County. A Garfield Club was organized also, and a grand procession planned, all before 2:30 p.m. The College took a holiday in honor of the nomination, and has the honor of organizing the first Garfield Club in the country.

Dignity of American Citizenship—Garfield's Eloquent Speech in Washington After His Nomination, Delivered June 16th, 1880.

Fellow-Citizens: While I have looked upon this great array, I believe I have gotten a new idea of the majesty of the American people.

When I reflect that wherever you find the sovereign power, every reverent heart on earth bows before it, and when I remember that here, for a hundred years, we have denied the sovereignty of any man, and in place of it we have asserted the sovereignty of all in place of one, I see before so vast a concourse that it is easy for me to imagine that the rest of the American people are gathered here to-night; and, if they were all here, every man would stand uncovered and in unsandaled feet in the presence of the majesty of the only sovereign power in this Government under Almighty God; and, therefore, to this great audience I pay the respectful homage that in part belongs to the sovereignty of the people.

I thank you for this great and glorious demonstration. I am not for one moment misled into believing that it refers to so poor a thing as any one of our number. I know it means your reverence to your Government, your reverence for its laws, your reverence for its institutions, and your compliment to one who is placed for a moment in relations to you of peculiar importance. For all these reasons I thank you.

I cannot at this time utter a word on the subject of general politics. I would not mar the cordiality of this welcome, to which to some extent all are gathered, by any reference except to the present moment and its significance.

But I wish to say that a large portion of this assemblage to-night are my comrades in the late war for the Union. For them I can speak with entire propriety, and can say that these very streets heard the measured tread of your disciplined feet years ago, when the imperiled Republic needed your hands and your hearts to save it, and you came back with your numbers decimated, but those you left behind were immortal and glorified heroes forever, and those you brought back came carrying under tattered banners and in bronzed hands the ark of the covenant of your Republic in safety out of the bloody baptism of the war, and you brought it in safety to be saved forever by your valor and the wisdom of your brethren who were at home, and by this you were again added to the civil army of the Republic.

I greet you, comrades and fellow-soldiers, and the great body of distinguished citizens who are gathered here to-night, who are the strong stay and support of business, of prosperity, of peace, of civic order, and the glory of the Republic, and I thank you for your welcome to-night. It was said in a welcome to one who came to England to be a part of her glory, and all the nation spoke when it said:

> Normans, and Saxons, and Danes are we,
> But all of us Danes in our welcome of thee.

And we say to-night of all the nations, of all the people, soldiers and civilians, there is one name that welds us all into one. It is the name of an American under the Union and under the glory of the flag that leads us to victory and to peace.

"The Member from New York."

Gen. Garfield in his school days used to take the part of "the member from New York" in the miniature House of Congress which his elocution class had formed itself into. He is said to have enjoyed this exceedingly, and his oratory excelled that of all the others.

The Canal Story as Told by the Man Who Employed Young Garfield to Drive on the Tow Path.

The gentleman who employed young Garfield to drive on the "Tow path" is still living, and resides in Jersey City. His name is Jonathan Myers. He gives the following full account of "Jim Garfield's" canal labors:

"He was a driver for me on the Ohio Canal. I have watched his career ever since he left me, and have felt very much interested in him, and gratified to see what he has achieved.

The first time he ran for the Legislature of Ohio he was in my district, and I voted for him. After that I moved East, and that is the only time I ever voted for him. When he left me he did not 'boat' any more.

It is a mistake about his ever having been a steersman. He was not large enough for a steersman. When he was in my employ he was not more than 13 years of age.

I remember when he applied to me for a job on my boat. He was a stout, healthy boy, and his frank, open countenance impressed me so much that I at once employed him. He was always full of fun, and exceedingly good natured. I never saw him mad. He was with me about three months.

He was always very attentive to his business. He was also a great boy to read. If he was not busy he was always reading. I scarcely ever saw him idle. One day, as we were going up the canal, he came to me and said he would like to get a place where he could work and attend school.

I knew of a doctor by the name of Robinson who lived near me, who was in need of a boy to attend his horse and do chores about his place. I told "Jim" he had better go up and see the Doctor, and if he had not got a boy he had better get the place. I disliked to part with him, but I saw he was too intelligent a lad to be driving a canal-boat.

He went up, and the Doctor 'froze' to him at once. The Doctor was what you might call a minister. He was a Campbellite, and a very good man indeed.

During the first winter "Jim" was with the Doctor he got converted, and after he got converted they "froze" to him tighter than ever. When spring came, "Jim" wanted to get some work to enable him to buy some clothes, and he spoke to the Doctor about it. The Doctor told him he must not leave school—that he must go through now. "Jim" said:

"Doctor, but I haven't got any money." The Doctor told him that was all right—that he would stand behind him.

I remember that he was a very poor boy, and that I was very favorably impressed with him. These canal boys were generally a shiftless lot of fellows, and it was hard work to get a good boy. Our boats were different then from what they are now. We used to have them fitted up nicely to carry passengers as well as freight. My wife used to be on the boat with me, and she thought a good deal of "Jim."

The great difficulty we had with the drivers on our boats was that they would lie, but if you got anything from "Jim" you could always rely on it. I never caught him in a lie while he was with me. He was getting $10 a month and his board, and that was considered very big wages. He was born in Orange, Cuyahoga County, O. He came to me as any other boy to hire out.

The Turning Point in Garfield's Life, and How It Happened.

The following anecdote concerning Garfield's early life shows a critical period of the boy's experience:

Garfield was then a green, awkward boy of 16, and was

revolving in his mind the feasibility of taking a course of liberal study. He knew that Dr. Robinson was in town, and had seen him at his mother's house, and had confidence in his judgment. He called around, therefore, at the President's house, and asked for Dr. Robinson. The Doctor was at his dinner, but soon finished, and came out to see what his young friend wanted.

"I want to see you alone," said Garfield.

"Who are you?" asked the gruff but kind-hearted Doctor.

"My name is James Garfield, from Solon," replied the latter.

"Oh! I know your mother, and knew you when you were a babe in arms; but you had outgrown my knowledge. I am glad to see you."

The young man led the way toward a secluded spot on the south side of Hiram Hill; and, as they proceeded, the Doctor took a good look at his companion. He was a young man quite shabbily dressed, with coarse satinet pantaloons, which were far outgrown, and did not reach more than half-way down his cowhide boot-tops. His vest did not meet the waistband of his pants, and his arms reached far out through the sleeves of his coat. His head was clothed with a coarse wool hat, which had also seen much wear, and slouched upon his head.

"He was wonderfully awkward," said the good Doctor (who tells this story), "and had a sort of independent, go-as-you-please gait. At length we reached a spot that was covered with papaw bushes, and we took a seat on a log. After a little hesitation the young man said:

"You are a physician, and know the fibre that is in men. Examine me and tell me with the utmost frankness whether I had better take a course of liberal study. I am contemplating doing so. My desire is in that direction. But, if I am to make a failure of it, or practically so, I do not desire to begin. If you advise me not to do so, I shall feel content."

"I felt that I was on my sacred honor, and the young man looked as though he felt himself on trial. I had had considerable experience as a physician, but here was a case much different from any other I had ever had. I felt it must be handled with great care.

I examined his head, and saw that there was a magnificent brain there. I sounded his lungs, and found that they were strong and capable of making good blood. I felt his pulse, and saw that there was an engine capable of sending the blood up to the head to feed the brain. I had seen many strong physical systems, with warm feet, but cold, sluggish brain; and those who possessed such systems would simply sit around and doze. Therefore I was anxious to know about the kind of an engine to run that delicate machine, the brain. At the end of a fifteen-minutes' careful examination of this kind, we rose, and I said: 'Go on, follow the leadings of your ambition, and ever after I am your friend. You have the brain of a Webster, and you have the physical proportions that will back you in the most herculean efforts. All you need to do is to work. Work hard—do not be afraid of overworking—and you will make your mark.'"

The Doctor and the General visited the spot made thus sacred as the witness of the turning point in Garfield's life, on the day of the recent Hiram commencement.

"I invited the General to come to my house in Bedford, in order that I might talk the matter over more fully with him; and in a short time he did so. The General has often told me that the conversation gave him confidence in himself, which he had never had before, and he went on with his course, and, as is already known, won for himself the highest honors of his class, and of the world at large.

The Methods and Habits of Garfield While a Teacher—How He Played With the Boys, Shook Hands, Lectured, Etc.

The Rev. J. L. Darsie, of Danbury, Conn., was one of Garfield's pupils in his school days. He thus describes the habits and methods of Professor Garfield:

"I attended school at the Western Reserve Eclectic Institute when Garfield was Principal, and I recall vividly Gen. Garfield's method of teaching.

"He took very kindly to me, and assisted me in various ways, because I was poor and was janitor of the buildings, and swept them out in the morning and built the fires, as he had done only six years before, when he was a pupil at the same school.

He was full of animal spirits, and he used to run out on the green almost every day and play cricket with us. He was a tall, strong man, but dreadfully awkward. Every now and then he would get a hit on the nose, and he muffed his ball and lost his hat as a regular thing.

He was left-handed, too, and that made him seem all the clumsier. But he was most powerful and very quick, and it was easy for us to understand how it was that he had acquired the reputation of whipping all the other mule drivers on the canal, and of making himself the hero of that thoroughfare when he followed its tow-path ten years earlier.

No matter how old the pupils were, Garfield always called us by our first names, and kept himself on the most familiar terms with all. He played with us freely, scuffled with us sometimes, walked with us in walking too and fro, and we treated him out of the class room just about as we did one another. Yet he was a most strict disciplinarian, and enforced the rules like a martinet.

He combined an affectionate and confiding manner with a respect for order in a most successful manner. If he wanted to speak to a pupil, either for reproof or approbation. he would generally manage to get one arm around him and draw him up close to him.

He had a peculiar way of shaking hands, too, giving a twist to your arm and drawing you right up to him. This sympathetic manner has helped him to advancement. When I was a janitor he used sometimes to stop me and ask my opinion about this and that, as if seriously advising with me. I can see now that my opinion could not have been of any value, and that he probably asked me partly to increase my self respect, and partly to show me that he felt an interest in me. I certainly was his friend all the firmer for it.

I remember once asking him what was the best way to pursue a certain study, and he said:

"Use several text-books. Get the views of different authors as you advance. In that way you can plow a broader furrow. I always study in that way." He tried hard to teach us to observe carefully and accurately. He broke out one day with:

"Henry, how many posts are there under the building downstairs?" Henry expressed his opinion, and the question went around the class, hardly one getting it right.

He was the keenest observer I ever saw. I think he noticed and numbered every button on our coats.

A friend of mine was walking with him through Cleveland one day when Garfield stopped and darted down a cellarway, asking his companion to follow, and briefly pausing to explain himself. The sign "Saws and Files" was over the door, and in the depths was heard a regular clicking sound.

"I think this fellow is cutting files," said he, "and I have never seen a file cut." Down they went, and, sure enough, there was a man recutting an old file, and they stayed ten minutes and found out all about the process.

The Way Garfield Got His Military Education—Using Poles, Blocks, and Grains of Coffee for Drill Purposes.

It is a well-known fact that Gen. Garfield never had any military education previous to his taking command of the Forty-second Regiment, Ohio Volunteer Infantry. But the thorough disposition which he had cultivated, both as student and teacher, was with him here.

He purchased at the first opportunity a copy of some book on military tactics, and immediately inaugurated an entirely original method of learning the movements of bodies of men.

He prepared a large number of blocks, each representing columns of soldiers, and then went through with all the various movements described in the books, often working at the various problems until nearly morning.

When he had quite well mastered the rudiments in this way, he began to drill his officers by means of skeleton companies, as he called them. He had prepared long poles, and, giving the ends of these into the hands of the men who were being instructed, the marches, counter-marches, and various parades would be gone through with wonderful accuracy and dispatch.

"I have carried poles in this way many times," said Capt. C. E. Henry, one of his old officers, "and, if I do say so, we learned the movements as fast as the men of any other regiment, even though the others might have been presided over by West Point officers.

"Finally, he mislaid his blocks, and adopted grains of coffee, or corn, and still carried on his military maneuvers.

"I have heard West Point officers say that he was as thorough as any officer they ever saw in his knowledge of the common principles of military affairs. I never knew him to make a mistake in giving an order, or to hesitate in giving it."

The General Taking His Stand on Fugitive Slaves—A Story of the War.

A member of Gen. Sherman's staff is authority for the following incident, which is related as nearly as possible in his words:

"One day I noticed a fugitive slave come rushing into camp with a bloody head, and apparently frightened almost to death. He had only passed my tent a moment when a regular bully of a fellow came riding up, and, with a volley of oaths, began to ask after his 'nigger.'

"Gen. Garfield was not present, and he passed on to the division-commander. This division-commander was a sympathizer with the theory that fugitives should be returned to their masters, and that the Union soldiers should be made the instruments for returning them. He accordingly wrote a mandatory order to Gen. Garfield, in whose command the darky was supposed to be hiding, telling him to hunt out and deliver over the property of the outraged citizen.

"I stated the case as fully as I could to Gen. Garfield before handing him the order, but did not color my statement in any way. He took the order, and deliberately wrote on it the following indorsement:

"'I respectfully, but positively, decline to allow my command to search for, or deliver up, any fugitive slaves. I conceive that they are here for quite another purpose. The command is open, and no obstacles will be placed in the way of the search.'

"I read the indorsement, and was frightened. I expected that, if returned, the result would be that the General would be court-martialed. I told him my fears. He simply replied:

"'The matter may as well be tested first as last. Right is right, and I do not propose to mince matters at all. My soldiers are here for far other purposes than hunting and returning fugitive slaves.'"

Garfield's Letter Accepting the Republican Nomination for President.

Gen. Garfield forwarded to Senator Hoar, of Massachusetts, Chairman of Committee, the following letter of acceptance of the nomination tendered him by the Republican National Convention:

"MENTOR, O., July 10, 1880.—DEAR SIR: On the evening of the 8th of June last, I had the honor to receive from you, in the presence of the Committee of which you were Chairman, the official announcement that the Republican National Convention at Chicago had that day nominated me as their candidate for the President of the United States. I accept the nomination with gratitude for the confidence it implies, and with a deep sense of the responsibilities it imposes. I cordially indorse the principles set forth in the platform adopted by the Convention. On nearly all the subjects of which it treated my opinions are on record among the published proceedings of Congress.

I venture, however, to make special mention of some of the principal topics which are likely to become subjects of discussion, without reviewing the controversies which have been settled during the last twenty years, and with no purpose or wish to revive the passions of the late war.

STATE SUPREMACY.

It should be said that, while the Republicans fully recognize and will strenuously defend all the rights retained by the people, and all the rights reserved to the States, they regret the pernicious doctrine of State supremacy, which so long crippled the functions of the national government, and at one time brought the Union very near to destruction. They insist that the United States is a nation, with ample powers of self-preservation; that its Constitution and the laws made in pursuance thereof "are the supreme law of the land;" that the right of the nation to determine the method by which the Legislature shall be created cannot be surrendered without abdicating one of the fundamental powers of government; that the national laws relating to the election of Representatives in Congress shall neither be violated nor evaded; that every elector shall be permitted freely, and without intimidation, to cast his lawful vote at such election, and have it honestly counted; and that the potency of his vote shall not be destroyed by the fraudulent vote of any other person.

NATIONAL WELL-BEING.

The best thoughts and energies of our people should be directed to those great questions of national well-being, in which all have a common interest. Such efforts will soonest restore to perfect peace those who were lately in arms against each other; for justice and good-will will outlast passion. But it is certain the wounds of the war cannot be completely healed, and the spirit of brotherhood cannot pervade the whole country, until every citizen—rich or poor, white or black—is secure in the free and equal enjoyment of every civil and political right guaranteed by the constitution and the laws. Wherever the enjoyment of these rights is not assured discontent will prevail, immigration will cease, and the social and industrial forces will continue to be disturbed by the migration of the laborers and the consequent diminution of prosperity. The national government should exercise all its constitutional authority to put an end to these evils; for all the people and all the States are members of one body, and no member can suffer without injury to all.

The most serious evils which now afflict the South arise from the fact that there is not such freedom and toleration of political opinion and action that the minority party can exercise an effective and wholesome restraint upon the party in power. Without such restraint a party rule becomes tyrannical and corrupt. The prosperity which is made possible in the South by its great advantages of soil and climate will never be realized until every voter can freely and safely support any party he pleases.

POPULAR EDUCATION.

And next in importance to freedom and justice is popular education without which neither justice nor freedom can be permanently maintained. Its interests are intrusted to the States and to the voluntary action of the people.

Whatever help the nation can justly offer should be generously given to aid the States in supporting common schools; but it would be unjust to our people and dangerous to our institutions to apply any portion of the revenues of the nation or of the States to the support of sectarian schools. The separation of the Church and the State, in everything relating to taxation, should be absolute.

NATIONAL FINANCES.

On the subject of national finances, my views have been so frequently and fully expressed that little is needed in the way of additional statement. The public debt is now so well secured, and the rate of annual interest has been so reduced by refunding, that rigid economy in expenditures and the faithful application of our surplus revenues to the payment of the principal of the debt will gradually, but certainly, free the people from its burdens, and close with honor the financial chapter of the war. At the same time the government can provide for all its ordinary expenditures, and discharge its sacred obligations to the soldiers of the Union and to the widows and orphans of those who fell in its defense.

The resumption of specie payments, which the Republican party so courageously and successfully accomplished, has removed from the field of controversy many questions that long and seriously disturbed the credit of the government and the business of the country. Our paper currency is now as national as the flag, and resumption has not only made it everywhere equal to coin, but has brought into use our store of gold and silver. The circulating medium is now more abundant than ever before, and we need only to maintain the equality of all our dollars to insure to labor and capital a measure of value from the use of which no one can suffer loss. The great prosperity which the country is now enjoying should not be endangered by any violent changes or doubtful financial experiments.

CUSTOMS LAWS.

In reference to our custom laws, a policy should be pursued which will bring revenue to the Treasury and will enable the labor and capital employed in our great industries to compete fairly in our own markets with the labor and capital of foreign producers. We legislate for the people of the United States, not for the whole world, and it is our glory that the American laborer is more intelligent and better paid than his foreign competitor. Our country cannot be independent unless its people, with their abundant natural resources, possess the requisite skill at any time to clothe, arm, and equip themselves for war, and in time of peace to produce all the necessary implements of labor. It was the manifest intention of the founders of the government to provide for the common defense, not by standing armies alone, but by raising among the people a greater army of artisans, whose intelligence and skill should powerfully contribute to the safety and glory of the nation.

Fortunately for the interests of commerce, there is no longer any formidable opposition to appropriations for the improvement of our harbors and great navigable rivers, provided that the expenditures for that purpose are strictly limited to works of national importance.

The Mississippi River, with its great tributaries, is of

such vital importance to so many millions of people, that the safety of its navigation requires exceptional consideration. In order to secure to the nation the control of all its waters, President Jefferson negotiated the purchase of a vast territory, extending from the Gulf of Mexico to the Pacific Ocean. The wisdom of Congress should be invoked to devise some plan by which that great river shall cease to be a terror to those who dwell upon its banks, and by which its shipping may safely carry the industrial products of 25,000,000 of people. The interests of agriculture, which is the basis of all our material prosperity, and in which seven-twelfths of our population are engaged, as well as the interests of manufacturers and commerce, demand that the facilities for cheap transportation shall be increased by the use of all our great water-courses.

THE CHINESE QUESTION.

The material interests of this country, the traditions of its settlement, and the sentiments of our people have led the Government to offer the widest hospitality to immigrants who seek our shores for new and happier homes, willing to share the burdens as well as the benefits of our society, and intending that their posterity shall become an undistinguishable part of our population. The recent movement of the Chinese to our Pacific coast, partakes but little of the qualities of such an immigration, either in its purposes or its result. It is too much like an importation to be welcomed without restriction; too much like an invasion to be looked upon without solicitude. We cannot consent to allow any form of servile labor to be introduced among us under the guise of immigration. Recognizing the gravity of this subject, the present Administration, supported by Congress, has sent to China a commission of distinguished citizens for the purpose of securing such a modification of the existing treaty as will prevent the evils likely to arise from the present situation. It is confidently believed that these diplomatic negotiations will be successful, without the loss of commercial intercourse between the two powers, which promises a great increase of reciprocal trade and the enlargement of our markets. Should these efforts fail, it will be the duty of Congress to mitigate the evils already felt, and prevent their increase by such restrictions as, without violence or injustice, will place upon a sure foundation the peace of our communities, and the freedom and dignity of labor.

THE CIVIL SERVICE.

The appointment of citizens to the various executive and judicial offices of the Government is perhaps the most difficult of all the duties which the Constitution has imposed upon the Executive. The Constitution wisely demands that Congress shall co-operate with the executive departments in placing the civil service on a better basis. Experience has proved that with our frequent changes of administration, no system of reform can be made effective and permanent without the aid of legislation. Appointments to the military and naval service are so regulated by law and custom as to leave but little ground of complaint. It may not be wise to make similar regulations by law for the civil service; but, without invading the authority or necessary discretion of the Executive, Congress should devise a method that will determine the tenure of office and greatly reduce the uncertainty which makes that service so uncertain and unsatisfactory. Without depriving any officer of his rights as a citizen, the Government should require him to discharge all his official duties with intelligence, efficiency and faithfulness. To select wisely from our vast population those who are best fitted for the many offices to be filled, requires an acquaintance far beyond the range of any one man. The Executive should therefore seek and receive the information and assistance of those whose knowledge of the communities in which the duties are to be performed best qualifies them to aid them in making the wisest choice.

THE PLATFORM.

The doctrines announced by the Chicago convention are not the temporary devices of a party to attract votes and carry an election; they are deliberate convictions resulting from a careful study of the spirit of our institutions, the events of our history, and the best impulses of our people. In my judgment, these principles should control the legislation and administration of the Government. In any event, they will guide my conduct until experience points a better way. If elected, it will be my purpose to enforce strict obedience to the Constitution and the laws, and to promote, as best I may, the interest and honor of the whole country, relying for support upon the wisdom of Congress, the intelligence of the people, and the favor of God. With great respect, I am, very truly yours,

JAMES A. GARFIELD.

To the Hon. George F. Hoar, Chairman of Committee.

CHESTER A. ARTHUR.

A Sketch of the Life of the Republican Candidate for Vice-President.

Chester Allan Arthur is a native of Vermont, having been born at Fairfield, Franklin County, October 15th, 1830.

He was the oldest son of the Rev. William Arthur, D. D., a Baptist clergyman, and his mother's maiden name was Malvina Stone. His father was a native of the north of Ireland, and a graduate of the College of Belfast. He was a noted scholar and author of several books on philology.

The subject of this sketch was fitted for college mainly under his father's instructions, but also studied at Greenwich, Washington County, N. Y. He entered Union College, and graduated therefrom at the age of eighteen with high honors. He began the study of law soon after leaving college, in the office of the Hon. E. D. Culver, a former member of Congress from Pennsylvania, who was prominent in the anti-slavery struggles of thirty years ago. Gen. Arthur was admitted to the Bar in 1853, and began practice in New York.

As a young man he early took great interest in political

matters, and bore an active part in the Free-Soil agitation. He was a delegate from King's County (Brooklyn) to the first Republican State Convention held in New York, and gained considerable reputation from his connection with the litigation growing out of slavery and the rights of colored citizens.

He was attorney in the celebrated Lemon slave case, in which William M. Evarts acted as counsel, with Charles O'Conor as opposing counsel for the slaveholder, Jonathan Lemon, of Virginia, who, on his way to Texas, brought slaves with him into New York. This case, involving some of the most important principles of personal liberties and the comities of the States, was in the courts for many years, and was finally decided by the Court of Appeals against the slaveholder. Gen. Arthur prepared all the papers in the case and sued out the writ of habeas corpus by which the case got into court. He was also attorney in the case involving the right of the black man to ride in the cars, in which he was also successful in the Court of last resort.

He continued in the practice of his profession with good success until the breaking out of the war. During Gov. Morgan's administration he was for the first two years of the war Inspector and Quartermaster-General of New York. In this position he displayed remarkable organizing capacity in placing the New York troops in the field, and gained a high reputation as an officer.

Upon Seymour's election as Governor, Gen. Arthur returned to his practice, in which he continued until his appointment as Collector of the port of New York, in November, 1871. This appointment came to him unsolicited, and was an entire surprise. He discharged the duties of the place with signal ability, and to the entire acceptance of the commercial public. Business men of all parties petitioned for his retention in office, and he was reappointed in 1875, holding the position until his removal by President Hayes under circumstances with which the public is familiar.

He is a portly, middle-aged gentleman, with gray hairs and pleasant features, social and amiable, fond of a good dinner, and at home is agreeable company; quite frequently seen on public occasions in New York, and very active, but never obtrusive; altogether a public-spirited citizen and typical New York business man; rather slow of speech, but good in substance, and is one of Gen. Grant's intimate friends and admirers.

Mr. Arthur is now engaged in the practice of his profession. He has two children—a son of 14 and a daughter of 8 years of age. He had the misfortune to lose his devoted wife last January, whose death was sudden and unexpected. Mrs. Arthur was a daughter of the late Capt. Herndon, of the United States Navy, the intrepid explorer of the river Amazon, who was lost at sea while in command of the steamship Central America on her trip between Havana and New York in 1857.

Gen. Arthur's Letter of Acceptance.

Gen Arthur forwarded to Senator Hoar, Chairman of the Committee, the following letter of acceptance:

DEAR SIR: I accept the position assigned me by the great party whose action you announce. This acceptance implies an approval of the principles declared by the Convention, but recent usage permits me to add some expression of my own views. The right and duty to secure honesty and order in popular elections is a matter so vital that it must stand in the front. The authority of the National Government to preserve from fraud and force elections, at which its own officers are chosen, is a chief point on which the two parties are plainly and intensely opposed. Acts of Congress for ten years have in New York and elsewhere done much to curb the violence and wrong to which the ballot and count have been again and again subjected, sometimes despoiling great cities, sometimes stifling the voice of a whole State, often placing not only in Congress, but on the Bench and in Legislatures, numbers of men never chosen by the people.

The Democratic party, since gaining possession of the two Houses of Congress, has made these laws the object of bitter, ceaseless assault, and despite all resistance has hedged them with restrictions cunningly contrived to baffle and paralyze them. This aggressive majority boldly attempted to extort from the Executive his approval of various enactments destructive of these election laws by revolutionary threats that a constitutional exercise of the veto power would be punished by withholding appropriations necessary to carry on the Government, and these threats were actually carried out by refusing needed appropriations and by forcing an extra session of Congress, lasting for months and resulting in concessions to this usurping demand, which are likely in many States to subject the majority to the lawless will of a minority. Ominous signs of a public disapproval alone subdued this arrogant power into a sullen surrender for the time being of a part of its demands.

The Republican party has strongly approved the stern refusal of its representatives to suffer the overthrow of statutes believed to be salutary and just. It has always insisted, and now insists, that the Government of the United States of America is empowered and in duty bound to effectually protect the elections denoted by the Constitution as National. More than this, the Republican party holds as the cardinal point in its creed that the Government should by every means known to the Constitution protect all American citizent everywhere in the full enjoyment of their civil and political rights. As a great part of its work of reconstruction, the Republican party gave the ballot to the emancipated slave as his right and defense. A large increase in the number of members of Congress and of the Electoral College from former slave-holding States was the immediate result.

The history of recent years abounds in evidence that in many ways and in many places, especially where their number has been great enough to endanger Democratic control, the very men by whose citizenship this increase of representation was effected have been debarred and robbed of their voice and their vote. It is true that no State statute or Constitution in so many words denies or abridges the exercise of their political rights, but bodies employed to bar their way are no less effectual.

It is a suggestive and startling thought that the increased power derived from the enfranchisement of a race now denied its share in governing the country, wielded by those who lately sought the overthrow of the Government, is now the sole reliance to defeat the party which represented the sovereignty and nationality of the American people in the greatest crisis of our history. Republicans cherish none of the resentments which may have animated them during the actual conflict of arms. They long for a full and real reconciliation between the sections which were needlessly and lamentably at strife. They sincerely offer the hand of good will, but they ask in return a pledge of good faith. They deeply feel that the party whose career is so illustrious in great and patriotic achievements will not fulfill its destiny until peace and prosperity are established in all the land, nor until liberty of thought, conscience, and action, and equality of opportunity shall not be merely cold formalities of the statute, but living birthrights which the humble may confidently claim, and the powerful dare not deny.

CIVIL SERVICE.

The resolution referring to the public service seems to me deserving of approval. Surely no man should be the incumbent of an office the duties of which he is for a cause unfit to perform, who is lacking in ability, fidelity, or integrity, which a proper administration of such office demands. This sentiment would doubtless meet with general acquiescence, but opinion has been widely divided upon the wisdom and practicability of various reformatory schemes which have been suggested, and of certain proposed regulations governing appointments to public office. The efficiency of such regulations has been distrusted mainly because they have seemed to exalt mere educational and abstract tests above general business capacity and even special fitness for the particular work in hand. It seems to me that the rules which should be applied to the management of public service may be properly conformed in the main to such as regulate the conduct of successful private buisness. Original appointments should be based upon ascertained fitness. The tenure of office should be stable. Positions of responsibility should, so far as practicable, be filled by the promotion of worthy and efficient officers. The investigation of all complaints, and the punishment of all official misconduct, should be prompt and thorough.

These views, which I have long held, repeatedly declared, and uniformly applied when called upon to act, I find embodied in the resolution, which of course I approve. I will add that by the acceptance of public office, whether high or low, one does not, in my judgement, escape any of his responsibility as a citizen or lose or impair any of his rights as a citizen, and that he should enjoy absolute liberty to think, and speak, and act in political matters according to his own will and conscience, provided only that he honorably, faithfully, and fully discharges all his official duties.

FINANCE.

The resumption of specie-payments—one of the fruits of Republican policy—has brought a return of abundant prosperity and the settlement of many distracting questions. The restoration of sound money, the large reduction of our public debt and the burden of interest, the high advancement of the public credit—all attest the ability and courage of the Republican party to deal with such financial problems as may hereafter demand solution. Our paper currency is now as good as gold, and silver is performing its legitimate function for the purpose of change. The principles which should govern the relations of these elements of the currency are simple and clear. There must be no deteriorated coin, no depreciated paper, and every dollar, whether of metal or paper, should stand the test of the world's standard.

POPULAR EDUCATION.

The value of popular education can hardly be overstated.

Although its interests must of necessity be chiefly confided to voluntary effort and individual action of the several States, they should be encouraged so far as the Constitution permits by the generous co-operation of the National Government. The interests of a whole country demand that the advantages of our common-school system should be brought within the reach of every citizen, and that no revenues of the Nation or the State should be devoted to the support of sectarian schools.

TARIFF AND INTERNAL IMPROVEMENTS.

Such changes should be made in the present tariff and system of taxation as will relieve any overburdened industry or class, and enable our manufacturers and artisans to compete successfully with those of other lands.

The Government should aid works of internal improvement, national in their character, and should promote the development of our water-courses and harbors wherever the general interests of commerce require.

THE REPUBLICAN PARTY.

Four years ago, as now, the nation stood at the threshold os a Presidential election, and the Republican party, in soliciting a continuance of its ascendency, founded its hope of success, not upon its promises, but upon its history. Its subsequent course has been such as to strengthen the claims which it then made to the confidence and support of the country. On the other hand, considerations more urgent than have ever before existed forbid the accession of its opponents to power. Their success, if success attend them, must chiefly come from the united support of that section which sought the forcible destruction of the Union, and which, according to all the teachings of our past history, will demand ascendency in the councils of the party to whose triumph it will have made by far the largest contribution.

There is the gravest reason for the apprehension that exorbiant claims upon the public Treasury, by no means limited to the hundreds of millions already covered by bills introduced in Congress within the past four years, would be successfully urged if the Democratic party should succeed in supplementing its present control of the National Legislature by electing the Executive also.

There is danger in intrusting the whole law-making power of the Government to a party which has in almost every Southern State repudiated obligations quite as sacred as those to which the faith of the Nation now stands pledged.

I do not doubt that success awaits the Republican party, and that its triumph will assure a just, economical, and patriotic administration. I am, respectfully, your obedient servant, C. A. ARTHUR.

To the Hon. George F. Hoar, President of the Republican National Convention.

INAUGURAL ADDRESS

OF

PRESIDENT JAMES A. GARFIELD.

President Garfield delivered the following inaugural addrsss at Washington, D. C., March 4th, 1881:

FELLOW CITIZEN: We stand to-day upon an eminence which overlooks a hundred years of National life—a century crowded with perils, but crowded with the triumphs of liberty and love. Before continuing the onward march, let us pause on this height for a moment to strengthen our faith and renew our hope by a glance at the pathway along which our people have traveled.

It is now three days more than a hundred years since the adoption of the first written Constitution and perpetual union. The new Republic was then beset with danger on every hand. It had not conquered a place in the family of Nations. The decisive battle of the War for Independence—whose centennial anniversary will soon be gratefully celebrated at Yorktown—had not yet been fought. The Colonists were struggling not only against the armies of Great Britain, but against the settled opinion of mankind; for the world did not believe that the supreme authority of the Government could be safely intrusted to the guardianship of the people themselves.

We can not overestimate the fervent love or the intelligent courage, having the common sense with which our fathers made the great experiment of self-government. When they found, after a short time, that a confederacy of States was too weak to meet the necessities of the glorious and expanding Republic, they boldly set it aside, and in its stead established a National Union, founded directly upon the will of the people, endowed with future powers of self-preservation and with ample authority for the accomplishment of its great objects. Under this Constitution the boundaries of freedom enlarged, the foundations of order and peace have been strengthened, and growth in all the better elements of national life has vindicated the wisdom of the founders, and given new hope to their descendants. Under this Constitution our people long ago made themselves safe against danger from without, and secured for their mariners and flag equality of rights on all the seas. Under this Constitution twenty-five State-houses have been added to the Union, with Constitutions and laws framed and enforced by their own citizens to secure the manifold blessings of local and self-government. [The jurisdictions of this Constitution now covers an area fifty times greater than that of the original thirteen States, and a population twenty times greater than that of 1780.

The trial of that Constitution came at last under the tremendous pressure of civil war. We ourselves are witnesses that the Union emerged from the blood and fire of that conflict purified and made stronger for all beneficent purposes of good government And now, at the close of this first century of growth, with the inspirations of its history in their hearts, our people have lately reviewed the condition of the nation, passed judgment upon the conduct and opinions of political parties, and have registered their will concerning the future administration of the Government. To interpret and to execute that will in accordance with the Constitution is the paramount duty of the Executive. Even from this brief review it is manifest that the nation is resolutely facing to the front, resolving to employ its best energies in developing the great possibilities of the future, sacredly preserving whatever has been gained to liberty and good government during the century. Our people are determined to leave behind them all those bitter controversies concerning things which have been irrevocably settled, further discussion of which can only stir up strife and delay the onward march.

The supremacy of the nation and its laws should be no longer a subject of debate. That discussion, which for half a century threatened the existence of the Union, was closed at last in the high court of war, by a decree from which there is no appeal; that the Constitution, and the laws made in pursuance thereof, shall continue to be the supreme law of the land, binding alike on the States and the people. This decree does not disturb the autonomy of the States, nor interfere with any of their necessary rules of local self-government; but it does fix and establish the permanent supremacy of the Union. The will of the nation, speaking with the voice of battle and through the amended Constitution, has fulfilled the great promise of 1776, by proclaiming: "Liberty throughout the land, to all the inhabitants thereof."

The elevation of the negro race from slavery to the full rights of citizenship is the most important political change we have known since the adoption of the Constitution of 1776. No thoughtful man can fail to appreciate its beneficial effect upon our people. It has freed us from the perpetual danger of war and dissolution. It has added immensely to the moral and industrial forces of our people. It has liberated the master as well as the slave from a relation which wronged and enfeebled both. It has surrendered to their own guardianship the manhood of more than five million people, and has opened to each one of them a career of freedom and usefulness. It has given new inspiration to the power of self-help in both races, by making labor more honorable to the one and more necessary to the other. The influence of this force will grow greater and bear richer fruit with coming years.

No doubt the great change has caused serious disturbance to our Southern community. This is to be deplored; but those who resisted the change should remember that in our institutions there was no middle ground for the negro between slavery and equal citizenship. There can be no permanent disfranchised peasantry in the United States. Freedom can never yield its fullness of blessing so long as the law or its administration places the smallest obstacle in the pathway of any virtuous citizenship. The emancipated race has already made remarkable progress. With unquestionable devotion to the Union, with a patience and gentleness not born of fear, they have "followed the light as God gave them to see the light." They are rapidly laying the material foundations of self-support, widening the circle of intelligence, and beginning to enjoy the blessings that gather around the homes of the industrious poor. They deserve the generous encouragement of all good men. So far as my authority can lawfully extend, they shall enjoy the full and equal protection of the Constitution and laws.

The free enjoyment of equal-suffrage is still in question, and a frank statement of the issue may aid its solution. It is alleged that in many communities negro citizens are practically denied the freedom of the ballot. In so far as the truth of this allegation is admitted, it is answered that in many places honest local government is impossible if a mass of uneducated negroes are allowed to vote. These are grave allegations. So far as the latter is true, it is no palliation that can be offered for opposing freedom of the ballot. Bad local government is certainly a great evil, which ought to be prevented; but to violate the freedom and sanctity of suffrage is more than an evil—it is a crime which, if persisted in, will destroy the Government itself. Suicide is not a remedy. If in other lands it be high treason to compass the death of a King, it should be counted no less a crime here to strangle our sovereign power and stifle its voice.

It has been said that unsettled questions have no pity for the repose of nations. It should be said, with the utmost emphasis, that this question of suffrage will never give repose or safety to the States or to the nation until each, within its own jurisdiction, makes and keeps the ballot free and pure by the strong sanctions of law. But the danger which arises from ignorance in the voter can not be denied. It covers a field far wider than that of negro suffrage, and the present condition of that race. It is a danger that lurks and hides in the sources and fountain of power in any State. We have no standard by which to measure the disaster that may be brought upon us by ignorance and vice in citizens, when joined to corruption and fraud in the suffrage. The voters of the Union, who make and unmake Constitutions, and upon whose will hangs the destiny of our Governments, can transmit their supreme authority to no successor save the coming generation of voters, who are the sole heirs of sovereign power. If that generation comes to its inheritance blinded by ignorance and corrupted by vice, the fall of the Republic will be certain and remediless.

The census has already sounded the alarm in appalling figures, which mark how dangerously high the tide of illiteracy has arisen among our voters and their children. To the South the question is of supreme importance; but the responsibility for the existence of slavery does not rest upon the South alone. The nation itself is responsible for the extension of suffrage, and is under special obligations to aid in removing the illiteracy which it has added to the voting population. For North and South alike there is but one remedy: All the constitutional powers of the nation and of the States, and all the volunteer forces of the people should be summoned to meet this danger by the saving influence of universal education. It is the high privilege and the sacred duty of those now living to educate their successors, and fit them by intelligence and virtue for the inheritance which awaits them. In this beneficent work sections and races should be forgotten, and partisanship should be unknown. Let our people find a new meaning in the Divine Oracle which declares that "A little child shall lead them," for our little children will soon control the destinies of the Republic.

My countrymen, we do not now differ in our judgment concerning the controversies of the past generations, and fifty years hence our children will not be divided in their opinions concerning our controversies. They will surely bless their fathers and their fathers' God that the Union was preserved, that slavery was overthrown, and that both races were made equal before the law. We may hasten or we may retard, but we can not prevent the final reconciliation. Is it not possible for us now to make a truce with them by anticipating and accepting its inevitable verdict? Enterprises of the highest importance to our moral and material well-being invite us, and offer ample powers. Let all our people, leaving behind them the battle fields of dead issues, move forward, and in the strength of liberty and restored Union win the grandest victories of peace.

The prosperity which now prevails is without parallel in our history. Fruitful seasons have done much to secure it, but they have not done all. The preservation of the public credit and the resumption of specie payments, so successfully obtained by the Administration of my predecessors, has enabled our people to secure the blessings which the seasons brought. By the experience of commercial Nations in all ages it has been found that gold and silver afforded the only safe foundation for a monetary system. Confusion has recently been created by variations in the relative value of the two metals; but I confidently believe that arrangements can be made between the leading commercial Nations which will secure the general use of both metals. Congress should provide that the compulsory coinage of silver, now required by law, may not disturb our monetary system by driving either metal out of circulation. If possible, such adjustment should be made that the purchasing power of every coined dollar will be exactly equal to its debt-paying power in all the markets of the world. The chief duty of the National Government in connection with the currency of the country is to coin and to declare its value.

Grave doubts have been entertained whether Congress is authorized by the Constitution to make any form of paper money legal tender. The present issue of United States notes has been sustained by the necessities of war; but such paper should depend for its value and currency upon its convenience in use and its prompt redemption in coin at the will of the holder, and not upon its compulsory circulation. These notes are not money, but promises to pay money. If the holders demand it, the promises should be kept. The refunding of the National debt at a lower rate of interest should be accomplished without compelling the withdrawal of National Bank notes, and thus disturbing the business of the country. I venture to refer to the position I have occupied on the finance question during a long service in Congress, and to say that time and experience have strengthened the opinions I have so often expressed on these subjects. The finances of the Government shall suffer no detriment which it may be possible for my Administration to prevent.

The interests of agriculture deserve more attention from the Government than they have yet received. The farms of the United States afford homes and employment for more than one-half of our people, and furnish much the largest part of all our exports. As the Government lights our coasts for the protection of mariners and the benefit of commerce, so it should give to the tillers of the soil the lights of practical science and experience. Our manufacturers are rapidly making us industrially independent, and are opening to capital and labor new and profitable fields of employment. This steady and healthy growth should still be maintained. Our facilities for transportation should be promoted by the continued improvement of our harbors and great waterways, and by the increase of our tonnage on the ocean.

The development of the world's commerce has led to urgent demands for shortening the great sea voyage around Cape Horn by constructing ship canals or railroads across the isthmus which unites the two continents. Various plans to this end have been suggested, and will need consideration; but none of them have been sufficiently matured to warrant the United States in extending pecuniary aid. The subject is one which will immediately engage the attention of the Government, with a view to thorough protection to American interests. We will urge no narrow policy, nor seek peculiar or exclusive privileges in any commercial route; but, in the language of my predecessors, I believe it to be "the right and duty of the United States to assert and maintain such supervision and authority over any inter-oceanic canal across the isthmus that connects North and South America as will protect our National interests."

The Constitution guarantees absolute religious freedom. Congress is prohibited from making any laws respecting the establishment of religion, or prohibiting the free exercise thereof. The Territories of the United States are subject to the direct legislative authority of Congress, and hence the General Government is responsible for any violation of the Constitution in any of them. It is, therefore, a reproach to the Government that in the most populous of the Territories the Constitutional guarantee is not enjoyed by the people, and the authority of Congress is set at naught. The Mormon Church not only offends the moral sense of mankind by sanctioning polygamy, but prevents the administration of justice through the ordinary instrumentalities of law. In my judgment, it is the duty of Congress, while respecting to the uttermost the conscientious convictions and religious scruples of every citizen, to prohibit within its jurisdiction all criminal practices, especially of that class which destroy the family relation and endanger social order. Nor can any ecclesiastical organization be safely permitted to usurp in the smallest degree the functions and powers of the National Government.

The Civil Service can never be placed on a satisfactory basis until it is regulated by law for the good of the service itself, for the protection of those who are intrusted with the appointing power against the waste of time and the obstruction of public business caused by the inordinate pressure for place, and for the protection of incumbents against intrigue and wrong. I shall at the proper time ask Congress to fix the tenure of minor offices of the several executive departments, and prescribe the grounds upon which removals shall be made during the terms for which incumbents have been appointed.

Finally, acting always within the authority and the limitations of the Constitution, invading neither the rights of the States nor the reserved rights of the people, it will be the purpose of my Administration to maintain authority, and in all places within its jurisdiction to enforce obedience to all laws of the Union and in the interests of the people; to demand rigid economy in all expenditures of the Government, and to require honest and faithful service of all executive officers—remembering that offices were created, not for the benefit of the incumbents or their supporters, but for the service of the Government.

And now, fellow-citizens, I am about to assume the great trust which you have committed to my hands. I appeal to you for that earnest and thoughtful support which makes this Government, in fact, as it is in law, a Government of the people. I shall greatly rely upon the wisdom and patriotism of Congress, and of those who may share with me the responsibilities and duties of the Administration; and upon our efforts to promote the welfare of this great people and their Government, I reverently invoke the support and blessings of Almighty God.

ASSASSINATION

—OF—

PRESIDENT GARFIELD.

Full Particulars of the Terrible Event.

It was on Saturday morning, July 2, 1881, at 9:28, in the Baltimore & Potomac depot at Washington, D. C., that occurred the tragic attempt to assassinate President Garfield. It was the President's intention that morning to have started for Long Branch, where he expected to meet Mrs. Garfield and spend a season of pleasant recreation. The day opened with refreshing breezes, and it is said the President was never more happy; but alas! ere its sun had set, the whole nation and civilized world were stricken with unspeakable sadness at what was believed to be the momentary death of one of God's noblest of men, James A. Garfield.

An eye witness of the terrible tragedy says: "I was coming down Pennsylvania avenue when I saw a carriage coming up the avenue, the horses running so fast that I thought they were running away. Just as the carriage arrived in front of me a man put his head out of the window and said, 'Faster, faster, faster, damn it!' After hearing this remark I thought there was something wrong, and ran after the carriage. When it reached the depot a man jumped out and entered the ladies' room. He had not been there more than three minutes when the President arrived, stepped out of his carriage, and also entered the ladies' room. The President, after passing through the door, was just turning the corner of a seat when the assassin, who was standing on the left of the door, fired. The ball struck the President in the back. The President fell forward. I ran into the depot, and just then the man fired again while the President was falling. The moment the President fell a policeman, who had been standing at the depot door keeping the way clear for the President and his party, grabbed the assassin by the neck, and, as he pulled him out of the depot, another policeman came to his assistance. Just after firing the shot the assassin exclaimed, 'I've killed Garfield! Arthur is President. I am a stalwart!'"

The first person to reach the President after he had fallen upon the floor, was Mrs. Sarah B. White, a lady in charge of the ladies' waiting room, who saw him enter and saw the would be assassin raise his hand and fire. She raised up the head of the stricken man and he was soon placed upon a mattress and borne to an upper room of the depot building.

Gen. Garfield, as he lay upon his mattress in the upper room, is said by those who were about him to have been brave and cheerful. His first impulse was to have his wife informed, and he dictated a dispatch to Col. Rockwell, in which he informed her that he had been wounded, how seriously no one could tell; that he desired her to come immediately. He was conscious and sent his love. At the same time another dispatch was sent to Maj. Swain, Judge Advocate-General, who had charge of Mrs. Garfield, informing him of the nature of the shooting, and directed him to keep the information from Mrs. Garfield. While this was being done, the carriage of one of the Cabinet officers who was present was driven with great speed to the office of Dr. Bliss, on F street, who, with his instrument-case, was hastily driven to the depot, and was the first of the physicians to arrive. He instantly pronounced the wound a dangerous one, but not necessarily fatal. Afterwards he said it was a wound of exceedingly severe character, and all the physicians concurred with him. Garfield manfully and cheerfully talked with his friends, among whom was Col. Robert Ingersoll, to whom he cordially extended his hand and said, "I am glad you came."

It was then found, upon examination, that both shots fired by the assasin had taken effect. The first was well aimed. It had entered the back, just above the kidney, and had perforated the liver. The second shot was fired while the President was falling, and went under the left arm, barely grazing the skin.

It was evidently Guiteau's purpose to shoot Garfield several times, for in the confession which he left sealed, he says that he shot the President several times.

The surgeons, of whom a dozen had arrived, agreed that the President should be taken to the White House as speedily as possible before his strength should fail. Gen. Sherman, who had also come, had already provided an ambulance, and Secretary of War Robert Lincoln, with remarkable sagacity, had ordered a company of troops from the arsenal to help preserve order. A large squad of mounted police had been summoned. They cleared the way for the ambulance, riding up the avenue at a furious gallop. The ambulance containing the President was driven at great speed, to avoid a possible crowd. It entered the White House grounds at the lower gate, the President reclining upon the mattrass. As he was lifted out he saw, at a window, his private secretary and a number of friends who were at the White House looking out, who had already been notified by telephone from the depot, of the attempted assassination. The President, raising his head from his improvised litter, waived his hand in greeting to those who were so anxiously watching his arrival. He showed, even in this supreme moment, the same tender consideration for those around him which has always characterized his private and public career. He was immediately brought into the house by the lower entrance, and carried to the room occupied by the President, in the southwest corner of the second floor; there his clothes, which were very much soiled with blood, were removed, and he was placed upon his bed. Those who saw him say that the trace of the bullet was very plainly visible in a murderous looking hole above the hip.

Preparations were immediately taken to preserve quiet and order. The large force of police cleared the White House grounds and barred the gates. A company of artillerymen arrived, and were ordered to camp in the ground, and to guard them. The gates were closed to carriages, and no persons were allowed to enter the grounds of the Executive Mansion without passes from the private secretary of the President, which were granted to every person having any reason except that of idle curiosity to be there. Every member of the Cabinet followed the President to the White House, and the ladies of the Cabinet officers performed the tender womanly offices, in the absence of the wife who was approaching the National Capital with all the speed that steam can give. Officials of all grades and prominent persons in the city assembled in the White House ante-room, some of them being even permitted to enter the President's chamber. It was thought that the wound might be probed immediately after the President had been brought back to the White House, but this was not deemed safe. There were many indications of internal hemorrhage. The temperature increased rapidly and the pulse was greatly quickened. Soon after the return from the depot there was great hope that the bullet might not prove fatal, but when it was discovered that the physicians declined to make a search for it, and postponed any further examination until 3 p. m., it became apparent that the President was too weak to submit to the operation, and the hopes of recovery rested first in the location of the bullet and next in a strong constitution. Meanwhile everything was done to relieve the sufferer His head was clear and he was very comfortable, complaining of nothing except of pain and twitching in his feet, which the surgeons said was not a good symptom.

Soon after he had been placed upon the bed Mr. Blaine came in. He had stopped in the ante-room long enough to write in his own hand dispatches to Minister Lowell at London, and to the principal diplomatic representatives abroad, stating that the President had been shot. "I never saw,' said Postmaster-General James afterwards, "a man of such extraordinary nerve as Mr Blaine. He stood beside the President when he was shot, and he was the only man in all that depot-building who was not almost paralyzed with terror. He stood calm and collected in the midst of that surging, panic-stricken crowd, and gave his orders as coolly as if he had been commanding a battle, and he was within a few inches of the assassin's bullet himself." "I never thought of myself at all at the time," said Mr. Blaine afterwards. "I only thought of our poor, dear President." When Blaine entered the President's chamber, the President hardly turned. Throughout the entire day he always tried to turn whenever a friend entered the room, and extended his hand to him. The Secretary of State approached the bedside of the rapidly sinking man, when the President placed his arm about him, as nearly as he could, and said: "How I love you!" It was not until then that Blaine, the strong man broke down. The eyes that had refused to fill during the intense excitement of the preceeding hour were suffused with tears, and the voice was choked when the great man stricken down embraced him and said: "How I love you!" "It was a moment" said Mr. Blaine, "that I never shall forget in all my life." The Secretary of State soon retired, for he did not wish to excite the wounded man by an exhibition of emotion.

The afternoon was spent in the White House in an agony of suspense. The entire Cabinet remained there all the time. The physicians were in constant consultation. There were some hyperdermic injections, after which it was noticed that the President vomited, a circumstance said to be explained by the fact, subsequently discoverd, that the ball had perforated his liver. For nourishment he was given champagne and ice.

The President talked all the evening as much as they would allow him to talk. Mrs. Secretary Blaine, Mrs. Attorney-General MacVeagh, Mrs. Postmaster-General James, and Mrs. Secretary of War Lincoln, were in constant attendance, and the Cabinet officers occasionally went in to see the President. To one of the ladies of the Cabinet the President said:

"What do you suppose he wanted to shoot me for?"

She answered that it was charitable to suppose he was a crazy and disappointed office-seeker.

The President said, quoting "Penzance" and cheerfully smiling, "I expect that he supposed that 'it was a glorious thing to be a pirate King.'"

The President told Col. Rockwell, soon after the shooting, that he feared that the shot was fatal, and that he was prepared for the worst. During the afternoon he referred very seldom to his condition. His greatest anxiety was to see his wife. As often as every fifteen minutes he would turn to his attendants and ask how soon they expected her to arrive. Bulletins from the rapidly-approaching train were received at least every half hour. The tracks had been cleared, and the operators at every station along the road had been instructed to telegraph directly to the White House operator at Washington the progress of the train. When it was learned that Mrs. Garfield could not, at best, arrive before 7 o'clock, and to do that it would be necessary to cover the distance between there and Philadelphia in three hours, the President was disappointed. The moments seemed to hang heavily with him after 5 o'clock p. m., as at that hour, he had learned definitely that the physicians did not think that he had much chance to recover. The President, at his own earnest request, was informed of this fact by Dr. Bliss. The President said:

"I am not afraid to die. I want to know what you think of my condition. Tell me the worst."

The doctor replied that his condition was very serious, but he had some chances of life, but that he would do well to prepare for the worst.

One of the ladies of the Cabinet afterwards cheerfully said to the President, "We expect to pull you through, Mr. President."

Gen. Garfield answered, "And I am going to try to help you pull me through." He never lost his spirits, not even when the doctor informed him that he, perhaps, had not many hours to live. He said: "Then God's will be done; I am content;" but from the moment that he learned that he might not live, his thoughts turned more anxiously to the arrival of his wife.

During the afternoon the Cabinet officers seriously discussed the situation. It was noticeable that their thoughts were turned chiefly to the sufferer, and very little to the political results which might follow from the death of the President.

Mr. Kirkwood sat silently much of the time, smoking in the ante-room. He was very calm and sad. Secretary

Blaine did not leave the room except to take a lunch, and he conversed freely about the occurrence, and paid an eloquent tribute to the great qualities of his chief. He was very calm. His greatest regret seemed to be for the family of the President and for the country. Postmaster-General James was especially effected. He was frequently heard to say; "God save the poor country!"

Robert Lincoln, painfully reminded of the tragic death of his own father, in the same position, said, in the Cabinet Council chamber, while sitting beneath that statue of his father which looked down upon him, to a colleague in the Cabinet and some friends: "It is a curious fact that the President has lately talked a great deal about my father. At a dinner the other day, to which a number of us were invited, his conversation was full of story-telling. He narrated, among other things, his experiences at the time of the assassination in New York, and said he strolled out of his room and almost unconsciously attended the meeting which was called in Wall street, and made that remarkable speech which had such an effect in quieting the mob."

Mrs. Garfield's meeting with her husband on her arrival from Long Branch, is described as an effecting scene.

Attorney-General MacVeagh and Mrs. James went to the door to meet her as the carriage drove up at the south entrance.

"How is he?" she said, as she placed her hands in those of Mrs. James.

"We think he is greatly improved," said the Attorney-General.

Mrs. Garfield walked quickly up the stairs along which her husband had been borne, faint and bleeding, and she was directed to the room where he was lying. The door was thrown open and she entered. The President opened his eyes and saw who it was. Mrs. Garfield knelt by the side of the bed and threw her arms around him. "It is all right now," she exclaimed, "I am here."

The President murmured an almost inaudible expression of love and returned her embrace as best he could. The single witness of the meeting was moved to tears, but Mrs. Garfield's bearing was such as to inspire confidence in those around her. She refused to entertain the idea that her husband might die.

"How does she bear it?" asked the President to Mrs. James when Mrs. Garfield had left the room.

"Nobly. She is full of courage," was Mrs. James' reply.

"Thank God for that," said the President, "I would rather die than be the cause of bringing on a relapse of her illness."

At this time the President was at the most critical state since the shooting. The physicians had abandoned all hope of his living more than two or three hours at the most. The pulse was mounting higher and higher. There were signs of internal hemorrhage and the temperature of the body constantly increasing. The members of the Cabinet were sending dispatches to different points announcing the speedy dissolution of the President. Within the short space of half an hour, however, nature asserted herself, and the work of improvement began.

Col. Rockwell's Story of the Attempted Assassination.

Col. A. F. Rockwell, the Private Secretary of Gen. Garfield and intimate friend of the President, gives the following account of the attempted assassination:

"The boys, James and Harry (sons of the President), started off in the President's carriage to pick up Dr. Hawks, their tutor, who was stopping on F street. The President had arranged the night before for Secretary

Blaine to call at the mansion to go to the depot with him. The Secretary came round in his own carriage. Mine was in reserve and followed just behind the Secretary's. I had several pieces of baggage to dispose of, and so drove directly to the baggage-room, and was getting the checks, when I heard a crack, crack, with an interval between the shots as long as it would take to cock a pistol. On the sill of the door leading from the ladies' parlor into the general reception room, or main hall, stood Secretary Blaine, calling for me and pointing to the would-be assassin, Guiteau. It was a terrible thought, but nevertheless one which flashed across my mind that the President had been shot. Quickly I had the President's carriage brought to the main door, the cushions arranged to make the President as comfortable as possible, and was prepared to take him directly to the mansion. The physicians advised against it and for the best. After I had written from his dictation a touching telegram to his wife, and a hasty examination had been made up stairs, he was removed to the ambulance. The President put his hand in mine and the driver was cautioned to proceed slowly over the cobble-stone pavement until we reached the concrete at Seventh street. We had traveled but two squares from the depot when he asked, 'How far are we now?' and in a subdued voice said: 'It hurts, oh! it hurts.' At Thirteenth street he again asked:

"Where are we now?" I told him and he urged us to go a little faster.

"It is impossible to describe Mrs. Garfield, the heroic wife and mother. She, too, realizes the restraint which the medical advisers have been compelled to put upon her visits to the President's bedside. The sympathy detween them, the union of their hearts, impels the President to want to exert himself, and then we have to protest, and the good woman retires."

"It is true, that on the morning before the deed, the President turned a handspring over his bed!"

"It was the morning before, this day week, Jimmie, there the fellow sits," pointing to Private Secretary Brown's desk, "came into his father's chamber half-dressed, and in his nimble way turned a handspring over the bed and back again." "See here, papa," he said, "if you were not so stout, you might do that, too, couldn't you? The President kept on with his toilet, until Jim's bantering somewhat nettled him, and, before the boy could realize it, the President had turned gracefully from one side of a large double bed to the other, and came down with a thump on the floor. "There, my boy, the son is not greater than his father; now finish your dressing." "I suppose," continued the Colonel, "the story was told to illustrate the strength and suppleness of the President at his age of life. Very few men of 50 years (for the President will be that old on the 9th day of November next) would care to undertake such a feat. But the story has a thrilling secret. You know, the ladies' room, where the shots were fired, is about twenty feet wide—that is, from the door-sill to the opposite hall. The aisle-way leading to the main hall is formed by a double row of seats, heavily cushioned and of large frame work.

When the President entered the depot with Secretary Blaine, he was in his cheeriest mood. He passed half way down the aisle, Blaine preceding him a very few steps. Guiteau stood at the inside end of the row of seats near the main entrance on the left, when he fired the first shot, which did the President no harm, for he turned to see from whence the sound came, and saw Guiteau advancing. He was preparing to leap over the seat, that is, he realized when he turned partially around that the man had fired at him. He instantly determined to attack the man. The next instant the President would have been face to face with Guiteau. His confidence in his ability to spring over the barrier, for the back of the seats is about four feet high, flashed upon him, and his whole muscular strength was strained for the act when he fell forward struck by the second shot. Guiteau was behind him. The instant he pulled the trigger the first time he stepped forward four feet. It was but the very fraction of a second between the explosion and the President's alarm. The fraction was on the side of the would-be assassin.

His purpose was also to fire a second shot, and he stepped quickly forward to get as near the President as possible. They were not six feet apart, so that the instant the President realized the situation his intense activity of mind and muscle made him aggressive, and it was at that instant he received the staggering bullet and fell forward against the wainscoting of the reception-room, at the head of the aisle leading to the main hall. Till now the impression seems to have gained a hold that Guiteau's act was done so quickly that the President did not comprehend what was going on. It is true, as I told you a while ago, that the reports of the firing were so close together that it could not have been longer than it would take to cock a pistol, yet during this time Guiteau was advancing and the President preparing to advance upon his assailant.

Anyone who will take his watch and carefully observe the beats of the second-hand, will be surprised at the distance one can get over in a second if impelled by a strong motive. The position in which Guiteau stood made it necessary for him to shoot at nearly an angle of 40 degrees while the position of the body of the President was also at about the same angle with the seats when the ball struck his right side. With this understanding of the position of the two, it is evident that the ball met with great resistance and was deflected. Its natural course would have been through the body, passing out over the pelvis, so it is a reasonable theory that, upon entering the interior of the body, its force had been exhausted, and the internal injury is less than it was at first supposed. All of which gladdens us with increased hope and conviction that his recovery is now only a question of time."

Scenes and Incidents on the Sick-Bed.
"NOT SO WELL AS I THOUGHT."

One day before a chill, the President was speaking words of hope and enjoying the soft breeze tempered by the rays of the sun that flowed in so gratefully through the window. He had said:

"I feel better. The rigor yesterday was at the best but a trifle." The President asked what they were about to write of his condition. Bliss announced:

"We are going to give the public good news to-day.'

"You are not likely, responded the patient, to make it too strong. I feel ever so much better."

"Directly afterwards the chill came. When the rigor passed there was no apparent rally on the part of the patient, who lay exhausted in a stupor. For a time it seemed as if the end had really come, and that out of that state of unconsciousness the President would never awake. The treatment, however, had its effect in time, although nearly three hours after the chill had gone by."

Perspiration that followed the chill was profuse, but the mind was clear, and he seemed to bear up bravely, though aware of his condition. He said half jestingly, "I am not not so well as I thought I was, am I?"

THE PATIENT'S WATCHFULNESS.

When Dr. Bliss was taking the temperature one evening, an operation which consumes exactly ten minutes, he remarked to General Swaim after nine minutes had passed:

"I can't make it about normal."

"Well," said the President, "you have just one minute more."

The Doctor was surprised by the accuracy of the patient's information regarding the lapse of time.

"How do you know?" he asked.

In reply the President pointed to a little clock sitting on the mantel, a present from some friend the presence of which the Doctor had not discovered until that moment.

LAST OF EARTH.

General Swaim tells the story of the death-bed scene from his own observations. He was General Garfield's watcher for the night, and Dr. Bliss had gone across the passage to his own room to prepare for Swaim, before going to bed, a written memoranda of what was to be the treatment of the case for the night. A few moments before ten o'clock, while the President was sleeping, Swaim put his hand under the bed-clothes, and finding that the patient's limbs were slightly cold he immediately applied warm cloths. At ten o'clock the President awoke from pain in the region of the heart, and placing his hand upon his left breast said: "I have a terrible pain," and asked for a glass of water. Before the water could be handed to him he exclaimed: "Oh Swaim," and with his hand pressed upon his heart at once lost consciousness.

Dr. Bliss and the other physicians were promptly summoned, and did what they could to revive him, although it was evident that death was upon him. He lay there, his breath passing in sighs. Mrs. Garfield stood there, and fully realizing the calamity that was present, said: "Why am I called upon to bear this sorrow?" At 10:35 life was extinct, and Mrs. Garfield passed from the chamber. Afterward she returned and remained for two hours with the body of her dead husband.

THE MEDICAL RECORD.

PULSE, TEMPERATURE AND RESPIRATION.

The following table, compiled from the official bulletins, shows the variations of the pulse, temperature and respiration of President Garfield each day since he was wounded. The highest pulse recorded, it will be seen, was 130, which was 60 pulsations above the normal rate of the patient, and the lowest was 94, which was 24 pulsations too many.

Month	Time	Pulse	Temperature	Respiration	Month	Time	Pulse	Temperature	Respiration	Month	Time	Pulse	Temperature	Respiration
July					July					August				
2.....	6.00 p m	140			23.....	7.00 p m	118	101.7	25	22.....	8.30 a m	104	98.4	18
	8.30 p m	128	99.1	22	24.....	8.15 a m	98	98.4	18		6.30 p m	110	100.2	19
	11.20 p m	120	98.	18		12.00 a m	118	99.8	24	23.....	8.30 a m	100	98.4	18
3.....	2.45 a m	124	98.	18		7.00 p m	104	99.2	23		6.30 p m	104	99.2	12
	8.00 a m	115			25.....	8.30 a m	96	98.4	18	24.....	8.30 a m	100	98.5	17
	10.10 a m	114	98.	18		7.00 p m	110	101.8	24		6.30 p m	108	98.2	19
	3.00 p m	104			26.....	8.30 a m	109	98.4	18	25.....	8.30 a m	106	98.5	18
	10.45 p m	120	100.	20		7.00 p m	104	100.7	22		6.30 p m	112	99.8	19
4.....	8.15 a m	108	99.4	19	27.....	8.00 a m	94	98.4	18	26.....	8.30 a m	108	99.1	17
	12.30 p m	110	100.	24		7.00 p m	96	98.5	20		6.30 p m	116	99.9	18
	7.45 p m	120	101.9	24	28.....	8.30 a m	90	98.4	18	27.....	8.30 a m	100	98.4	22
	10.00 p m	124	101.	24		7.00 p m	94	100.5	20		6.30 p m	114	79.9	22
5.....	8.30 a m	114	100.5	24	29.....	8.30 a m	92	98.4	18	28.....	8.30 a m	100	98.4	17
	12.30 p m	110	101.	24		7.00 p m	98	100.	20		6.30 p m	110	99.7	20
	8.30 p m	106	101.9	24	30.....	8.30 a m	92	98.4	18	29.....	8.30 a m	100	98.5	18
6.....	8.30 a m	98	98.9	23		7.00 p m	94	100.2	20		6.30 p m	110	100.5	18
	12.30 p m	100	99.7	23	31.....	8.30 a m	94	98.4	18	30.....	6.30 p m	112	98.5	18
	8.30 p m	104	100.	23		7.00 p m	94	99.	20		6.30 p m	109	99.5	18
7.....	9.15 a m	94	99.1	23	August					31.....	8.30 a m	100	98.4	18
	1.00 p m	100	108.	23	1.....						6.30 p m	109	98.6	18
	8.30 p m	106	101.2	23		8.30 a m	94	98.4	18	Sept.				
8.....	8.30 a m	96	99.2	23		7.00 p m	94	99.5	20	1.....	8.30 a m	100	98.4	17
	12.30 p m	108	104.	24	2.....	8.30 a m	94	98.4	18		6.30 p m	108	99.4	18
	8.00 p m	108	101.3	24		7.60 p m	94	100.	20	2.....	8.30 a m	100	98.4	17
9.....	8.30 a m	100	99.4	24	3.....	8.30 a m	94	98.4	18		6.30 p m	104	99.2	18
	1.00 p m	104	101.2	22		7.00 p m	108	100.8	19	3.....	8.30 a m	104	98.6	17
	7.30 p m	108	101.9	24	4.....	8.30 a m	90	98.4	18		6.30 p m	102	98.6	18
10.....	8.00 a m	106	100.	23		7.00 p m	102	100.2	19	4.....	8.30 a m	108	98.4	18
	1.00 p m	102	105.5	22	5.....	8.30 a m	88	98.4	18		6.30 p m	110	99.	18
	7.00 p m	107	101.9	24		7.00 p m	102	100.4	18	5.....	8.30 a m	102	99.5	18
11.....	8.00 a m	98	98.2	24	6.....	8.30 a m	92	98.4	18		6.30 p m	108	99.8	18
	1.00 p m	108	99.8	24		7.00 p m	102	101.8	19	6.....	8.30 a m	112	99.8	18
	7.00 p m	108	102.3	24	7.....	8.30 a m	96	98.7	18		6.30 p m	124	101.2	18
12.....	8.00 a m	97	99.6	22		7.00 p m	100	98.7	18	7.....	9.00 a m	106	98.4	18
	1.00 p m	100	100.8	24	8.....	8.30 a m	94	98.7	18		6.00 p m	108	101.	19
	7.00 p m	104	102.4	24		7.00 p m	108	100.8	19	8.....	8.30 a m	104	98.7	18
13.....	8.30 a m	90	98.5	20	9.....	8.30 a m	96	99.8	18		5.00 p m	110	99.1	18
	1.00 p m	92	100.6	22		7.00 p m	102	101.9	19	9.....	8.30 a m	100	98.5	18
	7.00 p m	100	101.6	24	10.....	8.30 a m	94	98.5	19		6.00 p m	100	98.6	18
14.....	8.30 a m	90	99.8	22		7.00 p m	108	101.	15	10.....	8.30 a m	104	99.4	18
	1.00 p m	94	99.5	22	11.....	8.30 a m	100	98.6	19		6.00 p m	108	98.7	19
	7.00 p m	96	101.	23		7.30 p m	108	101.2	20	11.....	8.30 a m	104	98.8	20
15.....	8.30 a m	90	98.5	18	12.....	8.30 a m	100	98.6	19		6.00 p m	110	100.	20
	1.00 p m	94	98.5	18		7.00 p m	108	101.2	20	12.....	9.00 a m	100	98.4	20
	7.00 p m	98	100.4	20	13.....	8.30 a m	104	100.8	19		12.00 m	100	99.2	18
16.....	8.30 a m	90	98.5	18		6.30 p m	100	99.8	19		5.30 p m	100	98.6	20
	7.00 p m	94	98.4	19	14.....	8.30 a m	100	100.2	19	13.....	8.30 a m	100	99.4	20
17.....	8.30 a m	90	98.4	18		8.30 a m	108	100.2	19		5.30 p m	100	98.6	19
	7.00 p m	96	100.2	20	15.....	6.30 p m	110	98.6	19	14.....	9.30 a m	100	98.4	21
18.....	8.30 a m	98	98.4	18		7.00 p m	110	102.6	18		6.30 p m	112	99.2	20
	7.00 p m	107	100.7	21	16.....	6.30 p m	106	99.2	18	15.....	8.30 a m	101	98.4	22
19.....	8.30 a m	90	98.5	18		8.30 a m	110	98.5	18		5.30 p m	104	98.2	21
	7.00 p m	96	99.8	18	17.....	6.30 p m	106	98.6	18	16.....	8.30 a m	110	98.6	21
20.....	8.30 a m	90	98.4	18		8.30 a m	108	99.6	19	17.....	5.30 p m	104	99.8	24
	7.00 p m	96	99.6	19	18.....	6.30 p m	108	100.	18		5.30 p m	102	98.5	18
21.....	8.30 a m	88	98.4	18		8.30 a m	106	99.9	17	18.....	9.00 a m	116	100.6	20
	7.00 p m	90	99.6	19	19.....	6.30 p m	100	98.4	18		6.30 p m	102	98.5	22
22.....	8.30 a m	88	98.4	17		8.30 a m	106	100.	18	19.....	8.00 a m	100	98.4	22
	6.30 p m	99	100.3	20	20.....	6.30 p m	110	101.4	18		12.30 p m	104	98.2	20
23.....	7.00 a m	92	98.4	19	21.....	6.30 p m	108	100.4	18					
	10.00 a m	110	101.1	24										
	12.30 p m	125	100.4	26										

The Run to Long Branch.

Private Secretary Brown makes, in substance, the following statement of the trip from Washington to the Elberon:

Upon leaving the executive mansion the President seemed to enjoy the scenery and looked around inquiringly. He noticed several employes standing in front of the mansion and waved his hand to them, at the same time smiling as if it were very gratifying to him to leave the scene of his long illness. All the way to the depot he was a very anxious observer of everything, and this he was not prevented doing. Upon arrival at Sixth street and Pennsylvania avenue the patient was removed from the express wagon and placed on a spring mattress which had been prepared for his reception.

The President experienced little or no disturbance in being transferred from the vehicle to the car, and his pulse, although slightly accelerated, reaching about 115, fell to about 106 before the train started, and shortly after fell to 104, and again to 102.

The first stop of the train was made at Patapsco, at which point the parotid gland was dressed.

The pessengers on the special train besides the President were: Mrs. Garfield and Miss Mollie; C. O. Rockwell, the President's brother-in-law; Col. A. F. Rockwell, wife and daughter; Gen. D. G. Swaim, Secretary Brown, Col. H. C. Corbin and Warren S. Young, assistant to Secretary Brown. The surgeons in charge, namely, D. W. Bliss, J. K. Barnes, J. J. Woodward, Robert Reyburn and D. Hayes Agnew; nurses, Drs. S. S. Boynton and Edson; domestics,

Dane, Sprigg, Mary White, and Eliza Cutter; T. N. Ely, superintendent of motive power of the Pennsylvania railway, in charge of the train; Charles Watts, assistant in charge of the train; James T. Elder, chief inspector of air brakes; George Albright, inspector of air-brakes; J. P. Syster, carpenter; E. M. Berrell, porter of President Roberts' car, porter; Andrew James, assistant porter, and J. Sharp, assistant trainmaster of the Baltimore and Potemac railroad; William Page, engineer; E. Grinnell, fireman; J. Mason, fireman; G. K. Dean and James Kelly, brakemen on the Baltimore and Potomoc. Extract of beef was administered at 10:10 a. m.

A stop of four minutes occurred at Lamokin for fuel, the only time coal was taken in on the trip. At 10:30 a stop of five minutes was made at Gray's Ferry for water. Between Philadelphia and Monmouth Junction the special train made several miles at the rate of seventy miles per hour.

Bay View was reached at 8:05, and a brief stop was made to enable the surgeons to make a dressing of the wound. It was found to have suffered no derangement by travel. The dressing was soon accomplished, and the train, aftet leaving Bay View, was run at the rate of fifty miles an hour. The track in this locality is very straight, and in excellent condition, and, though the speed was at times greater than fifty miles an hour, the vibration of the President's bed was no more than it would have been had the train been moving at twenty miles per hour. The attending surgeons felt very much gratified with the manner in which the removal was conducted, and were generally of opinion that, with the exception of being slightly fatigued, the President would endure the journey exceedingly well.

A gentleman who was on board the President's train said that when Philadelphia was passed **Mrs. Garfield came into** the car. The President was lying in a half doze, but seemed to recognize her presence, and immediately opened his eyes and said: "Well, Crete, this is quite a journey."

"Do you feel any bad effects of the ride," she asked kindly.

"Not a bit. This is many times better than the confinement of that horrible room in the White House."

Before that, and while passing through Chester, he noticed from the elevation on which he lay, and which enabled him to look out through the window, a large crowd at the depot. It was, in fact, the only place where there was a crowd on the line of route. He was very much interested; in fact, his interest partook of the nature of excitement. Dr. Bliss stepped forward and dropped the curtain of the window.

"Put it up," said Mr. Garfield, pettishly. "I want to see the people."

At this time the train was running at the rate of fifty-five miles an hour. There are a number of switches here, and the only jolt that had been felt was experienced as the train dashed over the rails of the freight-yard at the north side of Washington. He placed his hand on his stomach and said:

"It feels qualmish."

The doctors were afraid that a recurrence of the vomiting, which boded such disastrous results, was about to come. He was given a considerable quantity of stimulant, and, under its influence, he fell asleep and rode fourteen miles in fourteen minutes, without waking. When he opened his eyes he said:

"Where are we?—half way?"

Col. Rockwell, who was beside him, said: "Yes, more than half way," and he replied:

"Well, this is the most interesting day I have had since I was shot."

At Gray's Ferry, three miles south of Philadelphia, the journals on the President's car had become so heated that it was necessary to repack them. When the train started again they were not to stop until they reached Freehold, sixty miles nearer the point of destination.

Once, when traveling at the rate of sixty miles an hour, Dr. Bliss said to him:

"Mr. President, if the movement affects you in any way, we will reduce the speed."

"No," he answered, "let her go."

Afterward Dr. Bliss remarked that we would stop and give him his bath.

"No," said the President, "to get to the end of this trip is more important now than the bath."

The President was given food regularly every two hours during the journey, but he had no enema given him. His food consisted of from two to four ounces of beef extract each time.

A track 3,500 feet long had been laid from the regular station to the front door of the cottage where he was to stop. Although the sun was broiling hot and Long Branch has seldom experienced such sultriness, the long line of roads was lined with carriages, and with men and women on foot, of all ages and from every class in society, each bent on showing reverence to the President. It was known that he would not be seen, and the mere sight of a moving train would have drawn none of them, but it was a spontaneous movement on the part of all within reach to stand quietly and in a respectful attitude while the Nation's sufferer passed. The track had been laid not only to the grounds, but through them and close up to the porch where he was to be received.

Shortly after one o'clock the train was seen coming slowly round the curve out from the apple orchard through which the branch track passes. When within two hundred feet of the cottage the train stopped. The last car, containing Mrs. Garfield, her daughter Mollie and Mrs. and Miss Rockwell, was uncoupled and pushed by the railroad laborers a little beyond the cottage. Then the President's car was detached, and a hundred citizens sprang forward and surrounded it. It was moved gently, and stopped right before the ocean-side entrance to the cottage at 1:31 p. m., having occupied almost exactly six hours in its trip from Washington. First several utensils were taken out by attendants. At last all was ready, and the President was carefully lifted from the car on a stretcher, which was carried by the surgeons into the cottage beneath canvas awnings which ran out from the entrance to the car and concealed the sight from the crowd, which soon began to disperse.

The Engineer's Story.

William Page was the man who brought the President through safely from Washington to Long Branch. He was a most striking figure on the train as it pushed up in front of the Elberon. His long beard was floating in the wind, which was blowing in from the sea, and his swarthy face was covered with dirt and cinders. He stood erect and firm, and with an air of conscious pride in every feature, that showed he was conscious of a duty well performed.

"Did she behave well to-day on the trip?" was asked.

"Behave? Well I should say so. She seemed to feel all

that was required of her. When, on ordinary occasions, I take her over the road she starts off with a jerk like, and raising herself, and goes galloping down, puffing and snorting, but this morning she glided away as gentle as a lady's mare, and even when I put her to her best, and she went on at the rate of a mile in fifty-three seconds, she seemed to hold her breath." As he said this he leaned out of the cab and looked at his engine as kindly as a rider would his favorite horse.

"Then you limited the speed to forty-five miles an hour, which was intended?"

"Oh, no! that you see, would only have been three-fourths of a mile to a minute, and a good deal of the way we made more than a mile a minute."

"Did the doctors and the President know you were going at that speed?"

"They did not the first time I let her go; and I'll tell you," he said, after a moment's hesitation, "how I came to do it. We left Washington at 6:37 this morning. We ran down to Patapsco, thirty-seven miles out, at a limited rate. There we stopped three minutes. This stop, like all the other stops made on the way up, were to change crews, to water, and allow the physicians to attend on the President. I saw one of the attendants, I guess it was Col. Rockwell, coming down the platform, and I called out to him, 'How is the President?' You see though I was not sure who he was, I felt kind of safe in calling him Colonel. 'He is doing finely, Page,' came back the answer.

'Does he feel the motion?' 'Not at all. Why, you are going as smoothly as a carriage over an asphalt pavement.'

"Was it then you began to think of running a little faster?"

"Well, yes; but as Bayview, our next stopping place, was only eight miles further, I did not try until we started from Bayview to Perryville, seventy-eight miles out from Washington. They sent word that the President had been doing better and better as the distance from the White House was increased, so I thought I would water the engines, and, if she went smoothly, try one mile a little faster. Lamokin, the next halt, was forty-six miles further on. The engine behaved beautifully, and was half way between Bayview and Lamokin. I went on with the trial, and went one mile in fifty-three seconds. I did not feel a jolt or jar as she went tearing down the track, but I knew then that if the President had a mind he might get the sea-breeze sooner. We stopped seven minutes at Lamokin. I called out to one of the attendants: 'Did you notice any extra motion when we were going faster?'

"'Why, no,' was the reply. Were we traveling faster than forty-five miles an hour?'

"'Yes, sir,' says I, 'we went one mile in fifty-three seconds.'

"'Well,' says he, 'I did not notice it, and I am sure the President did not. I will go and ask.'

"Pretty soon I saw him coming down the platform.

"'Whip her up, Page, whip her up,' he called out. The President did not feel any extra motion. They were all delighted to hear that we were getting along faster, and the President said: 'Tell him to go ahead. I want to get there.'

"'Does he continue to improve?' I asked.

"'Yes. He said a short time ago: 'I feel as if I were on the road to recovery.'"

"After these stops," was asked, "you went pretty much at the speed you thought best, according to your knowledge of the road?"

"Pretty much as I thought best, and the engine behaved well right through to Elberon—yes sir, right straight through. She ran more smoothly than she is running now, and I warrant you'er not being much shaken at this mo- moment."

" I suppose after this she will be the most famous engine on the road?"

"Yes, sir, and she ought to be. I guess she has earned a National reputation to-day."

The Last Day's Bulletins.

The following bulletins were issued during the day on which the President died. The last one, it will be noticed, was sent at 10:10 p. m. At 10:35, the great and good man was dead.

ELBERON, N. J., Sept. 19, 9 A. M.—The condition of the President this morning continues unfavorable. Shortly after the issue of the evening bulletin he had a chill lasting fifteen minutes. The febrile rise following continued until 12 midnight, during which time his pulse ranged from 112 to 130. The sweating that followed was quite profuse. The cough, which was quite troublesome during the chill, gave him but little annoyance the remainder of the night. This morning at 8 o'clock his temperature is 98.8, pulse, 106 and feble; respiration, 22. At 8:30 another chill came on, on account of which the dressing was temporarily postponed. A bulletin will be issued at 12:30 P. M. D. W. BLISS,
D. HAYES AGNEW.

12:30 P. M.—The chill from which the President was suffering at the time the morning bulletin was issued lasted about fifteen minutes, and was followed by febrile rise of temperature and sweating. He has slept much of the time, but his general condition has not materially changed since. Temperature, 98.2; pulse, 104; respiration. 20. D. W. BLISS.
D. HAYES AGNEW.

2 P. M.—Dr. Boynton says the President is perceptibly weaker

than yesterday. There was considerable mental disturbance last night, and there has been more or less delirium to-day, There is nothing encouraging to report so far this afternoon. He takes his nourishment and stimulents as usual.

6 P. M.—Though the gravity of the President's condition continues, there has been no aggravation of the symptoms since the noon bulletin was issued. He has slept most of the time, coughing but little and with more ease. The sputa remains unchanged. A sufficient amount of nourishment has been taken and retained. Temperature, 98.4; pulse, 102; respiration, 18.

6:40 P. M.—In an interview a few minutes ago, Attorney-General MacVeagh said there was no new grounds for hope, and the President could not last long in his present weak condition. He is weaker now than at any time, and the Attorney-General has the greatest apprehensions. The mind of the President has been perfectly clear all day. There is no reason now to believe he will have another chill. The Attorney-General says he understands every precaution has been taken during the day to prevent recurrence of the rigors. At 6:30 Miss Mollie Garfield was walking on the lawn with several ladies.

7:25 P. M.—Dr. Agnew said he does not feel much encouraged by the evening bulletin. The case is still critical.

THE LAST WHILE ALIVE.

10:10 P. M.—The President thus far has passed a comfortable night. He is now sleeping with pulse at 120 and no indications of another chill.

The Death-Bed Scene.

The death-bed scene of the President was a peculiarly sad and impressive one. As soon as the doctors felt there was no longer hope, the members of the family assembled. Dr. Bliss stood at the head of the bed with his hand on the pulse of the patient, and consulted in low whispers with Dr. Agnew. The Private Secretary stood on the opposite side of the bed, with Mrs. Garfield at the bedside, she at times leaning on his arm. Miss Lulu Rockwell and Miss Mollie Garfield came into the room at the time the President lost consciousness. Afterward they went into the hall, the door of which remained open, and waited there. What conversation was had was conducted in whispers. Those about the bed occasionally went into the corners of the room and spoke to each other. The solemnity of the occasion fully impressed itself upon them. There was no sound heard except the gasping for breath of the sufferer, whose changing color gave indications of the near approach of the end.

LAST WORDS.

After he had repeated "It hurts," he passed into a state of unconsciousness, breathing heavily at times, and then giving a slight indication that breath was still in his body. The only treatment that was given was hypodermic injections of brandy by Dr. Agnew, assisted by Dr. Boynton. Occasionally they spoke with Dr. Bliss in quiet whispers. The President suffered no pain after the time he placed his hand upon his heart. He passed away almost quietly. The time between life and death was not marked by any physical exhibition or any word. There was absolutely no scene. The intervals between the gaspings became longer, and presently there was no sound. Everyone present knew death had come quickly, without pain. When it became evident that he was dead, Mrs. Rockwell placed her arm around Mrs. Garfield and led her quietly from the room. She uttered no word. One by one the spectators left the scene, the doctors only remaining in the room, and the windows were closed.

AROUND THE DEATH-BED.

The following persons were present when the President breathed his last: Drs. Bliss and Agnew, Mrs. Garfield and her daughter Mollie, Col. Rockwell, O. C. Rockwell, Gen. Swaim, Dr. Boynton, Private Secretary J. Stanley Brown, Mrs. and Miss Rockwell, Executive Secretary Warren Young, H. L. Atchison, John Ricker, S. Lancaster and Daniel Spriggs, attendants—the last named colored.

Mrs. Garfield sat in her chair shaking convulsively, and with the tears pouring down her cheeks, but uttering no sound. After a while she arose, and, taking hold of her dead husband's arm, smoothed it up and down. Poor little Mollie threw herself upon her father's shoulder on the other side of the bed, and sobbed as if her heart would break. Everybody else was weeping. At midnight Mrs. Garfield was asked if she would like to have anything done, and whether she desired to have the body taken to Washington. She replied that she could not decide until she became more composed.

The Autopsy.

It was 3 o'clock when the special train which had gone to Sea Girt to meet the physicians summoned from Washington to attend the autopsy arrived at Elberon. The surgeons, Drs. Reyburn, Barnes, Woodward, and Lamb were driven at once to the hotel, and, after a short consultation with the other doctors, it was decided to proceed with the autopsy at once, as the sun was already declining in the West, and it was desirable to perform the work during the daylight. The physicians, therefore, proceeded at once to their work. At 4 o'clock the body was laid out for the examination. There were present Drs. Agnew, Bliss, Barnes, Reyburn, Woodward, and Lamb. The examination proved a slow and dangerous one, the poisonous condition of the flesh, notwithstanding being carefully prepared for the work, rendering it exceedingly dangerous to handle. It was fourteen minutes to 8 o'clock before the physicians concluded their work. They then came out to lunch, and returned to prepare their report.

THE OFFICIAL REPORT.

ELBERON, N. J., Sept. 20.—The following official bulletin was prepared at 11 o'clock to-night by the surgeons who have been in attendance upon the late President:

By previous arrangement the post mortem examination of the body of President Garfield was made this afternoon in the presence and with the assistance of Drs. Hamilton, Agnew, Bliss, Barnes, Woodward, Reyburn, Andrew H. Smith, of Elberon, and Acting Assistant Surgeon D. S. Lamb, of the Army Medical Museum, Washington.

The operation was performed by Dr. Lamb.

It was found that the ball, after fracturing the right eleventh rib, had passed through the spinal column in front of the spinal canal, fracturing the body of the first lumbar vertebræ, driving a number of small fragments of bone into the adjacent soft parts, and lodging just below the pancreas, about two inches and a half to the left of the spine and behind the peritoneum, where it had become completely encysted.

The immediate cause of death was secondary hemorrhage from one of the mesenteric arteries adjoining the track of the ball, the blood rupturing the peritoneum, and nearly a pint of blood escaping into the abdominal cavity.

This hemorrhage is believed to have been the cause of the severe pain in the lower part of the chest, complained of just before death. An abscess cavity, six inches by four in dimensions, was found in the vicinity of the gall bladder, between the liver and the transverse colon, which were strongly inter-adherent.

It did not involve the substance of the liver, and no communication was found between it and the wound.

A long suppurating channel extended from the external wound between the loin muscles and the right kidney almost to the right groin. This channel, now known to be due to the burrowing of pus from the wound, was supposed, during life, to have been the track of the ball.

On examination of the organs of the chest, evidences of severe bronchitis were found on both sides, with broncho-pneumonia of the lower portions of the right lung, though of much less extent of the left.

The lungs contained no abscesses and the heart no clots. The liver was enlarged and fatty, but free from abscesses; nor were any found in one other organ, except the left kidney, which contained near its surface a small abscess about one-third of an inch in diameter. In reviewing the history of the case in connection with the autopsy, it is quite evident that the different suppurating surfaces, and especially the fractured spongy tissue of the vertebra, furnish sufficient explanation of the septic condition which existed.

D. W. BLISS,
J. K. BARNES,
J. J. WOODWARD,
ROBT. REYBURN,
FRANK H. HAMILTON,
D. HAYES AGNEW,
ANDREW H. SMITH,
D. S. LAMB.

The Mother and Her Dead Son.

Mother Garfield, who was at Solon, Ohio, with her daughter Mrs. Larrabee, watched anxiously for the 6 o'clock bulletin Monday evening, feeling, if it was favorable, that she might hope on. Worn out by anxious days and sleepless nights, her strength became so exhausted that the administration of stimulants was found necessary. Though hoping against hope, she could not realize that her son was in immediate danger. "He will live," she said but yesterday. "God makes so few men like him that he will not take them away when they are living lives of usefulness. There are so many who are of no use to any one who live on that I cannot believe God will take my James away when he is much needed."

Shortly after eight o'clock Tuesday morning Mrs. Garfield arose, and after dressing, spent some time reading her Bible, as customary. Then she went into the dining-room where her breakfast was being prepared. Refreshed by a night of rest, she was more cheerful than for several days. Mr. Larrabee, unable to conceal his emotion, left the room in tears. Mother Garfield walked about, looking out of the windows. Finally she turned to her daughter, saying: "Is there any news yet this morning, Mary?" Mrs. Larrabee's heart failed. She could not blast the hope expressed in that voice and exhibited in that dear old face.

"Eat your breakfast, mother, it is ready now," she said.

"But I want to hear from James first," said the loving mother.

The telegram that was soon to bring grief and anguish to her hopeful heart lay on the shelf, and seeing it she took it, and was about to read, saying, "Here it is now, I must read it before I eat."

Her grand-daughter, Ellen Larrabee, fearing that so sudden a shock would be fatal, took the dispatch from her hand, and said, "I will read it to you grandma. Are you prepared for bad news?"

"Why, no," said grandma, "I am not prepared for bad news, and there isn't any bad news this morning, is there?"

"Yes, grandma."

"Oh, Nelly, he is not—he cannot be dead?"

"Grandma, his spirit passed away last night."

"Oh, it cannot be; it must not be. I cannot have it so.

My James, my James dead! I cannot believe you. Let me see the dispatch."

The dispatch read as follows:

"ELBERON, N. J., Sept. 19.

"*Mrs. Eliza Garfield:*

"James died this evening at 10:58. He calmly breathed his life away. "D. G. SWAIM."

She took and read it, dropped the message on the floor, and fell backward into the chair, moaning and wringing her hands, and bitter tears coursing down her cheeks. For some time she gave way to uncontrollable grief, but at length subdued her feelings in a measure.

Mother Garfield then said: "To-morrow I will be eighty years old, but I will not see the beginning of another year; James is gone, and I shall not be long after him."

After that she succeeded in somewhat controlling her emotions until the arrival of James Palmer, husband of a grand-daughter now dead, a daughter of Mrs. Larrabee. When he entered she again burst into tears, and between sobs repeated, over and over, in her anguish: "He is gone; he is gone. O, I cannot have it so."

When the morning paper arrived, although advised by her daughter not to read it, she insisted on it, and eagerly scanned the dispatches for awhile, and then, throwing it down, exclaimed, "I cannot read any more."

Then she went to her room and laid down, but soon arose and requested a grand-daughter to read to her further, listening with blinded eyes and a breaking heart, making noble effort to restrain her emotions.

During the afternoon somebody remarked to her that it seemed very still to-day.

"Still?" responded she. "Yes, but it is the stillness of death."

Mr. Larrabee, the President's brother-in-law, said he had known James A. Garfield since he was three years old, and added: "One thing gives me slight comfort to-day—my belief that he was a sincere and earnest Christian if ever there was one."

In the Francklyn Cottage at Long Branch.

At half-past nine o'clock Chief Justice Waite, Secretary and Mrs. Blaine, Secretary and Mrs. Windom, Secretary and Mrs. Hunt, Postmaster-General and Mrs. James, and Secretaries Lincoln and Kirkwood, and Attorney-General McVeagh arrived at the Francklyn Cottage, and the doors were closed to visitors. Religious services were conducted by the Rev. Charles J. Young, of Long Branch, at the request of Mrs. Garfield. There were present, besides the family and their attendants, members of the Cabinet, their wives, and a few personal friends, numbering in all not more than fifty. When the moment for the services was announced, the windows and doors were closed, and the most solemn silence prevailed.

"The Scripture reads," said the pastor, "Blessed are the dead who die in the Lord. Yea, saith the spirit, that they may rest from their labors, and their works do follow them." "We know that if our earthly house of this tabernacle were dissolved, we have a building of God—a house not made with hands, eternal in the Heavens. Therefore, we are also confident of knowing that whilst we are at home in the body we are absent from the Lord. We are confident, I say, and willing, rather, to be absent from the body, and to be present with the Lord. For me to live is Christ, and to die is gain. I am in the strait betwixt the two, having a desire to depart and to be with Christ, which is far better. There the wicked cease from troubling, and there the weary are at rest; and there shall be no more death, neither sorrow nor crying; neither shall there be any more pain; and there shall be no night there, and they need no candle, neither the light of the sun, for God giveth them light, and they shall reign forever and ever. Behold, I show you a mystery. We shall not all sleep, but we shall all be changed in a moment, in the twinkling of an eye, at the last trump. For this corruptible must put on incorruption, and this mortal muts put on immortality. So when this corruptible shall have put on incorruption, and this mortal shall have put on immortality, then shall be brought to pass the saying that is written: Death is swallowed up in victory. O death, where is thy sting? O grave, where is thy victory? The sting of death is sin; the strength of sin is the law; but thanks be to God who giveth us the victory, through our Lord Jesus Christ. Let us pray.

THE PRAYER.

O, Thou, who walked through the grave of Bethany—that open grave of the brother in Bethany! O, Thou, who hadst compassion on the widow of Nain—she bore her beloved dead! O, Thou, who art the same yesterday, to-day, and forever; in whom is no variableness nor shadow of turning! have mercy upon us in this hour, when our souls have nowhere else to fly. But we fly to Thee. Thou knowest these sorrows that we bow under. O, Thou God of the widow, help the stricken heart before Thee. Help these children, and those that are not here. Be their father. Help her in the distant State who watched over him in childhood. Help this Nation that is to-day bleeding and bowed in sorrow before Thee. Oh, sanctify this heavy chastisement to its good. Help those associated with him in the Government. O Lord, grant from the darkness of this night of sorrow there may arise a better day for the glory of God and the good of man. We thank Thee for the record of life that is closed; for its heroic devotion to principle. We thank Thee, O Lord, that he was Thy servant; that he preached Thee by a noble life and example, and that we can say of him now, "Blessed are the dead who die in the Lord; their works do follow them." Now, Lord, go with this sorrowing company in this last sad journey. Bear them up and strengthen them. O God, bring us all at last to the morning that has no shadows; the house that has no tears; the land that has no death; for Christ's sake. Amen."

The Body in State in the Rotunda at Washington.

The day was very warm, and the sun poured down without mercy on those who stood in the line waiting their turn to enter the rotunda. By 1 o'clock the double line was over half a mile long. From the door of the rotunda two ropes extended across the porch and formed a passageway beginning a hundred feet from the foot of the steps. From this point the line continued in a serpentine course, zigzagging back and forth, until it reached a street, and then ran from First to Second streets. By reason of the curious winding form of this closely packed double column, its actual length was more than twice that of the distance in a direct line which was covered. As the crowds continued to arrive, they either took their places at the end of the line as it moved slowly along, or formed part of the great multitude of onlookers who, on account of the great length of the line, had despaired of entering it.

It was a motley throng. More than half of those who stood here for hours and reached the Capitol by slow shuffling steps over the asphalt, were black.

There were men, women, children, and infants in arms, the infirm and aged cripples from the war, some of them wearing badges of service, and ladies in Swiss muslin dresses, and young girls in pretty costumes, along with ragged street urchins and a few tramps. The weak and crippled old darkies in whose faces reverence and awe were expressed, hobbled on crutches and canes with difficulty up the broad marble steps.

The sight of their sincere mourning was pathetic. There was no levity, and but little conversation as the patient line dragged its slow length along. Those who early in the morning started at the extremity of the line did not reach the rotunda until three weary hours later, and yet they moved along up the steps of the Capitol at the rate of 6,000 persons an hour, and this was continued from very early in the morning all through the hot day.

It is believed that over one hundred thousand persons viewed the remains of the late President while they lay in the rotunda.

A short time before the coffin was closed, Mrs. Secretary Blaine and Mrs. Secretary Windom entered the rotunda and viewed the remains. Both were shocked at the change, and suggested to the gentlemen composing the guard of honor that the casket be closed at once. This, they replied, could not be done without an order from the Cabinet. In a short time the order came. Two thousand were in line, and for half an hour they continued to pass the bier before it became generally known among the throng outside that the face could no longer be seen. When the coffin lid was closed the beautiful floral offering of Queen Victoria was placed above it.

Services at the Vault in Cleveland.

THE SCENE.

The State militia were stationed at the entrance to the cemetery and on either side of the driveways leading to the vault. The steps leading to the vault were carpeted with flowers, and on either side of the entrance were an anchor of tuberoses and a cross, while smilax and evergreens were festooned above. A heavy black canopy was stretched over the steps from which the exercises were to be conducted. At 3:30 o'clock the procession entered the gateway, which was arched over with black, with appropriate inscriptions. In the keystone were the words: "Come to rest." On one side were the words: "Lay him to rest whom we have learned to love." On the other: "Lay him to rest whom we have learned to trust." A massive cross of evergreens swung from the centre of the arch.

The United States Marine Band, continuing the sweet mournful strains it had kept up during the entire march, entered first. Then came the Forest City Troop, of Cleveland, which was the escort of the President to his inauguration. Behind it came the funeral car with its escorts of twelve United States artillerymen, followed by a battalion of Knights Templar and the Cleveland Grays. The mourners' carriages and those containing the guard of honor comprised all of the procession that entered the grounds. The cavalry halted at the vault and drew up in line, facing it with sabres presented.

At 3:30 the great funeral car drawn to the front and a little beyond the vault. The twelve black horses, covered with heavy folds of black drapery move so slowly that the tread of their feet can hardly be heard, and the wheels of the huge somber cab pass noiselessly over the soft roadway.

All that is left now to complete the final act of the great tragedy occupies but twenty-five minutes, and the scene is as solemnly sad as the burial of the great dead must be, but fitly. It happens that no manifestations of violent grief disturb the last scene in the burial of this pure and gentle man.

The carriage, which carries on one seat, side by side, the mother and the wife of the President, and on the front seat three of his boys, Harry, Jimmie, and the little Abram, is drawn up on the carpet of flowers at the very door of the vault. Harry and Jimmie, the two older boys, get out and stand upon either side of the carriage doorway, with faces that are so white as to startle those who look upon them. They remain motionless as they watch the coffin of their father carried to its resting-place. Mrs. Garfield takes the vacant seat, and side by side the face of the grand old mother and the brave wife are seen in the open doorway of the carriage. As the military escort lifts the coffin from the car the band play "Nearer My God to Thee." They watch with strained eyes the passage of the body to the tomb and until it is lost to sight within, when Mrs. Garfield drops her veil and sinks back upon her seat, but the old mother still watches at the window, and her beautiful but calm, sweet face, is a picture there which the people watch in loving, sympathetic interest until the benediction is pronounced.

After the body is laid upon its bower of roses, the pall-bearers range themselves upon each side of the raised entrance to the vault. Behind them upon the right Mr. Blaine stands, with a few Senators and others who were in the near carriages. In front of this line Swaim, Rockwell, and Corbin stand, nearest Marshal Henry, who is one of the pall-bearers. Harry and Jimmie leave their mother's carriage and remain near them. On the other side, behind the opposite line of pall-bearers, Hinsdale, Errett, and Jones are seen, while on the lower ground to the right C. O Rockwell and wife, Mrs. Garfield's sister, and Dr. Boynton take position. The rest of the relatives and friends remain in their carriages under the drizzling rain. From one of them, near Mrs. Garfield, the calm, restful face of her father, Uncle Zeb Rudolph, can be seen.

The ceremonies which followed were of the briefest kind. It is a subject of congratulation among all that the last moments at the cemetery were so quite and full of gentle silence. It was not to Mrs. Garfield the burial of her husband. Sometime she will bury him, when he shall be taken from the vault, and unattended by pomp or the presence of the curious multitude, and laid in his last resting place. She only saw him laid upon a bed of flowers, to stop a little longer before he is laid on the high hill near by that she has chosen for the long rest.

J. H. Robinson, as President of the day, opened the exercises by introducing the Rev. J. H. Jones, Chaplain of the Forty-second Regiment O. V. Infantry, which General Garfield commanded, as follows: "The Rev. J. H. Jones, the Chaplain of the Forty-second Regiment, who went out with General Garfield, will offer some remarks." Mr. Jones said:

THE CHAPLAIN'S ADDRESS.

Our illustrious friend has completed his journey's end, a journey that we must all soon make, and that in the near future; yet, when I see the grand surroundings of this occasion I am led to enquire was this man the son of an emperor, of the king that wore a crown, for in the history of this great country there has been nothing like this seen by the people, and perhaps no other country. Yet I thought, perhaps, speaking after the manner of men, that he was a prince, and this was offered in a manner after royalty.

He was not, my friends. It is not an offering of a king, it is not as we are taught an offering to earthly kings and emperors. Though he was a prince and a freeman, the great commoner of the United States, only a few miles from where we stand, less than fifty years ago, he was born in the primeval forests of this State and in this county, and all he asks of you now is a peaceful grave in the bosom of the land that gave him birth.

I cannot speak to you of his wonderful life and his work. Time forbids and history will take care of that, and your children's children will read of this emotion when we have passed away from this earth, but let me say when I was permitted with these honorable men to go to Pittsburg as a committee to receive his mortal remains, I saw from that city to Cleveland hundreds and thousands of people, and many of them in tears, and this reflection came to me, that there was a dearth over the lands. The soil for 500 miles was moistened with tears, as we passed from the city of Washington to Cleveland. Then I asked myself the meaning of all this, for I saw the workingmen come out of the rolling-mills, with dust and smoke all over their faces, their heads uncovered, with the tears rolling down their brawny cheeks.

With bated breath I asked: What is the meaning of all this? because it casts down a workingman. He was a workingman himself, for he has been a worker from his birth almost. He has fought his way through life at every step, and the workingman he took by the hand, and there was sympathy and brotherhood between them. I saw, in small cottages as well as in splendid mansions, drapings on the shutters, and may have been the only vail which the poor woman had, and with tears in her eyes she saw us pass. I asked. Why, what interest has this poor woman in this man? She had read that he was born in a cabin, and that when he got old enough to work in the beech woods he helped to support his widowed mother.

Then I saw the processions and the colleges pour out. The local professions attended, and there was civic socities and military all concentrated here, and he has touched them all in his passage thus far through life, and you feel that he is a brother. He is, therefore, a brother to you in all these regards, but when a man dies his work usually follows him. When we sent General Garfield to the Capitol at Washington he weighed 210 pounds. He had a soul that loved his race; a splendid intellect that almost bent the largest form to bear it. You bring him back to us a mere handful of some eighty pounds, mostly of bones, in that casket.

Now, I ask you why is this? I do not stop to talk about the man that did the deed. "Vengeance is mine, saith the Almighty God; I will repay." He sees the terrors of a scaffold before him, probably, and the eternal disgrace that falls to the murderer and the assassin, and he is going down to the judgment of God and the frowns of the world.

But where is James A. Garfield that we lent to you seven months ago? Many of you were there at the time of his inauguration, and witnessed the grandest pageant that ever passed in front of the Capitol, and the grandest that was ever had in the Nation was had on that occasion, and now comes that unwelcome but splendid exhibition that will be read of all over the world with regret. For Secretary Blaine, in a business-like manner, to-day made out that there were at least 300,000,000 of people of the world mourning the death of President Garfield and offering us sympathy. But where is he? Here is all that is left of him, the grand, the bright, and brilliant man. Now that soul that loved, that mind that thought, and has impressed itself upon the world, must come back, for if thoughts live will that precious thought cease to be dead. In reason he speaks and in example lives. His thoughts and mighty deeds still flourish in structure. We shall get him back, fellow citizens.

In conversation with the one nearest and dearest to him, she said, when she thought of his relations as a husband and as a son and as a statesman, having reached the highest pinnacle to which man can be elevated by the free suffrage of our 50,000,000 people, there was no promotion for her beloved but for God to call him home. He has received that promotion.

He believed in the immortality, not only of the soul, but of the body and that the grave will give up the dead. He must live, and, my friends, that was the hope that sustained him. I was with him in the war, and the enemy never saw his back. He was fortunate in that every contest he was on the victorious side, but the grandest fight he ever made was in the last eighty days of his existence, fought not because he himself personally expected to live, but the doctors told him to hope.

He loved his wife and children, and he hoped. "I am not afraid to die, but I will try," said he, "to live," and then he was not conquered even except by simple exhaustion. It seems to me that no good man by the name of Abraham can be the President of the United States and can be long out of Abraham's bosom, for both of them have been called, and early, too, to the paradise of God, and his spirit looks down upon us to-day, and he is in the society of Washington and Lincoln and the immortal hosts of patriots that stood for their country.

Let me say, in conclusion, there was a man in ancient Biblical history that killed more in his death than he did in his life, and I believe that to be true with James Abram Garfield, I doubt whether there is a page that equals this in sympathy and love, not only in this country, but all over the world. Have you ever read anything like this. You, brethren, here of the South, I greet you to-day, and you brethren of the North, East, and West. Come, let us lay all our bitterness up in the coffin of the dead man. Let him carry them with him to the grave in silence, till the angels disturb the slumbers. Let us love each other more, our country better. May God bless you and the dear family, and, as they constitute a great family on earth, I hope they will constitute a great family in the kingdom of God, and where I hope to meet you all in the end.

At the close of Jones' address the venerable Dr. Robinson announced that the hymn which was General Garfield's favorite, "Ho, Reapers of Life's Harvest," would be sung, and, as the melody of the grand old song rings and echoes among the forests and hills, it falls upon the ears of all.

GARFIELD'S FAVORITE HYMN.

Ho, reapers of life's harvest,
  Why stand with rusted blade
Until the night draws round thee
  And the day begins to fade?

Why stand ye idle waiting
  For reapers more to come?
The golden morn is passing,
  Why sit ye idle, dumb?

Thrust in your sharpened sickle
  And gather in the grain;
The night is fast approaching
  And noon will come again.

The Master calls for reapers,
  And shall he call in vain?
Shall sheaves lie there ungathered
  And waste upon the plain?

> Mount up the heights of wisdom
>   And crush each error low;
> Keep back no words of knowledge
>   That human hearts should know.
>
> Be faithful to thy mission
>   In service of thy Lord,
> And then a golden chaplet
>   Shall be thy just reward.

Once during Chaplain Jones' address, and in the midst of his masterly review of the march of the dead from the log cabin to the Presidency, the face of Mrs. Garfield appeared at the window by the side of the mother of Garfield, and both looked, with calm, clear eyes, upon the speaker as he told the story of their hero's achievements.

The Latin Ode from Horace was then sung as follows, by the United German Society:

> Integer vitae scelerisque purus
> Non eget Mauris jaculis neque arcu,
> Nec venenatis gravida sagittis,
>   Fusce, pharetra,
> Sive per Syrtes iter aestuosas,
> Sive facturus per inhospitalem
> Caucasum, vel quae loca fabulosus
>   Lambit Hydaspes.
> Namque me silva lupus in Sabina,
> Dum meum canto Lalagen et ultra
> Terminum curis vagor expeditis,
>   Fugit inermem:
> Quale portentum neque militaris
> Daunias latis alit aesculetis,
> Nec Jubae tellus generat, leonum
>   Arida nutrix.
> Pone me pigris ubi nulle campis
> Arbor aestiva recreatur aura,
> Quod latus mundi nubulae malusque
>   Jupiter urget.
> Pone sub curru nimium propinqui
> Solis, in terra domibus negata;
> Dulce ridentem Lalagen amabo,
>   Dulce loquentem.

The following is a literal translation of the ode:

The man of upright life and pure from wickeddess, O Fuscus has no need of the Moorish javelins or bow, or quiver-loaded with poisoned darts. Whether he is about to make his journey through the sultry Syrtes or the inhospitable Caucasus, or those places which Hydaspes, celebrated in story, washes. For lately, as I was singing my Lalage, and wandered beyond my usual bounds, devoid of care, a wolf in the Sabine wood fled from me, though I was unarmed; such a monster as neither the warlike Apulia nourishes in its extensive woods, nor the land of Juba, the dry nurse of lions, produces. Place me in those barren plains, where no tree is refreshed by the genial air; at that part of the world which clouds and an inclement atmosphere infest. Place me under the chariot of the too-neighboring sun, in the land deprived of habitation, there will I love my sweetly-smiling, sweetly-speaking Lalage.

Mr. Robinson then announced the late President's hymn, "Ho, Reapers of Life's Harvest," which the German vocal societies of Cleveland sang with marked effect.

The exercises closed with the benediction by President Hinsdale, of Hiram College, who was introduced by Dr. Robinson, as follows: "Friends and Fellow-Citizens: From the heart-broken friends of the deceased, I tender you their thanks. Mr. Hinsdale, will you dismiss?"

Mr. Hinsdale said:

"Oh, God; the sole experience of this day teaches us the truth of what Thou hast told us in Thy word. The grave is the last of the world and the end of life. Earth to earth, dust to dust, ashes to ashes. But we love the doctrine of the immortality of the soul, and in the power of the endless life therefrom. Oh God, our Father, we look to Thee now for the greatest blessing. We pray that the fellowship and salvation of the Lord Jesus Christ our Savior, and the inspiration of the Holy Spirit, the Comforter, may be with all who have been in to-day's assembly. Amen."

The final dirge is sung, and friends and relatives standing

by move nearer to the sepulchre. Blaine steps nervously to the very door of the vault, and his white face is pitiful evidence of the agony of that moment, while he looks for the last time upon even the casket which contains the remains of him who was both friend and chief. Mrs. Garfield does not look from the carriage; perhaps she finds comfort there in thoughts of the quieter, more secluded hour, when she, instead of the Nation, shall bury the man so beloved.

At rest at last—the hymn is done, the melody is hushed, the doors of the vault are noiselessly closed. President Burke Hinsdale reaches out his hands in final invocation for Divine support and pity, and it is the end.

The End.

J. G. HOLLAND.

A wasp flew out upon our fairest son
And stung him to the quick with poisoned shaft;
The while he chatted carelessly and laughed,
And knew not of the fateful mischief done.
And so this life, amid our love begun,
Envenomed by the insect's hellish craft,
Was drunk by death in one long, feverish draught,
And he was lost—our gracious, priceless one!
Oh, mystery of blind, remorseless fate!
Oh, cruel and of a most causeless hate!
That life so mean should murder life so great!
What is there left to us who think and feel,
Who have no remedy and no appeal,
But damn the wasp and crush him under heel?

The World Wide Sympathy.

It may be safely said that the death of President Garfield called forth a greater expression of sympathy from the great rulers and nations of the earth, from eminent persons, and from the various fraternities and associations of men, than the death of any other man. And this is not only an evidence of the great worth of the man, but also an evidence of a progressive civilization. It is estimated that over 300,000,000 persons mourned the death of James A. Garfield. The following are a few of the dispatches of condolence·

QUEEN VICTORIA TO MRS. GARFIELD.

Words cannot express the deep sympathy I feel with you. May God support and comfort you, as He alone can.

THE QEEN, Balmoral.

The Queen also cabled at once to the British Minister to have a floral tribute prepared and presented in her name. It was soon received at the Capitol and placed at the head of the bier of the President. It was very large, and was an exquisite specimen of the florist's art. It was composed of white roses, smilax, and stephanotis. It was accompanied by a mourning card bearing the following inscription: "Queen Victoria, to the memory of the late President Garfield—an expression of her sorrow and sympathy with Mrs. Garfield and the American Nation. Sept. 22, 1881."

GEN. GRANT.

NEW YORK, Sept. 19.—*Wayne MacVeagh, Long Branch:* Please convey to the bereaved family of the President my heartfelt sympahty and sorrow for them in their deep affliction. A nation will mourn with them for the loss of the Chief Magistrate so recently called to preside over its destiny. I will return to Long Branch in the morning to tender my services, if they can be made useful. U. S. GRANT.

Affecting Incidents.

"I WANT TO SEE MYSELF."

After a rigor had passed the President fell asleep, and although his pulse was still beating about 120, yet his temperature had not decreased more than a tenth of a degree or so below the normal point. He awoke in about twenty minutes and said to Dr. Bliss,

"Doctor, I feel very comfortable, but I also feel dreadfully weak. I wish you would give me the hand-glass and let me look at myself."

Gen. Swaim said, "Oh no, don't do that, General. See if you cannot get some sleep."

"I want to see myself," the President replied.

Mrs. Garfield then gave him the hand-glass. He held it in a position which enabled him to see his face. Mrs. Garfield, Dr. Bliss, Dr. Agnew, Gen. Swaim and Dr. Boynton stood around the bed, saying not a word, but looking at the President. He studied the reflection of his own features. At length he wearily let the glass fall upon the counterpane, and with a sigh, said to Mrs. Garfield:

"Crete, I do not see how it is that a man who looks as well as I do should be so dreadfully weak."

"LITTLE MOLLIE FELL OVER LIKE A LOG."

In a moment or two he asked for his daughter Mollie. They told him that she would come to see him later in the day. He said, however, that he wanted to see her at once. Thereupon Don Rockwell went to the beach, where Miss Mollie was sitting with Miss Rockwell, and told her that her father wanted to see her. When the child went into the room she kissed her father and told him that she was glad to see that he was looking so much better.

He said, "You think I do look better, Mollie?"

She said, "I do, papa," and then she took a chair and sat near the foot of the bed.

A moment or two after Dr. Boynton noticed that she was swaying in the chair. He stepped up to her, but before he could reach her she had fallen over in a dead faint. In falling, her face struck against the bed post, and when they raised her from the floor she was not only unconscious, but also bleeding from the contusion she had received. They carried her out where she could get the fresh breeze from the ocean, and after restoratives were applied she speedily recovered. The room was close, the windows were closed, and Miss Mollie had not been very well, and all these causes combined with anxiety, induced the fainting fit.

The President, they thought, had not noticed what had happened to his petted child, for he seemed to have sunk into the stupor which has characterized his condition much of the time. But when Dr. Boynton came back into the room he was astonished to hear the President say:

"Poor little Mollie; she fell over like a log. What's the matter?"

They assured the President that the fainting fit was caused by the closeness of the room, and that she was quite restored. He again sank into a stupor, or sleep, which lasted until the noon examination. This stupor was not healthy sleep. The President frequently muttered and rolled and tossed his head upon th epillow.

Garfield's Birthplace—How It Looked on the Great Day of the Funeral—Interesting Incidents in Garfield's Early Life.

[Written by one of Garfield's most Intimate Friends, at Orange, Ohio.]

Here, at the birth-place of Garfield, what memories sweep over us when we recall the scenes of his birth and boyhood! On the place where stood the log hut in which he first saw the light is a pole floating a flag at half-mast. The old log house is gone, the frame house that succeeded it is gone, and now all that marks the spot where James A. Garfield was born, fifty years ago, is a whitewood pole rising from the green fields. All around are the groves and fields in which the farmer's boy began that noble history which is ended so abruptly, so cruelly.

Here he was born, here he worked in the field by day and studied by night, here stood the log school house where he first attended school. It is gone now, and a brick one stands in its place, but it will never be forgotten, for " Garfield went there first to school."

THE FRIEND OF HIS BOYHOOD.

Next to the field in which the national colors now sadly wave is the farm of Mr. Henry Boynton, Garfield's cousin, and a brother of Dr. Boynton. He was more than a cousin. While their mothers were sisters and their fathers half-brothers, there was another tie that bound them more closely than the bonds of kinship. Amos Boynton was all to Garfield that a father could be after the death of his father, when James was but over a year of age. Henry Boynton and James A. Garfield were all to each other that brothers could be.

Mr. Boynton was found at his home in the afternoon, and although much affected by the tragic death of the loved companion of his boyhood, seemed to be pleased to relate incidents of his early life.

Mr. Boynton said: James and I were constant companions from the time that he was old enough to talk, down to the time that he went into active political life. I know, perhaps, more of his boyhood and early manhood than any person. In our boyhood we were said to bear a striking resemblance to each other.

HIS EARLY LIFE.

James was always noted from his earliest childhood for his desire to be the leader in whatever he undertook. At school he was never satisfied to have another boy ahead of him, but would strain every nerve to overtake and pass one who seemed to have the advantage of him, and always succeeded in doing so. He always managed to be the leader, in every circle, whether it was social, intellectual or moral. He first went to school at the little log school house which stood where you now see yonder brick school building. He then worked mornings and nights and attended school through the day. One little incident I never shall forget. There was a spelling match in the little log school house in which James, who was thirteen years old, took part. The teacher told her scholars that if any whispered she would send them home. The lad standing next to James became confused, and to help him, James told him how to spell his word. The teacher saw this and said:

"James, you know the rule. You must go home."

James picked up his cap and left. In a very few seconds he returned and took his place in the class.

"Why, how is this, James? I told you to go home," said the teacher.

"I know it, and went home," said James.

BEGINNING AS A FARM HAND.

When fourteen years old he began working as a farm laborer for Mr. Daniel Morse, who lived near here. While working here, he one evening remained in the sitting room to listen to the conversation of a young gentleman who had called on Miss Morse. Miss Morse, observing him, told him it was time for servants to go to bed. This galled his sensitive feelings, and the next day he left there, telling me that some day he would show them that he was not to be looked down upon.

ON THE CANAL.

He now went to work on the canal, with Captain Letcher for a master. Soon after starting at this work he whipped the burly Irishman, Murphy, as you have heard many times, I suppose. An incident occurred one night which showed his innate love of justice. One night when approaching a lock he was called on by the captain to help fight the crew of another boat, which had reached the lock at nearly the same time, for the first use of it.

"Who has the right to it?" asked James, as he prepared for action.

"Well, I guess they have, but we can lick them and get it," said the captain.

James drew on his coat again, and said: "No, sir; I won't help if it justly belongs to them."

He staid on the canal but a short time, as he suffered a severe attack of fever and ague, which obliged him to return home. All winter he staid at home, shaking with ague chills, but studying all the time. Between his chills he would go over to the school house and recite, and at the end of the term stood at the head of the class. In the spring he intended to return to the canal, but by the arguments and advice of Mr. Bates, his teacher, was persuaded to give up this idea and attend school.

Assassination Record of Rulers for the Last Thirty Years.

The following is a list of attempts upon the lives of rulers since 1848:

1848—Nov. 26—The life of the Duke of Modena was attempted.

1849—June 21—The Crown Prince of Prussia was attacked at Minden.

1850—June 28—Robert Pate, an ex-Lieutenant in the army, attempted to assassinate Queen Victoria.

1851—May 22—Sefeloque, a workman, shot at Frederick William IV., King of Prussia, and broke his arm.

1852—Sept. 24—An infernal machine was found at Marseilles, with which it had been intended to destroy Napoleon III.

1853—Feb. 18—The Emperor Francis Joseph of Austria was grievously wounded in the head while walking on the ramparts at Vienna, by a Hungarian tailor named Libzens.

1853—April 16—An attempt on the life of Victor Emmanuel was reported to the Italian Chamber.

1853—July 5—An attempt was made to kill Napoleon III. as he was entering the Opera Comique.

1854—March 20—Ferdinand Charles III., Duke of Parma, was killed by an unknown man, who stabbed him in the abdomen.

1855—April 28—Napoleon III. was fired at in the

Champs Elysees by Giovanni Pianeri.

1856—April 28—Raymond Fuentes was arrested in the act of firing on Isabella, Queen of Spain.

1856—Dec. 8—Agesilas Milano, a soldier, stabbed Ferdinand III. of Naples with his bayonet.

1857—Aug. 7—Napoleon III. again. Barcoletti, Gibaldi, and Grillo were sentenced to death for coming from London to assassinate him.

1858—Jan. 14—Napoleon III. for the fifth time. Orsini and his associates threw fulminating bombs at him as he was on his way to the opera.

1861—July 14—King William of Prussia was for the first time shot at, by Oscar Becker, a student of Baden-Baden. Becker fired twice at him, but missed him.

1861—Dec. 18—A student named Dossios fired a pistol at queen Amalia of Greece (Princess of Oldenburg) at Athens.

1863—Dec. 24.—Four more conspirators from London against the life of Napoleon III. were arrested at Paris.

1865—April 14 — President Lincoln was shot by J. Wilkes Booth.

1866—April 6—A Russian named Kavarasoff attempted Czar Alexander's life at St. Petersburg. He was foiled by a peasant, who was ennobled for the deed.

1867—The Czar's life was again attempted during the great Exposition, at a review in the Bois de Boulogne, at Paris.

1867—June 19—Maximilian shot.

1868—June 10—Prince Michael of Servia was killed by the brothers Radwarowitch.

1871—The life of Amadeus, then newly king of Spain, was attempted.

1872—August— Col. Gutieriez assassinated President Balla, of the Republic of Peru.

1873—Jan. 1—President Morales, of Bolivia, was assassinated

1875—August—President Garcia Maeno, of Ecuador, was assassinated.

1877—June—President Gill, of Paraguay, was assassinated by Commander Molas.

1878—May 11—The Emperor William, of Germany, was shot at again, this time by Emile Henri Max Hoedel, alias Lehmann, the Socialist. Lehman fired three shots at the Emperor, who was returning from a drive with the Grand Duchess of Baden, but missed him.

1878—June 2—Emperor William shot at by Dr. Nobiling, while out riding. He received about thirty small shots in the neck and face.

1878—April 14—Attempted assasination of the Czar at St. Petersburg, by one Solojew. He was executed May 9.

1870—Dec. 1—The assassination of the Czar attempted by a mine under a train near Moscow.

1879—Dec. 30—The King of Spain was shot at while driving with the Queen.

1880—Feb. 17—Attempt to kill the Royal family of Russia by blowing up the Winter Palace. Eight soldiers killed and forty-five wounded.

1881—March 14—The Czar killed by a bomb.

1881—July 2—President Garfield shot by C. J. Guiteau, an eccentric lawyer of doubtful sanity, who is said to have been born at Freeport, Ill., and who was licensed at the bar in Chicago.

ASSASSINATION
OF
PRESIDENT LINCOLN.

The attempted assassination of Gen. Garfield naturally recalls the assassination of President Lincoln, and will go down to posterity allied to that terrible event. The particulars of that dreadful tragedy are as follows:

It was on the evening of Friday, April 14, 1865, that President and Mrs. Lincoln, with Miss Mary Harris and Maj. Rathbun, of Albany, son-in-law of Senator Harris, visited Ford's Theatre, at Washington, for the purpose of witnessing "The American Cousin," which was running at the theatre. The fact that this distinguished party was to be present at the performance had been duly announced in all the local papers, and the theatre was densely crowded. The Presidential party occupied a box on the second tier. The scene was a brilliant one, and all went merry with the audience and actors alike until the close of the third act, when the sharp report of a pistol was heard, and an instant afterward a man was seen to spring from the President's box to the stage, where, striking a tragic attitude and brandishing a long dagger in his right hand, he cried out, "Sic semper tyrannis!" and then, amid the bewilderment of the audience, rushed through the opposite side of the stage and made his escape from the rear of the theatre. The screams of Mrs. Lincoln told the audience but too plainly that the President had been shot. All present rose to their feet, and the excitement was of the wildest possible description. A rush was made to the President's box, where, on a hasty examination being made, it was found he was shot through the head. The President was quickly removed to a private house opposite the theatre, where, on further examination, his wound was pronounced to be mortal. This tragic occurrence, of course, immediately put a stop to the performance, and the theatre was closed as quickly as possible. The assasin, in his hurried flight, dropped his hat and a spur on the stage. The hat was identified as belonging to J. Wilkes Booth, a prominent actor, and the spur was recognized as one obtained by him at a stable on that day. One or two of the actors and members of the orchestra declared that the assassin was no other than Wilkes Booth, and the evidence almost momentarily accumulating fixed him beyond doubt as the author of the bloody tragedy. Almost before the audience had left the theatre it was known that the assasin, after he got out, made his escape on horseback.

SECRETARY SEWARD'S ESCAPE.

The news of the hideous tragedy spread like wild-fire, and the greatest excitement prevailed throughout the city, dense throngs of people congregating in the locality of the house where President Lincoln was lying. While the general excitement was at its height, it became known that an attempt had been made to assassinate Mr. Seward, Secretary of State. At about 10 o'clock a man called at the Secretary's house, stating that he had been sent by the family physician with a prescription for the Secretary, who was sick, at the same time stating that he must see him personally, as he was instructed to give particular directions concerning the medicine. He pushed his way past the servant, who had told him Secretary Seward could not be seen, and rushed up stairs to Mr. Seward's room, where he whs met by the Secretary's son, Mr. Fred. Seward, who said he would take charge of the medicine. The man dealt him a heavy blow, and rushing past him into Secretary Seward's room, sprang upon the Secretary as he lay in bed and stbabed him several times in the neck and breast. Maj. Seward, another of the Secretary's sons, rushed to his father's assistance, and got badly cut in a tussle with the ruffian, who after a hard struggle managed to escape from the house, and mounting the horse he had left at the door, galloped off, shouting out, "*Sic semper tyrannis.*" Surgeon General Barnes was immediately sent for, and pronounced the Secretary's and Maj. Seward's wounds not fatal, but the injuries which the desperado had inflicted on Frederick Seward and the servant of the house were considered more serious. When it was known that Secretary Seward was not dangerously wounded, the general anxiety was centered on President Lincoln, and while the scene in the streets was one of the wildest excitement and confusion, within the chamber where President Lincoln was lying all was sadness and stillness. Several members of the cabinet had hastened to his side. Medical and surgical aid were obtained, and exerything was done to relieve the suffering President. It was soon ascertained, however, that it was impossible for him to survive, the only question being how long he would linger. All through the weary hours of the night and early morning the President lay unconscious, as he had been ever since his assassination. He was watched by several faithful friends, in addition to near relatives. At his bedside were the Secretary of War, Secretary of the Navy, Secretary of the Interior, Postmaster General, and the Attorney General, Senator Sumner. Gen. Farnsworth, Gen. Todd, cousin of Mrs. Lincoln; Maj. Hay, M. B. Field, Gen. Halleck, Maj. Gen. Meigs, the Rev. Dr. Gurley, Gen. Oglesby, of Illinois, and Drs. E. N. Abbott, R. K. Stone, C. D. Hatch, Neal, Hall, and Lieberman.

MRS. LINCOLN'S GRIEF.

In the adjoining room were Mrs. Lincoln, her son, Capt. Robert Lincoln, Miss Harris, Rufus S. Andrews, and two lady freinds of Mrs. Lincoln. Mrs. Lincoln was under great excitement and agony, exclaiming again and again: "Why did he not shoot me instead of my husband?" She was constantly going back and forth to the bedside of the President, crying out in the greatest agony: "How can it be so?" The scene was heartrending in the extreme, and all were greatly overcome. Mrs. Lincoln took her leave of her husband about twenty minutes before his death. When she was told he had breathed his last she exclaimed: "Oh! Why did you not tell me he was dying?" The surgeons and members of the Cabinet, Senator Sumner, Capt. Robert Lincoln, Gen. Todd, Mr. Field, and Mr. Andrews were standing at his bedside when he died. The surgeons were sitting on the foot of the bed, holding the President's hands and with watches observing the slow declension of the pulse, and such was the stillness for some minutes that the ticking of the watches could be heard in the room. At twenty-two minutes past 7 a. m. on April 15, the looked for but dreaded end came, and as he drew his last breath the Rev. Dr. Gurley offered up a prayer for the deceased's heart-broken family and the mourning country. The President died without a struggle, passing silently and calmly away, having been in a state of utter unconsciousness from the time he was shot till his death. All present in the silent death chamber felt the awful solemnity of the occasion, and the scene was heartrending and touching. Mrs. Lincoln, shortly after her husband's death, was driven, with her son Robert, to the White House, where, but the evening before, she left for the last time with her honored husband, who was never again to enter that home alive.

Long before the President expired the authorities were perfectly satisfied as to who committed the terrible deeds, and the city and military authorities commenced the investigation, and while the Cabinet and other ministers were watching over the

President every effort was made to capture the murderers. Couriers mounted on fleet horses rushed to and fro, and the sound of the hoofs of horses was heard in all directions. The city and military authorities worked with energy and vigilance, and the tidings at last came that one of the horses had been captured, nearly exhausted, at the outskirts of the city, and that its bridle was covered with blood. The animal was identified as the horse ridden by the assassin from Seward's residence. This gave a good deal of hope that the author of the horrible crime might be captured.

THE EFFECT OF THE PRESIDENT'S DEATH.

The news of the President's death fell like a pall over the city, and before long every house was draped in mourning. It seemed that all were engaged in the sad tribute to the departed. The Department buildings were tastefully draped, the War Department being literally covered. The pillars and the entire front were richly festooned with black. The hotels, private residences, and places of business were also appropriately dressed. In short, a mantle of gloom was thrown over the entire National Capital. Flags from the Departments and throughout the city floated at half-mast, and nearly all private and public business was suspended. The grief felt was widespread, and the deepest gloom and sadness prevailed on all sides. The President's corpse was removed to the White House before noon, and a dense crowd accompanied the remains. After an autopsy had been made on the corpse it was embalmed and placed in a handsome mahogany coffin, on which was a silver plate bearing the inscription:

```
ABRAHAM LINCOLN,
Sixteenth President of the United States.
Born February 12, 1809.
Died April 15, 1865.
```

In the evening City Councils, clergy, and others held meetings to officially express regret at the President's death. Although nothing was talked of during the day but the atrocious assassination and attempted assassination made by Secession sympathizers and desperadoes, there was no disturbance of any kind, and by night time the streets were quiet and the excitement gradually subsiding. In the meantime every effort was being made to capture the assassins. Every road leading out of Washington was strongly picketed, and every avenue of escape thoroughly guarded, and steamboats about to start down the Potomac were stopped. A rumor prevailed that Wilkes Booth had been captured, and this helped to keep the indignation of the people as fierce as ever; and to keep up the excitement, though the rumor turned out to be without foundation.

THE NORTH IN MOURNING.

Sunday, the 16th, was a solemn and mournful day in Washington, as also in every city in the States. The churches were crowded, and not a sermon was preached but the tragic occurrence was touchingly alluded to. During the day it was learned that all members of the Seward family were recovering from their injuries, and general satisfaction was expressed that Secretary Seward had not fallen a victim to the assasin's blow. The interior of the White House all day presented a scene of overwhelming sadness. The body of the Chief Magistrate of the Nation was temporarily laid out in one of the upper rooms of the house. The body was dressed in the suit of plain black worn by him on the occasion of his last inauguration, while on his pillow and over the breast were scattered affectionate offerings in the shape of white flowers and green leaves. During the evening it was made known that the funeral services would take place Wednesday, the 19th, and that the President's body would be interred at Springfield, Ill. On Monday the person who assaulted Secretary Seward was arrested as he was about to enter the house of Mrs. Surratt in the little village of Uniontown. An intense excitement prevailed when it was learned that detectives were on Booth's tracks. Several persons supposed to be concerned in these murderous outrages were placed under arrest. On Monday the body of the murdered President lay in state in the coffin, which was placed on a grand catafalque erected in the East Room of the White House. The room was heavely draped in mourning and a guard of honor surrounded the coffin. The populace by thousands gathered at the White House and there viewed the body. The trains during the night and morning rought hundreds of distinguished visitors to the city from all portions of the North. All the streets leading to the White House were thronged with people from early morn till late at night wending their way to the spot where rested the sarcophagus in which was confined the cold and motionless form of him who but a few days since had hold of the helm of the ship of State. The universality of the mourning was remarkable. Old and young, rich and poor, all sexes, grades and colors, united in paying their homage to the great and illustrious dead, and one of the most touching sights was that of the wounded soldiers from the hospitals, who came to have a long, last look at the face of the late President and honored Commander-in-Chief.

THE FUNERAL SERVICES.

On Wednesday morning a funeral service was held at the White House, at which were present a large number of clergymen representing various sections of the country. The heads of Bureaus, the Sanitary and Christian Commissions, the Governors, Assistant Secretaries, Congressmen, officers of the Supreme Court, the Diplomatic Corps, the Judges of the local Courts, the pall-bearers, ladies of the Government officials, the chief mourners, President Johnson and Cabinet, the members of the family, and the ushers. The whole scene presented in the room was one of solemnity, and a single feeling appeared manifest among all, and that was grief. The services were conducted by the Rev. Dr. Hall, of the Episcopal Church, in the city, and the funeral oration was delivered by the Rev. Dr. Gurley, pastor of the Presbyterian Church in the city, which Mr. Lincoln and his family were in the habit of attending. At the close of these services the the funeral cortege started for the Capital. Every window, housetop, balcony, and every inch of sidewalk on either side was densly crowded with a living throng to witness the procession. The beat of the funeral drum sounded upon the street, and the cortege marched with solemn tread and arms reversed. The procession consisted of a large military escort, including a body of dismounted officers of the army and navy and marine corps. Following these came the civic authorities, and after them the funeral car, drawn by six gray horses. A long line of sad and weeping relatives of the deceased followed in carriages. Next came President Johnson, accompanied by Mr. Preston King, of New York, with a strong cavalry guard on either side. The rest of the procession consisted of the Cabinet and diplomatic corps, Judges of the Supreme Court, and clerks of the Departments, and was closed by 1,500 well-dressed negroes of various organizations. The procession was one hour and a half passing a given point; it contained 18,000 persons, and was witnessed by *at least 150,000 people. After the body had been placed in the Capitol, the Rev. Dr. Gurley read the burial service, at the close of which the outside procession slowly dispersed. The body of the late President lay in state in the Capitol all that day and through the night, attended by a guard of honor and viewed by an immense number of citizens.

Early on Friday morning, the 21st, the body was carried to the depot of the Baltimore & Ohio Railway, and the distinguished party that was to accompany the remains to Springfield, Ill., left on their sad errand by the half-past 7 a. m. train. The route was as follows, and the arrangements were all carried out to perfection, there being no delays on the journey: From Washington to Baltimore, Baltimore to Harrisburg, Harrisburg to Philadelphia, Philadelphia to New York, New York to Albany, Albany to Buffalo, Buffalo to Cleveland, Cleveland to Columbus, Columbus to Indianapolis, Indianapolis to Chicago, Chicago to Springfield. All the towns along the route were draped in mourning, and at the cities above mentioned, where the funeral train stopped, the coffin was removed from the funeral car and borne in solemn and majestic procession through the streets to the principal public building in each city, where suitable ceremonies were performed, and the sad procession in each city witnessed by thousands of citizens and visitors from neighboring towns. The funeral train reached Springfield, Ill., on the 4th of May, on which day the body of the deceased President was interred in the Oak Ridge Cemetery amid much funeral pomp and ceremony.

THE ASSASSINS ARRESTED.

It was some days after the assassination of President Lincoln before the indignation of the public was somewhat calmed at learning of the arrests of those implicated in the assassination of the President and in the assaults on the Seward family. A reward of $50,000 was offered for the arrest of Booth, $25,000 for the arrest of Atzerot, and a like sum for that of D. C. Harrold, the latter two being known to be specially implicated in the assassination and the attempted assassination. Lewis Payne was arrested April 15 at Washington, at the house of Mrs. Surratt. On being taken before the servant at Mr. Seward's house he was immediately recognized as the person who attempted to assassinate Secretary Seward. With him were arrested Mrs. Surratt and others in the same house. Atzerot was arrested on April 20 near Middlebury, Montgomery Co., Md. On April 25th J. Wilkes Booth was overtaken by a party sent out by Col. L. C. Baker, special detective of the War Department. Booth and Harrold had been traced together across the Rappahanock River at Mathias Point, Md., and were found on Tuesday evening, April 25, in a barn about three miles from Port Royal. The barn was surrounded, and, although Harrold was willing to give himself up, Booth refused to surrender. Finally the barn was fired. Harrold then gave himself up, but Booth prepared to defend himself. Lieut. Docherty, commanding the party, ordered Sergt. Corbett to fire, which he did through one of the crevices and shot Booth through the head. Upon being shot Booth exclaimed, "It is all up now; I'm gone!" He was found to be wounded in the head, and died about two hours after he was shot. The other important arrests made were Dr. Mudd, at whose house Booth was known to have stopped when in Maryland; Edward Spangler, of Ford's Theatre; Michael O'Laughlin, and Samuel Arnold. These, with Atzerot, Harrold, and Mrs. Surratt, were arraigned on Saturday, May 13, and after a lengthy trial, Harrold, Payne, Atzerot, and Mrs. Surratt were sentenced to be executed, and were hanged on July 7 at Washington.

Garfield's Maxims.

—I WOULD rather be beaten in Right than succeed in Wrong.

—I FEEL a profounder reverence for a Boy than for a man. I never meet a ragged Boy in the street without feeling that I may owe him a salute, for I know not what possibilities may be buttoned up under his coat.

—PRESENT Evils always seem greater than those that never come.

—LUCK is an *ignis-fatuus*. You may follow it to Ruin, but never to Success.

—A POUND of Pluck is worth a ton of Luck.

—FOR the noblest man that lives there still remains a Conflict

—THE principles of Ethics have not changed by the lapse of years.

—GROWTH is better than Permanence, and permanent growth is better than all.

—IT is no honor or profit merely to appear in the arena. The Wreath is for those who contend.

—AFTER the battle of Arms comes the battle of History.

—THERE is a fellowship among the Virtues by which one great, generous passion stimulates another.

—THE privilege of being a Young Man is a great privilege, and the privilege of growing up to be an independent Man in middle life is a greater.

—No Man can make a speech alone. It is the great human power that strikes up from a thousand minds that acts upon him and makes the speech.

—WE hold reunions, not for the Dead, for there is nothing in all the earth that you and I can do for the Dead. They are past our help and past our praise. We can add to them no glory, we can give to them no immortality. They do not need us, but forever and forever more we need them.—*Speech at Geneva, Aug. 3, 1880.*

—NOTHING is more uncertain than the result of any one throw; few things more certain than the result of many throws.

—IF the power to do hard work is not Talent, it is the best possible substitute for it.

—OCCASION may be the bugle-call that summons an army to battle, but the blast of a bugle can never make Soldiers or win Victories.

—THINGS don't turn up in this World until somebody turns them up.

—WE cannot study Nature profoundly without bringing ourselves into communion with the Spirit of Art, which prevades and fills the Universe.

—IF there be one thing upon this Earth that mankind love and admire better than another, it is a brave Man—it is a man who dares to look the Devil in the face and tell him he is a Devil.

—IT is one of the precious mysteries of Sorrow that it finds solace in unselfish Thought.

—TRUE ART is but the anti-type of Nature—the embodiment of discovered Beauty in utility.

—EVERY character is the joint product of Nature and Nurture.

—HE was one of the few great Rulers whose wisdom increased with his power, and whose spirit grew gentler and tenderer as his Triumphs were multiplied.—*Oration on Abraham Lincoln.*

—THE Problems to be solved in the study of human life and character are these: Given the Character of a Man and the conditions of life around him, what will be his Career? Or, given his Character and Career, of what kind were his Surroundings? The relation of these three factors to each other is severely logical. From them is deduced all genuine History. Character is the chief element, for it is both a Result and a Cause—a result of Influence and a cause of Results.

—POWER exhibits itself under two distinct forms—Strength and Force—each possessing peculiar qualities and each perfect in its own sphere. Strength is typified by the Oak, the Rock, the Mountain. Force embodies itself in the Cataract, the Tempest, the Thunderbolt.

—THE possession of great Powers no doubt carries with it a contempt for mere external Show.

—To a young Man who has in himself the magnificent possibilities of life it is not fitting that he should be permanently commanded; he should be a Commander. You must not continue to be *the employed.* You must be an employer! You must be promoted from the ranks to a command. There is something, young Man, which you can command—go and find it and command it. Do not, I beseech you, be content to enter upon any Business which does not require and compel constant intellectual Growth.

—In order to have any success in life, or any worthy success, you must resolve to carry into your work a fullness of Knowledge—not merely a Sufficiency, but more than a Sufficiency.

—Be fit for more than the Thing you are now doing.

—If you are not too large for the Place you are too small for it.

—Young Men talk of trusting to the Spur of the Occasion. That trust is vain. Occasions cannot make Spurs. If you expect to wear Spurs you must win them. If you wish to use them you must buckle them to your own heels before you go into the Fight.

—The Student should study himself, his relation to Society, to Nature and Art—and above all, in all, and through all these, he should study the relations of Himself, Society, Nature and Art to God the Author of them all.

—Great Ideas travel slowly and for a time noiselessly, as the gods whose Feet were shod with wool.

—The world's history is a Divine Poem of which the history of every Nation is a canto and every Man a word. Its strains have been pealing along down the centuries, and though there have been mingled the discords of warring, cannon and dying men, yet to the Christian, Philosopher and Historian—the humble listener—there has been a divine melody running through the song which speaks of hope and halcyon days to come.

—Truth is so related and correlated that no department of her realm is wholly isolated.

—Liberty can be safe only when suffrage is illuminated by education.

—The scientific spirit has cast out the Demons and presented us with Nature, clothed in her right mind and living under the reign of law. It has given us for the sorceries of the Alchemist, the beautiful laws of chemistry; for the dreams of the Astrologer, the sublime truths of astronomy; for the wild visions of Cosmogony, the monumental records of geology; for the anarchy of Diabolism, the laws of God.

—The American people have done much for the Locomotive, and the Locomotive has done much for them.

—I love to believe that no heroic sacrifice is ever lost, that the characters of men are moulded and inspired by what their fathers have done; that, treasured up in American souls are all the unconscious influences of the great deeds of the Anglo-Saxon race, from Agincourt to Bunker Hill.

THE WORLD'S EULOGIES

ON

PRESIDENT GARFIELD.

(1)

GEN. JAMES A. GARFIELD.

MRS. JAMES A. GARFIELD.

GEN. GARFIELD'S FORMER RESIDENCE AT HIRAM, OHIO.

MARY.   JAMES.   HARRY.   IRWIN.   ABRAM
GENERAL GARFIELD'S CHILDREN.

GEN. GARFIELD'S RESIDENCE AT MENTOR, OHIO.

THE WORLD'S EULOGIES

ON

PRESIDENT GARFIELD,

—BY—

REV. ISAAC ERRETT,   EX-GOV. C. K. DAVIS,
PROF. SWING,   RABBI LILIENTHAL,
DR. TALMAGE,   JOHN G. WHITTIER,
PRESIDENT HINSDALE,   LORD BISHOP OF MONTREAL,
HON. J. H. RHODES,   REV. T. K. NOBLE,
HENRY WATTERSON,   JAMES FREEMAN CLARKE,
HENRY WARD BEECHER,   JUDGE REA,
ROBERT COLLYER,   SENATOR VORHEES,
HON. EMERY A. STORRS,   BISHOP CLARKSON,
HON. R. M. MATHEWS,   EX-GOV. OGLESBY,
CHAS. T. BUCK,   HON. ROGER A. PRYOR,

AND MANY OTHERS.

EDITED BY

J. B. M^cCLURE.

CHICAGO:
RHODES & McCLURE, PUBLISHERS
1881.

COPYRIGHT, RHODES & McCLURE,
A. D. 1881.

Preface.

The reader will find in this volume some of the most eloquent and pathetic words that have ever fallen from the lips of man, called forth by the life and death of one whose career, from the cabin to the White House, forms the brightest pages in human history. Life's grandest lessons, its highest aspirations, holiest love, noblest ambition, manifold duties, patient labors and fullest rewards, are exhaustively portrayed, by orators the most eminent, as they gaze upon the colossal figure. In this one single life the whole world seems beckoned to a higher civilization. Says Watterson: "To-day, for the first time in fifty, aye, in sixty years, the people of the United States are one with one another, and stand hand in hand and heart to heart." " In the scenes of these few days," says Swing, " we must mark some signs of a more sensitive brotherhood;" and the eloquent Storrs, in his eulogy, declares that "Never since we have been a people—indeed, since this world has had a history—has there been a mourning so universal, a grief so deep and so profoundly sincere." And the basis of all is touchingly told in another eulogy, where a little child, seeing the mourning emblems on every side in its native village, said, in all the sincerity of its heart:

"Mamma, is there somebody dead in everybody's house to-day?"

"No, dear," said the mother, "there is not some one dead in everybody's house to-day, but everybody has lost a friend."

The eulogies in this volume have been pronounced by the best orators of the day, upon one of the grandest themes of the age—a perfect man—which necessarily called forth the best possible effort. For eloquence, pathos and general instruction—so far as we may learn from the example of an upright man—they are as unparalleled in the history of literature as is the great "Memorial Day," with its three hundred millions of sorrowing hearts, unparalleled in the history of human sympathy.

J. B. McCLURE.

CHICAGO, Oct. 10, 1881.

CONTENTS.

A GRAND LIFE AND ITS GREAT LESSONS.
REV. ISAAC ERRETT, CINCINNATI.
        PAGE

The Funeral Address at the Pavilion, in Cleveland—Time of unparalled Mourning—Why do we Mourn?—A Thrilling Incident—Virtue and its Rewards—A Rounded Life—The Great Lesson—Truth the Eternal Foundation—The Mother—The Wife—The Children—The Divine Benedictions, ... 17

A COLOSSAL FIGURE.
PROF. SWING, CHICAGO.

Human Greatness and Sorrow—Young Garfield and Liberty—Lessons for the Young—Man's Dignity and Greatness—Signs of a Higher Civilization—Garfield's Religion—Garfield and Lincoln—The White Pages of History, ... 30

MIGHTIER DEAD THAN LIVING.
DR. T. DE WITT TALMAGE, BROOKLYN.

Sampson, the Hercules of Greece—Garfield's Remarkable Death—Shaking Hands across the Palpitating Heart—Valuable Lessons for All—The Limits of Science and Sympathy—Mrs. Garfield's Heroism—Eloquent Peroration, ... 41

GARFIELD'S GREATNESS OF NATURE.
PRESIDENT HINSDALE, HIRAM COLLEGE.

An Unparalleled History—Garfield's Many-sidedness—Young Garfield at Hiram—Garfield's Simplicity—Garfield's Last Letter to President Hinsdale—The Noble Wife—A Mystery, . . . 51

GARFIELD'S BEAUTIFUL LIFE.
HON. J. H. RHODES, CLEVELAND.

Garfield at Hiram—In the Class-room—How He Learned—Born in the Right Age—Pleasing Incidents—Love of Poetry—Stopping the Carriage on the Old Bridge, ... 58

CONTENTS.

THE NATION'S FRIEND.
HENRY WATTERSON, LOUISVILLE.
PAGE

Heart to Heart—Every Inch a Man—A Blow that Missed the State and Struck the Man—Watterson Loved Him—Personal Reminiscences—We Stand on Common Ground—Saluting the Star-Spangled Banner—"God Reigns and the Government Still Lives," . 63

THE CROWN OF MARTYRDOM.
REN. HENRY WARD BEECHER, BROOKLYN.
(In Peekskill.)

A World in Mourning—Garfield's Birth-gifts—The Conflict Ended—Four Conspicuous Names, ... 69

GARFIELD'S GREATNESS.
REV. HENRY WARD BEECHER, BROOKLYN.
(In Brooklyn.)

The Prayer—Shortness of Life—The Lion and the Lamb—The Funeral March—Comfort in Sorrow—Unity of Mankind—Instructive Lessons—A Word on Guiteau—The Sorrowful Family Group, 73

COMFORT IN SORROW.
ROBERT COLLYER, D.D., NEW YORK.

The President is Dead—The Shining Portals—A Shadow over the Day—Hard to Submit to the Doom—Garfield's Love for his Country and Family—Kissing his Mother—The Tokens of Sympathy—Waiting and Watching, ... 80

OUR GOOD PRESIDENT.
HON. EMERY A. STORRS, CHICAGO.

Unparalleled Sorrow—Universal Brotherhood of Humanity—Garfield Made the Whole Circuit of American Life—A Record Pure and Spotless—The School-boy and the Teacher—The Preacher and the Soldier—Meeting Garfield During the Campaign—Meeting Him at Mentor—Anecdotes—Meeting Him at the White House—Interesting Incidents—Garfield Without an Enemy—His Firmness—The Friend of All—Standing by the Open Grave—The Past is Secure—His Memory is Ours, ... 83

GARFIELD'S LIFE AND DEATH.
HON. R. STOCKETT MATHEWS—BALTIMORE.

Picturesque Phases in Garfield's Life—An Inspiration—A Hero—The Genius of Free Institutions—The Long Distance Between the Tow-path and the Executive Mansion—Twenty Years—The

Coronation—Firing the Temple of Ephesus—James A. Garfield the Most Perfect Man of the Century—Meeting him Eighteen Years Ago in Monument Square—Meeting him a Few Days Before the Assassination—The Christian Politician—Christian Statesman—The Dying Hero, ... 97

IN MEMORIAM.
CHARLES F. BUCK, ESQ.—NEW ORLEANS.

A Bright Morning—A Great Nation—Garfield's Election—His Inauguration—His Martyrdom—A Review of his Life—Extract from Garfield's Speech to Restore Jefferson Davis to the Right of Citizenship—On the Greenback Question—His Personal Characteristics—His Domestic Life, ... 114

THE MAN OF HIS TIME.
PHILLIPS BROOKS, D.D.—BOSTON.

Days that Stand Apart in History—A Common Grief—A Half Century of Noble Life—Garfield in War—His Fidelity to the Right—Garfield a Philosopher—His Love for Literature—His Love for Jesus Christ—A Word to the Young, ... 127

A NATION MOURNS.
EX-GOV. C. K. DAVIS—ST. PAUL.

The Trappings of Woe—A Leading Statesman—A Pratical Man—A Noble Ambition—Garfield's Imagination—His Scholarship—An Incident in the Chicago Convention—The Duty of the Hour—The Three Martyred Presidents—The Halls of History—The Lesson we Must Learn to Live—Warning Words, . . . 133

GARFIELD'S DOMESTIC LIFE.
REV. L. W. BRIGHAM—LA CROSSE.

Garfield's Home Life—His Good Mother—Mrs. Garfield's Wifely Devotion—Scene at the Inauguration—Full Realization of a Mother's Hopes—Garfield's Tender Affection—His Remark on the Fatal Morning: "I Should Rather Die than that She Should Have a Relapse," 141

A PICTURE.
HON. JOHN H. CRAIG—SAN FRANCISCO.

Looking Across the Intervening Space—States Bowed in Reverence—The Eloquence of Grief—The Dearest Name in History—Looking at the Picture—A Glimpse at Garfield's Family Life—A Representative Man, ... 145

GARFIELD'S LEGACY.
RABBI LILIENTHAL—CINCINNATI.

The Divine Poem—The Coffin-Pulpit—"God Reigns, and the Government at Washington Still Lives"—American Aspiration and Success—Fortitude in Suffering, ... 149

THE TYPICAL AMERICAN.
PROF. SHATTUCK—GREELEY.

Garfield's Boyhood—On the Farm—Swinging the Ax—"I will go Through College"—Garfield's Remarks on Williams' Old Log Cabin and Mark Hopkins—His Kindness of Heart—Incidents Illustrating the Greatness of the Man—His Moral Courage—Studying the Good of the Republic, ... 154

TRUE TO HIMSELF—FALSE TO NONE.
HON. R. F. PETTIBONE—BURLINGTON.

Garfield Followed his Convictions—What we Love him For—A Vision of the Past—Garfield's Devotion to his Wife—Graphic Picture of a Scene in the Chicago Convention—On the Bed of Suffering—The Nation his Memorial, ... 160

THE HOUSEHOLD STORY.
CHANCEY M. DEPEW—NEW YORK.

The Wickedest Crime of the Century—Garfield the Highest Type of Manhood—His Life a Great Incentive to the Young—Salutary Influence of Garfield's Death—The North and South Rise from Bended Knees to Embrace—The Queen, ... 166

A MAN FOR THE PEOPLE.
REV. T. K. NOBLE—SAN FRANCISCO.

An Army Chaplain to his Comrades—A Grand Life—Garfield's Religion—A Happy Home, ... 169

A LIFE THAT SHINES.
JAMES FREEMAN CLARKE, D.D.—BOSTON.

Garfield Side by Side with Washington and Lincoln—The Worldwide Sorrow—Loyalty to the Government, . . . 176

CONTENTS.

THE IMMORTAL NAME.
JUDGE JOHN P. REA—MINNEAPOLIS.

The Sad Requiem—A Tribute Laid Upon a Fresh-made Grave—Human Love, ... 180

THE ILLUSTRIOUS DEAD.
SENATOR VOORHEES—INDIANA.

Every Nation a Mourner—Meeting Garfield on the Political Field—Personal Character—Intellectual Abilities—Incidents, . . 184

AN UNPARALLELED SPECTACLE.
REV. G. H. WELLS—MONTREAL.

We Share the Grief—Growing Intercourse—Garfield, the Boy—The Man—The President—Not Ashamed of his Religion—Domestic Life—Love for Mankind, ... 189

LESSONS FOR THE YOUNG.
BISHOP CLARKSON—IOWA.

Among all the Wonders of History this Hour Stands Alone—A Great Example—The Victory—Honest Manhood—Earth's Highest Civic Honors, ... 201

LINCOLN AND GARFIELD.
EX-GOV. OGLESBY—ILLINOIS—(Delivered in Leadville, Col.)

A Nation's Sorrow—Two Great and Good Men—Lincoln and Garfield—Both in the Affections of all Lovers of Liberty Throughout the World, ... 205

GARFIELD, THE CHRISTIAN.
REV. J. W. INGRAM—OMAHA.

Influence of His Life—The Christian Statesman—At Home in Mentor—His Faith—Example, ... 212

THE FUNCTIONS OF GREAT MEN.
REV. DR. RANKIN, WASHINGTON.

Garfield Grew into Greatness—His Power Never Degenerated—A Loving Heart, ... 217

WHY WE MOURN.
N. R. HARPER, ESQ., LOUISVILLE.

How the Colored People in Louisville, Ky., Observed the "Memorial Day"—Garfield a Tried Friend, ... 221

WE ALL MOURN.
CAPTAIN HENRY JACKSON, ATLANTA.

Twenty Years Ago—Resolutions by the Cœur de Leon Commandery —Garfield a Knight Templar, ... 225

THE PERFECT MAN.
ELDER J. Z. TAYLOR, KANSAS CITY.

Grandeur of a Great Life—From the Tow-path to the Presidential Chair—Garfield Never Missed from his Place of Worship in Washington—How he Sang "All Hail the Power of Jesus' Name," when leaving Mentor, ... 229

THE LAMENTED PRESIDENT.
HON. ROGER A. PRYOR, BROOKLYN.

A Melancholy Pleasure—An Unclouded Promise—Tokens of a Union of Hearts, ... 232

IN LONDON.
MINISTER LOWELL'S ADDRESS IN EXETER HALL.

A Paradox—Womanly Devotedness—The Queen—The Death Scene Unexampled—Joseph and Garfield—Destiny of the American Republic, ... 233

PERSONAL TRIBUTES TO GEN. GARFIELD.

John G. Whittier—Lord Bishop of Montreal—Dr. Franklin Noble—Dr. H. A. Edson—Gen. Sibley—Rev. J. P. Bodfish, . . . 237

A PUPIL'S TRIBUTE.
BY U. F. UDELL, ST. LOUIS.

Interesting Incidents by one of Garfield's Scholars in Hiram College, 247

A WISE MAN.
BY DR. SPROLE, DETROIT.

Preliminary Statement—A Man Present who has Attended all the Funerals of the Presidents, including that of Washington—Duffield's Poem, ... 250

IN CONCLUSION.

Garfield's Poem on Memory, ... 253

"OH! sir, there are times in the history of men and nations when they stand so near the veil that separates mortals and immortals, time from eternity, and men from their God, that they can almost hear the beating and feel the pulsations of the Infinite. Through such a time has this Nation passed. When two hundred and fifty thousand brave spirits passed from the field of honor through that thin veil to the presence of God, and when at last its parting folds admitted that martyred President to the company of the dead heroes of the Republic, the Nation stood so near the veil that the whispers of God were heard by the children of men."—*President Garfield, on the occasion of the assassination of his illustrious predecessor, Abraham Lincoln.*

THE WORLD'S EULOGIES

ON

PRESIDENT GARFIELD.

A GRAND LIFE AND ITS GREAT LESSONS.

By Rev. ISAAC ERRETT, of Cincinnati.

FUNERAL ADDRESS,
DELIVERED AT THE PAVILION IN CLEVELAND, SEPTEMBER 26, 1881, IN THE PRESENCE OF 250,000 PEOPLE.

UNPARALLELED MOURNING.

This is a time of mourning that has no parallel in the history of the world. Death is constantly occurring, and every day and every hour, and almost every moment, some life expires, and somewhere there are broken hearts and desolate homes. But we have learned to accept the unavoidable, and we pause a moment and drop a tear, and away again to the excitement and ambitions, and forget it all. Sometimes a life is called for that plunges a large community in mourning, and sometimes whole nations mourn the loss of a king, or a wise statesman, or an eminent sage, or a great philosopher, or a philanthropist, or a martyr who has laid his life on the altar of truth, and won for himself an envious immortality among the sons of men. But there was never a mourning in all the world like unto this mourning. I am not speaking extravagantly when I say—for I am told it is the result of calculations carefully made from such data as are in possession—that certainly not less than 300,000,000 of the human race share in the sadness, and lamentations, and sorrow, and mourning that belong to this occasion here to-day. It is a chill shadow of a fearful calamity that has extended itself into every home in all this land, and into every heart, and that has projected itself over vast seas and oceans into distant lands, and awakened the sincerest and profoundest sympathy with us in the hearts of the good people of the nations, and among all people. It is worth while, my friends, to pause a moment, and ask why this is?

WHY DO WE MOURN?

It is doubtless attributable in part to the wondrous triumphs of science and art within the present century, by means of which time and space have been so far conquered, that nations once far distant and necessarily alienated from each other, are brought into close communication, and the various ties of commerce, and of social interests, and of religious interests bring them into a contact of fellowship that could not have been known in former times.

It is likewise unquestionably partly due to the fact that this Nation of ours, which has grown to such wondrous might and power before the whole earth, and which is, in fact, the hope of the world in all that relates to the highest civilization, that sympathy for this Nation and respect for this great power leads to these offerings of condolence and expressions of sympathy and grief from the various nations of the earth, and because they have learned to respect this Nation, and recognize that the Nation is stricken in the fatal blow that has taken away our President from us. And yet this will by no means account for this marvelous and world-wide sympathy of which we are speaking. Yet it cannot be attributed to mere intellectual greatness, for there have been and there are other great men; and, acknowledging all that the most enthusiastic heart could claim to our beloved leader, it is but fair to say that there have been more eminent educators, there have been greater soldiers, there have been more skillful, and experienced, and powerful legislators and leaders of mighty parties and political forces. There is no one department in which he has won eminence where the world might not point to others who attained higher and more intellectual greatness. It might not be considered more righteously here than in many other cases; yet, perhaps, it is rare in the history of men and in the history of nations that any one man has combined so much of excellence in all those various departments, and who, as an educator, and a lawyer, and a legislator, and a soldier, and a party chieftain, and a ruler, has done so well, so thoroughly well, in all departments, and brought out such successful results as to inspire confidence and command respect and approval in every path of life in which he has walked, and in every department of public activity which he has occupied.

Yet I think when we come to a proper estimate of his character and seek after the secret of their world-wide sympathy and affection, we shall find it rather in the richness and integrity of his moral nature, and in that sincerity, in that transparent honesty, in that truthfulness that laid the basis for everything of greatness to which we do honor to-day. I may state here what perhaps is not generally known as an illustration of this:

A THRILLING INCIDENT—GARFIELD ENLISTING UNDER THE BANNER OF CHRIST.

When James A. Garfield was yet a mere lad in this

county, a series of religious meetings were held in one of the towns of Cuyahoga County by a minister by no means attractive as an orator, possessing none of the graces of an orator, and marked only by the entire sincerity, by good reasoning powers, and by earnestness in seeking to win souls from sin to righteousness. The lad Garfield attended these meetings for several nights, and after listening night after night to the sermons, he went one day to the minister and said to him:

"Sir, I have been listening to your preaching night after night, and I am fully persuaded that, if these things you say are true, it is the duty and the highest interest of every man, and especially of every young man, to accept that religion and seek to be a man. But really I don't know whether this thing is true or not. I can't say I disbelieve it, but I dare not say that I fully and honestly believe it. If I were sure that it were true, I would most gladly give it my heart and my life." So, after a long talk, the minister preached that night on the text, "What is Truth?" and proceeded to show that, notwithstanding all the various and conflicting theories and opinions in ethical science, and notwithstanding all the various and conflicting opinions in the world, there was one assured and eternal alliance for every human soul in Christ Jesus, as to the way of the truth and the life that every soul of man was safe with Jesus Christ; that he never would mislead; that any young man giving Him his hand and heart and walking in his pathway would not go astray, and that whatever might be the solution of ten thousand insoluble mysteries, at the end of all things the man who loved Jesus Christ and walked after the footsteps of Jesus, and realized in spirit and life the pure morals and the sweet piety, that he to-night was safe, if safety there were in the universe of God; safe, whatever else were safe; safe, whatever else might prove unworthy and perish forever. And Garfield seized upon it after due reflection, and came forward and gave his hand to the minister in pledge of acceptance of the guidance of Christ for his life, and turned back upon the sins of the world forever.

The boy is father to the man, and that pure honesty and integrity, and that fearless spirit to inquire, and that brave surrender of all the charms of sin to conviction of duty and right, went with him from that boyhood throughout his life, and crowned him with the honors that were so cheerfully awarded to him from all hearts over this vast land.

VIRTUE AND HER REWARDS.

There was another thing. He passed all the conditions of virtuous life, between the log cabin in Cuyahoga and the White House, and in that wonderful, rich and varied experience, still moving up from high to higher, he has touched every heart in all this land in some point or other, and he became the representative of all hearts and lives in this land, and not only the teacher but the interpreter of all virtues, for he knew their wants, and he knew their condition, and he established legitimately ties of brotherhood with every man with whom he came in contact. I take it that this law lying at the basis of his character, this rock on which his whole life rested, followed up by the perpetual and enduring industry that marked his whole career, made him at once the honest and the capable man who invited in every act of his life, and received the confidence and the love, the unbounded confidence and trust, of all who learned to know him.

A ROUNDED LIFE.

There is yet one other thing that I ought to mention here. There was such an admirable harmony of all his powers; there was such a beautiful adjustment of the physical, intellectual, and moral in his being; there was such an equitable distribution of physical, intellectual, and moral forces, that his nature looked out every way to get at sympathy with everything, and found about equal delight in all pursuits and studies; so that he became, through his industry and honest ambition, really an encyclopedia. There was scarce any single word that you could touch to which he would not respond in a way that made you know that his hands had swept it skillfully long ago, and there was no topic you could bring before him, there was no object you could present to him, that you did not wonder at the richness and fullness of information somehow gathered; for his eyes were always open, and his heart was always open; and his brain was ever busy, and equally interested in everything—the minute and the vast, the high and the low. In all classes and professions of men he gathered up that immense store, and that immense variety of the most valuable and practical knowledge that made him a man, not in one department, but in all rounds, everywhere his whole beautiful and symmetrical life and character. But, my friends, the solemnity of this hour forbids any further investigation in that line, any further detail of a very remarkable life. For these details you are familiar with, or, if not, they will come before you through various channels hereafter.

THE GREAT LESSON.

It is my duty, in the presence of the dead, and in view of all the solemnities that rest upon us now in a solemn burial service, to call your attention to the great lesson taught you, and by which we ought to become wiser, and purer, and better men. And I want to say, therefore, first of all, that there comes a voice from the dead to this entire nation, and not only to the people, but to those in places of trust—to our legislators and our governors, and our military men, and our leaders of parties, and all classes and creeds in the Union and in the States, as well as to those who dwell in the humblest life, qualified with the dignities and privileges of citizenship.

The great lesson to which I desire to point you can be expressed in a few words. *James A. Garfield went through his whole political life without surrendering for a moment his Christian integrity, his moral character, or his love for the spiritual.*

Coming into the exciting conflicts of political life with a nature capable as any of feeling the force of every temptation, with temptations to unholy ambition, with unlawful prizes within his reach, with every inducement to surrender all his religious faith and be known merely as a successful man of the world—from first to last, he has manfully adhered to his religious convictions and found more praise, and gathers to him in his death all the pure inspirations of the hope of everlasting life.

I am very well aware of a feeling among political men, justly shared in all over the land by those who engage in political life, that a man cannot afford to be a politician and a Christian. That he must necessarily forego his duty to God, and be abandoned in different measures of policy that may be necessary to enable him to achieve the desired result. Now, my friends, I call your attention to this grand life, as teaching a lesson altogether invaluable just at this point. I want you to look at that man. I want you to think of him in his early manhood. He was so openly committed to Christ and the principles of the Christian religion that he was frequently found, among a people who allow large liberty, occupying a pulpit, and you are within a few miles of the spot where great congregations gathered, when he was as yet most a boy, just emerging into manhood, week after week, and hung upon the words that fell from his lips with admiration, wonder and enthusiasm. It was that when he was known to be occupying this position they invited him to become a candidate for the Ohio State Senate. It was with the full knowledge of all that belonged to him in his Christian faith and his efforts to lead a Christian life, that this was tendered to him; and without any resort to any dishonorable means he was elected, and served his State and began his legislative career.

When the country was called to arms, when the Union was in danger, and his great heart leaped with enthusiasm and was filled with holiest desire, and ambitious to render some service to his country, it required no surrender of the dignity and nobleness of his Christian life to secure to him the honors that fell on him so thick and fast, and the successes that followed each other so rapidly as to make him the wonder of the world, though he ventured upon that career wholly unacquainted with military life, and could only win his way by the honesty of his purpose and the diligence and faithfulness with which he seized upon every opportunity to accomplish the work before him. Follow him from that time until he left the service in the field. The people of his district sent him to Congress, their hearts gathering about him without any effort on his part, and they kept him there as long as he would stay, and they would have kept him there yet if he had said so. He remained there until, by the voice of the people of this State, when there were other bright, and strong, and good names—men who were entitled to recognition and reward, and worthy every way to bear senatorial honors—he was sent to the United States Senate. Yet there were such currents of admiration, and sympathy, and trust, and love, coming in from all parts of the State, that the action of the Legislature at Columbus was but the echo of the popular voice when by acclamation they gave him that place, and every other candidate gracefully retired.

And then, again, when he went to Chicago to serve the interests of another; when, I know, his ambition was fully satisfied, and he had received that on which his heart was set, and looked with more than gladness for a path in life which he thought his entire education and culture had prepared him; when, wearied out with every effort to command a majority for any candidate, the hearts of that great convention turned on every side to James A. Garfield. In spite of himself and against every feeling, wish, and prayer of his own heart, this honor was crowded upon him; and the Nation responded with holy enthusiasm from one end of the land to the other; and in the same honorable way he was elected to the Chief Magistracy under circumstances which, however bitter the party conflict, caused all hearts of all parties not only to acquiesce, but to feel proud in the consciousness that we had a Chief Magistrate of whom they need not be ashamed before the world, and unto whom they could safely confide the destinies of this mighty Nation.

TRUTH IS THE SURE AND ETERNAL FOUNDATION.

Now, gentlemen, let me say to you all, those of you occupying great places of trust who are here to-day, and the mass of those who are called upon to discharge the responsibilities of citizenship, year by year, the most invaluable lesson that we learn from the life of our beloved, departed President is that not only is it not incompatible with success, but it is the surest means of success, to consecrate heart and life to that which is true and right, and rise above all questions of mere policy, wedding the soul to truth and right, and the God of truth and righteousness in holy wedlock, never to be dissolved.

I feel, just at this point, that we need this lesson, in this great, wondrous land of ours, this mighty Nation, in its marvelous upward career, with its ever-increasing power, opening its arms to receive from all lands the people of all languages, all religions, and all conditions, and hoping, in the warm embrace of political brotherhood, to blend them with us, to melt them into a common mass, so that, when melted and run over again, it becomes like the Corinthian brass, and in one type of manhood, thus incorporating all the various nations of the earth in one grand brotherhood, presenting before the nations of the world a spectacle of freedom, and strength, and prosperity, and power, beyond anything the world has ever known.

But let me say that the permanency of the work and its continued enlargement must depend on our maintaining virtue as well as intelligence, and making dominant in all the land those principles of pure morality that Jesus Christ has taught us. Just as we cling to that we are safe, and just as we forget and depart from that we proceed toward disaster and ruin, and this, now when we see what has been accomplished in a mighty life like this, is an instance of the power of truth and right which spreads from heart to heart, and from life to life, and from State to State, and finally from nation to nation, until, these pure principles reigning everywhere, God shall realize his great purpose, so long ago expressed to us in the words of prophecy, that the kingdoms of this world are become the Kingdoms of our God and of his Christ; so that, then, over the dead body of James A. Garfield may all the people join hands and swear by the Eternal God that they will dismiss all unworthy purposes, and love and worship only the true and the right, and in the inspiration of the grand principles that Jesus Christ has taught, seeking to realize the grand ends of the high civilization to which His word of truth and right continually point us. I cannot prolong my remarks to any great extent.

There are two or three things that I must say, however, before I close. There is a voice to the Church in this death that I cannot pause now to speak of particularly.

There is a tenderer and a more awful voice that speaks to the members of the family—to that sacred circle within which really his true life and character were better developed and more perfectly known than anywhere else. What words can tell the weight of anguish that rests upon the hearts of those who so dearly loved him, shared with him the sweet sanctities of his home—the pure life, the gentleness, the kindness, and the manliness that pervaded all his actions, and made his home a charming one for its inmates, and for all that shared in his hospitalities. It is of all things the saddest and most grievous blow, that those bound to him by the tenderest ties in the home circle, are called to yield him to the grave, to hear that voice of love no more, to behold that manly form no longer moving in the sacred circle of home, to receive no more the benefit of the loving hand of the father that rested upon the heads of his children, and commended the blessings of God upon them.

THE MOTHER.

The dear old mother, who realizes here to-day that her four-score years are, after all, but labor and sorrow—to whom we owe—back of all I have spoken of, the education and training that made him what he was, and who has been led from that humble home in the wilderness, side by side with him in all his elevation, and assured him the triumph and the glory that came to him step by step, as he mounted up from high to higher, to receive the highest honors that the land could bestow upon him; left behind him, lingering on the shore where he has passed over to the other side, what words can express the sympathy that is due to her, or the consolation that can strengthen her heart and give her courage to bear this bitter bereavement?

THE WIFE.

And the wife, who began with him in young womanood,

who has bravely kept step with him right along through all his wondrous career, and who has been not only his wife, but his friend and counselor through all their succession of prosperities and his increase of influence and power, and who, when the day of calamity came, was there, his ministering angel, his prophetess and his priestess, when the circumstances were such as to forbid ministrations from other hands, speaking to him the words of cheer which sustained him through that long, fearful struggle for life, and watching over him when his dying vision rested upon her beloved form, and sought from her eyes an insuring gaze that should speak when words could not speak.

THE CHILDREN.

And the children, that have grown up to a period when they can remember all that belonged to him, left fatherless in a world like this; yet, surrounded with a Nation's sympathy and with a world's affection, and able to treasure in their hearts its grand lessons of his noble and wondrous life, may be assured that the eyes of the Nation are upon them, and that the hearts of the people go out after them. While there is much to support and encourage, it is still a sad thing, and calls for our deepest sympathy, that they have lost such a father, and are left to make their way through this rough world without his guiding hand or his wise counsels. But that which makes this terrible to them now is just that which, as the years go by, will make very sweet, and bright, and joyous memories to fill all the lips of the coming years. By the very loss which they deplore, and by all the loving actions that bound them in blessed sympathy in the home circle, they will live over again ten thousand times all the sweet life of the past, and, though dead, he will live with them, and though his tongue be dumb in the grave will speak anew to them ten thousand beautiful lessons of love, and righteousness, and truth.

THE DIVINE BENEDICTIONS.

May God, in His infinite mercy, fold them in His arms and bless them as they need in this hour of darkness, and bear them safely through what remains of the troubles and sorrows of the pilgrimage unto the everlasting home, where there shall be no more death, nor crying, neither shall there be any more pain, for the former things shall have forever passed away. We commit you, beloved friends, to the arms and to the care of the everlasting Father who has promised to be the God of the widow and the father of the fatherless, in His holy habitation, and whose sweet promise goes with us through all the dark and stormy paths of life: "I will never leave thee nor forsake thee." I have discharged now the solemn covenant trust reposed in me many years ago, in harmony with a friendship that has never known a cloud, a confidence that has never trembled, and a love that has never changed. Fare thee well, my friend and brother; "Thou hast fought a good fight; thou hast finished thy course; thou hast kept the faith. Henceforth there is laid up for thee a crown of righteousness, which the Lord, the Righteous Judge, will give to thee on that day, and not unto thee only, but unto all them also who love His appearing."

JAMES A. GARFIELD—A CITY SET ON A HILL.

By Prof. Swing.

Delivered in Music Hall, Chicago, Sept. 25, 1881. (Full report.)

"A city set on a hill cannot be hid." Matt. 5:15.

IN that part of our earth which was made memorable by the presence of Jesus, many of the cities and towns were located upon the summit of a hill or mountain. The oppressive temperature of the summer months, and military considerations, and also a sense of the beautiful, led those who were about to found a village or a city to seek not always some river-bank or lake-shore, but some hill, or crag, or mountain. Nazareth, the town of Christ's early life, was on a height, and on one side there was a fearful precipice, down which the offended citizens threatened to throw Him who had rebuked their sins. The two mountains, Moriah and Sion, remind us that Jerusalem was seated upon lofty heights, and was a grand spectacle to the traveler who was journeying thither in its palmy days. The Temple of Solomon, the palaces of the King and his court, with the walls and watch-towers, made up an impressive scene to all coming along the valleys of Kedron and Hinnom, and fully justified the thought of Christ that "a city set on a hill cannot be hid."

The domain of Christ was spiritual; when He spoke of material things He had the spiritual qualities of our world in His mind. He wished that His disciples might possess virtues so great and so active that all society might behold and enjoy their righteousness and benevolence. The ages had been full of diminutive persons who lived only for self and for all small results—persons like to lighted candles placed under a bushel. It was time other forms of soul should appear; time for the world to have minds and hearts that should be as large and visible as cities upon mountains.

Soon after the great Palestine Teacher had uttered His wish and had given the nations a specimen of a soul too large and too lofty to be concealed, the dream began to find fulfillment in many of the departments of human life. Thought and sentiment began to be enlarged, history began to record greater actions and to receive into its storehouse greater biographies. There came along in the living tide men whose heads rose above the multitude like the tall cliff which "midway leaves the storm."

HUMAN GREATNESS AND SORROW.

Our Nation mourns to-day the loss of one too lofty to be concealed. All the grades of society, looking up from the door of cottage or palace, see this outline of a scholar, and statesman, and soldier, and President, and all mourn that the image is no longer to be seen in life, but only in death's pallor. The spectacle is made unusual, not only by the merit of the dead man, but also by the savage cruelty of the wound that robbed this citizen of his existence. The eighty days of physical and mental suffering, of alternate hope and fear, days which reduced a powerful man to the powers of only an infant, add their awful part toward placing this name fully before the civilized portion of the world. Made conspicuous by his character and works, Mr. Garfield becomes conspicuous by his misfortune. Thus this figure stands as upon a hill, and it will require centuries full of men and of events to hide its colossal outline from the gaze of mankind. Man is drawn toward the pathetic. What touches his heart, touches also his memory. Pity often makes up a large element in love. Had Mr. Garfield died of disease or by the limitation of nature, he would have been a large subject of study, but millions will read his biography in coming years because it ends in the awful cloud of tragedy. What do we witness to-day, and what will those behold who shall in future times run over the black and white page in history—black with misfortune, white in virtue? It must come to us as a peculiar fact that two of the greatest of American names are now made more sacred by the sadness of their deaths. As though the overruling Providence desired that the young men of this era and of future times should study deeply the lives of Garfield and Lincoln, their deaths were made tragic to allure the student toward their chapters in the annals of society.

YOUNG GARFIELD AND LIBERTY.

Looking at this man, not easy to be hidden, we see the ability of our country to produce a high order of manhood. That liberty which in name has been the ideal condition of all ages, here verifies all the old hopes and produces a symmetrical character strong on every side. When a lad, this Garfield enjoyed the free play of all his intellectual and emotional faculties. He was free to move toward books, and profession, and wisdom. All the gates to success would open to him as they had opened to a Webster or a Clay. He was not imprisoned by birth nor by caste. The path to law or statesmanship was as free to him as the path along the canal, and out of this freedom of a continent came an ambition of great power. Often when distinguished visitors appear in London they are given the freedom of the city in a gold box—an elegant letter, before which the doors of galleries, and libraries, and parliaments, and cathedrals fly open.

To this youth, poor and unknown, the Nation gave the freedom of the whole circle of human acquisition, from the study of Greek to a place in the army; from the hall of the law-maker to the chair of a President; and his ambition and energy were inspired by the generous offer. Freedom does not confer merit, but it affords an opportunity, and even allures the heart along by its possible rewards. It creates a landscape which charms the eye of each one setting out upon the journey of life. Despotism offers a desert to all the humble of birth. If poor and of low parentage, the mind sees only an arid plain, without tree or blossom, but the liberty and equality of this land make it optional with the traveler whether the plain he is to pass over shall be a desert or a magnificent garden. All is left to personal taste, and industry and will. And this taste, and industry, and personal power, are developed by the many, and great rewards offered to their growth. Mr. Garfield is one more witness in this great spiritual trial, and his testimony is direct, that the liberty of America is the greatest opportunity ever offered to man as man. Elsewhere rewards are offered to the few; here all are invited to the best feast of earth.

LESSONS FOR THE YOUNG.

In this eminent man the youth of to-day may learn that early poverty and hardships, instead of breaking the heart, need only sober the judgment and compel that common sense to come early and richly, which to the children of luxury comes scantily and comes late, if ever it finds a dawn. We can now look back and perceive that the hardships in the youth of him who died as a President was only a condition of things which made all the philosophy which came to the young man assume a practical form. It was not thought a philosophy unless it held in its solution much of human happiness; for when a toiler along a canal meditates, it will be for the welfare of man; just as when a slave thinks, he thinks of liberty; just as when a fever-patient dreams, his dream is about cold water. It has been stated recently that the dreams and laws of reform and all welfare do not come down from the rich and great, but up from the poor. Therefore those statesmen who have tasted some of the bitter things of the world know best how badly the waters need sweetening. This patient toiler wrought out an economy for the millions of youth here and everywhere. He showed what will and industry and exalted purposes can accomplish in this wide land—that all the young need ask as an endowment is mental and physical health. That is the essential capital upon which to base a large business in things either mental or spiritual.

MAN'S DIGNITY AND GREATNESS.

Out of energy and taste comes the real dignity of man. This dead President carries us back to the theory of old Plato, that motion or energy lies at the origin of the universe; that the starry skies and the variegated earth are only expressions of the self-moved mind. To this notion this one heart brings us back, for out of its self-moved depths there issued a moral world of great attractiveness. Education, learning, religion, politics, duty, honor, and high office emerged from the mind which began its career far down in weakness. That force made all the humble days and years to be rich veins of the later silver and gold.

As in the theology of nature we gather up the infinite phenomena of land, and sea, and sky, and say the One mind made all these wonderful and beautiful things, so in reading this biography, whose last page has just been written in tears, the reader will say, Behold what goodness and greatness have moved out of that one heart in royal pageantry!

Was James A. Garfield great? Ask those early years, when adverse winds always assailed his bark; ask the nights of study; ask the schools where he taught; ask the place where he worshiped; ask the halls where he helped enact wise laws; ask the battle-fields where he led soldiers; ask the magnificent Capitol where he was crowned as republicans crown their chieftains; ask the cottage where he died.

If out of the answers to these questions there comes not the witness of greatness, the human heart must henceforth toil and long in vain. Earth has no greatness. And yet all this human excellence grew up out of our national resources, as though to show the world the peculiar richness of the soil; and grew inland so far that we cannot say that England or Europe combined with America to cause this character.

The boy and man lived in the heart of the continent all surrounded by his country; and he lies in his coffin to-day a dead child of his Nation. The country mourns to-day, not only because a man has died, and died unjustly and painfully, but also because that man was her son. She had reared him, she saw her own likeness in his face, she loved him; in him were a mother's hopes. This land herein shows not only the power of its institutions to fashion a noble character, but that power of appreciation and grief that can weep for one thus overtaken by death.

SIGNS OF A HIGHER CIVILIZATION.

In the scene of these few days we must mark some signs of a higher civilization and a more sensitive brotherhood. Looking at the assassin we might despair of the present and the future. We might wonder what is the value of school-house, and church, and literature, and freedom, and the eloquence over human rights, if out of these beautiful things there can stalk a man much more cruel than a brute

But while the heart wonders and sinks over the name of that one savage, it is cheered by seeing a whole civilized race moved by a divine pity.

One vile human creature wished to remove Garfield from life, but millions upon millions wished him to live—live happily and live long. Men of wealth and men of poverty, men of learning and men of scanty education, men of all the political parties, men in the South and men in the North, and the crowned Kings and Queens, loved the life of this one man, and would, by their esteem, have carried him beyond the common three-score years of pilgrimage. His death was desired by the lowest one of the human race; it is lamented by the entire population of two continents.

If we count or measure these tears, if we see the Queen of England ordering her court to put on the emblems of mourning, we cannot but conclude that the hate of the one assassin is sublimely outweighed by the esteem of the world. In the presence of such an uprising of brotherly esteem the murderer finds his proper depth of infamy. In the light of a universal love we see the dark cruelty of the crime.

But we must not forget that we have assembled to-day in the name of the weekly service of God. If in this life of a President any quality of Christianity is placed upon a mountain top, that quality cannot remain hidden. In our times, when there is threatened an eclipse of faith, all religious minds must be happy to recall the public man who in his best manhood saw the power of a belief in God. He realized the perfect grandeur of the words: "The Lord Reigns." He uttered them in an hour of great national darkness, and the populace needed no other eloquence; and when in July last the one who had offered consolation in calamity needed some refuge for himself, he said he was ready to die or to live. Not the details of any church faith came, but the great ideas of the Christian religion grouped themselves around his bed—the best angels of those sad nights, for they were to help him when the skill of man should fail.

GARFIELD'S RELIGION.

It would be unjust to the name of Christ to say that Mr. Garfield's religion was only that of Nature, only such general thoughts as were cherished by Greek and Roman pagans. His faith came to him through the Church of the age as it communicates its ideas through pulpit and press and the Testament, as it is wont to surround and teach the young all through the days of formation, of passion, and temptation. That Church encompassed this youth with its hymns, and morals, and trust, and hope, and if at last the world saw evidences of that honor so conspicuous in the Sermon on the Mount, and that belief in Heaven so visible in Jesus Christ, it is under some obligation to confess that Christianity helped form that character which to-day all admire and lament. Beyond doubt, daily association with learned men of all the different religious sects, and the daily discovery that many creeds made only one kind of religious manhood, turned Mr. Garfield away from the distinctive doctrines of a denomination, and led him into the concord of faith rather than into its discord; but in estimating the greatness of his character we must declare that his moral symmetry was Christlike, and Christlike his repose in the hope of a second life. From his official and personal height he reminds the whole land that there should be church doors open to all the youth, inviting them away from the sins of the street and from the freezing touch of a Godless air—there should be a Sunday secured to the young and old, that there might be some hours of sunlight for these delicate plants—faith and spirituality. If our Nation, destined in a generation or more to surpass all upon the globe in power, material and men tal, desires to be governed by able and good men, it must see to it that the school-house and the church, with its day of rest, are kept open, for through these the youth pass on their way to all great beauty of character and usefulness of life.

GARFIELD AND LINCOLN.

It has been the reproach of our country that it is not rich in history; that the mind must look beyond the ocean or travel beyond the ocean to reach the presence of all that is deemed impressive. We have no venerable architecture, no historic church, no places of fame, no throne-rooms, or prisons, or towers, or crowns, or jewels, made affecting by the annals of a thousand years. This objection to our new world is well made; but this poverty of our country is being rapidly exchanged for riches—the riches seen in such men as Lincoln and Garfield, and similar moral products of the Republic. A nation will not long remain without history when the lives of such men are rapidly entering into the great open page. The Old World in its thousand-year period, reaching from the tenth century to the nineteenth, cannot point us to better names—names which stand for a better union of intelligence, and ability, and integrity, and charity, and heroism. Old history can point us to violent deaths of rulers, and can say: here Charles I. was beheaded, here Mary, Queen of Scots, died, here Marat was slain; but our two great Presidents have been slain, not by a multitude which was wronged, but by private fanatics, in their attack as unauthorized as beasts of prey; and, while old history abounds in instances where men died for some sins or wrongs, our new history points us to two great leaders who were the unhappy victims each of a single wicked heart; and died to gratify no party, but amid the tears of all parties and factions of the land.

THE WHITE PAGES OF HISTORY.

Rapidly is our country making up a history which will surpass those books we read in our early years. It cannot be affirmed of many of these illustrious ones whose names besprinkle the records of human life that they surpassed this Garfield in the power to measure the wants of society, and in the sympathy that cannot forget the welfare of the people. Where ancient great men trampled about in the living fields, this man walked softly, fearing lest some flower might be crushed. That attachment to the aged mother, that measureless attachment to the wife, were only evidences that this President was the type and product of a new age which was putting aside ferocity, and was reaching a sensibility as to human rights which was not present in the men who ruled once those nations which now boast of possessing history. The American pages may not be many, but comparatively they are white.

Must we not to-day read anew the lesson of mortality ? Must not we who have come into this church from the many paths of the world, along which paths we, too, are allured by some one of the many forms of ambition and hope, feel deeply the undeniable fact that we are all hastening to the end ? The closing scene may not be tragic, but it is coming. We are asked to think of these things by the memory of both Lincoln and Garfield, for they were both half-melancholy men—the former loving pathetic poetry, the latter even writing it. Lincoln in the height of his fame would say :

> "The hand of the king that the sceptre hath borne,
> The brow of the priest that the mitre hath worn,
> The eye of the sage and the heart of the brave,
> Are hidden and lost in the depths of the grave.
>
> "The peasant whose lot was to sow and to reap,
> The herdsman who climbed with his goats up the steep,
> The beggar who wandered in search of his bread,
> Have faded away like the grass that we tread."

And Mr. Garfield, in the hight of his success, looked out upon the earth of his triumph with sad eyes. He was unable to forget that he and all he loved were being borne along by arms mysterious and powerful. All sensitive minds are pathetic and almost superstitious in their hours of meditation. The dictates of reason are not able to counteract fully the deep attachments of the heart to life and friends and all the loved ones. When the great are warmhearted they are melancholy and most plaintive. May you all possess such a pathetic estimate of our earth; may you all see the tombward march of man, so read the vanity of riches, and fame, and home, and love, that you shall be compelled to become children of God and of Jesus Christ, and thus children of the final country that knows no funeral pageants, no days of bitter disappointment.

JAMES A. GARFIELD—"MIGHTIER DEAD THAN LIVING."

By Dr. T. De Witt Talmage.

Delivered in Brooklyn Tabernacle, Sept. 25, 1881—(full report.)

And the dead which he slew at his death were more than they which he slew in his life. Judges, 16:30.

Sampson in the text was deified and became the Hercules of Greece. He was a giant warrior born to be a leader, and Paul applauds him as a man who through faith subdued kingdoms. "He was a friend of God and an enemy of unrighteousness." But the most memorable scene in his life was the death scene. The Philistines, his enemies, gathered round him in a great building to mock him. With supernatural strength he laid hold of the pillars and flung everything into ruin, destroying the lives of the 3,000 scoffers, among them the Lords of Philistia. He had slain many of the enemies of God during his life, but my text says his last achievement was the mightiest. "So the dead which he slew at his death were more than they which he slew in his life." It is sometimes the case that after a most industrious, useful and eminent life, the last hours are more potent than the long years that went before. In the overshadowing event of this day, we find illustration of my text.

President Garfield, as many orators will say, was all his life the enemy of sin, the enemy of sectionalism, the enemy of everything small-hearted and impure and debasing. He made many a crushing blow against those moral and political Philistines, but in his death he made mightier conquest.

The eleven weeks of dying made a more illustrious record than the fifty years of living. "So the dead which he slew at his death were more than they which he slew in his life." As a matter of inspiration and comfort, I propose to show you that President Garfield's expiration is a mightier good than a prolonged lifetime possibly could be. Mind you, there was no time at which his death-bed could have been so emphatic. If he had died a few years before, his departure would not have been so conspicuous. If he had died one month before, his administration would not have been fairly launched. If he had died six months later, his advanced policy of reform would have cut the friendship of a great multitude, and if he had died years after he would have been out of office and in the decline of life. But he died at the time when all parties had turned to him with unparalleled expectation. There has not been a time in all the fifty years of his past when his death-bed could have been so effective, and in the next fifty years there could not have been a time when his death-bed would have been so impressive.

GARFIELD'S REMARKABLE DEATH.

First, our President's death, more than his life, eulogizes the Christian religion. We all talk about the hope of the Christian, and the courage of the Christian, and the patience of the Christian. Put all the sermons on these subjects for the last twenty years together, and they would not make such an impression as the magnificent demeanor of this dying Chief Magistrate. He was no more afraid to die than you are to go home this morning. Without one word of complaint he endured an anguish that his autopsy alone could reveal to the astonished world. For eighty days in inquisition of pain, yet often smiling, often facetious, always calm; giving military salute to a soldier who happened to look in at the window, talking with Cabinet officers about the affairs of state, reading the public bulletins in regard to his condition, watching his own pulse, and so undisturbed of soul that I warrant if it had not been for his dependent family and the Nation, whom he wanted to serve, he would have been glad to depart any time. O, sirs! all he ever did in confirmation of religion in days of health was nothing compared with what he did for it in this last crisis. James A. Garfield learned his religion from his mother, when she was trying, in widowhood and poverty, to bring up her boys aright; from that same old mother who sat with her Bible in her lap in her bed-room last Tuesday, when the news came that her son was dead.

James A. Garfield had no new religion to experiment with in his last hours. It was the same gospel into the faith of which he was baptized, when in early manhood he was immersed in the river, in the name of the Father, of the Son, and of the Holy Ghost. That religion had stood the test through all the buffetings and persecutions, through the hard work of life, and it did not forsake him in the tremendous close. There have been thousands of death-beds as calm and beautiful as this, but they were not so conspicuous. This electrifies Christendom. This encourages the pain-struck in hospitals, and scattered all up and down the world, to suffer patiently. The consumptive, the cancered and the palsied, and the fevered and the dying of all nations lift their heads from their hot pillows and bless this heroic, this triumphant, this illustrious sufferer. The religion that upheld him under surgeon's knife, and amid the appalling days and nights at Long Branch and at Washington, is a good religion to have. Show us in all the ages among the enemies of Christianity a death-bed that will compare with this radiant sunset.

"SHAKING HANDS ACROSS THE PALPITATING HEART."

Again, our President's death will do more for the consummation of right feeling between North and South than all his administration of four years could have accomplished. This is not "shaking hands across the bloody chasm" according to the rhetoric of campaign documents; this is shaking hands across the palpitating heart, that was large enough to take in both sections. This expiring man took the hand of the North and the hand of the South and joined them together, and practically said, with a dying pathos that can never be forgotten, "Be brothers!" Where now are the flags at half-mast? At New Orleans and Boston, Chicago and Charleston. There is absolutely to-day no Republican party and no Democratic party. A new party has swallowed up all—a party of national sympathy. The bulletins on the south side of Mason and Dixon's line have been as carefully watched as on the north side. We have been trying to arbitrate old difficulties and settle old grudges, yet the old quarrel has ever and anon broken out in a new place, but this requiem which shades the land forever drowns out all sectional discords.

After all that has been done and said during the last eleven weeks, the people of the South will be welcome in all our homes as we shall be welcome in theirs. He who tries hereafter to kindle the old fires of hatred will find little fuel and no sulphurous match. Alabama and Massachusetts! stand up and be married. South Carolina and New York! join hands in betrothal. Georgia and Ohio! I pronounce you one. Whom God hath joined together let no man put asunder. The seal is set by the cold and emaciated hand of our dead President. No living man could have accomplished it. More of the sectional prejudices and the misinterpretations and the bitternesses of old war times have perished in the last eleven weeks than in all the seventeen years since the war ended, and so the dead which Garfield slew at his death were more than they which he slew in his whole life.

VALUABLE LESSONS FOR ALL.

Again, President Garfield's sickness and death have educated the world, as all his life and the life of a thousand men beside could not have educated it, in the wonders of the human body. For the last two months all Christendom have been studying anatomy and physiology. Never since the world stood has there been so much known about respiration, about pulsation, about temperature, about gunshot wounds, about febrile rise, about digestion, about convalescence. The vast majority of the race have hitherto wandered about stupidly ignorant of this master-piece of God, the human mechanism. The last eleven weeks have educated 10,000 nurses for the sick. The invalids of all lands for this experience will have better attendance, more kindness, more opportunity of restoration. Never has there been such examination of dictionaries to find the meaning of a medical phrase. One new word of the morning bulletins has set the leaves of all the lexicons in America a-flutter.

Since the time when David, the psalmist, probably returned from an Oriental dissecting-room, wrote the autopsy, "we are fearfully and wonderfully made," and Solomon, who was wise in physiology as in everything else, called the spinal marrow the silver chord—(or "ever the silver chord be loosed") and called the head the "golden bowl" because the skull, is round like a bowl, and the membrane which contains the brain as yellow like gold—(or "the golden bowl be broken")—and called the veins of the human body a pitcher, because they carry the crimson liquid from the heart, the fountain through all the organs of the body —("or the pitcher be broken at the fountain")—and called the lungs a wheel, because they draw to itself and let go away like a well-bucket, and called the stomach the cistern—(the "wheel broken at the cistern,")— and showed that he knew what Harvey thought he was discovering thousands of years after concerning the circulation of the blood, I say, since those obscure times down to these days, when physicians are busy instructing the people, and all medical colleges and all high schools are scattering physiology and anatomical information, there never has been so much wisdom on these subjects as to-day, and the most potent of all the doctors has been the sick and dying bed of your President. He had often spoken and lectured on these subjects in college and on the lyceum platform, and was a scientist in all these fields. But in the last eleven weeks he has overthrown more ignorance on these important subjects than during all his half century of existence. "And so the dead which he slew in his death were more than they which he slew in his life."

THE LIMITS OF SCIENCE AND SYMPATHY.

Again, these last scenes must impress the world as no preachment ever did, that when our time comes to go the most energetic and skillful physician cannot hinder the event. Was there ever so much done to save a man's life as the life of President Garfield ? Is the season too hot ? There is manufactured for his sick room in August an October day. Is he to be transported to the seaside ? All the wheels and all the steam whistles, and all the voices along the line of progress are hushed for 200 miles, and a new section of railroad is built to let him pass over. Added to the medical skill of the capital are the skill of Philadelphia and New York.

All the medical ingenuity of the last 300 years flashes its electric light upon the wound. Paris and London and Edinburgh applaud the treatment. He had all the courage that comes from the hand of a wife who was sure he would get well. He had physicians who did not stand with cold, scientific calculation, studying the case; but splendid men, whose hearts grew strong or faint as the patient's pulse was strong or faint, and they were as great nurses as they were great surgeons. But the doctors could not keep him. His wife could not keep him. All the arms of his children hung around his neck could not keep him. His great spirit pushes them all back from the gates of life and soars away into the infinities. My Lord and my God! solemnize us with this consideration.

My hearer, if you and I were sick, I am sure we would have good medical attendance and good nursing, plenty of watchers and plenty of attendants. The world is naturally very kind to the sick. We who have good houses would have sympathetic, though trembling, hands to hold ours in the last exigency. We all have those who love us as we love them, and when the time fixed by the merciful God arrives, we must be off.

There is no need of our getting nervous about it, or fretting about it. All we have to do is to keep our hearts right with God and do our best, and then be as unfluttered as was our dying President. If after the mightiest surgery of America and the world, he had to surrender on Monday night at the stroke of the Death Angel, surely we cannot resist it. In the emphasizing of all these great truths, James A. Garfield is mightier lying on his catafalque at Cleveland than in the White House, receiving the honors of foreign embassage.

Who knows but that this death will save millions of people for this world and the next? Fifty millions of people—nay, North and South, America and Europe and parts of Asia—called to thoughts of mortality and the great future! Who knows but it may awaken whole nations from the death of sin to the life of the gospel? When, last week, I saw one line of mourning from Detroit, Mich., to Brooklyn, I wondered if God would not use this great grief for the purification of the Nation. "O, Lord, revive Thy work in the midst of the Nation." Enough of the Sabbath-breakings and the impurity and the blasphemy and the official corruption in this country! By the scowl of this terrific event let these dogs of hell be driven back to their fiery kennels; against all these evils this Presidential giant is mightier dead than when alive.

POOR MRS. GARFIELD.

But, while the Nation has this comfort, there are three words that will leap to our lips, and they have been reiterated oftener than any other words for the past few days: poor Mrs. Garfield! More pathetic words I never read than those in the Friday newspapers which said that, with two of her children, she had gone over to the White House to get the property of her family, and have it sent to her home in Ohio. Can you imagine anything more full of torture than the walk through the rooms filled with associations of her husband's kindnesses, of her husband's anxieties, and of her husband's long-continued physical anguish? She had, with her womanly arms, fought by his side all the way up the steep of life. She had helped him in their economies when they were very poor; with her own needle clothing their family, with her own hands making him bread. When the world frowned upon him in the days of scandalous assault she never forsook his side. They had together won the battle, and had seated themselves at the very top to enjoy the victory. Then the blow came. What a reversal of fortune! From what midnoon to what midnight! It is said that this will kill her. I do not believe it. The God who has helped her thus far will help her all the way through. When the broken circle gathers in the future days at the old home at Mentor, the mighty God who protected James A. Garfield at Chickamauga, and in the fiery hell of many battles, will protect his wife, his children, and his old mother.

Upon all the seven broken hearts let the grace descend! What consolations they have! It was a great thing to have had such a son! It was a great thing to have been the wife of such a man! It was a great thing to have been the children of such a father! While theirs and ours is the grief, I am glad on his account that he has gone. He had suffered enough. Enough the cuts of the lancets and the thrusts of the catheter, and the pangs of head and side and feet and back! Ascend, O disenthralled spirit, and take thy place with those who "came out of great tribulation, and had their robes made white in the blood of the Lamb!"

ELOQUENT PERORATION.

This Samson of intellectual strength, this giant of moral power, had—like the one in the text—in other days slain the lion of wrathful passion, and had carried the gates of wrong from the rusted hinges. But the peroration of his life is stronger than any passage which went before. The dead which this giant slew in his death were more than those whom he slew in his life. May we all learn the practical lessons with which our subject is filled! Oh, behold the contrast between Friday, the 4th of March, 1881, and Friday, the 23d of September, 1881. On the former day Washington was ablaze with banners. Each State in the Union had its triumphal arch. Great men of this country and vast populations filled the streets; procession such as had never moved from the White House to the Capitol; military display that would have confounded hostile nations; the city shaken with cannonading by day, and the night on fire with pyrotechnics! Thousands of all political parties who congratulated the President, pronounced that 4th of March the brighest day that had ever shone on American institutions. That night, or soon after, in some room of the Presidential Mansion, I warrant you there assembled, husband and wife and five children and the aged mother, taking a long breath after the excitement of the inauguration. But, behold, Friday, Sept. 23d, the dead President in the rotunda, his bereaved wife at a friend's house, a dangerously sick child 400 miles away at Williamstown, Mass.; military on guard around the casket; hundreds of thousands of people gazing on the face so emaciated that none would know it; the poor, black woman falling on her knees beside the coffin, expressing the anguish of speechless multitudes when she said: "Oh, dear! how he must have suffered!" Friday, 4th of March, 1881! Friday, Sept. 23, 1881! Of all the words of comfort I have uttered to-day I have this lesson, which seems to sound out from the tramp of pall-bearers and from the rolling of the draped rail train moving westward, and from the open grave now waiting to receive our dead President: "Put not your trust in princes. nor in the sons of men, in whom there is no help. His breath goeth forth, he returneth to this earth; in that very day his thoughts perish." Fare thee well, departed chieftain!

GARFIELD'S GREATNESS OF NATURE.

By President Hinsdale, of Hiram College, Ohio.

Delivered before the soldiers of Garfield's regiment (42nd Ohio), students of Hiram College, and of Williams College, and Garfield's neighborhood friends, in the First Presbyterian Church, Cleveland, Sept, 25th. 1881.

AN UNPARALELLED HISTORY.

BRETHREN in the Hiram Fellowship: There was never but one man who could fitly preside at a Hiram re-union; and he was the man whom we have gathered, not to honor, but to remember. With what felicity did he always open the service; with what aptness did he guide all our thoughts and feelings in right courses? Can you think of Garfield as presiding at his own obsequies, not knowing that they are his own? If you can, please to consider that I have resigned the chair, and that he is present and presiding in our midst.

James Abram Garfield: born November 19, 1831; a student at Hiram in August, 1851, at Williamstown in 1854; president of the Eclectic Institute in 1857; an Ohio senator in 1859; a soldier in 1861; elected a representative in Congress in 1862, and re-elected each two years succeeding until 1878; chosen United States Senator in January, 1880; nominated by the Republican party for the Presidency in June of the same year; elected to that high office in No.

vember following; inaugurated Chief Magistrate of the great Republic March 4, 1881; shot by the assassin July 2; died at Long Branch September 19—these facts and dates are the salient points of a career that, in all the points of high character, noble achievement, lofty promises not yet fulfilled, beautiful romance, generous enthusiasm, pure ambition, and a final euthanasy, have no parallel in the history of the world.

Were I limited to one phrase in which to describe James A. Garfield, I should say: Greatness of nature. With what wealth of noble faculties was he endowed! Close observation, high analytical and generalizing ability, solidity of judgment, depth and purity of feeling, strength of will, power of rhetorical exposition, artistic sense, poetic sentiment, reverence of spirit, and noble courage—these are only a few of his great gifts. Were I allowed a second phrase of description, I should add: Richness of culture, fullness of knowledge, breadth of attainment, discipline of all the great faculties of the mind, ripeness of experience—are phrases that describe but imperfectly what study and the friction of life had done for him. Greatness of nature and richness of culture, together fitly describe his life and character. And this is in perfect harmony with his own maxim: "Every character is the joint product of nature and nurture."

GARFIELD'S MANY-SIDEDNESS.

One of the most striking facts pertaining to this noble product of nature and nurture was his many-sidedness. Tennyson said of the Duke of Wellington:

> He stood four-square to every wind that blew."

This is a striking figure, and it admirably expresses the poet's thought. But General Garfield had many more sides than four. You can hardly take up a point of observation where you will not discover something in him both interesting and striking. He seemed to face in all directions. He faced to law and policy, to science and literature, to arms and the camp, to religion and the Christian ministry, to the Senate and the forum, to the farm and the arts, to the social circle and domestic life, and in as many more directions as the diamond from its polished facets flashes its lustrous beauty.

But, brethren in the Hiram Fellowship, we are not come together to remember the late President in all the phases of his great life and character. To-day we leave the soldier to soldiers, the lawyer to lawyers, the statesman to statesmen. Mr. Garfield faced towards Hiram, and to us this will always be the most engaging side of his life. Here we recall the sound scholar, the great teacher, the discreet administrator, wise counsellor, sure guide, faithful friend, and noble man. Under circumstances that make the world weep, are we gathered to hold memorial service for him whose fourfold connection with our college, as pupil, teacher, president and trustee, has made the humble name of Hiram known all over the land.

Rapid as was General Garfield's march upon the nation still the public as a whole was slow in finding him out. They never did fully find him out until his life was ebbing away to the music made by the Atlantic sobs. Nay, they have not fully done so yet. But I may fairly claim that the students of Hiram had discovered his greatness long before the year 1860. They were, in fact, the original discoverers of James A. Garfield. Years ago a Hiram poet sang at one of our reunions:

> "Right proud are we the world should know
> As hero him we long ago
> Found truest helper, friend."

YOUNG GARFIELD AT HIRAM.

Young Mr. Garfield first came to Hiram in August, 1851. The next school year he became one of the teachers, and continued such until 1854, when he went to college. On his graduation, in 1856, he returned as teacher, and the next year became the principal. From this time to August, 1861, when he left his class room for the camp, he was the head of Hiram. Within these years, especially lies the service that we should remember. I can only say, in general, that it was fully marked by all the great qualities of his later life, wealth of knowledge, buoyancy of spirits, dignity of carriage, wisdom in counsel, kindness and justice, faithfulness of friendship. I sketch the outline and leave it for you to fill in the picture.

Of my own obligations to him, first as a pupil, next as a co-teacher, then as friend—nay as a brother, I cannot trust myself to speak. Only he who chanted the elegy over the fallen Jonathan could do justice to the theme: "How are the mighty fallen in the midst of the battle. O, Jonathan, thou wert slain in thine high places. I am distressed for thee, my brother Jonathan; very pleasant hast thou been to me; thy love to me was wonderful, passing the love of women."

GARFIELD'S SIMPLICITY.

One of the very grandest phases of this grand man was his great simplicity of character. This he retained unsullied to the end. Nothing could corrode or taint his original honest fiber. Principalities and powers, dynasties and dominion, were nothing to him in comparison with the fellowship of his early friends. His love for the old school continued to the very end. He last visited Hiram not long before his final departure for Washington. He made one of his beautiful speeches in the chapel. He spoke of the memories that lay under the snow; said never since he went to the army had he left Hiram with similar feelings; said he was about to sail out into unknown seas, but that he felt that, on the Hiram promontory, he had built a cairn from which he could draw supplies throughout the voyage. He called for the singing of "Ho! Reapers of Life's Harvest," joined heartily in the song, shook hands with all present, and was driven away homeward.

HIS LAST LETTER TO PRESIDENT HINSDALE.

The last autograph letter that he wrote me came in the midst of the great political tempest, and was in these words.

"DEAR BURKE: I throw you a line across the storm to let you know that I think, when I have a moment between breaths, of the dear old quiet and peace of Hiram and Mentor. Let me hear from you. Inclose your letter in an envelope to Crete. As ever yours,

J. A. GARFIELD."

How he longed for this "dear old quiet and peace" in all storms, was well known to all his closer friends, and how he sighed for it as he lay upon his bed of pain in the heart of Washington and by the shore of the far-resounding sea, the reporters have told the world.

THE NOBLE WIFE.

There is one person who must not be forgotten here. And who is this? You all anticipate my answer. She is a Hiram student, one of our Fellowship, the lamented President's noble wife. Hiram claims two thousand daughters, many of whom have done virtuously, but Lucretia excels them all. Wheresoever his history shall be read in the whole world, there shall also be told what this woman has done for a memorial for her. In behalf of all who are in the Hiram Fellowship, I wish to thank Mrs. Garfield for her heroic devotion, unfaltering courage and immortal hope in the sick chamber of her husband. It was not for yourself and your children alone that you wrought, you wrought for the Nation, for the world, and for us. We recognize, but can never pay our deep debt of obligation.

But it is all over. Black care, that perched like the night raven in our homes the evening of July 2, sits in them still. In 1865 I stood with General Garfield in the pouring rain on Dr. Robison's door steps, on Superior street, April 28, when the hearse of President Lincoln passed by to the public square. Yesterday I passed the same place as I followed Garfield's hearse. To-day his remains lie where Lincoln's lay. And it is left for us, and it is left for all his friends, to adjust ourselves to a world that contains no living Garfield. He has left us his life and his spirit. Storm, and war, and strife are all over, and he has entered upon a quiet and a peace that neither Hiram nor Mentor knew. He is thrice happy and doubly immortal; immortal in life and immortal in death.

A MYSTERY.

Finally, let me ask, why was all this permitted? Why was the assassin allowed to strike him down? Why were not the prayers of the people granted? Why did the night-raven never lift his wings and fly away? Why was the Most High deaf, and why did the heavens give no sign? What a strange providence! How can it fit into any plan of Divine wisdom and love! Thus far I have scarcely tried to answer these questions, though they have pressed upon me many an hour. It is a great test of faith in God. But Garfield believed in God. He thought that an unceasing purpose runs through the ages and comprehends the lives of men; and I think so, too. Still, hitherto I have been able to do little more than say, "Lord, I believe; help Thou mine unbelief!" For myself, I must leave the problem to the future. History will no doubt discover and disclose what passes our power to comprehend.

I have dwelt upon the darker side of the great tragedy. True, there are great elements of good in the story. These I hope will be duly emphasized, for we must not dwell too much upon the cypress. In Garfield's young days at Hiram, when he was full of bounding life, this saying of Emerson's was a great favorite with him: "To-day is a king in disguise. Strip off his robes and enjoy him while he is here." And I think I hear him who presides over us, in spirit, say: "Be not so carried away with grief, so paralyzed with sorrow, so blind with weeping that you cannot discover the good that is in it all." Still for one I must declare:

> "I falter where I firmly trod,
> And falling with my weight of cares
> Upon the great world's altar—stairs,
> That slope thro' **darkness up to** God.
>
> "I stretch lame hands of faith, **and grope**
> And gather dust and chaff, **and call**
> To what I feel is Lord of all,
> **And** faintly trust the **larger hope.**"

GARFIELD'S BEAUTIFUL LIFE.

By Hon. J. H. Rhodes—His Schoolmate, of Cleveland.

Delivered at the Hiram Memorial Service, Sept. 25, 1881.

GARFIELD AT HIRAM.

To THOUSANDS of men and women these words bring swift and happy visions of the golden age, the world over, when memory is not busy with the dead past, but when life is eager, joyous, standing on tip-toe to catch each new bright morning. Then surely it was true, as he often said, "Each day is a king in disguise."

It always seems to me now, that from boyhood he was almost conscious of his high destiny in life. He was born to lead and command. He captured all hearts as naturally as he breathed. He could not help winning them if he would.

It is not now the time for critical analysis or historic preciseness. We see him only through the mist of tears. We cry out in our despair, like infants in the night crying for the light, but generations hence his memory and his life, hallowed by the lapse of years, and looked at through a long line of succeeding events, like some grand mountain peak, viewed from afar, will not be less grand, will rise into the heavens with equal glory as now.

To many who are here to-day, visions come again of Garfield in the class-room or the chapel at Hiram. They see a fair-faced, blue-eyed young man in the robust vigor of early manhood, overflowing with animal spirits and breezy, cheerful good nature, standing before a class, and irradiating the room with the grand enthusiasms for knowledge and ideas which made each pupil feel as if he were in an atmosphere highly electrified, out of which he passed, feeling that life had new meanings to him, and longing for the return of the next lesson. The crayon often became a magic wand with which new worlds were disclosed to the young explorer in search of new continents.

Observe all things, and question all men, were maxims he daily illustrated. No man was so humble, he often remarked, but something new can be learned by talking with him. With all men he was, therefore, social. If he did not learn anything from another, young Garfield had already learned that ideas can only be clearly held when they can be clearly clothed in words, and, as long as he could find a good listener, he delighted to pour forth his own thoughts in words, thus crystalizing ideas and opinions already formed. Many a man has wondered at the wealth of conversation with which he was flooded. Many a small audience thought it strange he should speak as abundantly and as eloquently to them as if there were thousands to be moved. All men were foils for his own swift blades, and so he grew daily in strength and breadth.

He died young, but he was born at the right time. His young manhood began with the great stir in modern thought which had already revolutionized the world. The age of invention and discovery had just begun to usher into our modern life the triumphs of electricity and steam. The ferment of scientific research had opened up a thousand new fields of inquiry. The conflict between old decays and new creations in the world of politics was at hand. Literature had just had a new birth, and the modern period of books and newspapers had been inaugurated. I can remember how, in 1855, 1856, 1857, 1858, 1859 and 1860, the very air seemed surcharged with the new life that already threatened storms and hurricanes. I never heard him wish he had been born in another age. He did not sigh that his lot had not been cast amid the stirring scenes of ancient Rome or modern Europe. He was born in America and for America, and he lived long enough to see the dawn of the modern life and thought, full-orbed and high, advanced in the day. He went away from Hiram at twenty-four to Williamstown, to return in the fall of 1856, with the baptism of fire from that new heaven on his heart and head. For two years after his graduation at Williams we roomed together at Hiram. The old office in the orchard is more hallowed to me by those two years of companionship than any temple made by human hands. It was both an education and an inspiration to hear him at this period.

PLEASING INCIDENTS.

It was after his return from Williams College that he began to preach. Preaching was a vent for the overflow of his energies and activity. In preaching he had a range of thought that gave more scope than the school room. The effect of two years at the feet of that great teacher, Mark Hopkins, was very marked. His thoughts ranged through wider circles, whilst the distinctive dogmas of the church at Williamstown did not seem to have attached themselves strongly; the philosophic and metaphysical methods of President Hopkins became a part of his own methods. The result of this was that his preaching had a new charm for the people who heard him.

It was during the years that followed his return from Williamstown that he found so much inspiration and strength from that remarkable woman, Almeda A. Booth, whose intellectual grasp and range of thought were only second in Hiram to his own. He owed much to her, and he has made public acknowledgment in a beautiful tribute to that woman, whom he compared to Margaret Fuller.

Whilst teaching at Hiram and preaching in various places in Northern Ohio, his mind had turned to the law as a life profession, and among the legacies I have of this period are synopses made by us of the first two volumes of Bouvier's Institutes. The law, in its great principles, its broad generalizations, its sacred regard for life and property, its conservative influence and power in maintaining order and peace in society, had a great charm to his mind, and I distinctly remember that he would synopsize the institutes so thoroughly as to cover every doctrine laid down. In subsequent years he achieved distinction for his success in the law. But politics, in the higher and almost forgotten meaning of the word, had become a subject of great interest to him.

The great struggle in the land had already begun, which ended in the downfall of American slavery. He was intensely absorbed in this great controversy, and soon entered as State Senator, upon that public career with which the world is so familiar. Into this he poured his energies, as he had formerly into teaching and preaching.

Here, too, in Hiram was continued that devotion to the little woman whose name is revered in every home in the civilized world. It began a few years earlier at Chester. Writing to me in 1871, in the midst of his public life, and nearly thirteen years after his marriage, he said:

"There is not a day when I do not certainly fear such completeness will not be allowed to last long on this earth." "Verily, she was the rainbow on his storm of life, the anchor on its sea."

His mind was imaginative, and his temper poetical. The fresh beauties of "In Memoriam" were his delight, and thousands of times did I hear him recite, in those early days, the passage beginning: "The tide flows down, the wave again is vocal in its wooded walls; my deeper sorrow also falls, and I can speak a little there."

The Cuyahoga, above the rapids at Hiram, will forever be associated with him, where once we stopped our horse and carriage on the old bridge, and looked up the stream and saw from the tall trees on either side what Tennyson meant by "wooded walls."

I must be pardoned for not dwelling further, as there are many you wish to hear. It is hard to find any reconciliation to the fact that men say he is dead, and that his bodily form will no more be visible on earth. It may be that his outward frame may be resolved again to dust, and become, in the long processes of nature, flowers and fruit, clouds or frost, but I never can conceive of him as dead. I do not belive he is dead. Death has no definition or limitations which can include so great a soul. Immortality was no myth with him. His voice is still heard.

THE NATION'S FRIEND.

By Henry Watterson (Editor Louisville Courier-Journal).

Delivered in Jeffersonville, Ind., Sept. 26, 1881.

HEART TO HEART.

To-day, for the first time in fifty, aye, in sixty years, the people of the United States are one with one another, and stand hand in hand, and heart to heart, by the open grave of their murdered President. This vast assemblage, these paraphernalia of public lamentation, these muffled drums and mournful cadences of dead marches—your own sad faces and tearful eyes—are not the offerings of a locality, nor the offsprings of party feeling. They are universal. Everywhere throughout our dear land—and not alone where men are wont to congregate—everywhere—and not anywhere broken by geographic stops or sectional lines—everywhere, in the market places and the churches, in the great mansions of the rich and the humble cots and cabins of the poor, and on the rock-ribbed ridges where the sumach and the maple twine their boughs in pious benediction over the bended head of New England to the rice-farms and cotton-fields of the kneeling South, where the live-oak stands as a guard of honor and the magnolia sends its fragrance up to God—everywhere, and with all classes, all sects, all conditions, all ages, but one sight is to be seen this day, but one sound is to be heard—the solemn march, the solemn music, which bears to their last earthly home the mortal remains of James A. Garfield.

Nor is this grievous spectacle of grief the product of our country only, and confined within her borders and to her people. The stranger arriving on our shores to-day would not need to ask, with *Hamlet:*

> "—Who is it that they follow,
> And with such maimed rights?"

Across the seas, as if borne by the magnetic tides that in electric currents ebb and flow beneath the waves, the sorrow of America has thrilled the heart of Europe; nor yet there alone among crowned heads, uncertain of their crowns, and courts, unknowing when their turn may come, since murder strikes so close and indiscriminate; but high among the crags, where the free Switzer sings of liberty, and in the storied groves and sweet meadows of Old England, where bells that rang for Hampton and the Iron Duke, for Wordsworth, the gentle poet, and Albert, the good Prince, are ringing into Anglo-Saxon song and legend, the name of James A. Garfield.

Why, why is all this? I answer, because he was a man, and every inch a man, who stood as the representative of manhood and the State.

> "What constitutes a State?
> Not high-raised battlement nor labored mound,
> Thick wall and moated gate.
> * * * * *
> No; men, high-minded men,
> With powers so far above dull brutes endued
> In forest, brake, or den,
> As beasts excel cold rocks and brambles rude;
> Men who their duties know,
> But know their rights, and, knowing, dare maintain."

The blow that struck down Garfield, struck at the State, and, though it missed the State, it hit the man, and, through him, touched the manhood and the womanhood, yea, and the childhood, of our time; and so, we are come to do honor to his memory, to take comfort one from another in our sorrow, on this, as it were, his last day upon earth, our hero and our martyr—who went down because he was clad with our sovereignty—our Peasant Chieftain—whose glory America gives to the world!

WATTERSON LOVED HIM.

I knew him well. I knew him, and I know now that I loved him. He was a man of an ample soul, with the strength of a giant, the courage of a lion, and the heart of a dove. Never lived a man who yearned more for the approval of his fellow men, who felt their anger more. Never lived a man who struggled harder to realize Paul's ideal, and to be "all things to all men." Nor did ever the character sketched by Paul find a nobler example, for he was "blameless, vigilant, sober, of good behavior, apt to teach, not given to filthy lucre." No one without the little family circle of relatives and friends in which he lived will ever know how a certain dismal, though in truth trivial, episode in his career cut him to the soul. Born a poor man's son, to live and die a poor man, with opportunities unbounded for public pillage—with licensed robbery going on all about him, and he pinched for the bare means to maintain himself, his wife and his little ones, with decency and comfort—to be held up to the scorn of men as one not honest. He is gone now, and, before he went, he had outlived the wounds which party friends, alike with party foes, had sought to put upon his honor; and mayhap, to-day, somewhere among the stars, he looks down upon the world, and sees at last how false, how sordid, how selfish and unreal were the assaults of those in whose way he stood. It is a pleasure to me to reflect, amid these gloomy scenes, that some friendly words of mine gratified him at a moment

5

when he suffered most. Not in the last campaign, for it would have been a crime in me to have hesitated then. But away back, when no vision of the Presidency had crossed the disc of his ambition, and when the cruelest blows were struck from behind.

INCIDENTS.

It is also a pleasure to me to remember the last time I saw him. It was an all-night session of the House, when, in company with Joseph Hawley, of Connecticut, Randall Gibson, of Louisiana, and Randolph Tucker, of Virginia, we took possession of the committee-room of Proctor Knott, who joined us later, and buried all bickerings and jars in happy forgetfulness of section and party, and in joyous return to nature, and the contemplation

> "——Of poesy and philosophy,
> Arts which I love, for they, my friend, were thine."

I do well remember how buoyant he was that night in spirit and how robust in thought; how full of suggestion, quick in repartee, unaffected and genial ever; how delighted to lay aside the statesman and the partisan, and be a boy again; and how loth he was, with the rest, to recross the narrow confines which separate the real and ideal, and to descend into the hot abyss below. I could not have gone thence to blacken that man's character any more than do another deed of shame; and, Republican though he was, and party chief, he had no truer friends than the brilliant Virginian, whom he loved like a brother, and the eminent Louisianian, whose counsels he habitually sought.

I refer to an incident, unimportant in itself, to illustrate a character which unfolded to the knowledge of the world through affliction and death, has awakened the admiration and love of mankind. All know now that he was a man of spotless integrity; who might have been rich by a single deflection, but who died poor ; who broadened and rose in hight with each rise in fortune ; who was not less a scholar because he had wanted early advantages ; and who, not yet fifty, leaves as a priceless heritage to his countrymen the example of how God-given virtues of the head and heart may be employed to the glory of God and the use of men by one who makes all things subordinate to the development of the good within him. I do not mean to be panegyrical. I mean to be just, for I would draw from this dire experience its true lesson, as that relates to our private no less than our public life.

On all these points we think together. There are not two opinions. We stand upon common ground. We shall separate and go hence, and each shall take his way. Interests shall clash; beliefs shall jar; party-spirit shall lift its horrid head and interpose to chill and cloud our better natures. That is but a condition of our being. We are mortal and we live in a free land. Out of discussion and dissention ends are shapen, we rough-hewing. In spite of us, however, occasions come which remind us that we have a country and are countrymen, which tell us we are a people bound together by many kindred ties. No matter for our quarrels. They will pass away. No matter for our mistakes. They shall be mended. But yesterday we were at war one with the other. The war is over. But yesterday we were arrayed in angry party conflict. Behold how its passions sleep in the grave with Garfield.

I am here to-day to talk to you of him, and through him, and in his memory and honor, to talk of our country. He was its Chief Magistrate, our President, representative of things common to us all, stricken down in the fullness of life and hope by wanton and aimless assassination. He fell like a martyr; he suffered like a hero; he died like a saint.

Be his grave forever and aye a trysting place for the

people, and from the sods that burst thereon to let the violets through, spring flowers of peace and love for all the people. Citizens, the flag which waves over us was his flag, and it is our flag. Soldiers, standing beneath that flag and in this armed fort of the Republic, I salute your flag and his flag reverently. It is my flag.

I thank God, and I shall teach my children to thank God, that it did not go down amid the fragments of a divided country, but that it floats to-day, though at half-mast, as a symbol of union and liberty, assuring and reassuring us that, though the heart that conceived the words be cold and the lips that uttered them be dumb, " God reigns, and the Government at Washington still lives."

THE CROWN OF MARTYRDOM.

By Rev. Henry Ward Beecher.

Delivered in Peekskill, N.Y., Sept. 23d, 1881.

A WORLD IN MOURNING.

The time will come when we shall have a right to expect from competent minds a careful and elaborate biography of President Garfield. It ill becomes us at this time, when we are all under a cloud, in deep sympathy with one another, that I should take the time in flights of fancy and in eloquent periods. This is a funeral service. We are gathered together to-night as a household would be gathered where the father had been stricken down. We are not alone in our sorrow. The world to-day mourns. Not even when Lincoln was slain was there such universal sympathy. America was then disesteemed by many, little esteemed by more, loved by few; but now no other nation commands more universal respect, and respect not for the trappings of monarchy, not for governmental display, but because she has become at once full of strength, brave, honest, and noble; and there is not an organized Government in the universal world that has not had its pulse quickened by the impending sorrow that has come upon us. Crowned heads, chief Ministers, men of Legislatures everywhere, and Parliaments, the noblest and the highest, and chiefly the noble

Queen of our Mother Country, all have taken home this sorrow into their own household and made it their own, and to-night we are one with the English speaking world; we are one with the civilized world, speaking in every tongue, but with one heart and one thought of sorrow and sympathy. The brave man has gone.

I would not say that President Garfield was endowed before all men, but he inherited the best gifts that God ever gives to man when he is born, for that which his mother bestowed upon him was a wholesome constitution, an equable temperament, and a noble example of virtue, industry, and frugality. These were as birth-gifts given to him, and he did not fritter them away. From his earliest life he has shown the one trait of high ideals and perseverance. He fought against poverty and trod it under foot. He rose from obscurity, and shone as a star. He fought against every adverse circumstance. When the country demanded that none of her sons should quail, he pressed forward, and his military history is marked with the same traits that are so conspicuous throughout his whole career; and now he that stood where mighty batteries were belching forth death on every side, and on the field where thousands of bullets were flying, has fallen beneath the single bullet of a dastardly assassin, and when he lay upon the bed of sickness, the same traits were conspicuous. He met death, and grappled with it. For a long time it looked as if he would master death. Alas! no. He was ripe. The measure of his glory had been filled to him. There was given to him, as to the illustrious Lincoln, the crown of martyrdom.

There is not a man worthy of the name that does not just as much honor the name of Garfield as if he had helped to elect him. There is no more conflict, only the calm of universal peace. I look with admiration on the man, with profound sympathy upon those who are nearest to him, but even greater admiration upon the Nation of which he was the illustrious head. He was taken as if in a moment, but nothing fell with him—no law, no practice, no institution, no interest. The vast machinery did not even stop for one single moment; every wheel in its place still went on, for the Government of the United States is the people of the United States, and no man can move or assume an authority which restricts or supplants the universal citizenship. He has left his post to another and an honored man, for whom let us invoke all sympathy from a Divine source while he takes upon himself the onerous duties that he must perform. But Garfield has ascended. We may weep for him that shall never weep another tear. We may crown our reverence with all tokens of admiration, but in the Divine presence he now stands. What would be to him the tribute of the round world when he has ringing in his ears the command of the Father to ascend higher! Sweeter than a mother's voice, sweeter than earth's most affectionate tone, is the voice of God in approval.

FOUR CONSPICUOUS NAMES.

Four names in the line of presidents will stand conspicuous in history—Washington, Jefferson, Lincoln, and Garfield. They have each been men of mark and left their impress on the National character. In the few weeks that he presided over the destinies of this people he showed the possession of yet deeper power than any had anticipated; had attracted universal attention and had given promise of the richest harvest in the after days. He had proven himself a nobleman. He had gained a name for all time— as an officer in the military service, as a member of the greatest Legislatures, as President, as a Christian gentleman, as a canonized Martyr. For him no more toil. We go on still treading the dusty path. For us are sorrows to be nobly borne; for us weariness; for us sickness, infirmity, and, by-and-by, death. These are no more for him. He walks the golden street, has thrown down the mantle of doubt and trouble, and put on the robes of grace; he has gained the rest for which we all pray; he has gone to his God. I join with you as fellow-townsmen, for Peekskill is my home. I know that it is not the scene of my chief labors, but I desire, when I am incapacitated for labor, to live here and then die among you, and I shall deem it a privilege here to-night to open my heart and let streams of sympathy flow with yours, to ponder with you on the lesson that we have that he, the hero of great or less renown, in his death his works will follow him, and that good and noble deeds never die.

GARFIELD'S GREATNESS.

[The following is the address of Henry Ward Beecher on President Garfield, delivered in Plymouth Congregational Church, Brooklyn, Sept. 25, 1881.]

THE PRAYER.

In his opening prayer, Mr. Beecher said: "Thou hast laid Thy hand heavily upon this Nation. Thy servant Thou hast taken to Thyself in a way that fills us with shame and horror. We have thanksgiving to offer in our sorrow that there is no more turmoil and torment for him, no more strife for life on a couch of suffering, that rest and eternal blessedness are finally his. We thank Thee that there has been no shock, no disorganizing of the affairs of this great Nation by this event. We believe that Thou art anointing this great people, and by this great sorrow raising us to a higher plane. For Thy handmaid, the mother, for the wife and counselor, for the children, we pour out our prayers, and beg Thee to take them into the arms of Thy consolation. Let it come it to pass that they may rest in the bosom of love of this great people; that they may be cherished and consoled. Bless Thy servant who has suddenly been called to fill an exalted station. Spare his life; defend him from harm; may he have the wisdom of God to guide his footsteps. Grant in this emergency that he may gird himself up, not in his own strength, nor in the strength of counselors, but in the strength of the Lord Jesus."

Mr. Beecher read selections from the 102d and 103d Psalms:—"I said, Oh my God, take me not away in the midst of my days." "As for man, his days are as grass; as a flower of the field, so he flourisheth. For the wind passeth over it, and it is gone; and the place thereof shall know it no more. But the mercy of the Lord is from everlasting to everlasting upon them that fear Him, and His righteousness unto children's children; to such as keep His covenant, and to those that remember his commandments to do them."

THE DISCOURSE—SHORTNESS OF LIFE.

How short is human life at the longest. We spend years in gathering knowledge, and die just as we get ready to use it. We learn how to live only to pass on. Yet we are not allowed to live even the short life allotted to man. A full life is accounted fourscore years, yet the average one is not more than twoscore. The babe grows up to maturity, but the web is broken, and man stumbles on the threshold of his usefulness. Moralists and poets have filled the world with sad strains at the shortness of life, and to-day we stand before a strange manifestation of Providence. Why is it that the good man dies, apparently in the beginning of his usefulness? Why is it that the hero to whom we pinned our faith has passed away? We had gone through the war victoriously, and had lived through reconstruction; we had fought the fight against greenback money and won; we had just entered on the skirts of our promised land, when our leader, our Joshua, was stricken down.

GARFIELD'S GREATNESS.

He was a man who united the best elements of his fellow

countrymen; he was firm, yet gentle, and in him the lion and the lamb seemed to lie down together; he was not an empty partisan, but he looked at all questions with a calm and unbiased mind; he had a love for learning, and he had acquired it by hard and incessant labor; he had been bred upon hardship and poverty, and he had lived by the sweat of his brow; moreover, he had been a preacher of righteousness. With almost the first sound of the trumpet he had gone forth to defend his country, and he earned a name as one of her leading generals. Later he entered the highest councils of the Nation, and from that time on his name was found connected with every advanced measure.

At length the Republic called Garfield to its highest office, because he was the very man for the place. Call the names of all the men honorable and useful in the courts, the army, and the navy, or in mercantile life—was there any one of them more needed than he was? Four months only he presided over the Nation, but his administration gave splendid promises of usefulness. But that bright vision has vanished. "Garfield has been shot!" flashed along the telegraph wires, and the whole world wept with his family. The drama is now ended. For weeks he lay fighting for his life. There were no more laurels to put on his brow, and God took him. After twenty years the train bore him westward. He who entered Washington four months before amid the clanging of bells and the joyous shouting of the people was borne away in silence. Such a funeral march as that was never seen. Along its route men forgot to sleep, and watched its passage at all times of the night with bowed heads and in silence. "Blessed are the dead that die in the Lord." For them there are no more burdens or sorrows. Around the burial place of this man let mothers gather with their children, to teach them to be brave and to be honest.

COMFORT IN SORROW.

But let us turn to the sublime God from these human measurements. What is time to Him? Man's life is like the bubble on the sea, which rises to the surface and gleams brightly in the sun, but only to burst. God measures all events by eternity, so that which may seem to us to be confusion is a benefit in His eyes. And so some benefit may arise to us from this disaster. Sometimes a single act may outweigh the rest of a man's life. So from Garfield's death we may gain something, although not in an exactly similar way. Washington is revered for his life, but how much more elevated his memory would have been if he had met with a tragic death for his country. Wise and gentle as our Savior's life was, His death was of much more importance. Although we hoped to reap so much from Garfield's life, we may reap even more from his death. The North and South have felt for the first time the healing balm of mutual sympathy and grief. The wounds left by the war, and not yet healed over, will be mollified. There has been no division in the Nation's sorrow, and it's whole heart has beaten together. Charleston has felt the loss as bitterly as Philadelphia, and New Orleans has been as sincere in her grief as New York. Nor have party lines divided this sympathy.

UNITY OF MANKIND.

But still more striking than the unity of the Nation in its grief has been the unity of mankind. When Lincoln was shot, the world was shocked rather than grieved. England had not yet learned wisdom, while the hands of France were still red with the blood of Mexico. But now no nation has been so obscure that it has not expressed its sorrow. From Russia and Turkey on the East to Japan on the West, there has been a common sorrow. I think that never before has the heart-blood of the world been so stirred. But if this is the first time, may it not be the last?

This sympathy had also a moral comfort. Were there ever before so many prayers offered up? The Mussulman, the Catholic, the Protestant—all prayed to God as they knew Him, and in their own formality. But did God refuse to answer them, and is prayer a fiction? In the lower sphere God gave no answer; but in the higher one He did. Is there no other answer of prayer save in continuance of life? Could we not be more fortified and strengthened by President Garfield's death than by his life? Is this not a more sublime answer to our prayers? We see people dying everywhere; but except in the case of near relations or friends we scarcely feel that death is an affliction. But why should Garfield not die? Because we looked upon him as a tree from which we should gather only good fruit? But is it not better to have its branches raised higher so that it will benefit the whole world?

INSTRUCTIVE LESSONS.

There are some lessons to be drawn from President Garfield's death, and there is one which I wish particularly ambitious young men should profit by. Our Government may be compared to a stately mansion which many are desirous of entering. Some walk boldly up to its front entrance and go in; but others seek to enter by the back way, from which all the refuse comes. By the nature of our Constitution we are obliged to send men to our legislative bodies, and sometimes the ones selected are not the most suitable persons. But we cannot bear to have the public ideal destroyed and the opinion prevail that he who would enter politics must give up his honor, and advance by ignoble means. And when we behold a man struggling honorably for a political career and equipping himself as a statesman, it is an example that honor and integrity are not incompatible with political advancement, and that man's life will be an example as Washington's has been.

In the simplicity of our habits, there has been no need of protection around our Presidents. And it is still true that public opinion, with us, is better than the guard of any European monarch. There is no sense here of wrongs inflicted upon generation after generation to stir men up to madness against their rulers. Our laws are of our own making, and can be changed. Then only a short time must pass before we are freed from the most hateful ruler. Yet our legislation is incomplete. I would not have a guard if I were the President, for I had rather take the bullet than be protected from my fellow-citizens. But an attempt on the life of a man whom we have elected as our leader, and upon whom we all rely, should be treason, and its punishment should be death. But let this be done by law. No man has any more right to assassinate Guiteau than he had to assassinate President Garfield. Let us stand for the administration of justice. When the Rebellion ceased, neither bullet, sword nor halter slew one man, and the moderation of our people impressed the whole world. And if Guiteau should die unlawfully there would be a spot upon our escutcheon. I have been angry with the miscreant, but I have obeyed the command of the Lord not to let the sun go down on my anger. Indignation has had its day; now let law have its day. I have a right to speak thus of Guiteau. He once was with us, but not of us. He sat in this sanctuary among the worshipers. Robert Burns expressed a faint hope in one of his poems that the devil might yet be turned around the corner and be saved. Let us hope that Guiteau's life will not be ended suddenly by that wanton sentiment into which you have blown a breath.

But what shall we say of that sorrowful group, Garfield's family; of the mother, whose son preceded her, and of the wife, who had shared her husband's elevation? Love needs the presence of the loved one, and chastened though she is, there is no one that needs our prayers more than she. May the blessing of God, enriched by the tears of a whole people, rest upon his children, and may his sons follow in his footsteps.

COMFORT IN SORROW.

By Robert Collyer, D.D.

Delivered in the Church of the Messiah, New York, Sept. 25, 1881.

We can meet no more as we did last Sunday, with some gleam of hope left, that a joyful word would soon come to whisper that God would give back the President to us. What we have feared so long has come upon us. Out of the midnight came the sad cry, "The President is dead." After the tossing to and fro unto the close of day the Angel came, and the gates of eternal morning opened swiftly on our midnight, and he was free from pain. Angels welcomed him as he passed through the shining portals into his final home.

There was a little ray of hope, but as I looked down upon your faces last Sunday I could only think it had burned in your hearts as in mine, to the last spark, hidden in the white embers, and nothing less than a miracle could make it kindle up again into a flame that would live day by day. In the heart of the Church and of the Nation I do not think the blow, when it did come, was so severe as we had expected, for we were doing what we have done so often when the threads of life were breaking, and at last only one is left—we saw that while there was life there was hope; but in this case, that life was death. Yet we would not admit that the pain and suffering of our President should end in dissolution, but still I think at last we came to that point that we could pray that he might be spared much suffering. He became so helpless, and there was only one way out of it, and that way prevailed.

When the news came, troubling the night and casting a shadow over the day, I think there came over us a dumb thanksgiving that the struggle was over. We watch those we love while they live in the tabernacle, and we cling to the dust when they are gone, and while they are safe in the heart of the great Divine wonder; yet we turn to the face and kiss it, because, we say, it is all we have left.

While there is some consolation in all this, it is not enough, and where shall we find enough? I confess it is as hard for me as for you to submit to the doom. We are not resigned, as he was not resigned. We may say, "God's will be done," but we cannot say that it is God's will that he should be taken from us in that infernal way, taking out the heart of the Nation and flying our banner at half-mast. It is a consolation to us not to be resigned, and when ministers in the pulpit say: "God is in all this," let us cry out: "How do you know? Where is your authority for saying so?" Garfield himself did not wish to give up the world, for three reasons. He loved his life, he loved his country, and he loved his family. He loved his life in the West, his farm, the fruits of the earth, the milk and honey, the sweet-smelling odors found about an old farm house, that aroma that comes from the fields and from the woods. He loved Ohio better than "the fields beyond the swelling flood." His love for the Nation was blended with his love for life. He was ready to work for the Nation when the bullet came. The love of country and of his life was crowned with his love of those at home. After taking the oath of office he turned and kissed his mother. With some men that would have been only clap-trap, but in him it was taking the sacrament. All were proud of him. How he battled against death for their sakes! The heart could not be broken as the body was, for he loved his life and his country, and above all his home, and for their sakes wished to live. Let evil work its worst, it could not slay the heart.

Another spring of consolation comes from the tokens of sympathy and good will which came pouring in as he slowly sank into the grave. If all this had been revealed to him—that the old smoldering fires of resentment between North and South, between England and America, were being quenched by the tears of sympathy for him and his family—would he not have welcomed his death? Another intimation of consolation arises from the fact that the Nation will now inquire after the root of this evil, and will search out the cause. The problem is no longer how shall we govern, but how shall we govern ourselves, and must our President be destroyed in doing this?

There is consolence for his widow in that he is waiting and watching for her; for his children, in that in the future their father will be spoken of and placed among the names of Washington and Lincoln. Had he served out his term he would probably have made mistakes, for a weary time was waiting for him, and our ex-Presidents do not get much praise. Our hopes were that fairer days were in store for him; but he has gone to fairer days above.

OUR GOOD PRESIDENT.

By Hon. Emery A. Storrs.

Delivered in the First M. E. Church, Chicago, Sept. 25, 1881.

Be sure, my friends, I am entirely conscious of the impossibility of giving anything like adequate expression to that great sorrow which weighs upon your hearts, and upon the hearts of 50,000,000 of people to-night. I know that no language that I can possibly employ—I know, indeed, that no language that falls short of inspiration in its character—could fittingly tell the grief in which this great people is involved. Never since we have been a people—never, indeed, since this world has had a history—has there been a mourning so universal, a grief so deep, and so profoundly sincere; and how tame and weak, in the presence of such a sorrow, which weighs upon the hearts of all our people like lead, how tame and weak, I say, mere words seem, to voice and to give it expression! I shall not voice your feelings to-night if I speak of the great dead merely as the dead President. I shall not voice your sorrows to-night if I speak of the martyred President as the noble husband, as the patriotic citizen, and as one filling high station, as the great statesman, as the devoted Christian. Not all these combined would fill the requisition which you would make upon him to whom you look for the expression of

(83)

your sorrow and your grief; but to all these must be added, and every sentence must be deeply freighted with words of kindliest personal regard and expressions of tenderest personal friendship.

I wish to supplement what your pastor has said. The Christian Churches do not merely honor the memory of President Garfield because he believed in the Bible, in which you believe and I believe, nor because he believed in that blessed Savior in whom you believe and I believe. It honors him, not merely that he was a believer, nor merely because he was a preacher of its doctrine, but it honors him above all things and beyond all things because in the lowliest station and in the highest station, in his daily walk and conversation, he illustrated the majestic truths of the Bible in which he believed, and the divine character of the blessed Savior whose example he followed.

What is there that makes this mourning so universal? The whole world is filled with it, and during these long, sad, dreadful, weary weeks through which we have passed, Gen. Garfield has come to be something more than our President. He has been enshrined in every home, and folded with an infinite loving tenderness into every heart. Tottering old age has left its corner, prattling childhood has abandoned its sports, to inquire, "How is the dear, good President to-day?" And prayers, and hopes, and fears have filled all the atmosphere, and enveloped us like it, until at last the dreadful shock came; and the mighty sob, heard all over the continent, which is carried all around the globe, and in which every civilized people have joined, teaches us the blessed truth of the universal brotherhood and humanity of man.

I cannot speak alone to-night of Gen. Garfield as President of the United States. I cannot speak of him merely as legislator. I cannot speak of him, if I fitly express our feelings, as Senator, or as Congressman, or as statesman, or as politician, or as lawyer, or as citizen. I must speak of him in a connection dearer than all else to me. When I think of him there comes rushing back upon my mind the memory of these past years; and let me, my good friends, lay at your feet to-night, poor as it may be, the tribute of one who loved him tenderly and well.

Gen. Garfield made the whole circuit of our noblest and best American life. He described it all. He suffered and he rejoiced. He strove and he succeeded. He tried and he failed like all the rest of us. Disappointments, triumphs—all these checkered his splendid life as we look back upon it as a completed whole; but the marvelous feature of that life seems to me to be after all, as we look upon it now, its wonderful and its absolutely perfect naturalness.

He never reached a position that he did n't seem naturally to fill. He never achieved a single elevation that did not seem to be so thoroughly due to him. He never aspired—in its vain, mean sense—to place, but place came to him. No man in all this broad land is any poorer to-day for what James A. Garfield has been. No ambitious man in all this continent is any lower to-day because of the splendid heights which James A. Garfield reached. He entertained no rancors toward a single human being. And when their hearts were probed, no single human being held a rancor against James A. Garfield. He never despised a living creature, and no living creature ever contemned him. He never harmed a human being, and, but for the one, no human being would ever have wittingly harmed James A. Garfield. He never selfishly stood in any human being's way, and when great bodies of men disagreed, hundreds and thousands of human beings got out of his way, and asked him to stand up higher.

A little more than one year ago, in a great convention—

the grandest in some of its aspects the world has ever witnessed—we strove and strove, day after day, and day after day, each one pursuing his own choice and his own ambition, but when the final end came, James A. Garfield had offended no man, James A. Garfield had wounded no one, and when the rushing tide came, every heart in that great body and this great Nation said Amen. In the contests of his own State the word "contest" ceased, and there was no contest. In the conflicts of the legislative forum the word "conflict" ceased to have a meaning, and there was no conflict. There was no bitterness in his heart, and there was never slander on his tongue.

You may search the record of that pure and spotless life, and all through it you cannot find one unkind or one ungenerous word uttered of a human being. My friends, challenge your memories. How bright and spotless will this simple record some of these days become, growing from the ground up, suffering with the people, of the people, sympathies quick for the people; of towering, and I might almost have said of a colossal, but a noble ambition. Assailed as but very few men have been assailed, yet his gentleness and his nobility disarmed them all, and the slanders of his enemies fell harmless and worthless at his feet.

Pursue his career in his own State. How marvelous it seems to be to-day, and how natural. The school boy, the teacher, the preacher, the soldier, as brave as he was modest and as modest as he was brave. His soul, his life itself, as he periled it, he held in slight esteem when the honor of his Nation was involved. He knew not what fear was; but of all the pities that angels ever felt, none were softer and tenderer than that of James A. Garfield for a vanquished foe. And thus everybody came to love him; thus it is that everybody does love him; thus it is that through all the homes, on every hillside, in every valley of this great land, there is no spot in which the memory of our dear dead President is not enshrined as the most sacred and blessed among all their possessions.

I have said how natural his life was—how easy was its flow. There were no leaps; there were no sudden advances. There was nothing theatric nor dramatic in his manner. It was one day of honest, earnest, patriotic well doing, following right along after the other, in as noiseless and as beautiful a succession as, under the hands of the Almighty, the seasons make their courses as the ages roll on. This is our dead President. I have said to you that above and beyond all the honor that I have for him in every department of life that he has filled, there is something that comes much nearer my heart when I remember him as I have seen him. I know how simple the story of reminiscence must be, and I know that no eulogy is so fitly or so expressively spoken as the simple language of the simple days that great men have lived. During the last campaign I met the General, as we all called him, again and again. From the day that he received the nomination here at Chicago I never saw him look, and I never heard him express a doubt—not a whisper nor a suggestion of a doubt. I never heard him make an unkind criticism, although I did hear him again and again and repeatedly insist upon it that whatever the result might be no man in all this Union would be so thoroughly satisfied with it as himself, provided every man beneath the flag, high or low, rich or poor, black or white, should vote precisely what he thought, and that his vote should be counted as it was cast.

I remember meeting him at Mentor. I think I shall never forget that. Reaching Cleveland just upon the eve of the election in Ohio, thoroughly fatigued, in some way or other Gen. Garfield had learned that I was almost disabled for further exertion, and there came into my room late that night, or rather about two o'clock in the morning, a dispatch from the General, saying that I must go down to Mentor in the morning, and so down to Mentor I went. We had heard the news from Maine. You know how bad it was—how discouraging it was. I met him at the station, and a cheerier, heartier, breezier man, it seemed to me, I never met in all my life. I went to his home with him, and we talked a little of politics, but very little. He had been reading Burke, and he took down a volume of Burke in his library, and called my attention to one or two of those splendid passages of his, in one of which—and I shall always remember it—occurred the wise expression: "He who accuses all mankind as being guilty of corruption is sure to convict but one." How wise, the General said, this was, and how well it would be could the captious fault-finders of the country thoroughly appreciate what that greatest and most substantial of all reformers said. And so we spent the day, talking over the campaign, looking through his books, going about his farm—talking less of politics, a great deal less, than of literature; and the time came when I must go, for I was to speak that night at Cleveland, and he got out that good, old, honest, country horse of his, as honest and plain as his owner, and drove me to the station. I remember his speaking of what his friends had done for him, the time they had spent, and the earnestness that they exhibited; and putting his arms around my shoulder, and calling me by my first name, he said: "I should be guilty of the greatest ingratitude—I know I never can do it—I must always remember what through all this country all these people have done."

I saw our poor President again not until April, calling upon him, of course, immediately upon my arrival in Wasnington, as it was my pleasure and my duty to do.

There was no opportunity whatever for conversation. He asked me to come to the White House that night, and of course I went; but there was no talk of politics. Senators were there, and other people who took his attention, and we simply talked of his pictures; but again, at his request, I went. His wife was in New York; his mother was there. He asked me to lunch, and I spent three hours with him that day, almost alone. Nobody, indeed, came in, except Dr. Baxter, of whose name you have heard so much. As we were about half through with our conversation, Dr. Baxter came in, and the President complained of difficulty with his head, pain in the back of his neck, and said that he was feverish. Dr. Baxter looked at him, and the President passed out. A little alarmed, I asked the Doctor what was the matter—if there was anything the matter with the spine, or anything of that sort. He said, "No, not the slightest; the poor man has been absolutely run over, beseiged unto death almost by seekers after office. All he wants is quiet and rest, and," said Dr. Baxter, "he is good for fifty years."

Some allusion has been made to it here, and almost the first thing that he said, I remember, as we got into the library, was his utter disgust for that part of his official duties—utter and complete. He looked it, and he felt it. He threw up his hands as he spoke in a sort of despair, and he said: "When can I ever get rid of this? How insignificant it all seems to me to be!" And then, sitting down, he said: "You know we are something alike in one respect—we like a stupendous debate on some question of doctrine, have it settled, shake hands and make up, and go along and settle another question. But these dreadful things, it seems to me, never will be settled." "Why," I said, "Mr. President, I am not as good a mannered man as you are, I am not as gentle a man as you are. You have asked me to talk to you quite plainly. Why don't you disperse this mob?" He said: "How can it be done?" I said: "Divide it into seven parts. You have seven members of your Cabinet. Divide the mob up into seven parts, and if there is danger of one-seventh of the mob killing any of your Cabinet officers, have them hire help, and have subdivisions all the way down until it is one at a time, if it is necessary for your relief." And so we went all over the field of politics. There were a great many troubles in the political sky at that time. I am not going to talk about them now, but I will tell you how gently and affectionately he spoke of everybody.

There was not a man who was considered his enemy at that time that he did not speak of him in the gentlest and most affectionate terms. And I told him what a gentleman whom he had supposed was at enmity with him, had said about him—some kind, pleasant word. I said to him: "Mr. President, I am not here, it is no part of my mission, to tell you disagreeable things, but I want to tell you what Senator so-and-so said to me no longer ago than yesterday —a good, kind, manly recognition of your qualities"—and he was as pleased and delighted at it as a boy; and he spoke of the same Senator words freighted with good feeling, and of those who were supposed to be in hostility to him, mentioning them by name. Not one single syllable dropped from his lips that I did not feel it a most exquisite pleasure to convey to the men concerning whom he had spoken.

And again and again I saw him. I can't recall it all. It would take all night if I undertook to do it. I never can describe to you the exquisitely friendly manner that he had. Those who have ever known Gen. Garfield loved him as you would love a wife, as you would love a daughter. It was not a mere feeling of admiration. It was a feeling of deep, intense personal affection and regard.

And the idea that he could do anything that was wittingly unjust seemed to me to be utterly impossible.. Knowing the man as I did, seeing him as I have, I don't think, so conspicuously free, and clear, and honest was his nature, that it would have been possible for James A. Garfield to have done an unjust thing if he had tried. I recall the day when the children of Washington had a festival; and I remember it now because it was one of the little events worth while recollecting, while I was in Washington. Some notes were brought in to him from the children, asking that they might be allowed to roll their eggs on the White-House lawn. It is a great festival day in Washington, and a custom peculiar, I think, to Washington alone. There were a great many notes, and they were answered in the President's charming manner. And when we went into the library and got a view of the lawn—it slopes very gently, as those who have been there will remember—there seemed to be thousands of children engaged in that curious sport of rolling eggs down the lawn; and there was no child there half so delighted, half so charmed, with the sport as the dear, good President, who had opened the White-House grounds for the innocent play of the day. And there he was so burdened with all these tremendous cares.

But let me say one thing more. It was perfectly clear to my mind, notwithstanding all this gentleness of demeanor, notwithstanding all this tenderness of feeling for friend and for foe, that, when the President had finally made up his mind as to what was the fitting and the proper course for him to pursue, he was going to adhere to it undeviatingly and unswervingly unto the end. When I left him I had no mistake about it. I was in no sort of doubt. I knew that certain things would be done. I knew perfectly well that certain things would not be done. There was no anger about it. It was a feeling infinitely loftier and holier than anger. There was no passion whatsoever in it. He made up his mind on those grave questions without compassion. I think I can say it truthfully—he was almost absolutely impersonal. I had known him for years, but the iron strength of that solid resolution down in his soul, and encysted with that tenderness of spirit, never exhibited itself to me before as it did that day.

And so the days went on, and he was President. I know we talked; he delighted as a boy over the wonderful reception that his Administration had met in its opening days from the people, and he compared it to a great ship. He said: "How splendid it seemed. A crew faithful to the last, the winds all favoring, the skies all clear, triumphal music sounding upon its white and stainless decks, floats from the shore," and he said, "and it would be some honor, out in the depths of the ocean, smitten by storm and enveloped by seas, to go down gurgling to the bottom; but," he says, "we cannot afford to be stranded in the bay. The ship must go out to sea." And I know that his wish was—it was the solid prayer of his heart every hour—that the great party of which he was the head—the elected and the selected head—and which he believed was the custodian for the years to come of the priceless treasure of free government among men—might rule the country; but he loved the great Nation better than he loved the party. He was in no sense a factionist, and never could be. He loved the party because he believed its existence was indispensable for the prosperity of the country, and, to secure it, he would have sunk party faction—all other interests—deeper than ever plummet sounded, if it became necessary.

And thus, my friends, it comes to pass again that the sorrow over the death of our good President comes from no section of the country. The grief is the same everywhere; the skies are as black South as they are North;

homes are stricken there as they are here; for they of the South know that that noble heart never throbbed that it did not pulse with love for the whole Union. They knew that while he wanted no solid South, he wanted no solid North. He wanted a great, splendid, God-fearing, prosperous and happy Nation. They knew that he would make them prosperous if they would but let him. Hardly a week had flown by when every man in the South, no matter how deeply in his heart rankled the bitterness of the old time, knew that if he had no friend elsewhere, he had in the President of the United States a friend upon whose wise counsels he could always rely. There was no laboring man in all this great land who toiled and sweated for daily subsistence, that did not know the President was his friend. There was no scholar struggling to a higher life and a clearer light, that did not know that Garfield was his friend, and sympathized with him. There was no statesman, looking for a broader and holier statesmanship, that did not know that he had a friend in the President of the United States. There was no oppressed and stricken man anywhere, whose rights the law failed to vindicate, that did not know that he could appeal to the great head of a great Nation, and that his prayer would be heard. There was not in all the South a cabin so low or a swamp so desolate, where the disfranchised citizen might be driven to escape from unrelenting foes, but that he knew that no matter how low his whisper, or how weak his cry, the quick ear of the President of the United States would be sure to catch them both. Thus the whole land loved him. Leaving the mighty cares which he had assumed, leaving the burden of this stupendous responsibility, with his past career illumined all the way with light, this good husband, this kind father, this brave soldier, this patriotic citizen, this profound scholar, this great statesman, this modest man, this true and faithful friend, turned his back upon his official place and power, and sought the college of his old days.

There is mixed with this dreadful bereavement something in the nature of a calamity, a feeling of utter shame and humiliation, that among all these 50,000,000 of people one miscreant heart could be found that would conceive, and one villain hand could be found that would execute, his death. Wounded unto death, they carried him back; and since these days there is not a home in all this land that has not had the spirit and presence of the poor suffering and wounded President within it. How we have watched through the days and through the nights, and and how the first thought, as dawn has broken upon us, was, "How has the President passed the night?" and the last prayer that we have uttered as we have sunk upon our couch was that the good President, the head of our great Nation, might rest sweetly and safely through the night! There is nothing, my friends, in all the history of this world half so tearful or half so sad. The world has never before witnessed anything like it; and if the spirit of these fifty millions of people could have taken bodily form and shape there, they would have been seen, with the angels from Heaven, hovering over the bed of pain of our dear President, from which, during all these hours of sore anguish and sorrow, there never came one complaint.

How dear he is to us, for the tender words that upon that dying bed he has uttered! No reproach has escaped his lips. He has watched his own life fast ebbing away. Taken from the malarious atmosphere of the Capitol, borne by the sounding sea, with his eyes resting upon its billows, there the life of the good President "went out with the tide." In these last hours that came to him, his poor, wrecked, shattered, and benumbed body, be sure, felt no pain. All agonies had ceased, all sufferings and sorrows had closed, and before that pure heart and across it the past seemed to swim like a hurrying vision. Back it carried him to the old school days—there was no reproach and no stain there; back to the early triumphs of his boyhood—there was no reproach there; back to his budding ambition—there was no shame nor dishonor there; back to the time when, feeling the honor of the land he loved so much assailed, he periled his life that the land he loved so much might know no dishonor—there was no discredit there; back to his long and splendid record as a legislator—no dishonor there; back to the achievement of the loftiest ambitions of earth—there was neither spot, nor blemish, nor any such thing there. The old memories of the old time filled his soul as if the sunshine coming from the throne of the eternal God had blazed all over it and the future lifted to our President—that future into which he soon went—and there, be sure, like the telegraphic message that runs from the heart of every living creature to the throne and bosom of the Eternal God, he heard that welcome, "Well done, good and faithful servant; enter into the joy of thy Lord."

The pinions of unseen angels bore him there, and there, this night, robed in spotless white and surrounded by the great of all the ages, stands our President and our friend, raining benedictions upon us who are mourning for him.

In the presence of such a sorrow, which is not unaccompanied with a holy and an almost ecstatic joy, how weak is the talk of party, and how mean the cry of faction! Standing by the open grave of this noble citizen and this patriot President, we may say: Hush strife and quarrel over this solemn scene. Enemies no longer, friends forever; and, linked hand in hand, take a solemn vow together that in that grave shall be buried all of bitterness and all of party hate. Over that pure life there shall come a penetrating perfume which shall, you may be sure, float all around the globe, and intoxicate every other nation with the hope of liberty.

Our good President is dead! The fires of his earthly tabernacle are all burned out, but burning with a clear, white light, we shall place the memory of that pure life, like a beacon light, upon the headlands of this world's history in all the ages to come.

My good friends, the very fact that throughout all our great land, in such halls as this, and under such sacred influences as these millions are this night gathered, would almost reconcile us to our mighty bereavement. The past of James A. Garfield is secure. No domestic enemy nor foreign foe can ever hurt him more. His memory is ours. His fame is ours, and I would take it to my heart and treasure it as the most priceless jewel in all our earthly possessions: Patriot, citizen, Christian gentleman, President, friend! All that we can say is, our hearts sound his dirges, God bless his name, and—farewell!

GARFIELD'S LIFE AND DEATH.

By Hon. R. Stockett Mathews.

Delivered at the Memorial Services in Grace M. E. Church, Baltimore, Sept. 26, 1881.

Over all the better portions of the vast earth the wisest and best of mankind are mourning as never before for the death of only one of the unnumbered millions of our race. Peasant and prince, kings and queens, hewers of wood and drawers of water, as well as the leaders of thought and discovery and progress, are turning their eyes towards the new continent and its young Republic with unaffected sorrow, almost as keen, well nigh as profound as our own.

Never before has just such an existence passed through so many picturesque phases to an ending so pathetically tragic, so violent, so appalling. He was the son of a widow, born in a cabin; he fell from that station which the citizens of the United States are wont to deem the zenith of earthly ambition, while the plaintive monody of grief which flows from the stricken heart of the Nation is repeated and echoed again and again, until its reverberations traverse the circumference of our planet, and return to mingle with the still fresh lamentations on our farthest shores. He possessed so many attractive qualities of personal character, united with so many and such varied capabilities for usefulness and distinction, that in the calamity of his death, the consolations of memory, as we ponder on what he was, and has achieved, are impotent to soothe the anguish of a thousand ungratified hopes, when we try darkly to foreshadow what he might have been and done. Nature and culture, each at its best, were to be seen in his full development, joining the graciousness of an even, unselfish temperament to the tender strength of constant affections, the generous enthusiasms of a large and liberal soul, with every grace, refinement and fascination of speech and manner which could be acquired by the pursuit of the noblest objects and familiarity with the most elevating books. "The two noblest things, which are sweetness and light," says Dean Swift; and of them, the man—the magistrate who has gone—had more than ample share, mingling in such harmony that while one deplores the perishing of the statesman by the ignoble hand of an assassin, one renders the homage of a genuine grief, of a stunning sadness, for which tears are only the eloquence to the son, the husband, the father, whose virtues have ennobled humanity in our own eyes.

It is an inspiration, as we contemplate his public course of a single score of years, not so much to emulate his intellectual attainments, or to take pattern after his eminent performances, but to become such as he was to those nearest to him, by the fireside, in the library—to fit ourselves to be trusted and respected as he was. Gentleness of disposition, a heart luminous with joy and manly cheerfulness, are potent to win and hold the attachments of all with whom we have to do. After all, to be able to forge the enduring bonds which are made fast and strong by the affinities of taste and sympathy and feeling, and to come back from toil or sacrifices or leadership into the privacy of the enchanting home, where love is master of all feasts and ceremonies, and genuine friends, however few, gather about us—this is, indeed, the richest compensation for every endeavor; the charm and unchanging delight of the highest form of life. It is because he shone conspicuous for these social and domestic attributes; because he had such a simple, symmetrical human personality that his taking-off, "a deed without a name," appeals with such pitiful intensity to all our better emotions, and we are not guilty of weakness when we weep over him, either in solitude or with the multitude.

Only a little while ago (here the speaker paused for a moment, and resuming, said:) I had written thus far, and nothing more, when the realization of the tremendous loss to which our people and all posterity have so suddenly been subjected came over me, and with it, in mental procession all its possible, saddest consequences, conjured by no willing imagination, I was forced to lay aside my pen and wait until I should come into the presence of an audience whose faith and prayers might drive the unwelcome visions from my thoughts. Only a little while ago—it seems as if we could reach the day by simply putting out our hands towards the invisible calendar—Washington beheld such a pageant as it had never witnessed in all preceding time.

Only a little while ago a young man, in the fullness of his physical bloom and beauty, who had not yet reached the ripeness and maturity of his transcendent intellect, stood in the presence of thousands of his admiring fellow citizens—the Chief Justice of the Supreme Court before him, Senators and Representatives of the Nation around him; just by his side the mother who had borne and raised him, and had carried him through privation and poverty; the wife whose gentle nature had tempered his own to a richer fineness, at his right hand. And when he had repeated the great oath, that he would see that the Republic should suffer no detriment, and it had been carried up to be recorded for all eternity, his first act of thanksgiving, of recognition to the instruments which had been most powerful in the moulding and the fashioning of his character, and the inspiration and the guidance of his career—his first act was to turn and kiss the woman whose lips had taught him the Lord's Prayer, and then the woman from whose lips he had drawn the first sweet baptism of that love which surpasses every rapture known on earth. And then he began this brief administration of the few months in which, with almost startling suddenness, he revealed to our people new qualities which are possible to public men; moral courage that was absolutely inflexible, a superiority to malign counsels and untoward influences, that would not for a moment permit him to stoop to any concession beneath the dignity of the Executive prerogative, although by dalliance or temporizing he might have bought peace and quiet for himself.

His secretary of the treasury, whose ability and long training are supplemented by the sound and accurate views of his superior, went on to finish that great act—of funding the national debt—which has made the students of finance in other States marvel beyond expression at the lessons of statesmanship which are being taught in our own, and everywhere, from Maine to California, from Oregon to Florida, although hosts of those who were seeking the substantial rewards for political activity went crowding to the capitol, this man of such extraordinary self-poise and self-reliance dismissed them by the thousand, remitted them to their dwellings, and was the first of our rulers for many successive administrations to announce as the guiding principle of his own, that no man should be disturbed in a subordinate office, so long as he was capable, honest, and faithful, until the end of his term expired, and even then his claims, his merits should be considered as fully and as conscientiously as those of others who might be applicants for the same place. And if he had done nothing else in his brief life, a moiety of which had been devoted to public service, he would have left a memory to the American people imperishable, precious, and which no coming man can eclipse.

Who was this hero? The bells of St. Paul's Cathedral of London speak with their resounding tongues, and the canons and prebendaries of the Cathedral, at Liverpool, are telling to our English-speaking kindred on the other side something of the sorrow which is being felt for our loss. In the villages, in the universities, and in the capital of Germany, the name which has been so frequently on our lips, is now pronounced as softly and as lovingly as in our own commonwealth. The English court is in mourning, the Spanish court is in mourning, while the recent republic of France sends to us, by the mouths of its President, its leaders, its statesmen, its great men, assurances of their sympathy and their grief. Even in the mosques of Constantinople, the Moslems are forgetting to bend their knees to the setting sun, are forgetting to lift up their alleluias to the Prophet, and are uttering benisons for the dead ruler of the free people of the United States. Was there ever, since the world begun, such another event as this? No distance so great, no people so far removed, no civilization so alien, no religion so restricting, no partition, no artificial barrier of any kind, sufficient to restrain the whole world from bending toward us, and bowing their heads in a sorrow that is unutterable, and craving for us a deliverance from its dreadful results, which can only come from the King of Kings and Lord of Lords. Oh, if the issues of life and death are ordained by a blind, fortuitous fate, how wretched are we to-day!

But, thank God, they are in the hands of a benignant and intelligent Providence, working out by grand laws His primeval scheme, throwing the whole majesty and grandeur of His sublime nature into the upward and onward progress of our race. We know that unless the mission of our Republic is ended, unless free institutions have fulfilled their predestined end, that the God who brought us into existence will still continue by His own laws, by His own purposes, antedating prehistoric ages—that he will yet bring us up to the fullness and the roundness of a career glorious in its objects, and that the death of General Garfield will be the advent of a new epoch and the beginning of a new era of better, wiser, farther-reaching, more salutary statesmanship.

It is one of the peculiar features of free institutions that no boy, however humble his birth, however narrow and confining the circumstances by which he may be surrounded, need fear that there is any insuperable necessity for his remaining in obscurity. To be able to lift up one's eyes and see the shining portal of the Temple of Fame; to be able to long for the strength to climb up to it, and the courage to enter it, constitute, after all, the best birthright; and the boy who has felt stirring within him the yearning to be something and to do something, has already half conquered the world. And if he act persistently and undeviatingly up to that aspiration, turning neither to the right to listen to the siren song of vice, nor to the left to satisfy mere sordid or mercenary impulses, but devotes himself to a life-work of nobility and utility, and keeping before him the great maxims and the great principles from whose motive power men gather pluck to reach high places and do grand things—before he has counted his half century he will be lifted to the top, and standing on the very loftiest heights of possibility and opportunity, turn and ask the world to look at him as the actual product of free institutions, and to behold in his career what may be accomplished by a freeman, with greater facility and assurance, than in those countries in which rank and caste, high associations and importunate influences are requisite to a brilliant service in the halls of Parliament or Assembly.

I would like to be able to tell you just how it was, and when it was, that he whose name I need not mention, whose image has melted into every soul, first came to realize that there was within himself something that the majority do not feel throbbing for recognition—a perceptibility and impression, ability, a capacity for the acquisition of knowledge, for the assimilation of truth, a perseverance of purpose, and willingness to deny himself, a readiness to submit to any privation that would only clothe and equip him with the mystic enginery of art and science, and of all the teachings of the great and good, until he could go out full and efficient and ready to take his place among men, and to assert his right to reputation, to become a "leader in the files of time."

It is not at close proximity between the tow-path of the canal and the Executive mansion. Long as is the physical distance between Lake Erie and Washington, the moral and intellectual stadia which he had to pass over were longer still; and yet it took but twenty years for him to travel the whole distance—and reach a place for which he did not intrigue or bargain, by any mean, illegitimate artifice or self-seeking.'

And when you remember from what low estate he started, and where he stood in modesty and docility only a few years ago, and what he became through the legitimate outgrowth of his own systematic and methodical use of those functions and capacities, aided, of course, and fructified by what he gained from contact with the world, it is seen that, given a sound heart, an honest disposition, not much more than ordinary faculties—that is, the seemingly ordinary faculties of childhood—and then by keeping at it all the time; by burning the midnight lamp; by the education of oneself to the perception of the invisible ends of life, to the intangible compensations, to things that cannot be transmuted into gold, or place, or position, for the time being; by an apprenticeship to high ideas; by working up to noble ideals little by little, hour by hour, year by year, and by never turning aside from them, he can at last reach the topmost height—be a man of mark; and, what is better still, he can do beneficent things, can by reason of his position, speak grand and assuring words of statesmanship into the ear of the universe.

Twenty years—think of it! Fatherless son of a poor widow; laborer; canal-boy; chopping wood at twenty-five cents a cord; mowing down the green grass of the meadows for fifty cents an acre; carpenter—a rough carpenter—hewing out the green logs of the forest to make the humble homes of the farmers in that far-off wilderness; student in a district school; certified teacher of those who had been his playmates and companions; scholar, neophyte in college, graduate, professor of languages, president of a college, running through the curriculum of humanities; Senator in the State Senate; at twenty-nine lieutenant-colonel of a regiment of volunteers, one whole company of which was composed of students who had sat under his teaching, and were willing to go out to death with him, if need be; helmsman of his own boat through forty-eight hours of peril, when no experienced pilot could be found to guide it through the rapids of a swollen river, to bear the needed succor to his beleaguered camp; steering it with a hand as firm and an eye as clear as though he were sitting here in the tranquillity of this sacred edifice; driving a leader more accomplished and perhaps more subtle than himself from his mountain fastnesses, and winning the first thrilling, magnetic victory of the war for the Union; then detached to join General Rosecrans as Chief-of-Staff, and acting with him until the fateful battle of Chickamauga, and then, when the right wing of the army under the Commander-in-Chief was pierced and disheveled and dissipated, made his way alone back through fleeing ranks, through brake and briar and forest, for eight miles, until he reached General Thomas, who was still fighting with an unbroken front against outnumbering legions, and aiding to hurl back their impetuous assaults until with his own hands he assisted General Granger to give the parting fusilade of artillery, which rang out triumphantly and told that the awful combat had closed with night and victory, and that new lustre had been shed upon the loyal troops; then, at thirty-one, a major-general; then a representative for six successive terms in the lower house of Congress; then a Senator-elect, and then President of the United States, in the forty-ninth year of his age. O beautiful youth! O grand and vigorous manhood!

Coming up from such an origin to take the coronation of a simple oath, and stand upon a level with kings and emperors by the suffrages of a free people—by the intelligent suffrages of a free people—for the vote which crowned him as chief ruler was the aggregate expression of the best conscience and intelligence of our Nation—never before did any candidate enter the White House more palpably and undeniably by the deliberate action and discriminating intelligence of the best classes of American communities. Here is a climax which surpasses the fables of heroes, the legends of ancient mythology. Here is an ascent which beggars description and impoverishes language.

I challenge you who are most conversant with the biographies of the great men of other ages and latitudes to find me a parallel with this almost marvelous rise to exalted station. Is it to be wondered at, that now, when he has suddenly disappeared from the theatre of the world's activities, that he has suddenly perished by the stroke of a reptile—whom it would be dignifying to call a monster? Is it wonderful that now, when all his acquisitions, all his attainments, all his varied and affluent scholarship, all his grand and rare traits of character, all that he was and might have been, are thus suddenly blotted out? Is it wonderful that our tears are flowing like rivers of water? Is it wonderful that this loss causes such an outpouring of inexpressible pain, that when it fully strikes us with its overwhelming force, in vain, in vain, almost, we call upon our faith in God, and ask Him as some surcease of sorrow, to vouchsafe us some medicament for this poignant woe. And yet, and yet, my friends, this terrible death may, after all be, we all hope, we all trust, we all would fain believe, that it may prove a great blessing to us, and to the generations yet to come.

We need this blessing. We need a benediction from heaven, for "all we like sheep have gone astray." We none of us are entirely guiltless in the sight of the great dispenser of good and ill, of our brother's blood.

If we had all been true, each and every one of us, high and low, to our duties of citizenship from our earliest youth to the present day; if we had been lending our energies to fashion virile public opinion and to mould robust public sentiment; if we had not lent ourselves to augment the rancor of parties and increased the hateful spirit of faction; if we had not perverted our privileges and stood silently by, time and again, acquiescent, passive, content to witness the elevation to power of men simply because they were glib-talkers; to see our whole elective system surrendered to the administration of "managers" and of "bosses;" if we had not been so long too willing to see unworthy representatives in

Congress; if we had always demanded that only delegates with cultivation and pure hands, of scholarly tastes, men who would be capable of devising additional advantages in our government, who could not only construe past laws, but introduce innovations by better statutes to remedy deficiencies in our jurisprudence, and make more homogeneous and symmetrical our civil polities, and beautify, and adorn, and enlarge all our institutions until they should be to their ultimate perfections and possibilities of good, this evil which has befallen us would not, could not, have happened; if we had not made idols of wood, and clay, and brass; if we had not been lured by mere orators who possessed something of dramatic force and the cunning chicane to please the ears of the multitude on the hustings; if we had not stood silently by and seen men working out their selfish schemes, and building before our very eyes what is called the "machine," whose wheels, howsoever well oiled, grated upon our ears; if we had not been subservient to intolerant, imperious, dictatorial politicians, who made their combinations expressly for the purpose of putting some one in the chief seat of authority who would promote their personal greed and interest; if every one had spoken through the press what ought to have been said of these things, or had called our fellow-citizens into town-meetings to reprobate pernicious methods for the profitable instructions and admonition of such false leaders; if we had sought to exalt the standards of citizenship, had stood upon the outposts and had cried aloud against our own dereliction and degeneracy—this fell, foul deed would not have occurred. For James A. Garfield has surely fallen a victim to the hate and intolerance of a single faction, whose heated denunciations, falling upon the distempered brain of that miserable dastard in the jail at Washington, impelled him to slay the conspicuous opponent of such methods and practices, as surely as Henri Quartre was a martyr to the Protestant opposition to the Jesuits, and was slain by the fanatical hand of Revaillac.

Just as in olden times another impious hand fired the Temple of Ephesus, that he might through such a conflagration inherit undying fame. Is it nothing that the great and good Ruler has given us such a country; has made us the heirs to such a Constitution and laws; has bestowed upon us, through the instrumentality of our forefathers, such franchises and opportunities; such rights to happiness, both individual and national? Do we not owe something in return to God for what He has made this land?

Are we to take all we see as matters of course in our daily life, such as are dew and sunshine and starlight, the early and the latter rain? Are we to look on and negligently behold so many mischiefs—to see great corporations rising to overshadow and corrupt legislation, traversing our land with continuous lines, and compelling the highways of commerce to become the mere agencies for speculation and the amassment of colossal fortunes, controlling our statesmanship, and binding and loosing statutes to suit their exigencies, and raise no voice to arrest them? Do we owe nothing of service and effort to Him and to the future to rightly use our liberties, and restrain their use within proper limits? Ought we not to cease to be indifferent to everything but party names and discipline, and resist and overthrow the spirit of faction?—that, taught by the terrible lesson of this untimely death, shocked by the appalling shedding of this innocent blood, which seems to have been sprinkled upon every door-post of every house in the land, that we should become only citizens and patriots, straining our utmost to fulfill every loyal obligation and responsibility?

If these solemn needs are apprehended, these warning lessons are appropriated by us, then our great and good President will not have died in vain. If they be not learned, it will be long indeed before heaven will vouchsafe such another to adorn private life and give brighter radiance to public station.

I consider the life of James A. Garfield—viewed either from its open or its private standpoint—the most perfect which has been lived in our century. I know of no man to-day in our land who is his equal. Nor is this a new opinion of mine. It is no fresh estimate, beaten out by the hand of the destroyer; it is no mere sentimentality which has come with the pangs of a crushing sorrow. On more than one occasion during the last canvass—I presume that, without immodesty, I may say it—I had the honor to address some of the largest audiences which gathered in this country. Twenty-seven times during last autumn I was permitted to stand before audiences, the least of which did not number less than twenty-five hundred people, and the burden of all my song, the theme of my warmest advocacy, was the personal life and character of the noble gentleman who was the candidate of the Republican party. I studied then the campaign biographies, in his speeches, in his essays, in the maxims of wisdom which had fallen from his lips.

I remember when I first saw him, eighteen years ago this November, on the platform of a meeting at Monument Square, and heard him presented to the people as the "brave General Garfield, fresh from the Army of the Tennessee." I was permitted to pass with him the whole of the evening on the Thursday in June before he went with Mrs. Garfield to Long Branch. I knew how absolutely frank and sincere he was—how straightforward and direct; what beautiful docility he united with firmness of will; what balance of judicial mind he had; that, although his perceptions were usually quick, his meditative faculties were equally as operative, and that the two sets worked in perfect poises; how that what he saw or thought passed into the chamber of judgment, and was chrystalized there before it came forth either in word or act; how that he was full of feeling and thought—an honest man, a Christian statesman, a perfectly upright politician. Some of you may smile when I give such a prefix to such absurd words—Christian politician, Christian statesman. Are they numerous? And yet, here was a man who never doubted the divine origin of the Christian system, the Atonement, the vicarious sacrifice of the founder, the inspiration of the Scriptures, the existence of a hereafter, of a future life, to which he looked forward always as to the time and place for the future development of his own character.

He turned aside from skepticism, from doubts and subtleties, from materialism, from positiveism, pantheism—believing with all the tenacity, all the persistency of his cultivated intellect, in one God, omnipotent and omnipresent, holding the ocean in the hollow of His hand and giving to the stars their courses. When science revealed to him distant spaces and new planets, and the myriad, multiform, sentient life of earth, and the stratifications which were being builded until the globe became a habitat of human beings, he only deepened in his reverence for the works of God, and enlarged his comprehension of the laws of creation.

Mr. Mathews then drew a graphic picture of the student life of the President, his ardent thirst for knowledge, and familiarity with great books, from Homer and Aristotle to Shakspeare, Bacon, Burke and Tennyson. He quoted the opinions of Lord Macaulay as to the value of learning even in the subordinates of a civil service, and said that he had been better accomplished for his grand work than any of his predecessors.

He then made a fervent appeal to his audience to put themselves into full correspondence with the spirit of the occasion, saying that there is darkness upon the land in spite of its sunshine. No man can tell what the next day may bring forth. The dropped curtain has upon it no clear landscape of hope. Let us, with thanksgiving for the manifold blessings of Heaven—with humiliation for our own shortcomings—trust that the day of our destiny is not over, the star of our fate not declined. I am no pessimist, no alarmist. We own ourselves citizens of a splendid nation; we boast that our children shall be heirs of a grand future; we say that ours is the only real Republic that has ever existed—that those of Greece and Rome, and Italy in the Middle Ages, were only phantoms when compared with our greater and freer institutions. Let us see that we do our best to preserve and perpetuate, to adorn and magnify the costly fabric of our liberties. I have already detained you beyond the proprieties of this occasion. It remains for me to say only a few words. I have spoken of the man—the public servant—in his life and work.

I come now to speak of the dying hero. I think that when every one comes to lie down to die, the example which he has left of fortitude will give us greater calmness with which to look the grim conqueror of all men in the face. Oh! what a glorious chamber that was at Washington or Elberon. No complaining, but resignation, manifested hour by hour, as the feeble strength and flickering were ebbing away so slowly, so slowly. You remember he asked the physicians when first wounded, "What are the chances?" And when Dr. Bliss replied, "But one in a thousand," the President responded, "We'll take that chance." The bitterness of death had passed to him when he parted from his wife to go into the war. It is a singular thing that during all the weary agony of his prolonged suffering, so little appreciated, because even the surgeons were ignorant of the cruel work done by the bullet, and that it was imbedded in a net-work of nerves, he never once mentioned the name of his assassin, but once, and then only in a single sentence, to express his utter inability to comprehend the provocation for his act. We think of his unfailing courtesy, of his unfaltering fortitude, of his patient heroism—of the smile which lighted his face when Mrs. Garfield came to him as heroic as he from her rapid journey from Long Branch; of his great affection for her—the last letter to his mother when he was almost on the brink of the beyond—all these things touch us too deeply for anything but tears. He has become now the subject for the historian. If of foreign nations, we know what the verdict of history would be, for foreigners have already published their admiration of the symmetry of his character, the lovely completeness of his private life.

And now he is sleeping beneath the fresh mold of the grave in Lakeview Cemetry. We have not seen the slow pace of the mournful procession; we have not heard the soft dirge of its march nor the requiem which has spoken peace to his slumbers. We have not stood by the open sepulchre' but I am not sure that many of you have not been sitting here, but in spirit listening only to sobs of breaking hearts around that memorable tomb. I seem myself to have been listening for the far-off articulation of that tender sorrow which friends and kindred, and children, wife and mother, will pour out above him. Dead! All his greatness has perished. His heart beats neither for his love nor his country. Well may we say, "What shadows we are! what shadows we pursue! Vanity of vanities; all is vanity!", Nay; not so. Such a life is never finished. He has added to the store of human knowledge. There is another lustrous name emblazoned upon the rolls of fame; another grand figure for monumental marble and bronze; another splendid example for the young to follow, for the older to emulate;

another great type of courage, of heroic endeavor and unenvied success. Dead, but living! Living forevermore to speak down the corridors of time and call the lowly to honor, the brave to victory, the pure in heart to the kingdom of this present life, and of the world to come.

8

IN MEMORIAM.

By Chas. F. Buck, Esq.

Orator of the day at the Memorial Service in New Orleans, La., Sept. 26, 1881.

It was one of nature's holidays. Calm and peaceful, resplendantly brilliant, rose the bright "monarch of day" on the 2nd of July, 1881, over a happy and peaceful country. There had been no "ominous tidings of mishap," no "lamentings heard in the air," nor prophesying with accents terrible—

"Of dire combustion and confused events."

Fifty millions of people went, rejoicing, to pursue their usual avocations. They compose the greatest nation known in the history of human development. They are a nation of rulers—of sovereign equals, governed only by the laws of their own making. From time to time they choose a worthy citizen of their number who must put the laws in operation and see them executed. He represents the executive sovereignty of the people. The man exalted to that station is honored above all mortals. The sceptre swayed by the chance of inheritance is a tinseled nothing, not worth the birth-right of the humblest American citizen; then how much greater than all is he, the chosen sovereign of a nation of sovereigns.

In the course of the appointed time such an one had just been singled out. There had been a fierce contest of opposition claimants, embittered by memories of the past; differences of the present, fears and misgivings for the future. But the will of the majority is the choice of all, and the successful candidate of a party becomes president of the people. James Abram Garfield, who now lies still in death, of the State of Ohio, candidate of the Republican party, received a majority of all the votes cast for President of the United States in the electoral college, and on the 4th of March, 1881, was installed in the duties of his high office. The grim asperities of conflict had already smoothed their "wrinkled front." The new President himself had said: "If there ever was a people on the earth who had reason to be tired and weary, to the bone and heart, of political contention, the bitterness of party malice, and all the evils that can be suffered from partisanship, it is the afflicted American people." And the people were tired of it all, "to the bone and heart."

The repose and quiet which followed the conquest, was the verdict of universal acquiescence. The chasm which divided the people was rapidly closing, making a smooth and common level for all to stand on. The soul of the chief-elect was full of the grandeur of this consummation. In his inaugural address he predicts that it will surely come. He appeals to the people with eloquence of tender entreaty. "Why should it not be now?" Let us recall what he says in this connection right here: "As countrymen we do not now differ in our judgment concerning the controversies of past generations, and fifty years hence our children will not be divided in their opinions concerning our controversies. They will surely bless their fathers and their fathers' God that the Union was preserved, that slavery was overthrown, and that both races were made equal before the law. We may hasten or we may retard, but we cannot prevent, final reconciliation. It is not possible for us now to make a truce with time by anticipating and accepting its inevitable verdict. Enterprises of highest importance to our moral and material well-being invite us, and offer ample scope for the employment of our best powers. Let our people, leaving behind them the battle-fields of dead issues, move forward, and, in the strength of liberty and restored union, win the grander victories of peace." Noble words; inspiration of the spirit of peace which hovers over the mounds where molder the bones of slain freemen. They went straight to the hearts of the people, because the people were ready for the day "of honorable reconciliation and peace," and the people throughout the land were happy and contented.

They accepted the inauguration of Mr. Garfield as the completion of the civil revolution which followed upon the revolution of arms, and as the commencement of the era of perfect pacification. The President had proclaimed himself the apostle of this new Union, and all honored him for it and all trusted him; no, not all: History is tragedy; the characters, peoples, the motive power of the action, the spirits of good and evil, out of the conflict of which the fate of the actors evolves itself. An infatuation, born of the spirits of evil, which destroy and build not up, possesses the brain and faculties of a being of flesh and blood like ourselves, with feet to walk upon, erect, in the image of God—it sounds like blasphemy to say so—and arms and hands to do his wicked will—an infatuation to kill the President of the United States in times of perfect peace. He follows the doomed man like his destiny. He is diabolical, cold and relentless as fate. He sees his victim in the peace of his home where he is happy, making others happy; the sight of it for the moment turns him from his purpose. Sophistry of the fiend! He is toying with his prey. He relaxes not his terrible design. He only defers its execution. He sees the doomed man at his devotions in the house of God, and thinks he will do it there. But no, the hour had not yet come. The dark shadow of destiny lurked, but struck not; but it never wavered in its purpose. The day came. It was decreed in heaven.

The mortal part of James A. Garfield was doomed to martyrdom and death. Two acts in the trilogy of the nation's trials had been concluded. The first—the conflict of blood—ended with the death of Abraham Lincoln; the second—the strife of the passions—closed on the inauguration of Garfield; the third—the expiation—begins with the sacrifice of the Apostle of Peace, whose soul had become the incarnation of the spirit of a better future. "The stars had said it." Twice the angels of mercy palsied the murderous hand; twice the conscious power of innocent and noble manhood awed the coward from his aim. But it was not to be. A third time the spirits of evil move their wicked instrument to his dark design. The victim is wholly unconscious of the shadow at his side. His soul is elated with the joy of a supreme happiness. He has rendered well the first duties of his high call. The seeds of a harvest of peace and plenty had been sown. Garfield felt himself the Chief Magistrate of a happy and united people.

He surveys his work and sees that it is good, and rejoices in it. He seeks respite from his labors; the father and the husband claim their natural due. He is on his way from the Halls of Power to enjoy his peace in the shrine of domestic love. At the fatal railway station, the cares of Government behind him, the consciousness of duty well done with him, the prospect of naught but what is good and beautiful to him, the President of the United States had reached the height of human happiness and glory.

> "Alas! the gods oft grudge what they have given
> And ne'er unmixed with grief has heaven
> It's joys on mortals shed."

In the moment of this supreme consummation of the toils of a life, the dark shadow of evil at his side became the avenging Nemesis of Fate, jealous of the happiness of men. The "unexpected" happened. Out of the clear sky of that bright and peaceful 2d of July, fell the thunderbolt. The assassin-instrument fulfilled his awful mission.

By noon on that ever memorable day the lightning messenger had spread the sad news over the civilized world. The President of the United States has been shot! Consternation filled the hearts of men and pallor blanched their cheeks. Was it treason, was it conspiracy, was it domestic broil? Thank God, no! It was the act of a madman; and by its fruits we shall know it is the decree of a Providence, working out after its own merciful manner the destiny of nations. "The blood of the martyr is the seed of the Church." "On the drenched graves of the battle-fields bloom the attributes of a great and free people."

Death was not instantaneous; the victim lingered between life and death for 78 long and painful days. Let us draw a veil over that weary struggle. It almost made one "waver in his faith" that the prayers of a nation availed naught; that fortitude, and patience, and resignation availed naught; that love and devotion availed naught. Agony and suffering were not even spared; yea, they seemed to overfill the fullest measure of woe that human flesh can bear. It shrunk and wasted from day to day, but the spirit kept its throne in all the grandeur of divine descent. "I cannot understand how I am so weak when I look so well." It continued to waste and waste away under the very hands of ministering love, till nothing remained but the coarse outer frame of "mortal coil" through which flowed no longer blood enough to warm the heart within; then the spirit took its flight, and the sacrifice was complete. The President was dead—dead by the assassin's bullet—and the

Nation is in tears! Sorrow for the dead is hallowed by sympathy with the living; a loving husband, a noble father, a faithful son, lies in death, lost to his dear ones, because he was President of the United States! That is the crime for which he died. Justice of Destiny, pardon us in our ignorance if we understand not the fitness of thy decree, and the people feel that he died for them, and so they mourn and honor him and make amends to his bereft.

James Abram Garfield was an extraordinary man of extraordinary career, and—fate, though cruel, remained true to him to the last—extraordinary in his death. Heroes have lived and died in all ages; great and good men have gone before, whose work still abides and bears fruit; excelling genius and intellect have reared pre-eminent and lasting monuments ere this, but the annals of recorded time furnish no parallel so comprehensive, so rounded and complete, as the life and death of President Garfield. Poets will delight to exalt, and statesmen, historians and philosophers pause to moralize on this singular life long after the generation which has witnessed his death shall have passed away. Garfield's life is the epitome of the struggle of mankind.

He came into the world with nothing but the privileges and attributes which he brought from his Creator. He left it at the topmost round of human glory—a character moulded to perfection in the school of adversity, through which he attained his eminence.

It becomes a part of my task, even at the risk of wearying you, not, I hope, by the subject, but I fear by my inability to do it justice, to review as briefly as I can the main incidents in the life and services of the honored dead to whose mortal remains we are now offering the last sad tribute of recognition and respect.

James Abram Garfield was born on the 19th day of December, 1831, in the township of Orange, Cuyahoga county, northeastern Ohio. His father, Abram Garfield, bought eighty acres of uncleared land in the midst of a forest, miles away from the habitations of men. On this he erected a log hut, about twenty by thirty feet, of the most primitive simplicity. Such was the birthplace of the President whose death the people mourn to-day, whose memory is honored by the world. The family consisted of six—the parents and four children. When James was two years old, the father died, and left the mother with four orphaned children, the oldest of whom, Thomas, was about nine years old. The 80 acres of land had not been paid for in full, and the mother sold 50 to get out of debt. This was the beginning. It is as memorable for the sacrifice which turned it onward and upward as for its lowliness. The widow knew privation and poverty were her lot and the lot of her elder children. Eliza Ballou, still living, mother of Garfield, is of the family of a heroic and gifted Huguenot, who fled from France after the revocation of the Edict of Nantes. Her love and her hopes centered on her youngest son. He, at least, shall be a man among citizen-men. He must be lifted out of the stagnation of isolated life to a sphere of action where prizes are gained and victories achieved. The elder brother gave himself up to this sweet fancy and offered himself, that James might go forward. This was the sacrifice. Cheerfully he followed his humble lot; he was content to be a tailor, a hewer of wood and a drawer of water, if only his young brother could be fitted for a better destiny.

That is the most instructive period of the deceased's career, which commenced when his brother led him by the hand to the country school, and ended when at the age of twenty-five years he graduated at Williams College. He worked his way through poverty and privation, but the end was ever clear to his mind. The struggles of to-day gave momentum to the effort of to-morrow; "character is a perfectly educated will," some one has said. Up to the age of 16 or 17 years, Garfield showed nothing extraordinary in his being, except that independence and individuality of will, without which no one ever became great. But his application had been desultory and his pursuits unsteady.

A strange fancy possessed him to adopt a seafaring life. It must have been the outgrowth of that indefinite yearning which compels great souls in that transition struggle from the vagaries of youth to the concentration of their faculties on some settled purpose. It ended by him becoming a canal-boat driver, of which he was cured by an accident which so nearly cost him his life that his escape seemed a miracle to him. He returned to his mother, whom he found in the silence of the night offering prayers by the fire-light for her wandering son. From that moment his character was formed, his "will was perfectly educated." He knew exactly what he wanted, and to resolve was to succeed. He set his heart on graduating in an Eastern college. He believed in thorough education as a great civilizer of nations and the maker of men. He had heard and read that Wellington said the battle of Waterloo was planned in the shades of Eaton College. The reasons he gave for selecting an Eastern college are characteristic. "Having always lived in the West, I think it will make me more liberal both in my religious and general views and sentiments to go into a new circle where I shall be under new influences." How he paid his way is known to all, partly by aid of kind friends, partly by the earnings of his labor at odd hours, and serving as janitor at the College.

In 1856, after his graduation, he became teacher of Latin and Greek at Hiram Institute. He soon became principal, and while so occupied in 1858, married the noble woman who is to-day the Nation's widow; all her greatness and glory and happiness shrunk into the cold and withered form of a murdered husband. At Hiram Institute, Garfield laid the foundation for that oratory, which gave him such readiness and command on all occasions. He lectured to the school extemporaneously, several times every week on history, literary or scientific subjects. Some time before this, he had written to a brother teacher, "Tell me, Burke, do you not feel a spirit stirring within you that longs to know, to do and to dare; to hold converse with the great world of thought, and hold before you some high and noble object to which the vigor of your mind and the strength of your arm may be given? Do you not have longings such as these which you breathe to no one, and which you feel must be heeded or you will pass through life unsatisfied and regretful? I am sure you have these, and they will forever cling around your heart, until you obey their mandate. They are the voices of that nature which God has given you, and which, when obeyed, will bless you and your fellow-men."

A man so gifted by nature and so perfected by study and reflection could not content himself with the professor's chair. The opening ambition of his life was accomplished; he was armed and equipped for the real struggle in which honor and distinction are won. This second period of his life he entered with an even chance, and soon distanced competition.

In 1859 he was elected a member of the State Senate of Ohio. When Lincoln's call for seventy-five thousand men was read, in the midst of clamor and confusion, he jumped to his feet and moved that twenty thousand troops and three millions of dollars be voted as the quota of Ohio. I refer to this to show a characteristic of his mind, the faculty to see and do the right thing at the right time, which is genius. He rose with every occasion, and mastered the situation at every turn. While preparing for his departure with his regiment he writes: "I have had a curious interest in watching the process, in my own mind, by which the fabric of my life is being demolished and reconstructed, to meet the new condition of affairs."

His military career was brief but brilliant. He rose rapidly to the rank of Major-General. He had but few opportunities of action, but whatever he did was done with the clearness of precision and self-reliance of the firm leader. There was inspiration in everything he touched. The mind's perception was clear and penetrating; the action that followed overwhelming and complete.

In 1863, while on duty with the armies of the North, he was elected to Congress by the Nineteenth District of Ohio. He did not leave the army until satisfied by the assurances of superior officers and the request of President Lincoln that he could do so with honor.

On the 4th of December, 1863, he took his seat in the House of Representatives, 32 years old, the youngest member of the House—as he had been the youngest general in the army, and the youngest member of the Ohio Legislature—after struggling twenty-five years of his life to gain an even start with his fellow-men.

The history of his congressional life is beyond the scope of this occasion. Nor will I attempt to describe his oratory. In this generation, when perhaps hundreds of thousands are living who have felt the power of his mind as it flowed a living current from his own lips, it would be folly on my part to repeat at second-hand the traditions of eye-witnesses. This I know, that clearness and precision and firmness never forsook him; that he acquired a confidence in his own judgment, which he always followed, not because he could not believe himself to be wrong, but because he made it a canon of his life's faith to please his own conscience above all other things or persons.

During all this time in Congress he was an advocate and leader to that policy of reconstruction of the Republican party, the scope and effect of which are well known. In the heat of discussion and the passion of reports, sharp and stinging words might sometimes cross his lips; but at the bottom of all he said or did was a stratum of justice and the image of liberty and equal rights. Uncompromising in his fealty to republican ideas, he never lost an opportunity to draw his hearers to the beauty of peace and the promise of reconciliation.

In 1875, during a bitter discussion on a motion to restore Jefferson Davis to the right of citizenship, he said:

"Mr. Speaker, I close as I began. Toward those men who gallantly fought us on the field, I cherish the kindest feelings. I feel a sincere reverence for the soldierly qualities they displayed on many a well-fought battle-field. I hope the day will come when their swords and ours will be crossed over many a doorway of our children, who will remember the glory of their ancestors with pride. The high qualities displayed in that conflict now belong to the whole Nation.

"Let them be consecrated to the Union, and its future peace and glory. I shall hail that consecration as a pledge and symbol of our perpetuity."

PAYING BONDS IN GREENBACKS.

Let one utterance suffice to illustrate the strength of his convictions on this subject. He had been absent in Europe. The Republican party of Ohio had been swept into "the greenback current," and had adopted a platform looking to the payment of bonds in greenbacks. He was told that there was no stemming the torrent. An indiscreet word might cost him the nomination. He returned to Ohio, attended a reception and was called upon to make a speech —and he said:

"Much as I value your opinions, I here denounce this theory that has worked its way into this State as dishonest, unwise and unpatriotic; and if I were offered a nomination and election for my natural life, from this district, on this platform, I should spurn it. If you should ever raise the question of re-nominating me, let it be understood."

One word more on Garfield's relations to the great questions of legislation which engaged the attention of Congress. I would not be just to the memory of the dead if I did not recall his position on the great financial problems. From the moment he entered Congress he foresaw the difficulties which were likely to come and he set himself to work to master the subject in advance. He reduced it to the simplicity of maxims: Pay your honest debts with honest money; paper money you may issue, but let your paper dollar be a certificate of actual value, convertible at the pleasure of the holder into a fixed amount of 'royal coin.' 'Fiat' paper money is a delusion and a snare; the more you issue the more you need, because the more there is of it the more worthless it gets. You can have my services only on the ground of the honest payment of this debt and these bonds, in coin, according to the letter and spirit of the contract."

In person the deceased is described as a model of perfect manhood. Of commanding stature and energetic mien, strong in repose, vehement in action; his moral nature was lofty as his intellect was grand. The grasp of his hand was strong and his heart was warm. His domestic life was pure and holy. He revered his mother with the devotion of a faith; he loved her, not as a child loves the parents, but the parents the child, for in the course of years he had become the stronger and she was his care as he had been hers.

His household was simplicity and faith and confidence and love. With small as with great things he carries the magnetism of genius and the presence of inspiration. It is his which has electrified the people of his country. This universal outpouring of sympathy and mourning, this grief so deep, so real, that men feel it but speak it not; this spontaneous consecration in fifty million human hearts to a fame, and a love, and a glory hallowed and undying; is it a false sentiment, a fancy of the moment? No, it is real, as it will be everlasting. It comes not from us alone, it springs from our hearts in response to the divinity that rediates from the manifestations of a soul grand in all the attributes which make man Godlike.

His strange, eventful life, with its struggles, its purities, its devotion, its success and its sacrifice, is a national possession and a national heritage. May its teachings be also a national blessing.

It remains for us to make it so. The President died because his mission was Peace. Let the object of the assassin be thwarted. By the memory of your sacred dead, consecrate yourselves to that Peace which he promised—the new Union which he foresaw—the new destiny of a re-united people. And when it is attained let the Nation rear a monument to Harmony and Concord, and on it inscribe in letters of everlasting gold, "Sprung from the blood of the predestined James Abram Garfield, Martyr President." Accursed be the generation that forgets the sacrifice; this is the sentence pronounced by the Justice of his country on his assassination.

"THE MAN OF HIS TIME.

By Phillips Brooks, D.D.

Delivered in Trinity Church, Boston, Sept. 25, 1881.

The events, thoughts and recollections of the time are those which we have never before brought into our church; they have given a color and tone to our service that is wholly unique. In every household that is closely united there will always be some days that stand apart in its history; there will be days that never came before, and that will never come again. If the Nation be a household, as it is, so there will be days for it also that will stand absolutely apart.

It is impossible now that one should not feel the sentiments, the thoughts, the mingling of intense sadness with the consciousness of nobleness that has filled these last days. All that we can do to-day is to come together to talk with one another of the common grief, to think together of the man whom God has called to Himself, and to look forward to the mercy that He has for all.

The President of the United States is dead at the hand of an assassin—not by one sudden blow, but after long weeks of watching and of painful alternations of hope and despair. He is gone; his death is something new in the history of America; it stands by itself; let us think of it as loving our President who is gone and God who has thus manifested Himself to him and to us. He has been and always will be ours; he is ours in a peculiar sense; we have for him a special feeling of familiarity. His life covered the last half century, and as we look back over those fifty years, I think we all feel that there have been no fifty years in the history of our country or of the world in which it has been such a privilege to live. The best characteristics of men have been called forth; the world has never seemed to have so noble a future before it; in attaining that future the life that has just ended here has had no inconspicuous part.

We cannot but let our minds run back, this morning, over the life of President Garfield. When he reached active manhood the national crime of slavery was just beginning to emerge into the necessary activity by which it was to be crushed out. He was on the side of the anti-slavery cause. He lived just too late to be one of those noble men who, when that cause seemed hopeless, lifted up their voices and declared this country must be free. In the year in which the war broke out he was 30 years old; it was impossible that such a man should not be in the service of his country. He was a brave soldier who left the army to strengthen it from the floor of Congress. He was identified with the drafts, with the emancipation of the black men, with the opinion that the liberated slave must be a citizen. By-and-by, when the war was stopped, there came other associations. The South was to be educated and reconciled, the financial obligations of the country were to be honored and redeemed. There has been no large cause in all the fifteen years since the war in which the heart of Garfield was not interested, and for the support of which his voice was not heard. We all know the story of his election, the history of his short administration, the dreadful manner of his death. What shall we say of his life and character?

In the first place, we cannot but remember how truly he was a man of his time. He recognized what was the next thing to be done. His recognition of what God was doing, and, therefore, of what a servant of God should be doing, is a striking feature in his history. Faithful to human freedom, loyal to the Union, faithful to the honesty of the country, insistent upon the purity of the Government, and determined that it should not be in the interest of a few but in that of the whole people—standing before all these issues, he quailed before none of them. With that record he stands in history glorified, indeed, by the death he has died, but having his real claim to fame in his eloquent, earnest, unswerving allegiance through all his life to these causes.

It is necessary that we should look not simply at this public life, but at the personal characteristics of the man. Think how the people have been studying him; think how through the closed door of his sick chamber they have studied him and understood him as scarcely anybody else has been understood. His intellectual life seems to have been singularly interesting. If there has been in the country any intellectual history that is thoroughly symmetrical it is this. He combined to a marvelous degree the practical and the philosophical.

There has been no man of affairs who so understood the philosophy underlying the things that lay about him. That is the secret of the power that made his intellectual life strong in the nation. There is also something beautiful about his moral life. He was not spared from temptation, but he has shown that it is possible for a man to live among us and be preserved from yielding to temptation. In the life of Garfield there was a positive devotion that saved him from those temptations under which his brethren, with broken reputations, were tumbling about him.

9

Then there came his social nature. It was genuine; it was the unsought utterance of his love. If he had gone on to old age he would always have gathered others around him to receive from him lessons of the past. He had a cordial sympathy with humanity, which showed itself in a friendly way to those who came in contact with him, and so those who were near him most loved him most. This is the highest eulogy of a man who led both a public and a private life.

Around him was a life of culture and refinement. He carried into the field with him a copy of Horace; he stole away from dull and unimportant debates in Congress into the library to dip into the rich wells of English literature. That meant enlargement and refinement of life. His thought was as fine as a woman's and as strong as that of a man. He was shaping the destiny of the Nation and of the world; his reputation, therefore, is not hard to account for.

And there is something else—the deep religiousness of President Garfield, with a profound honor for God, with a sincere love for Jesus Christ. Having united himself early in life with one of the simplest and smallest, but one of the most earnest and true religious denominations in our land, of it he lived an obedient servant of Jesus Christ. That religion was always present with him. The man who loved God and knew God has gone to God. These are characteristics of him; as we run over them we see they are not those of brilliant deeds. No man can tell when he began to be famous—when the country began to trust him as it did. Is there nothing noble in a reputation like this, standing before the world, made up of characteristics of admirable humanity—a reputation that is a combination in their mightiest proportion of those things which all true men strive for? He trusted and believed in his countrymen and in the world; there was shown the great power that enabled him to use all the characteristics of that life that has just been ended.

If one could stand now before the young men of America—those of the country rich only in their intellectual and moral attainments and possibilities, those of the cities paralyzed by the material riches they have not won—what would one want to put before them but the character of James A. Garfield? Let them know that in this Nation in which God has set their lives any man may run the road of truth and honor. Let them know from this life that it is possible to live in public life and to be honest; that where subtlety is futile, simplicity is great; that the country has called a straightforward man to its Presidential chair. Every man may be true, brave, earnest and simple; his country will honor him, and if it does not make him President, his influence will be felt through all time and will be for lasting good.

I have talked of Mr. Garfield as if he had passed away from us by some common fate. The dreadful tragedy that has closed that life, has caused a revelation of his character that otherwise might have been unseen except by the eye of God. The Nation grows strong by great sorrows. It has been stimulated by the struggle with the great Rebellion, by the slaying of that other President; it must be that it has something else of which to rid itself, that this life should be laid down to raise us up. This sorrow will leave for us a great fame and reputation in the land; it is a great thing for a nation to have one more man set in its pantheon. When we assemble to-morrow at the hour when the President's remains are laid in the ground, we should remember what his soul is doing; we should remember the influence with which he goes forth into the history of the country; we should remember the vast and unknown, but fascinating service into which he goes as the child of God. To-day let us sit around his coffin and say one to another, "He was faithful unto death." God has given unto him the crown of life. May God give us each the same faith and the same reward.

A NATION MOURNS.

By Ex-Gov. C. K. Davis.

Delivered at the Memorial Services in St. Paul, Minn., Sept. 26, 1881.

A NATION mourns to-day. A people goes with slow and measured steps through streets made sombre with the trappings of woe, under funeral arches, to the measures of disconsolate music, wailing its farewell lamentations, to bury and to praise—

"——the ruins of the noblest man
That ever lived in the tide of times."

The world is darkened to us. The designs of Providence move to their appointed ends through so vast an orbit that we cannot see through our tears the season of fruitage from such a desolation as that which this eclipse has caused. We somehow feel as if our very institutions are tainted by complicity with this monstrous crime, and are accessaries to it, and that the whole responsibility cannot be bounded by the nature of the vulgar murderer whose hand has drawn a pall over the land. It is as if some ancient fate, working to its ends through the agencies of innocence and guilt alike, had fulfilled a remorseless destiny and smitten down the dynasty of free government, while, like the chorus of some classic tragedy, a people chants the words of comfortless mourning. All are here. The laborer, the scholar, to whom no like catastrophe is told by history, the statesmen saddening over the fact that within twenty years two presidents have been murdered the business man, the woman, and the little child, wide-eyed with wonder and with grief—all are here to mourn.

The sermon, the eulogy, the dirge, the threnody will end, and the dead President will pass into history, with all his human faults atoned for, by his sacrifice. History often falsely sees the character of a man through the adit of such a death, for there is no prospective so distorting. It is probable that Garfield will always stand in this illusory and scenic light, and it is well, perhaps, for the force of example, that this should be so. Death teaches no finer precepts than are taught by the lives and death of men who, good and pure, and dedicated apparently to the consummation of a great career, are thus brought down untimely. It was so with him. He had finished no career. He had not fallen the leader of any disastrous political measure. He had been conspicuous, though not pre-eminent, in the press of political leadership. That he was capable to do all that men more self-assertive aspired to do every one knew. Still it was felt for years that he had at no time put forth all his strength. Upon all questions of statesmanship he stood in the van of the most advanced thought. Upon the fleeting questions of the hour, those mere expediences of the moment, he was seldom heard to speak.

He seemed to be a man in preparation and ripening slowly for the performance of some great, ultimate duty, which should surpass the daily tasks of other men, however well performed, and thus round out that crescent life to an orb of never fading light. But this was not to be. He has been stayed in his course. All hope of success or dread of failure is at an end, and we are free to consider the example of what this man might have become. From earliest life he was an assiduous student, and thus became next perhaps to the younger Adams, the most variously instructed man of all our presidents. It is exemplary to know the wide range of his studies. The classics had modeled his mind to antique simplicity and beauty of proportion. No speaker of English, on either side of the ocean, was his superior in the command of its resources. Whatever was to be known of the operation of those political forces of conservation or destruction which in all ages work upon all governments he knew. He was a student both diverse and minute. He was graced with the adornments of literature as well as armored in its panoply.

It was peculiar to this man that all he knew he knew how to use. He played many parts and received a plaudit in all. He had been a laborer with his hands, a college president, a theologian, a soldier, and a statesman. Each vocation was but a process in constructing the perfected man, and now that all externals have been taken away and the work has ended, we can see an edifice of such manhood, so widely spread, so spacious and so high that there are few such in the realm of history. The natural elements of the man were plainly discernible through the pellucid simplicity of his character. His perception of duty was clear, and his tendency to its performance was a moral gravitation.

He doubtless had great ambition, but it was to noble ends; it was the ambition which honors seek and which runs not after honors. Ready to serve but not self-serving, would be an appropriate motto for the man. He was not that padded statesman, too well known in our day, made up of newspaper commendations. Nor can any taint be found in his career of that dastardly self-promotion which wins its infamous way over the destruction of other men—that caitiff envy which spends its malignant force in the despoilment of larger and better natures. His logical processes seldom consisted in scholastic ability of deduction, but instinctive sense and exposition of the true relation of facts and situations to principals. They were constructive, selective and analogical, and the result was that his conclusions and the ways by which he reached them, argued for themselves as a perfect piece of architecture does.

This cursory estimate of this scholar, soldier and statesman would be imperfect if it failed to recognize an endowment which he had, and which is rarely possessed by men of affairs. He was endowed with the imaginative faculty to an extent unequalled by an American statesman. It was subtle, far seeing, and brought into correlative relations things most remote and diverse. The tributary forces of his scholarship were therefore always at his command, and the result was a wealth of illustrative power in which he resembled Edmund Burke. Who will ever forget the sentence which fell from his lips upon the tumultuary convention at Chicago: "But I remember it is not the billows, but the calm level of the sea, from which all heights and depths are measured." And that convention, measuring its duty from that standard, chose the man who doubtless represented best the calm level of popular thought. With his accession to the presidency an exceeding peace spread over the nation. Prosperity opened all her garners. It seemed as if our years of trial were past and gone, and that under the rule of this large-natured, generous man, the Saturnian days had come again.

But in a moment all was changed. The President, who by constitution and action, was showing himself to be an antagonist to every corroding political evil of the times, who combined the virtues of our best statesmen with the endowments of the ripe learning by which States are made great and governed well, was shot down by a disappointed office-seeker in the capital of the Nation. It was a brutal murder, like those assassinations which mark the annals of every corrupt state when office and plunder become the controlling forces of administration.

It becomes us at this moment, when sorrow makes every mind capable of instruction, to learn the lesson of the hour. For sometimes nations can be taught only by calamity, and this instructor cites us before her now. We must raise our processes of popular government to a higher plane, through reforms deep and permanent, or we are but at the beginning of calamities like this. It is the instruction of all time that when a government becomes personal, when it becomes merely the instrument of personal aggrandizement through few or many offices, corruption and violence strike hands together for its destruction. Since the foundation of this government three political murders have been committed, and the victim in every instance has been the personal exponent of what was best in public sentiment, killed by one of whom what was worst, had taken full possession.

Harrison, Lincoln and Garfield, each in their time represented the elements of thought which tended best toward our national greatness and perpetuity. Do not misunderstand me as alluding here to any of those temporary and incidental distinctions in the workings of American thought which have the name of party. The occasion and the fact prohibit this. I mean to say that these were men whose abounding love of country had wedded them to principles which rose above the fleeting party distinctions of the hour, and whose duty and love it was to place our institutions on a more lasting basis than mere party sentiment ever can. Each of these great men was a victim to the personal politics which preceded and disgraced their times.

These evils have debauched the public conscience for many years. The strife to get office, to retain office, or to dispossess from office, is the master passion of our politics. Our statesmen have become too often mere leaders of a personal following, who fight in the hope of reward. Our politics consist in mean advantages, in disreputable practices, in the use of men, in the assassination of character, and the enjoyment of office. For many years not one distinctive political issue has stirred the stagnant, rotting level of our political life. This lust and self-seeking for office has become the pyæmia of our system, and, predict recovery as we may, the patient is dying of political assassination.

The shot which has laid our hopes so low could never have been fired in the better times of the Republic. We have our duty to gather to our hearts the bloody instructions of our loss. Death has left us this to do. It grasped Garfield's noble heart and it is stilled forever, never more to beat high in triumphant anticipation of a country made greater and better by his powers. It trod the chambers of that massive brain and thought, and the soul left their earthly palace to live eternal in the heavens in a house not made with hands. It smote with its "petrific mace" that manly form, and it ceased to be the tabernacle of life. It is a sight to call up prophets to walk the land crying wo! wo! to all who live therein, for the evangelist of murder has come. Who could believe that here where schools abound, here where all men are free, here where religion teaches from more than ten thousand pulpits the lessons of heaven to earth, here where the awful sword and the righteous scales of justice are suspended high and untarnished over all, where thought and speech are free, that the fountain of official life could be changed to a pool of blood?

The genius of free government mourns over her slaughtered son. She calls up from the hells of history the assassins of past times for an excuse and parallel, but she finds none. They say, cite us not—we struck at evils when we struck at men; and she says as she gathers the ashes of Lincoln and of Garfield, and lays them reverently in the everlasting urn of history: "O, my children, it is you who have made possible these acts! The lessons which I taught you, you have forgotten! You are depraved with pride, lust for power, wicked ambitions, hatred, malice and all uncharitableness, and here is the bloody end. Unto your care, O people, I committed my choicest son from the sweet security of domestic life and set him to rule over you. He was gifted with the learning of ages; whatever was taught by the records of the ancient republic, or of later times, he knew for you.

"The love of country burned in that stainless heart like an altar flame; in him the North forgot its rancor, and the South its defeat. Charity ministered at his side with her sweetest works; prosperity was spreading over you like summer over a sterile land; all was well except your own rancorous hearts, and it is thus ye give him back! Listen, while I repeat the lesson which you must learn to live. States sink beneath the tide of time, not alone under the foreign invader, nor under the usurping ruler; nor under the debauched church, nor under providential annihilation. They are lost by their own abdication of that public spirit which works to noble ends. Show me that nation whose heart has become corrupt, who has made its liberties a procuress to its personal lusts for money or for place—where fraud rules in the mart, hypocrisy pollutes the temple, and corruption putrifies in the councils, and I will show you a people whose feet have taken hold on the paths which lead into the Gehenna of the nations—and so surely as I live ye have become such a people."

Well will it be for us to heed these warning words. Let us here, at this chastening hour, absolve ourselves from our rancor, our self-love, our party hate, our malignant greed for office, and come to know that we have that to save and perpetuate which is greater and more precious than our transitory personal interests—the state, our earthly all in all.

GARFIELD'S DOMESTIC LIFE.

By Rev. L. W. Brigham.

Delivered at the Memorial Services in LaCrosse, Wis., Sept. 26, 1881.

Ladies and Gentlemen:—I come to help weave the garland we place upon the brow of our illustrious dead. My theme touches the most tender and ennobling elements of his character. However great Mr. Garfield was as a soldier, scholar or statesman, he will be longest remembered as a loving obedient son, a devoted husband; as a true-hearted man in all the social relations. Unfortunately, the public know but little of this man in private life, except what was manifested during the last few weeks of pain and impending death.

We know that so noble and true a man as he, in all public trusts, must have made a good and pure home. All that we have seen during these last sad weeks confirms our expectations, and we understand and appreciate all Mr. Garfield's good qualities and sound religious principles. But what has touched and moved our hearts has been his tender consideration for those he loved more even than his own life. Not the least of his public service was his pure home-life, that to-day blesses and exalts every home in our land. The American people have never had such an experience before when we were all brought together around one bedside of suffering. The sick chamber of our President has its counterpart in every household. It recalls the hours of watching, waiting, hoping, praying and bereavement through which we have passed.

The real life of Mr. Garfield centered in his domestic relations, and his highest inspirations were drawn from the home. Mr. Garfield, like most men who have attained to eminence, could attribute his success to a good mother, and to a wise and fitting choice of a companion for life, and such was his nobility that he could prize a mother's love, and appreciate a good wife, making home the most sacred spot on earth.

Every step in his career from boyhood to manhood shows his first thought was of the loved ones at home. And as the honors come, his thought is of the pleasure it conferred on the home friends. They could never divide or alienate his heart from the old home. He was one of the few statesmen to whom a word of love and commendation from his mother and wife, was dearer than the honors of the world or shouts of the multitude. His tenderness of heart and Mrs. Garfield's wifely devotion have sanctified every home in the land, and there burns to-day upon the altar of every heart a purer, truer, holier and diviner love. His love had been tried by the ambitions and honors of the world, and lastly in the fiery furnace of heroic suffering.

His first act, after the oath of office had been administered in Washington, was to kiss his aged mother and wife. Here was he true to life. The first impulse of his noble heart in that supreme moment, when crowned with the highest honors the world could give, turned toward those he loved, and who, more than all the world besides, were interested in his promotion. They shared his honors as they had his cares and labors. The son and husband was here greater than the President or statesman; his heart-bonds stronger than all other ties. It was an honor to his manhood that he should first remember her who bore him; toiled and prayed for his success. She sowed in tears, that he might reap in honors.

He was the proud realization of all her mother-hopes, and no other person could so fully rejoice in his prosperity as that dear old mother, or, she who had toiled by his side through the days of poverty, darkness and obscurity, a help-meet, indeed; one now a rightful sharer in his harvest of honors. Who, more than they could feel for him; and what more sublime exhibition of manhood than, when James A. Garfield, the President of 50,000,000 people, gave this testimonial of the tenderness of his heart and nobility of his nature, in thus recognizing his mother and wife. All the subsequent events show that this act was a spontaneous tribute of a man, whose domestic nature was the strongest cord that bound him to life. It was this tenderness of love, this beauty of home life that has touched all hearts, so that his death became a personal bereavement to every man, woman and child.

Every home should mourn his loss and consecrate itself to a purer and diviner love. When stricken down by the assassin his first thought was of the wife, and so through all those weary days of pain, and patient waiting for death, the anxiety and solicitude of his heart was toward those dearer than life itself. On that fatal morning he says: "I had rather die than that she should have a relapse." In the heroic struggle for life, his heart turned toward the old home of his early years, full of tender memories and hallowed associations. Even when the hour had come that the silver cord was loosed, and his bark sent over the dark waters, the honors of the world and grand possibilities for future usefulness, now passing away forever, where lost from consciousness; but there survived to the last moment a vision of the old home, and the last dim consciousness of the dying hour placed him in the family circle, surrounded by mother, wife and children.

Thus he passed away to the higher life, there to wait till the home above is completed, and the family gathered in, one by one.

A PICTURE.

By Hon. John H. Craig.

Orator of the day at the Memorial Service, San Francisco, Sept. 26, 1881.

Ladies and Gentlemen:—As the beginning of these sad memorial services, what can I say to you? There are times when silence is more eloquent than any words which mortal tongue can utter. Though these lips of mine were touched with sacred fire, in vain would they try to give expression to the unspeakable pathos of this hour. After long weeks of agonizing suspense, the heart-rending tragedy is ended—the illustrious sufferer is at rest; and as the scene closes at his grave, and the curtain falls, the world is in tears.

Our physical presence is here to-day to do him honor, but our thoughts and our hearts are far away, where at this hour the mortal remains of our dead President are committed to the tomb. Our eyes look across the intervening space, and behold the autumn sun shining from heaven on the solemn, imposing scene. Before his open grave, uncovered, the Nation stands in tears, the majesty of these free and mighty States is bowed in reverence over it; and the homage of the civilized world, like an invisible presence, consecrates the beautiful spot, and makes it holy ground forever more.

> "Hush! the dead march walls in the people's ears;
> The black earth yawns, the mortal disappears.
> Ashes to ashes, dust to dust;
> And he is gone who seemed so great;
> Wearing upon his brow a truer crown
> Than any wreath that man can weave him."

This is not the hour to speak of his renown. We forget the glory of his example, and the inspiration of his fame, in the sad thought that his living presence has passed away forever from the earth. The hour of fresh sorrow is not the hour for eulogy. The universal grief of the Nation and the world speaks his eulogy, and at the eloquence of that grief the most gifted tongue falters and is mute. That grief has come to us all with the force of a personal bereavement. It has touched the hearts of men in this and other lands, and awakened them to better inspirations. Never was sorrow so universal and profound. Never was such homage paid at any mortal shrine—to any mortal name. Surely the man whose death has put the world in mourning needs no eulogy.

We are fast making history—our country is but a century old. We are yet in the morning of our national life. The full noontide of our national glory has not yet brightened the heavens above us. But our history is filled with achievements and examples which the world cannot afford to lose. Great events are crowded upon each other, which are shaping the world's destiny, and marking its progress. And great names have "leaped into the light," to shine forevermore. The names of heroes who, in defense of the right, have led the front of battle—of statesmen, "Who knew the seasons when to take occasion by the hand and make the bounds of freedom wider yet."

But this heart-rending tragedy is the saddest, most pathetic event in our history. Its effect on our future as a nation we know not. That will depend on the manner in which we improve the great and solemn lesson which it teaches. But this we know, that the example of the illustrious victim will be a lofty inspiration to all coming times, and generations yet unborn, as they read the page where it is written, will proudly weep, and find his name the dearest, tenderest memory in all our history.

Look at the picture which that page will present, and let me read it. It presents an extreme contrast. It is shaded from the extreme of human guilt to that of human excellence and glory. It is black with the darkest dye of human crime. It is stained with innocent blood, richer than the blood of kings. It is blotted with human tears. Is illumed with the tender light of human love, and radiant with glory born of suffering endured with a gentle, heroic patience almost divine. As it is presented to the world, no wonder that all hearts are stirred to their profoundest depths. There seems to be wanting not one single circumstance to heighten the pathos of the sad, tragical event. We shudder as we think of the vile, guilty wretch cowering in his cell. We pity and do homage to the great and martyred victim. Our tongues falter and our eyes are dimmed as we speak of the bereaved, orphaned children, the faithful, heroic wife, and the dear old mother, mourning for her noble son, and longing to lay down her weary head beside him in the grave.

The most touching thing connected with the assassination of President Garfield, next to his amazing sufferings and the gentle, heroic, amazing patience with which they were endured is the glimpse which it gave to the world into the privacy of his family life, and the tender relations which it disclosed. This, more than his high position and his fame, has won for him the homage of all true and loyal hearts. For we instinctively know that he, who in a long exalted public career, and even in the highest place on earth, is true to the gentle virtues of home, and the duties of a tender father, a loving husband, and a noble son, must be a true, a good and noble man. Rising by his own unaided powers from the humblest, lowliest lot in life to the most exalted place on earth, and filling his high seat with a gentle dignity and a lofty purpose, he was the representative of the supreme sovereignty of the American people.

But he was something more—he was the representative and type of gentle, cultured, resolute, self-reliant, noble American manhood. When the free choice of a great and free people is fixed on such a man, exalting him to be their ruler, no crowned and sceptered king, born of royal blood, to the heritage of an empire, commands from the world such honor while he nobly lives, or such homage when he nobly dies.

The hearts of the people all over this broad land, in the south as well as the north, are closer together to-day than they ever were before, joined in the sacred fellowship of a common sorrow. Past alienations are forgotten; old resentments are quenched in tears, and all dissentions are buried in the grave of him who has not lived or died in vain. Let us learn the great and solemn lesson of this hour, and follow the impulses and inspirations which it awakens, and so shall we be able, even in this dark hour of national bereavement, to forecast the years to come,

"And find in loss a gain to match."

GARFIELD'S LEGACY.

By Rabbi Lilienthal.

Delivered at the Memorial Service in Cincinnati, Sept. 26, 1881.

SHAKESPEARE, in his Romeo and Juliet, says:

> 'All things, that we ordained festival,
> Turn from their office to black funeral;
> Our instruments to melancholy bells,
> Our wedding cheer to a sad burial feast;
> Our solemn hymns to sullen dirges change,
> Our blooming flowers serve for a bury'd corse,
> And all things change them to the contrary."

The English bard has forstalled our grief, our mourning, a Nation's wailing! Who of us will and can ever forget that Monday night, when the bells of the city, with their heartless iron tongues, announced the death-knell of the Nation's patient! We had hoped against hope; we had had faith against fate—but then we added gloomy silence to the silent night, and lifted the tearful eyes unto the stars, and realized the crushing words sung by Barrett:

> "I tell you, hopeless grief is passionless.
> That only men, incredulous of despair,
> Half-taught in anguish, through the midnight air
> Beat upward to God's throne in loud access
> Of shrieking and reproach!"

Shrieking upward! it was so natural. A Nation's cry of agony and despair ought to be forgiven; but let us be silent, and listen in deepest humility to the great lesson, given in sublime eloquence by our lamented martyr President, when he said:

"The world's history is a divine poem, of which the history of every nation is a canto, and every man a word. Its strains have been pealing along down the centuries, and though there have been mingled the discords of warring cannon and dying men, yet to the philosopher and historian—the humble listener—there has been a divine melody running through the song, which speaks of hope and halcyon days to come."

This was our Garfield's faith, this his unshaken hope, this the word of comfort which he sends from his coffin and his grave, to his mourning countrymen.

Alas, we stand in bitter need of such a comforting, and cheering admonition. Let us listen to it; let us mind it, for it comes from the greatest and most impressive pulpit —the coffin! And not only we, the American people, his people, the whole world needs it; the parliament of man, the federation of the world which is thrilled with horror, which amidst the sighs and tears stands stupefied at the unnatural, foul and strange murder of our President.

Kings and emperors, in their marble palaces and on their golden thrones, must tremblingly ask: What will be our lot, our future, when the man not installed by the grace of God, but by the free choice of a free people, cannot escape the assassin's dagger, the assassin's bullet?

And the nations of the world, panting for freedom, must ask: What is all this boasted liberty for, when the chief of a Government of the people, by the people, and for the people, can be made the target of ruthless, premeditated murder? Shall mankind not despair? Must you not shroud the starry banner of human right and liberty in deep, deep mourning?

No such shrouding! No surrender! for, from the coffin-pulpit resound the other great words which James A. Garfield uttered, with patriotic voice and lofty spirit, when hearing of the death of Lincoln: "God reigns and the Government at Washington still lives!"

This is the great legacy he left to his people. These are the memorable words which the mourning yet grateful Nation shall engrave on the monument to be erected to his blessed memory. No, rest in peace, thou Martyr of the people; over thy grave, in yonder beautiful cemetery, shall shine like the eternal stars in heaven, that starry banner, for which thou hast fought, for which thou hast bled, under whose embracing folds thou hast died!

I shall not speak of his wonderful career, it has been told and repeated by thousands and ten thousands of tongues. The world is full of his praise. How befittingly have the press and merchants of the metropolis expressed the Nation's sentiment when they said:

"In the death of President Garfield the Nation loses one of its prominent citizens, a worthy representative of whatever is best in it, whose career has been singularly typical of the noblest American aspiration and success."

He will always be remembered, not only as a statesman of large experience and commanding abilities; not only as an orator, whose words of eloquent wisdom were effective and often controlling in debate; not only as a patriot soldier whose skillful generalship and unhesitating courage had been signally shown on the bloodiest fields, but also, more affectionately as a faithful man who had risen by his own efforts from the humblest station to the highest position; who had gained rare culture in spite of the sharp limitations of poverty, and who, having honored and adorned every office committed to him, has endeared himself as never before to the hearts of his countrymen by the fortitude with which in the eighty days of his suffering he has borne pain and faced without fear an imminent death.

This is the verdict of the country; what can we add to it but the beautiful words of Rowe:

> "What can I pay thee for this noble usage
> But grateful praise? so Heaven itself is paid."

I shall not dwell on the great success which in all departments of our Government distinguished his short career as our President. The Nation felt encouraged, hopeful, looking for still greater achievement. We rather say with Franklin:

> —"To the generous mind
> The heaviest debt is that of gratitude,
> When it is not in our power to repay it."

Still prompted by this filial and unpayable gratitude, the Nation throngs around his coffin and grave, to pay him the last tribute of honor and affection. The representatives of the people will accompany the earthly remains to their resting-place. Mountains of floral tributes will testify to the love, respect and veneration in which he was held by his mourning fellow-citizens; and from the Atlantic to the Pacific the melancholy bells, the sullen dirges, the gloomy processions will announce: "We mourn the Nation's loss."

But the flowers will fade; the sound of the dirges will pass away; the mourning crowds will disperse, and will this be all by which we intend either to honor his memory or to profit by the terrible lesson of his death?

Listen again to the warning voice, coming from his grave: "God reigns and the Government at Washington still lives;" and must live. Yes, must live; and it is our duty the sacred duty of the living ones, to guard and preserve it, and to execute the will of the departed Chief.

I have read this week some of the infamous doctrines first planted on American ground by Aaron Burr, and thenceforth spread with baneful activity throughout the land. Here are some of these maxims:

"Politics is a game, the prizes of which are offices and contracts."

"Fidelity to party must be the sole virtue of a politician."

"No man must be allowed to suffer on account of his fidelity to his party, no matter how odious to the people he may make himself."

"The end and aim of the professional politician is to keep great men down and put little men up. Little men, owing all to the wire-puller, will be governed by him. Great men, having ideas and convictions, are perilous even to tools."

This is the cancer which eats at the vitals of the Government and the country. It must be cut out, and marked by the dreadful example we have witnessed, the people in its majestic sovereignty must rise and must demand the undelayable reform; then we shall see day instead of the night of the grave, and the owls shall fly back into the haunts of darkness and nothingness.

Thus Washington's Government shall live, indeed; thus and then we shall love thy memory, sainted martyr; and in the name of all of us, I close with Carlyle's verses:

> "I find a pious gratitude disperse
> Within my soul; and every thought to him
> Engenders a warm sigh within me, which,
> Like curls of holy incense, overtake
> Each other in my bosom, and enlarge,
> With their embrace, his sweet remembrance."

Farewell! Farewell!

GARFIELD—THE TYPICAL AMERICAN.

By Prof. J. C. Shattuck.

Delivered at the Memorial Service in Greeley, Col., Sept. 26, 1881.

James A. Garfield was a typical American. He was born amid the forests. A great many generations, since the settlement of Plymouth and Jamestown, have been born in the forests, and have given the strength of their arms for the rendering of those forests fit for the habitation of man.

He was typical in his birth, and in his early boyhood learned to swing the axe amid the great trees that grew around his father's farm, which strengthened his muscles and rendered him vigorous of frame.

He was typical in the circumstances of his youth. No man can read his life, as millions to-day are hearing it, without being convinced that these circumstances and struggles were necessary to make him the man he was. Yet no circumstances could have swallowed up such a God-endowed man as James A. Garfield. I don't believe, however, that if he had been born to wealth and position, if he had been able to pave his way without difficulty through school and college with the temptations and surroundings of wealth, that he would have been less enervated, for I believe that to give him the fiber he possessed, and which made him essentially the great man that he was, standing prominently among the great men of the earth, there was needed just that determination which he early formed, and which was greatly fostered by the circumstances of his youth.

He had determined on a college course, and was told that probably in the course of twelve years, and by hard labor, he could work his way through college, without exterior help. Was he daunted? Oh, no! Says his biographer: "Every other impulse of his life became absorbed in that one—'I will go through college;'" and he went through college—not in twelve years, but in eight—working day and night, at farm-work, carpentering, or anything that came to his hand; never an idle moment until he got through his college career. The circumstances of his education were fortunate in this, that thereby he came to know Mark Hopkins.

On one occasion General Garfield said, "I rejoice, my friends, to see the great institutions of learning that are springing up out of the munificence of my countrymen all over this fair land, but I say to you that if I had it to do over again—to choose where I should attend college, and all these were to open their magnificent doors to me, and here stood Williams' old log cabin with Mark Hopkins in it as President, that would be college enough for me." Through our beloved martyred President, the influence of that one man, Mark Hopkins, will go on and on, blessing the human race long after the materials which now make the grand edifice called Williams College shall have crumbled into forgotten dust. So, too, with Garfield. He was typical in that he was among the very best, and his influence has changed the course of hundreds of young men. No one could come before him and listen to him without being drawn out of himself and up into the higher, nobler, purer sphere where he walked, and into the sweeter atmosphere which he breathed.

[The speaker here related the incident of Garfield's disobeying orders in regard to delivering up slaves who had escaped to our lines at the beginning of the war, and which, doubtless, was the first step that led to the proclamation of freedom. Also to show his kindness of heart and magnanimity, related the story of the non-commissioned officer who went to sleep while guarding the entrance to headquarters, and to whom Garfield apologized for falling over him, instead of placing him in the guard-house.]

One instance more, showing the greatness of this man, as well as the clearness and keenness of his judgment: You will remember how high the feeling ran, North and South, during the year succeeding the war. General Garfield was in his first term of Congress, and not so thoroughly known. Here came an issue which many of you will remember. Congress had passed an act providing that as fast as our lines were extended into the so-called Rebel States that the citizens thereof could form what was called a loyal government, and become States in the Union again; but President Lincoln vetoed the act. Soon after the veto old Ben Wade and Henry Winter Davis united in a letter which they published in the New York *Tribune*, very sharply and very bitterly criticising Mr. Lincoln for this action. General Garfield stood by Wade and against the President in this issue. His district upheld the veto and condemned the Wade and Davis letter.

The time drew nigh when the district convention should re-nominate Garfield or his successor; certain parties were very active, thinking they saw in this position that Garfield had taken, an opportunity for brushing Garfield out of the way. And they worked that thing up so thoroughly and well that when the convention assembled one of their first acts was to pass a series of resolutions indorsing the President and censuring Wade—thus involving Garfield.

Now mark the man. He was a young man, in the prime of his manhood, who had set aside a very promising military career, resigning his position as Major General in the army, and entered this new field. Now everything looked dark for the future. He recognized the dangers of his being set aside, and what did he do? He went to the convention—not to lobby or button-hole the members, but to express his decided opinions in regard to this matter. Before his arrival upon the train, these resolutions had been passed by a large majority, and when he put in his appearance at the convention he was invited to address them. He only used a few short sentences in which he stated his convictions firmly and clearly, placing himself distinctly upon the side of Wade in this issue and giving his reasons therefor, concisely and pointedly. He then passed from the platform down the aisle, through the hall down stairs, on to his hotel, and afterwards to the train, supposing that there was no possible hope of a re-nomination. But he had vindicated his manhood.

This man would not abate one jot of his private judgment upon a serious matter; no, not for the united voice of that district he loved so truly. What was the result? Ah! the master had been there. The leader of the opposition and promoter of the resolutions sprung to his feet before the sound of Garfield's footsteps had died away in the hall, and said:

"Mr. President and gentlemen of the convention: a man who has the moral courage to beard this convention in that manner deserves a nomination, and I move that General James A. Garfield be re-nominated by acclamation." And it was done, amidst great applause and enthusiasm. Such was the power of Garfield's influence, prompted by a depth of manhood and integrity seldom if ever excelled.

During the past eighty days millions of eyes, though dimmed with tears, have been going over the record of his life, and I dare any man to produce anything that stains the honor of this man, from the days of his boyhood until this sad nineteenth day of September, when this glorious record was closed. James A. Garfield was the highest type of a man we have been permitted to see. I have no expectation of ever again in my life seeing in the presidential chair a man so blameless in his private life, so noble in every phase of his character, so great in all lines of thought, and who has so strong a hold upon the hearts of this great people, as this man Garfield. I rejoice that I have lived to see such a man ; I rejoice that I am able to go over his career, day by day and year by year, and find it so faultless. I commend it to you, young and old. There is not a page of this eventful career that even the bitter hate of political passion can unfold that is not fair to the eyes and beautiful to all mankind.

He has done remarkable things for this country. No man of his day gave more careful, thoughtful study to the important problems affecting the welfare of the Republic; no man showed better judgment—so ripe and far-seeing. How we leaned upon him ! What a sense of security and confidence went over the country when we knew that his hand was guiding the helm. But to the honor of this man the Great Ruler of the Universe has thought it meet to add the martyr's crown. Lying there these eleven weeks in pain and suffering, he has been such a blessing to the United States of America and the civilized world, as neither he nor any other man could have been in the prime of his strength and glory. His activities have been stilled that the voice of his Creator might the more clearly be heard.

It is not what a man does in any one of his great successes that fixes his place among his contemporaries or in the judgment of posterity—oh, no! it is that something back of all these single actions that we call character; and it needed the assassin's pistol and the eighty days of suffering to put the appropriate crown upon this man's brow, to show to all the full measure of his power and the character he had built up.

And so, to-day, millions upon millions who gather to pay the last sad rites to this great and good and noble man, will say, "'Tis well."

TRUE TO HIMSELF—FALSE TO NONE.

By Hon. R. F. Pettibone.

Delivered at the Memorial Services in Burlington, Wis., Sept. 26, 1881.

Less than half a century ago James A. Garfield was a babe in his cradle—to-day he is the loved and honored dead of this Nation and of humanity.

What is the power that enabled him to tread this shining way from obscurity to world-wide renown? I know of no better answer than may be found in his own words: "During the twenty years that I have been in public life, I have tried to do one thing. Whether I was mistaken or otherwise, it has been the plan of my life to follow my convictions, at whatever personal cost to myself. I have represented for many years a district in Congress whose approbation I greatly desired, but, though it may seem perhaps a little egotistical to say it, I yet desired still more the approbation of one person, and his name was Garfield."

Yes, that is it; that is the secret of his power—true to himself, true to his own convictions of duty. And well did the world's great poet say:

> To thine ownself be true,
> And it must follow, as the night the day,
> Thou canst not then prove false to any man."

And the glorious path he trod from the forest clearing

to the White House—from humble oblivion to fame, wide as humanity, is open to the humblest. What an inspiration to every young man burning with the great and noble ambitions of life. Thanks to God and the fathers for institutions which make it possible that a day-laborer shall be chiefest and best valued among us.

We loved the hero for his splendid record written with steel amid the carnage and desolation of war.

We loved him for his wise and brave, his dignified and unsullied course in public life during the past twenty years, but most of all, we loved him for his high manhood displayed in all the relations of life, for his devotion to his home, the most sacred spot to him upon earth. O how pitiful was his longing for that Mentor home when his every nerve was racking pain!

And it was time that these old virtues were re-established. It is not the style in these later days to reverence an old mother. It is gone out of fashion for men to hold their wives above all other women, and it is not deemed necessary to continue the chivalry of love. Social vices abound. The home is no longer the dearest and most sacred spot upon earth. It is but a place to eat and sleep. But this man came bringing his quiet home to the first mansion in the land.

Though a mighty man and a ruler of rulers, his mother was honored and reverenced, his wife was loved and cherished, his children were tenderly cared for, his home was his holy of holies—for he remembered that all these were a part of him, and had helped to make him what he was. O, what a thought for us. Without the home and its influences a free government like ours is not possible for a day. In the true home center all the powers and forces that make men great. And when its pure influences stream forth into the current of public life, we know that the N. -

tion is safe—that "the government of the people, by the people, and for the people, shall not perish from the earth."

The past rises before me like a cloud. I see the babe in his humble cradle in the home of proverty and toil; I see the youth struggling for daily bread in the sweat of his brow; I see the young man step by step working his way forward through all discouraging hindrances to the rank of a scholar; I see the man still young amid the roll of drums and the roar of battle, as he leads his men at Sandy Creek and Piketon; I see him as he rides across the field of fire at Chickamauga; I see him in the Halls of Congress winning his way to the leadership of the House; I see the streets in New York crowded with maddened men: Lincoln was shot last night: thousands upon thousands are gathered in that great center of the Nation's commerce, furious with rage and burning for revenge; I see Butler of Massachusetts with crape streaming from his arm, and hear his voice choked with tears—"Gentlemen, he died in the fullness of his power." A telegram is read: "Seward is dead." I hear a wild cry from that frenzied throng which means death and desolation to hundreds. I hear a voice—"Another telegram from Washington," and in the moment's hush which follows, these words come with a clarion clearness:

"FELLOW-CITIZENS:—Clouds and darkness are around about Him. His pavilion is dark waters and thick clouds of the sky. Justice and judgment are the habitation of his throne. Mercy and truth shall go before his face. Fellow-citizens, God reigns, and the Government at Washington still lives!"

And the frenzy and madness of the throng are quelled by that divinely-gifted man. O, what a prophet's voice seems that utterance, as we stand in the presence and the mystery of his death.

We love him for his tenderness to his mother, for his devotion to his wife, who was to him the one woman above all other women, for his companionship with his children. Aye! for these things he came into our hearts.

Other men had been great leaders upon the battle-field and in legislative halls, but he, the great leader, was the filial son, the chivalrous husband, the kind father, the stanch friend. Who will forget that when the message was sent over the wires announcing his fall to that loved wife—it bore his words also to her: "He sends his love to you."

Again I see him as I saw him but yesterday at that historic gathering in the metropolis of the Northwest. The great building is packed with thousands upon thousands of men, an eager and yet fickle throng. The eloquent and regal senator from New York has finished his masterly and stirring presentation of the name of General Grant. From floor to rafter the building rocks with cheers. The world seems gone mad for the nomination of the Hero of Appomattox. The New York delegation seizes its banner and heads the procession down the aisles of the hall; delegation after delegation follow, waving flags and banners, until the floor of the convention is the parade ground of an army, while the majestic Conkling waves his hand to the admiring galleries as a signal for fresh tumults of cheers.

In the midst of this gigantic uproar, Ohio is called, and a delegate springs upon a table in front of the reporters. He is a man of fine physique, with a large head which seems more than half forehead; a clear eye, deep blue to his friends, but a cold gray to his foes, and his voice rings like a trumpet! His first words still the vast audience into the silence of death, and as he goes on towards a fitting climax, I hear him tell that Convention that not in Chicago, in the heat of June, but at the firesides of the Republic, in the days of November the contest will be decided, and that it is the calm level of the sea below the tumult and the storm, by which all heights and depths are measured. I felt that whatever the outcome of that contest, the great and wise man whose voice is sounding in my ears, is fitter than they all to be the ruler of this great people.

I see him as the flush comes into his face near the end of that memorable contest, when Wisconsin heads the break, and casts for him her seventeen votes—Thank God for Wisconsin,—and then Indiana wheels into line, and then State after State forgets its favorite, and hastens to his banner. I see him after he has taken the oath of office, and has spoken his inaugural tidings of conciliation and grand promise:

"The Nation is resolutely facing to the front, resolved to employ its best energies in developing the great possibilities of the future. Sacredly preserving whatever has been gained to liberty and good government, during the century, our people are determined to leave behind them all those bitter contentions concerning things which have been irrevocably settled, and the further discussion of which can only stir up strife and delay the onward march," then, forgetful of the great concourse, turning reverently to kiss that grand mother and devoted wife, under the gaze of the American people.

Who sneers at it now as sentimental? It was the man. Grander spectacle Nation never looked upon.

I see him upon his bed during the long agony of his martyrdom, and no word of complaint or purpose of revenge passes his calm lips. There he lies, the wonder and admiration of all nations, the hero of the world. I see him as he gasps, "O Swaim! what a terrible pain! Can't you do something for me?" And the pulse flutters and the breath grows faint. The light flickers and goes out, and the heroic woman strokes the nerveless arm of her dead. Aye! roll your surges, ocean, in ceaseless moaning for our hero. Hide your faces, stars of heaven, and let the earth be shrouded in darkness. Sweep your sable pinions across the sky, O clouds, and let not the sun look upon our beloved. And, men of every land, ring out the iron bells in peals of woe. Drape your houses and let your hearts be sad, for the friend of man is dead. Autumn shall wither the leaves, and winter shall hide the earth with snow as with a garment. Spring shall come again and wear her crown of verdure; and summer shall adorn the earth with flowers, and with the kindly fruit of the fields. Men shall sow the seed and reap the harvest; kingdoms shall fall and empires shall spring up, and all things ripen towards the end, but the gentle, courageous, humble, kingly man shall come back to us no more forever.

And now they lay him at rest in that beautiful spot by the blue waters of the lake upon which he gazed in boyhood. Cannon thunder a last tribute, and all that is mortal of James A. Garfield waits beneath the sod for the trumpet of the last day.

His death has brought sorrow to mankind, rest to a hero, duty to a nation. The standards he set we must never lower. We must see to it that Guiteau writes no page of American history. It is left for us to cherish the hero's memory and hand it down to the generations which shall come after us, as a dear possession for aye, to explore his character and reproduce it in our children, that when the stranger shall ask, "Where is his monument?" we may reply, "The Nation is his memorial;" to reap the fruit of his labors, garnered in our institutions and in our laws, and to write above all, "in letters of living light," "God reigns, and the Government at Washington still lives."

THE HOUSEHOLD STORY.

By Chancey M. Depew.

Delivered at the Memorial Service of the Grand Army of the Republic, New York, Sept. 26, 1881.

We have met together many times in the long years past on occasions, serious and trifling, sad and joyful; for the hot discussions of politics, for the purpose of commemorating historical and patriotic events, and to strew with flowers and eulogiums, the graves of our heroic dead; but never before have we assembled when we were only the units of universal and all-embracing grief. The sun, in its course, has for the past two months greeted with its morning rays, a never-ending succession of kneeling millions, supplicating the heavenly throne to spare the life of General Garfield; and, during the last forty-eight hours, it has set upon them, bowed in sorrow for his death.

This intense interest has been limited by neither boundaries nor nationalities. It has belted the globe with mourning. Why has this calamity touched the chords of universal sympathy? Heroes and statesmen have died before, but never before have all civilized peoples felt the loss their own. The glory of the battle-field has mingled exultation with the soldier's agony. Statesmen have closed a long and distinguished career, but the loss has been relieved by the reflection that such is the common lot of all. Lincoln's murder was recognized as the expiring stroke of a dying cause. The assassination of him who was the savior of

Holland, and the hope of the liberty of his time, was felt to be the fruit of implacable feud and religious strife; but the shot at Garfield was the most causeless, purposeless and wicked crime of the century. No section, no party, no faction, desired his death. It had no accessories in public vengeance or private malice.

The President was a strong, brave, pure man, in the prime of his power; the trusted Executive of fifty millions of people; the title to his office unquestioned; and the Nation unanimous in the purpose that he should develop his policy and fulfill his mission. Such a life and career, so ruthlessly broken, arouse horror and sympathy.

But the love, reverence and sadness of this hour are due to the fact that the man himself, in his strength and weakness, in his struggles and triumphs, in his friendships and enmities, in his relations to mother, wife and children, and in his battle with death, was the best type of manhood. He was not one of those historical heroes, with the human element so far eliminated that, while we admire the character, we rejoice that it exists only in books and on canvas; but a man like ourselves, with like passions and feelings, but possessed of such greatness and goodness, that the higher we estimated him the nearer and dearer he became to us. In America and Europe he is recognized as an illustrious example of the results of free institutions. His career shows what can be accomplished where all avenues are open, and exertion is untrammeled.

Our annals afford no such incentive to youth as does his life; and it will become one of the Republic's household stories. No boy, in poverty almost hopeless, thirsting for knowledge, meets an obstacle which Garfield did not experience and overcome. No youth, despairing in darkness, feels a gloom which he did not dispel.

No young man filled with honorable ambition can encounter a difficulty which he did not meet and surmount.

For centuries to come great men will trace their rise from humble origins to the inspirations of that lad, who learned to read by the light of a pine-knot in a log cabin; who, ragged and barefooted, trudged along the tow-path of the canal; and, without ancestry behind to impel him forward, without money or affluent relations, without friends or assistance, by faith in himself and in God, became the most scholarly and best-equipped statesman of his time— one of the foremost soldiers of his country, the best debater in the strongest of deliberate bodies, the leader of his party and the Chief Magisrate of fifty millions of people before he was fifty years of age.

We are not here to question the ways of Providence. Our prayers were not answered as we desired, though the volume and fervor of our importunity seemed resistless; but already, behind the partially-lifted veil, we see the fruits of the sacrifice. Old wounds are healed and fierce feuds forgotten. Vengeance and passion, which have survived the best statesmanship of twenty years, are dispelled by a common sorrow. Love follows sympathy. Over this open grave the cypress and willow are indissolubly entwined, and into it are buried sectional differences and hatreds. The North and the South rise from bended knees to embrace in the brotherhood of a common people and reunited country. Not this alone, but the humanity of the civilized world has been quickened and elevated, and the English-speaking people are nearer to-day in peace and unity than ever before.

There is no language in which petitions have not arisen for Garfield's life, and no clime where tears have not fallen for his death. The Queen of the proudest of nations, for the first time in our recollection, brushes aside the formalities of diplomacy, and descending from the throne, speaks for her own and the hearts of all her people, in the cable to the afflicted wife, which says: "Myself and my children mourn with you."

A MAN OF THE PEOPLE.

By Rev. T. K. Noble—Department Chaplain of the Grand Army of the Republic.

Delivered in San Francisco, at the Memorial Service of the Grand Army of the Republic, Sept. 25, 1881.

"Know ye not that there is a prince and a great man fallen?"—II Samuel, 3:38.

As I stand in your presence to-night, my comrades, there rises before me a Dantean picture of the touching scene it was my lot to witness in the general hospital of the Army of the Potomac on that awful day when the news reached us that our beloved Lincoln had been foully murdered. Only seven days before, it had been the privilege of those thousands of maimed and sick soldiers to look into his rugged but kindly face and feel the hearty pressure of his honest hand, and when the tidings came that he had been shot down like a dog, those bronzed and war-hardened veterans, raged like madmen, and then cried like children. This picture, dark as it is, has been duplicated, and in a period of profound peace. Despite a nation's wrath and a nation's woe, in less than a score of years, we are again smitten by a common blow, and bowed by a common grief. A dutiful son, a devoted husband, a revered father, a ripe scholar, a pure patriot, a sagacious statesman and a godly ruler has succumbed at last, after seventy-nine days of patient suffering to the bullet of the assassin, and strong men again have been crying in our streets. The Nation has lost its head, the people their President, and we of the Grand Army a comrade, honored and beloved. To use the words which Shakespeare puts in the mouth of Macbeth:

> ———"this Duncan
> Hath borne his faculties so meek, hath been
> So clear in his great office, that his virtues
> Will plead like angels, trumpet-tongued, against
> The deep damnation of his taking off."

HIS NOBLE LIFE.

But we are in God's house to-night, not to give utterance to useless invective, or expression to unavailing sorrow. The hour can be better spent in meditating upon his noble life and its inspiring lessons. And so I reiterate this old question of Holy Writ, "Know ye not that there is a prince and a great man fallen?" If we will rise to some just conception of his greatness, we must weigh his record as a man, a patriot, a statesman and a Christian ruler. Look, first of all, at his greatness as a man, a man among men, and a man of the common people. Born in a rude log cabin, a true son of the soil, his father a farmer, his elder brother a farmer, and his two sisters the wives of farmers, his superb physique inherited from robust ancestors, was magnificently developed by hard labor in the open air and at the workbench of the carpenter's shop.

Who that has ever looked upon him will ever forget his manly presence? The tall, but well rounded frame, the broad shoulders, the massive head, the full face, the clear blue eye, the kindly look, the affable and friendly ways, all these "bespoke elements so mixed in him that nature might stand up and say to all the world, this was a man!" Not a man of lead, heavy, dull, cold and unelastic; nor a man of iron, stern, hard, implacable and unattractive, but a man of steel, firm, but at the same time flexible, tenacious, but also tractile, and with all his powers and faculties so tempered and refined that whatever position in life he was called to fill, he always rose equal to the demands of the hour. Whether as a toiler upon the farm of his father, or as a driver of horses upon the canal, or as a teacher in our public schools, or as President of a College, or as a preacher of the Gospel of Peace, or as a General on the field of war, or as a Representative in the halls of Congress, or as President of fifty millions of people, by his ability, versatility and fidelity he has won imperishable honor as the fairest and finest representative of American manhood.

The speaker then proceeded to review at length President Garfield's greatness as a patriot and a statesman—calling public attention to the larger service rendered by him while a member of Congress, and to the wisdom, firmness and high manliness displayed by him during his brief occupancy of the Presidential chair.

THE PRESIDENT'S RELIGION.

He then said: I should be recreant to my duty as a Christian minister, did I not, on this memorial occasion, direct your thoughts to our dead comrade's beautiful loyalty to God, as well as to his large services to men. Never let it be forgotten that this noble life, which bore such blessed fruit, was rooted in Christian soil. It was Christian blood that flowed in his veins. It was a Christian mother that bore him. It was a Christian wife that ministered to him. It was a Christian home that sheltered him, and it was a Christian church of which he was a faithful and consistent member. His Bible was the Christian's Bible, and his God the Christian's God, and no day passed in which he did not, with bowed head, invoke the Divine blessing upon his home and upon the dear country of his life.

Even in his youth, while camping out with a few chosen companions, before the fire dies down, he takes from his pocket a well-worn Bible, reads a chapter aloud, and then, kneeling under the solemn stars, reverently commends himself and his young friends to the God of his fathers. It was this spirit of whole-souled loyalty to God that made our dead President so grandly great—great in peace, great in war, great in the sick chamber, and great in the presence of death. For, as Carlyle has said, "The chief question to be asked of a man or of a nation is, What was their religion?" Answering this question, he adds, "Give us the soul of their history, for the thoughts they had were the parents of the actions they did, and their feelings were the parents of their thoughts, and it is the interior and spiritual that determines the outward and actual."

I repeat it, my comrades, it was our dead President's stanch loyalty to God, that made him so truly great. This it was that imparted to his soul that lofty courage, that serene and beautiful equipoise of spirit, that is, the admiration of the world. "It will strike hard," he said to his college classmates, at the time of his inauguration. "It will strike hard, this mountain wave of political animosity," but he was anchored to his God, and in his soul there was peace. How hard it did strike, only the lips of his brave and bereaved wife can fully tell, and the unwritten history of those awful weeks of suffering adequately disclose. But he bore it with such knightly fortitude, such Christian patience, such unmurmuring submission to the will of the God he trusted, that it has touched the great heart of humanity in every quarter of the habitable globe. And, therefore to-night, as he lies in the repose of death, his worn, white face turned upward to those calm heights where sin and sorrow and pain are never known, "where the wicked cease from troubling, and the weary are at rest," all Christendom is mourning him. High and low, rich and poor, learned and unlearned, are bowing in the brotherhood of a common bereavement. It is our sorrowful privilege, my comrades, to honor him, not only as a man and a magistrate, but as a brother beloved—a faithful member of the Grand Army of the Republic.

And so, in the quiet of this holy Sabbath evening, we, the shattered remnants of this great fraternity, have come together to break the alabaster box of our honest affection over our dead comrade, and to anoint him for his burial. "He has fought a good fight, he has finished his course, he has kept the faith." He has entered into the joy of his Lord. In company with our revered Washington, and our martyred Lincoln, sacred triumvirate of noble souls, he will live forever in the hearts of the American people, as a man without guile, a patriot without selfishness, a statesman without corruption, and a President without fear.

THE LESSONS OF HIS LIFE.

And now, what are the lessons which ought to be drawn from our dead comrade's shining career? Among the many which press hard for recognition I name but three: First of all, are we not admonished afresh of the inherent excellence of the American ideas and institutions which made possible the character and career of James A. Garfield? In what other land upon the face of the earth do we behold an open highway, leading from the rude cabin of a pioneer farmer up to the Executive Mansion of a mighty nation? Where but in America do we see all the supreme prizes of life actually within the reach of the poorest and humblest? Where but in this dear land of our fathers do we find a free government, and a free church, and a free press, and free speech, and free schools? I know it is the fashion of the times to speak lightly of these prerogatives of the American people, and I do not forget that they have been abused, like other good things of earth.

But men do not gather grapes of thorns, nor figs of

thistles. And when I look upon the grand outcome of these ideas and institutions, as exhibited by our dead President, and also, I may add, by his predecessors in the high office, I discern new significance in these old ideas which our fathers died to establish, and their sons to maintain, and I find myself saying, in the strong language of Israel's King, "If I forget thee, oh, my country, let my right hand forget its cunning, and let my tongue cleave to the roof of my mouth."

The second lesson of our comrade's noble life—what is it but this: the inexpressible importance to our dear country of Christian homes—homes where the husband loves the wife as Christ the Church, and the wife reverences the husband with the sweet reverence of love; homes where children are taught to obey their parents "In the Lord, because it is right;" homes in which, as the shadows of evening fall, the household are gathered together, the word of Life is read, and the priest, the husband and father prays. If it were possible for the spirit of our departed President to speak to us to-night, I believe his message would be that America's supreme need is Christian homes like that in which his own young life ripened into such symmetrical and beautiful completeness.

And now, as we go forth into the world, let us take with us also the other inspiring lesson—the ever-increasing usefulness and the ever-widening influence of a genuinely unselfish and consecrated life. I open the Word of God, in which I am certain to find the very heart of truth, and I there read that "the path of the just is as a shining light, which shineth more and more unto the perfect day." How impressively is this truth illustrated in the life of our President! Beginning as a feeble rush-light, in a cabin in the West, it grew brighter and brighter as the years went by, illuminating successively the common school, the college, the field of battle, the halls of Congress, and the capitol of the Nation, sending its clear and steady beams over the whole land, and so letting this light shine, that men everywhere seeing the good works are glorifying their Father in heaven. And now, that the thin shade of the earthly tabernacle is at last dissolved, is not the pure spirit shining with a brightness and beauty and chastened radiance that belongs not to earth but to heaven? Faithful over a few things, he is made ruler over many things, and his blessed life is filling the whole world with fragrance. Oh, comrades and friends, is not the voice of our fallen leader speaking to us in this still hour, and saying to us calmly and solemnly, "Follow me ever as I have followed my great Master, Christ!"

A LIFE THAT SHINES.

By Rev. James Freeman Clarke, D.D.

Delivered in the Church of the Disciples, Boston, Memorial Sunday, Sept. 25, 1881.

"But the path of the just is as the shining light that shineth more and more unto the perfect day."—Proverb 4: 18.

The long trial is over; the great suspense is at an end, and our whole-souled and loved Chief has gone from us. The civilized world which has watched every fluctuation of the sick man's pulse, counted every throb, and asked anxiously every day for his welfare, turns sadly back to its usual avocations. Another name is written among the noble army of martyrs; another hero has been enrolled on the list of those whom this people reverences. Henceforth the memory of Garfield will stand side by side with those of Washington and Lincoln as one of the heroes of the Nation. All minds and hearts throughout the world are moved simultaneously by one sorrow and one sympathy. The mourning widow has condolence and sympathy from all the nations of the world, and has stood by his side faithfully. If her husband had remained a simple teacher in an Ohio academy she would have done no less; she could have done no more.

There is something wonderful and almost inexplicable in this expression of world-wide sorrow. In imagination we see the funeral. There is the casket surrounded by the pall-bearers, who are all his old boyhood friends. **Mrs.** Garfield passed over the distinguished gentlemen who would gladly have occupied these positions, and wisely chose those who knew him earliest. After them follow the wife, the mother and children, the faithful friends, the members of the Cabinet and the Governors of States; then there are present by their expressions of sincere sorrow, the Queen of England, and the Empress of India, the President of the great French Republic, the Kings of Italy and Belgium, the Parliament of Australia; crowded public meetings in every city and town in England send also their representatives. All these we see in our minds following lovingly and reverently the body of this man, who had no prestige except that which he won by his own worth. The world is better for such a scene as this; it is noble to see that in such an hour

"One throb of nature makes the whole world kin."

We see that the world is not so bad as it is represented to be, when such a wave of feeling sweeps over it, bearing all classes of men to one common point of meeting. Why is it? The assassination of the Czar, the ruler of a mighty empire, created no such feeling. The long weeks of sickness, of watching with untiring interest, may have something to do with it, but not all. He was a patient sufferer, but so were others. The assassination of Lincoln excited the passion of grief, but this universal sorrowing has a profounder source. It has been argued that the people of this Nation can have no feeling of loyalty toward a government represented by a man chosen from among themselves and placed at their head by their own votes. It is not the man to whom they are loyal, but his position. The place where he stands is their ideal position, and the divinity which hedges it round is not his personal character, but the divinity of the position which he fills. Whatever is good, grand and beautiful in the institutions of our country is represented by him, and if he leads a good and pure life, devoted to the interests of the country, then he is beloved and reverenced with a love greater than that of any other country. Such was he—our martyred chief. Other nations are moved by the sight of this upright man, who stands as the embodiment of the great hopes and future of this mighty republic. Whether or not this be the explanation, it is certain that this is a remarkable hour in the history of the Nation, and he has done more for us by his death than he would by living.

His death has extinguished the feeling between the North and South and made them one; it has stilled all animosity against him. We are rejoiced to see that the Republican and Democratic papers which opposed the policy and found fault with the administration of Garfield are acknowledging their mistakes openly; it is a mark of strength and not of weakness. If his death shall elevate the tone of political discussion, it will not have been in vain. It has helped to make mankind one. Every noble life which thrills the world with a common feeling tends to unite it, and goes far in the same direction with the atonement of Christ. The blood of Lincoln brought men, before estranged, nearer to each other; the blood of Garfield has united the North and South and brought the great spheres nearer together.

But we must carry this sentiment forward toward conviction. The principle for which Garfield died was that of truth. These funeral processions, mourning emblems and eulogies are all right and proper as far as they go, but we must not stop there in our tribute. The best monument which we can raise to his memory is to carry on the ideas and principles to which he was a martyr. It may be urged that the assassin was crazy, but his brain was filled with the notions of the spoils system, and it was in opposing that system that Garfield died. And now a man who has been known in the past as a supporter of that system has taken his place. We must not prejudge him. We can only hope that he has experienced a change of heart; but whatever he does, the people must not relax their vigilance; they must kill the spoils system. Hang the assassin if they will, but do n't stop there. A system well organized and well carried out for the reform of the civil service will be the best monument which can be erected to the memory of Garfield.

It is not a bad thing to die when death produces such results as these. Garfield was happy in his life, in his home, in his mother, in his wife, his church, his love for knowledge, his wise instructors; he was happy, too, in having the courage to leave these blessings to fight for his country; he was happy in his good sense, his sweet temper, his sound principles; but he was especially happy in the opportunity for death, when he had gained all and lost nothing. His life was bright and without a spot; his death was opportune and fortunate, since he has united the world in one great sentiment of pity and reverence. When such a man dies, it is not death, but a new life.

THE IMMORTAL NAME.

By Judge John P. Rea.

Delivered at the Memorial Services in Minneapolis, Minn., Sept. 26, 1881.

Just one week ago, way down by the sea, the wild waves of the mighty deep moaning their sad requiem in his ears, the grandest soul among men took its flight from earth to heaven.

This afternoon the body which that soul animated, ennobled and endeared for half a century, was laid to rest on the sloping shores that were his home by the lake he loved. Its restless murmuring waters are singing now as they will continue in calm or storm to sing forever, nature's anthem to his memory. In that little mound looking out upon that inland sea, he sleeps. There angel sentinels begin to-night their ageless watch above him. There by his faith, which is ours, we know that he will come forth in glory when the reveille of eternity sounds the dawn of immortality's morning.

I came not here to tell what James A. Garfield did, the world knows that by heart. I came not here to magnify his merits, or attempt by feeble words to burnish the dazzling lustre of his memory, but simply to lay a humble tribute from the heart upon his fresh made grave, and mingle a tear with those who weep that he is gone.

How feeble are words to express the emotions of the heart when stirred to the depth by the aggressive force of an overwhelming sorrow!

What pen can portray the anguish of a soul smitten by the hand of death? What language can convey from mind to mind, in all its acuteness, the grief that revels at this hour in the bosom of every American?

What heart here but feels upon its plastic walls the ruthless print of an iron hand? What ear but hears in the oppressive air about it the rustling of the black wings? What soul but feels the chilling presence of the inexorable angel of death? Upon what a scene in the world's drama the curtain falls to-day! Across the land draped in pall moves the funeral cortege of America's murdered President. In its trains are fifty million broken-hearted mourners. Chivalric soldiers who crossed with him in the fiercest conflict of the centuries are there. Proud men whom he met and conquered in the bitter contests of the political arena are there. Humble black men whom he helped to lift from bondage to manhood are there. The rich and the poor, the old and the young, the high and the low, the great and the humble, all are there, and all—all are weeping. All are moved by a common love and stricken by a common sorrow. Children strew flowers beneath the wheels of the car that bears the dead. The nations stand with bowed heads in silent sadness while the mighty procession passes, bearing to its tomb the lifeless form of him in whom was centered the tenderest love of the republic and the fondest hope of the world. The proudest Queen of Christendom wipes the tear from her cheek as she lays her floral tribute upon his bier, and millions of peasants in humble cots on mountain and lowland beyond the sea feel the gloom of an equal sadness and the touch of as tender a love. Eyes unused to weep are moistened. All humanity is in tears—through them its great, warm heart is breaking.

> "Aye, turn and weep: 'tis manliness
> To be heart-broken here,
> For the grave of earth's best nobleness
> Is watered by the tear."

We mourn not so much the loss of the ruler, as the death of the man. Looking through our tears upon his matchless career, the lustre of his triumphs as he carves his way from the cabin to the White House, dims by contrast with the golden glory that floods for months the chamber of patient suffering, of unselfish devotion, of conquered agony, where were revealed the immeasurable possibility of man's virtue and the unfathomable depths of woman's love. Oh! with what a delicate tenderness humanity will treasure away in the store-house of its memory the sacred incidents of loving self-denial and sublime fortitude that sparkle forth like heavenly gems through the black clouds of misery which envelop that scene. James A. Garfield won his way by no art but the true one of meriting honors. He commanded power by demonstrating his fitness for it. In its exercise he honors his country and his kind.

> "And to add greater honors to his age
> Than man could give, he died fearing God."

Barefooted orphan boy, delving in intellectual mines for the treasures of power; young teacher of the living truths that flash down the centuries from the martyr-crowned crest of Calvary; heroic soldier of freedom, snatching the inspiration of victory from the gloom of defeat, riding, king of the battle-storm, amid the death-revel that reigned supreme in the tangled fens of the Chickamauga; bold, honest, intelligent legislator, at the peril of popular displeasure, yielding obedience to the slightest commands of honor, teaching thy countrymen that "Aloft on the throne of God, and not below in the footprints of a trampling multitude, are the sacred rules of right, which no majorities can displace or overturn."

Chosen Chief Magistrate of the first republic of the world, standing on the sunlit portals of its capitol, in the full flush of new-born power, bending to imprint the kiss of filial love on the shrunken, shriveled cheek of the old mother—showing that true love has no season and no station; champion of liberty and law; lover of country and man; exemplar of virtue; teacher above all others of the limitless possibilities of rectitude and courage; incomparable President, faithful husband, tender father, loving son: Thy name shall be a household word to millions whose existence lies in the dreamy realms of the unborn centuries. We mourn thy tragic end! We behold with pride, the rising superstructure of the mighty fabric of thy fame. We cannot tell "thy doom without a sigh," and yet we know that

> "Thou art Freedom's now and Fame's,
> One of the few immortal names
> That were not born to die."

THE ILLUSTRIOUS DEAD.

By Senator Voorhees.

Delivered in the Opera House, Terre Haute, Indiana, Sept. 21, 1881.

Mr. Mayor and Fellow-citizens:—I cannot remain silent on such an occasion as this.

All that is mortal of him, who a few hours ago was the living head of the most powerful government on the globe, now lies cold and still in death. The sounds and emblems of mourning are encircling the earth to-day. Throughout the boundaries of the Republic, the bells are tolling for the illustrious dead, and following the track of the sun, wherever the dread intelligence finds the American flag, whether on the stately squadron, or coasting schooner; whether over the proud embassy, or the humble consulate, there it will droop at half-mast, and its brilliant folds will be shadowed in crape. And with American sorrow will be mingled the sorrow of the whole civilized world. Every nation will be a mourner at this saddest of all funerals in American history.

The President of the United States died in public, with the world looking on from hour to hour, counting his pulse-beats and his breathings, and in all the long tragedy he faced death so well, bore himself so manfully, without murmur of complaint, or word of vengeance, that civilized nations of every clime and kindred will stand uncovered as his funeral train carries him back to his beloved Western home.

Sir, I knew James A. Garfield well, and except on the political field, we had strong sympathies together. It is nearly eighteen years since we first met, and during that period I had the honor to serve seven years in the House of Representatives with him. I have been asked, in this hour of universal grief, to place some estimate upon his character. The kindness of his nature, and his mental activity, were his leading traits. In all his intercourse with men, women and children, no kinder heart ever beat in human breast than that which struggled on until half-past ten o'clock Monday night, and then forever stood still. There was a light in his face, a chord in his voice, and a pressure in his hand, which were full of love for his fellow beings. His manners were ardent and demonstrative with those to whom he was attached, and he filled the private circle with sunlight and with magnetic currents. He had the joyous spirits of boyhood, and the robust intellectuality of manhood, more perfectly combined than any one I ever knew.

Such a character was necessarily almost irresistible with those who knew him personally, and it accounts for that undying hold, which, under all circumstances bound his immediate constituents to him, as with hooks of steel. Such a nature, however, always has its dangers as well as its strength, and its blessings. The kind heart and the open hand never accompany a suspicious, distrustful mind. Designing men mark such a character for their own selfish uses, and General Garfield's faults, for he had faults, as he was human, sprang more from this circumstance, than from all others combined. He was prompt, and eager to respond to the wishes of those he esteemed his friends, whether inside or outside his own political party.

That he made some mistakes in his long and busy career is but repeating the history of every generous and obliging man who has lived and died in public life. They are not such, however, as are recorded in heaven, nor will they mar or weaken the love of his countrymen. The poor, laboring boy, the self-made man, the hopeful, buoyant soul in the face of all difficulties and odds, constitute an example for the American youth which will never be lost nor grow dim.

The estimate to be placed on the intellectual abilities of General Garfield, must be a very high one. Nature was bountiful to him, and his improvements were extensive and solid. He was an industrious, judicious student, and his rapidity of thought and activity of mind were at times amazing. He grasped a subject as quickly as any man who ever took part in the public affairs of the world. He had that fine mental courage which shrinks from no investigation. His acquirements were consequently rich and various. If I might make a comparison, I would say that with the exception of Jefferson and John Quincy Adams, he was the most learned President, in what is written in books, in the whole range of American history. This, in my judgment, will be the rank assigned him in the histories of the future.

The Christian character of General Garfield cannot, with propriety, be omitted in a glance, however brief, at his remarkable career. Those who knew him best in the midst of his ambition and his worldly hopes, will not fail now at his tomb to bear their testimony to his faith in God, and his love for the teachings of the blessed Nazarene. Though upon the summit of human greatness, he avowed his Master's cause and accepted the kingdom of Heaven in the spirit of a child. His chamber of death adds one more conspicuous illustration of the serenity and peace with which a Christian meets his fate. As the earth with all its honors, its loves and its hopes receded and disappeared, he was comforted by sights and sounds which this world can neither give nor take away.

It seems but yesterday that I saw him last, and parted from him, in all the glory of his physical, and mental manhood. His eye was full of light, his tread elastic and strong, and the world lay bright before him. He talked freely of public men and public affairs. His resentments were like sparks from the flint. He cherished them not for a moment. Speaking of one whom he thought had wronged him, he said to me, that sooner or later he intended to pour coals of fire on his head by acts of kindness to some of his kindred. He did not live to do so, but the purpose of his heart has been placed to his credit in the book of eternal life.

Sir, as to the public measures, and the recent vivid occurrences connected with his brief administration, I am not here now to speak. At other times, and in another forum, that task may perhaps be required, but not on this occasion of grief and commemoration.

General Garfield's career at the head of the Government was sad, stormy and tragic. He drank a bitter cup to its dregs. He realized, within his own party, in fullest measure, the harsh reward of an honorable and successful ambition.

> "He who ascends to mountain-tops shall find
>   The loftiest peaks most wrapped in clouds and snow;
> He who surpasses or subdues mankind
>   Must look down on the hate of those below.
> Though high *above* the sun of glory glow,
>   And far *beneath* the earth and ocean spread,
> *Round* him are icy rocks, and loudly blow
>   Contending tempests on his naked head,
> And thus reward the toils which to those summits led.'

But at last he has found rest and peace, the rest and peace of eternity to a Christian soul. As President, loving husband and father, affectionate son, and faithful friend, he will walk this earth no more. Alas! how pathetic was his death. At the high noon time of life, not quite fifty years of age, with a career already made, which would read like romance in any other country than this, and with a mission just before him in which he believed, and for which he longed to live, he fell by the hand of a wretch who had voted for him, and wanted some poor office in return. And then the long struggle with slowly approaching, but certain death! Whose eye has not wept, as the brave man was seen during the last eighty dreadful days, fighting his last great battle, and fighting it in vain? Like the strong swimmer in the surf of the sea, striving for the shore, he sometimes seemed to be nearing a point of safety, but with each ebbing wave he was carried further out, until at last he was gone forever from our anxious gaze on that tide which breaks alone on the high shores of immortality.

How gladly would a million of lives have been ventured for his rescue; but it could not be, and we bow our heads and our hearts in helpless submission. May God in his loving mercy have the bereaved wife and the orphaned children in His holy keeping.

I have no heart now to speak of the future administration of the government. I have faith in the American people, and all will be well. They are a source of power and of safety within themselves, and they can be trusted that no harm shall happen to the Republic. He who takes the place, under the Constitution, of the dead President, has my profound sympathy, and he will have my earnest support in all his efforts, to promote the welfare and glory of our common and beloved country.

AN UNPARALLELED SPECTACLE.

By Rev. G. H. Wells.

Delivered at the Memorial Services in Montreal, Canada, Sept. 26, 1881. In the pulpit were Revs. Gavin Lang, Dr. Sullivan, Dr. Clarke, H. Johnston, Dr. Stevenson, J. S. Black and W. S. Barnes, On the platform in front of the pulpit were the Lord Bishop of Montreal, Revs. Dr. McVicar, Canon Baldwin, Dr. Ussher, Prof. Shaw, J. L. Forster, W. W. Jubb, A. B. Mackay, Prof. Conssirat, E. A. Stafford, — Mallory, J. Nichols, and others.

My Friends:—We share a universal grief to-day. The American Nation bears its fallen President to his last resting-place, and the whole race of man forgets its differences and becomes a brotherhood beside his grave. The world has never seen a spectacle like this. The lines of country and of race seem blotted out.

It naturally reminds us of that former gloomy hour when, sixteen years ago, Lincoln fell by the assassin's hand. But there was difference of feeling then, both in his own and other lands. There is no division in opinion or emotion now. The world is one in condemnation of the deed and sorrow for his death. There have been many reasons for this fact.

The growing intercourse and unity of men never so deeply felt before; the sympathy awakened by the President's long suffering and his heroic fight for life, the perfect causelessness and madness of the crime have been large features in this grand result. But, quite beyond these things, there has been, too, a feeling which deepened as the weeks went by, and fuller light was thrown upon the case, until it ripened to conviction at the last, that the patient sufferer was a remarkable man, one of earth's truly noble and worthy sons—a man, who, quite aside from his exalted place and his tragic fate, deserved the high esteem of men, and whose death would be a general and heavy loss. A distinct, and important element in the great grief, is a tribute paid to his distinguished character and marvelous career. Men feel that there is a prince and a great man fallen this day in Israel, and they mourn for him as for a master and beloved chief. And this belief is amply justified by all the facts.

For some weeks past the world has been watching, and while they wondered at his gentleness and courage, they have searched his record in the past, and the more they have become acquainted with him the more have they admired and approved. No life could be more closely scanned than his has been with the keen vision of partisan political feeling, as well as with the gentler eye of pity, and no life ever bore the ordeal better, or came forth with purer fame. A calm review and candid estimate would rank him high among the great, good men. Think for a moment of his course, from the birth in a little clearing among the forests on the wild frontier—the humble home, so poor it sometimes lacked for necessary bread. His boyhood's hard and scantily rewarded toil, his small advantages of schools, and all the obstacles and hardships that hedged about his youth. Remember that he was a farm laborer, a wood chopper, a salt worker and a canal driver, in those days. And that, when yearning after something better for both heart and mind, he began a religious life, and entered on a course of study, he was compelled to struggle long and hard with poverty before he could attain the end.

His generous brother, and his almost more than human mother, gave him $17 for his first term in the Academy, and he made it suffice by sleeping on the floor and cooking his own food. In the vacation he earned $25 by cutting 100 cords of wood, to meet his next term's needs, and felt passing rich because he could afford to board. In the Collegiate Institute he did the work of janitor, and afterwards of tutor, as well as that of pupil, and gained a local fame as preacher and a speaker at political gatherings besides.

After graduating at an Eastern college among the highest in his class, he returned home to be a professor and soon President in the institution where he had been janitor six years before, and by his excellence in teaching lifted it at once to favor, and proved that he would become a great educator—the Arnold or the Taylor of the West, if he continued in the work. His admiring neighbors soon called him to public service, and he began his long political career in the Ohio Senate, of which he was the youngest member, as still later he was the youngest general in the army, and still later the youngest member of the National Congress.

He "let no man despise his youth," but was at once acknowledged in all these places as standing in the foremost rank. In the war he was an able and successful general, he was repeatedly promoted for gallantry, and eminent services, and might have risen to still higher place and won the name of a great commander had not his friends elected him to Congress, and President Lincoln urged that he could serve his country better in Washington than at the front. As member, first of the Committee of Military Affairs, where his experience in the army gave his counsels special worth, and, after the war, on the Committee of Ways and Means, which deals with the whole matter of revenue, and once more as Chairman of the Committee of Appropriations, which recommends and supervises the expenditures of Government, at a time when the annual outlay reached the sum of $300,000,000, he served his country in putting down rebellion and in defending the national honor and good name.

Last year, at the Chicago Convention, he led the delegation from his State, and urged the nomination of Secretary Sherman in a noble speech, and he continued loyal to his friend until all further strife was vain and he saw the choice of the convention was about to fall upon himself. Through the excited canvass that ensued he bore himself with dignity and delicacy that were as beautiful as they were rare. He never trumpeted his cause nor advocated his own claims, but retained his friendship with many in the opposing party, and kept the picture of the rival candidate hanging in his home throughout the whole campaign.

As President, he took the seat that had been made illustrious by Washington and Lincoln, and many other noble men, and has so filled it during these few months as to invest it with new honors, and to make it still more famous in the time to come. But who can worthily describe his conduct through these weeks of weary agony, while trembling in the balance between hope and fear, and watching at the very gates of death? His heroism here has beautifully closed, and crowned his whole career. He has shown how a man may stand sustained in every sphere of public life; he has shown now how a man may die without a fear. My friends, the person who has done this and yet has died before the age of fifty years, is surely of no common clay or mould. He had been tested on every side and everywhere found strong and true. Weighed in many balances, he was not found wanting.

Still more besides his active labors he found time for quiet study and research. He was a wide reader, a profound thinker, an accomplished scholar. He loved best to grapple with the great questions that belong to the national welfare, and affect the universal good. He had mastered history of both ancient and modern times. He was deeply versed in literature, both classical and recent. He kept pace with the discoveries of the present, and was an intimate friend of such scientists as Agassiz and Henry. He was a largely gifted, a richly stored, a ripely cultured man, who would have honored any age, and graced the choicest fellowship of mind.

And if we inquire for the finer moral qualities of heart, we shall find him still more rich in these. He was a singularly just, upright, affectionate and simple-minded man. He never asked an office or promotion in his life. Not that he lacked ambition, for he had as much of it as any great man should. He hoped that he might sometime be prepared to serve his country in high places—but others' estimate of him invariably outran his own, and before he was ready for it, honor came. When it was proposed to send him to the State Senate, he said: "If you elect me I will serve, but it must be entirely without my assistance." He was nominated and chosen to Congress while absent in the army and without being consulted in the matter. When, after many years of service as a representative, he might have been elected to the Senate, remained at the request of President Hayes to be administration leader in the lower house. When he saw he was to be nominated at Chicago he said: "I feel as if my death-warrant had been signed; I had thought I would like some time to be President, but I have just been chosen to the Senate, and might hope for many happy, useful years of labor there, but as ex-President I shall be shut out from public life."

In his case, the man never sought the office, but that ideal of patriotic philosophy was found, in which the office always sought the man. He sat in Congress for his native district, the 19th of Ohio. It is a region in the northeastern corner of the State, called the Western Reserve, or sometimes New Connecticut. It was settled largely by New England settlers, and has always been distinguished for high intelligence and moral worth. Joshua R. Giddings, one of the heroes of the anti-slavery conflict, had been its representative for twenty-five years. Here President Garfield had been born, and always had his home, most loved and trusted by his neighbors who knew him best, and here he will to-day be buried in the beautiful cemetery that overlooks the heaving lake. This district and its representative in Congress were mutually fond and proud of one another, but differences sometimes arose.

Some years after the close of the war the greenback heresy had risen, times were hard, and taxes heavy, and some even among the honest people of Ohio imagined that some easier method might be found. Garfield returned from Europe to find these opinions prevalent, and when he was to speak at a reception tendered him, some of his friends urged him to say nothing on the subject, lest he might injure his chances in the nominating convention that was soon to meet. There was no special need for him to speak, but he would not keep silent, when silence might be misconstrued, and he attacked the vital point at stake. He said: "My friends, much as I value your opinions, I here denounce this theory that has worked into this State, as dishonest. unwise and unpatriotic; and, if I were offered a nomination and election for my natural life from this district, on this platform, I should spurn it. If you should ever raise the question of re-nominating me, let it be understood that you can have my services only on the ground of the honest payment of this debt and of these bonds in coin, according to the letter and spirit of the contract."

Fortunately for themselves the people could appreciate his courage, and when the convention met he was re-nominated by acclamation. In one political address he said: "I wish to adopt doctrines that will endure. I should like to hold a belief that will live longer than I shall live, and that my children after me might believe as true, and say, 'this doctrine is true now, and it was true fifty years ago, when my father adopted it.'" But after all, it was in private and domestic life that he was best. Not many men seem greatest to those most intimately acquainted with them, but one who knew the President well, has told me that he never seemed to him so truly great as when sitting by his own fireside and holding converse with his nearest friends. His power of friendship was remarkable.

His regard for President Hopkins of Williams' College, where he studied, a great man and a great inspirer of youth, was beautiful in the extreme. Once the subject of the importance of enlarging the library and the collections was discussed; when asked for his opinion, he said: "Gentlemen, books and cabinets are very good, but put me in a log cabin with only one rude bench, and seat Mark Hopkins on one end of it and let me sit upon the other, and that will be a college good enough for me."

It is worth while to note the reasons that decided him to go East for an education, and to Williams rather than to some other college. It was naturally expected that if he wished for anything beyond the local schools, he would go to Bethany College, an institution connected with the church of which he was a member, and which had for its presiding officer Alexander Campbell, the founder and leader of that sect. He thus explains his change of destination in a letter to a friend: "There are three reasons why I have decided not to go to Bethany :

"1st. The course of study is not so extensive or thorough as in Eastern colleges;

"2nd. Bethany leans too heavily toward slavery;

"3rd. I am the son of Disciple parents; am one myself and have had but little acquaintance with people of other views, and having always lived in the West, I think it will make me more liberal, both in my religious and my general views, to go into a new circle, where I shall be under new influences." He then proceeds to say that he has written to the Presidents of three Eastern institutions, and has received similar replies, brief business notes from all, but adds, "President Hopkins concludes his letter with this sentence: 'If you come here, we shall be glad to do what we can for you.' Other things being so nearly equal, this sentence, which seems like a friendly grasp of the hand, has settled the question for me. I shall start for Williams next week."

Really this young man has got a very definite and just conception of his needs. He seeks for culture, liberality and freedom. He will not go where people lean toward slavery. To this thought he was consistent all his life.

One day, while he commanded a division in the Army of the Cumberland, a fugitive slave took refuge in the camp. It was early in the war, when some supposed that a chief duty of the Union forces was to capture and restore the slaves that ran away. So the commanding officer wrote an order to General Garfield, requiring him to find the fugitive and hand him over to his owner. He took the order and deliberately wrote upon the back these words:—" I respectfully but positively decline to allow my command to search for or deliver up any fugitive slaves; I consider that they are here for quite another purpose," and gave it to the orderly to carry back. A friend who saw the message expected him to be court-martialed on the spot, and begged him not to send it. He simply answered, "Right is right, and I will not mince matters. My people on the Western Reserve did not send my boys and myself down here to do that kind of work, and they will sustain me in my course." The refusal went to headquarters, but no reprimand was given, and nothing more was said about the case.

That yearning, too, for sympathy that made a kindly word appear the welcome of a friendly hand. He never lost that feeling, nor did he forget to sympathize in turn with other young men in circumstances like his own. Some of his choicest memories were of his success in encouraging and bringing forward some who were distrustful of themselves, and of winning some parents to consent to the education of their sons. One such unwilling parent of an economical disposition, he persuaded by assuring him that in a little time his boy could teach and so earn money for himself. Another, of religious principles, he gained by preaching in his hearing a sermon on the Parable of the Talents, urging that parents were responsible for the development and culture of their sons. To a young man who was almost discouraged and ready to give up the struggle for a college course, and who had asked him for advice, he wrote: "Brother, mind it is not a question to be discussed in the spirit of debate, but to be thought over, and prayed over, as a question out of which are the issues of life." And then proceeded to comfort and inspire in words that must have sprung out of his own experience. The rule of thought and prayer which he here prescribes to others, he followed rigidly himself.

On any matter that arose for settlement he sought the guidance of God's word and spirit. He was never ashamed of his religion, nor sought to put it out of sight.

One night a party of Williams College students were camping out upon a neighboring mountain to see the sunrise from the top. They sat beside a camp fire and spent the evening merrily in jest and song, until the hour for retiring came, when one of them drew a Bible from his pocket and said to his companions: "It is my habit to read a chapter and to pray before I go to bed. Will you not join me in this exercise to-night?" And so he read the sacred word and prayed with them upon the mountain top, and one who was a member of the group, and who described the scene, has lately said, "I never lost the influence of that hour." That student was James A. Garfield. He afterward confided to a friend that by a special arrangement with his mother they both read the same passage and prayed for one another every night.

But who may venture to describe the reverent regard, the tender, chivalric attention he ever manifested for that mother? His devotion to his wife was beautiful, and it is high encomium for him and her to say that they were perfectly united, and wholly worthy of each other. But towards his mother he displayed a love that seemed almost to be a worship. He never knew a father's care, and all his strength of soul went out upon the mother who had filled the place of both his parents to him. We all have read how, upon the day of his inauguration as President, when he had finished his discourse, he turned to his mother and his wife and kissed them both, as if in this, the proudest moment of his life, when the applause of the great multitude was hailing him the nation's chief, he found his sweetest pride and plaudits in their love. Most of us know that the only letter he wrote after he had received the fatal wound was a note to reassure and cheer his mother in her Ohio home, and have read those hopeful and courageous words. And he might well be a grateful and hopeful son, for in her character and the training that she gave were held, as in an acorn cup, his illustrious career.

He was highly favored in his parentage on both his

father's and his mother's side. His father's family were English yeomen from the Welsh borders, who came to America with the early Puritans, and who were always known as sturdy and God-fearing men. They were chiefly or entirely farmers—true sons and tillers of the soil. His mother's family were French Huguenots, driven from the country by the revocation of the Edict of Nantes. They were mostly preachers—men of great eloquence and intellectual power. And so the son inherited from the one side an admirable physique and perfect health, and from the other an instinct for study and for speech. English firmness and French fire, Saxon solidity and Celtic grace were blended finely in his frame.

God sometimes forms a great man as he makes a diamond, of one element, and the person, like the jewel, is of wondrous brilliancy and worth; but generally, at least, in these days, he combines many elements and traits together, and so secures variety and versatility of mind. This was pre-eminently true in him of whom we speak. He was a high, yet worthy representative of the people and the institutions of his native land.

His country mourns for him as for her favorite and chosen son. But with her tears, is mingled gratified pride that her soil can produce such men.

She thinks of Lincoln, of Garfield, her two murdered Presidents to-day, and like the Roman mother, points to them as her most precious gems. And that aged, widowed mother, sits desolate, yet glorified to-day, and while she weeps, she also must rejoice. She gave him to his country more than 20 years ago. When he decided to enlist he told her of his wish, and asked for her consent. For a while she could not give it—the struggle was severe. He could not go without her God-speed to the war, and she could not grant it. At last she said, "Go, my son, your life belongs to your country, not to me."

He has yielded his life, not upon the battle-field, but yet in his country's service and for her good. In her deep agony the mother to-day will rejoice that she pronounced those words. She will be glad that she had such a son to give and that she gave him for his country's good.

I should naturally fail in the feelings of this hour if I did not add a few words as the representative of my country and countrymen. Gratitude we all feel toward all our fellow-citizens for the outpouring of their sympathy in this the hour of our distress.

I never felt so deeply a love for all mankind as to-day. I never realized so much how many and how mighty are the cords that bind the Mother beyond the sea and the Daughter on this side, and how real are the common blood and the common sympathy.

And on behalf of myself I must be permitted to say to-day, with new emphasis and feeling, God bless Her Majesty the Queen, and all the sons of her realm that show themselves our brethren and fellow-mourners at this hour.

LESSONS FOR THE YOUNG.

By Bishop Clarkson, of Iowa.

Delivered at the Memorial Service, in Des Moines, Iowa, Sept. 26, 1881.

It may be safely said that history nowhere presents records of such a scene as this day's sun looks down upon. Fifty millions of people in actual mourning for one man, and the whole wide world, from end to end, bowed and silent in responsive sympathy.

Among all the wonders of history this hour's scene stands alone of its kind, and unapproachable in majesty and sublimity. Never has there been seen, heard or written of anything like it since the world began. Now, my friends, we take the position that all this remarkable condition of things that we see to-day on the American continent is not to be accounted for, simply because the man whose death we lament was the President of the United States, and therefore the representative of a great nation. Nor yet because his terrible taking-off was associated with such a startling and shocking tragedy, and with such continued and pitiable suffering, borne with a sublime heroism and a marvelous patience.

These facts have, no doubt, contributed largely to intensify the nation's sorrow, to evoke the world's sympathy and to swell everywhere the melancholy pageantry of to-day. But the real source of this unexampled exhibition of human grief lies deeper than all this. It is to be found in the universal and unchallenged estimate of the departed President's character, in the radiant beauty of his great and stainless life. From the fierce struggles of his lonely childhood up through all grades—" student, teacher, soldier, statesman, president," there was ever the same grand picture whose magnificent colorings were truthfulness, diligence, fidelity, purity, gentleness, unselfishness, dignity and clean-handedness.

And upon this grand picture of human life there has been cast, as Tennyson says, the shinings of the utmost possible daylight, and there it has ever stood and shall always stand, the same clear, unstained and wondrously beautiful and benignant. That is the reason why the uncounted thousands of the world's population stand to-day with uncovered heads and unspoken emotions, by the open grave that is to hide away from human sight so much greatness, so much goodness, so much loveliness, and so much true nobility. What an example to the young man here who feels that he has something in him that can lift itself above the mediocrity about him.

The laurels that wreathe this man's splendid career, the tributes that cover his name with glory, the tears that are wept over his tragic fate, are holier triumphs far than ever crowned the common politician, the average statesman, or the successful soldier—because they are the triumphs of character.

We hold up to you, young men, to-day, the inspiring name, James Abram Garfield. Not because he achieved success in gaining position and power, for this is not open to you all, but because he achieved success in preserving a record undefiled by a shadow of meanness or littleness, in securing the affectionate admiration of all who ever touched him in the manifold jostlings of life, and now in bringing upon his memory the benedictions of the ten times ten thousand who have been helped by his example upward to the right. This is the true victory of life.

And this victory is in some degree attainable by every young man before me—each one in his own sphere, standing, working and conquering in the lot where God has placed him.

One thought more. The mournful death which we this day lament, associated as it is with such relations of sadness and distress as to attract the gaze and the sympathy of the world, is not utterly deplorable. There is a bright side to it. Thank God there was among us—yes, even at our very head—such a man to live, yea, and such a man to die.

We hold that the world is vastly better to-day; that our common humanity has been lifted to a higher level; that our young men have been elevated in tone and purpose, because we have been bending in anxious grief for eighty days over the death-bed of such a man, watching with prayerful hope the flickering pulse of his parting life, and because we are now in the sacredness of a holy sorrow, laying him away to his final resting place, amidst the people who loved him the most, because they knew him the best. Life or death win equal honors for such a soul. Living, he was an inspiration. Suffering—we speak it reverently—he was Christ-like: for the sweet patience and the chastened resignation of that long agony was but the utterance of the sublime prayer, "Father forgive them, they know not what they do;" "and being dead he yet speaketh," and shall forever speak to American youth.

Sometimes the young man who is just entering upon his life's work, when he observes about him so much trickery in trade, so much corruption in politics, so much sham in religion, or when he is oppressed by the thought of how long and hard the fight is to be before he gains his goal—or when he seems to see about him the temporary advantage the False and the Wrong, and the crowding into the corner and the shade, the true and the good, he is tempted to lose faith in himself, faith in the right, faith in man and faith in the eternal realities. Oh, sad beginning this of many an immortal wreck. But I tell you, my young brother man, there is in this day's magnificent and mournful spectacle, and in the thoughts born of it, that ought to charm you back from a danger like this.

Here is first the spectacle of honest manhood, untiring labor, conscientious fidelity and incorruptible rectitude, crowned with this earth's highest civic honors, because of the Republic's confidence in these eternal virtues; here is the generous allaying of all party strife and the marvelous calming down of all political animosities in the presence of pain and danger to the chosen one, who represents to the Republic's eye these great principles, and embodies them in his person and life—here is a mighty people bereaved in his death as by a personal loss, beyond any precedent in history, because he was such a man—here is the measureless tide of human sympathy swelling towards the afflicted nation from all coasts and all shores, because he was such a man.

I tell you young man, when you think of these things and what they sprung from, and what they lead to, you may look above the struggles and the rivalries and the shams and the falsehoods around you; these are calculated to tone down your hopefulness and enthusiasm and say to yourself, "I have still faith in man, faith in myself, faith in the Nation, faith in the future, faith in the eternal power of right, and above all, faith in the Everlasting God who rules and reigns above, because such a man as James Abram

Garfield has lived and died and conquered, has been decorated with the Republic's choicest appreciation, and goes to his grave to-day garlanded with all that is holy, and all that is tender and all that is precious, in human sorrow.

LINCOLN AND GARFIELD.

By Ex. Governor Richard J. Oglesby, of Illinois.

Delivered at the Memorial Service in Leadville, Colorado, September 26, 1881.

Mr. Mayor, Brother Soldiers, Men of the Navy and Fellow-citizens: Wherever we turn our eyes we behold the signs and emblems of mourning, tokens of a nation's grief.

This sad day, observed throughout the Union, is also appropriately kept amid these mountains by these people, who never forget what is due, on all great occasions like this, of love to a president who has been assassinated in this great Republic.

It has been supposed tyrants were reserved for this crime. It is perhaps not admitting too much to say the world has felt relieved when known tyrants have been removed from the theatre of their bloody deeds. But what are we to think when we witness this crime in our own midst, in our day? Two men, great and good men, have fallen under our eyes, at our door, in the beauty and glory of perfect manhood—in the maturity of rounded and perfect lives, innocent of any wrong-doing to any human being. The breasts of both were filled with humanity for all mankind. And if it be the hand of Providence, are we to be taught the hard lesson that republics are not favored of God? This is unendurable—this is manifestly untrue. If, then, it be the mysterious hand of Providence, are we to learn that no distinction is taken between tyrants and the truly great benefactors? or shall we not rather understand from this experience—these great national bereavements—that this, regarding alike the law of God and man, assassination is the instigation and the work of cruel and abandoned men, who neither understand nor care for the institutions of government or the lives of men? But if Providence is still discernible in this heart-rending crime, may we not catch the sunlight of the holy purpose breaking through the dark cloud in the dawn of a more perfect and fraternal national sentiment. For have we not witnessed during this great calamity the most beautiful and touching manifestations of sympathy and sorrow from all political parties, and from all men and associations of men of all countries and all nationalities of the nations of this earth?

But a few years ago Abraham Lincoln fell by the hand of an assassin—that great, God-like, sainted man, who illuminated the whole earth by his illustrious character, and when he fell a dark suspicion also fell upon our Southern fellow citizens who had lately been arrayed against us. It was a long time that the South, I feel constrained as an honest man to say, suffered under the suspicion of participation in that national and cruel crime.

Let me here to-day, in the most copious and open manner, declare as only a private American citizen can declare, that in my opinion and in the opinion of most of the living thoughtful men of the day, the South had nothing whatever to do with the assassination of Abraham Lincoln.

James A. Garfield has fallen. I fear a dark suspicion lurks in the mind of thoughtful women and thoughtful men, that perhaps agencies may have been at work, deep and direful, to bring about this awful result. I believe it due to the dignity of this occasion, I believe it due to the patriot, and to the trustworthiness of American political history, to say for one, and for only one, but still that one speaking from the high plateau of American citizenship, that political parties, however variant and however different in their opinion of their hostilities, have had nothing under God's heaven, under God's free, shining sun, either secretly or otherwise, with the foul agency that resulted in the death of our late President.

These great facts, fellow-citizens of Leadville, these great, astonishing and terrifying historical facts, will live. History will astonish and mortify the world long after you and I and these people shall have passed into the grave of oblivion. These terrible facts will endure as long as American history shall endure, and let us, you and me, let the women and men to-day of this country and of this State contribute whatever we can in the way of truth, in the way of open and honest declaration, to divest that history of all foul and unnatural suspicion. But they fell—both of them fell, by the hands of wicked, cruel, individual, irresponsible men, and it is neither becoming the dignity of this occasion, the solemnities of this all-pervading day, nor your character, nor mine as an American citizen, that we should fritter away the dignity of the awful hour in unworthy and unbecoming imprecations upon the foul heads of the worthless men who brought these great disasters upon our God, our country and our liberty.

Of the miserable Guiteau, what does it concern you or me as to what his fate shall be? Whether he shall die as he ought to die, and a wronged and outraged sentiment be avenged by a wronged and outraged people, or at the hand of some other assassin, or by the due process of law—it matters not. His poor, worthless life, his poor, worthless character, his poor, unworthy ending, can in no possible event be any compensation for the calamity he has brought upon the republican institutions. No, ladies! no, no gentlemen! I will not spend an hour or a minute upon his fate; it is totally unworthy of the notice, the reflection or the consideration of the humblest and most unpretentious individual within the reach and reverberation of my voice. God in heaven that rules to-day, as he has ever ruled, as you are taught by the lispings of the touching and eloquent prayer to which you have just listened, will see that not only the destiny of nations, but the destiny of republics among nations, shall be wisely and forever cared for.

Women and men of these mountainous regions, whom I am from to-day learning to love so well—you women and men gathered from all the States and Territories of the nations of this world, in these isolated, remote and lofty regions do not forget your allegiance to yourselves; do not forget your allegiance to civilization; do not forget your allegiance to republican institutions, and do not forget your allegiance to God in heaven.

As sure as time rolls on, as sure as the sun shall rise and illuminate with its gorgeous rays those lofty peaks that rear their heads heavenward above us, and continues its course until it reaches the West and sinks behind those mountains that are to endure forever, remember, fellow citizens, one and all, that justice, and right, and humanity, and law, and order, and piety, and virtue, will in the end, triumph over all.

Our government is a government of the people; our government is a government for the people; our government, thank God, is a government by the people. If it be not the best on earth, if it shall not finally triumph in the onward march of civilization, then has humanity been created in vain; then has every man lived to no purpose; for I am sure, poor and infirm man as I am, I am sure that God in heaven intended the lowest and commonest, and the most ignorant of mankind, should share equally and fully and finally in the glorious existence, and in the full enjoyment of human life and human liberty.

The death of Lincoln, the death of Garfield, the death of any man or combination of men who have lived, cannot affect the onward march of a free, patriotic and honest people. A government resting upon the hearts of honest men, a government firmly grounded in the affections of a pure people, cannot rust and perish away.

We live, fellow citizens, and we can only live by the institutions of government. You may, many of you, feel as I have felt; you may, all of you have felt sometimes that the ways of government and the ways of constitution and the ways of laws are hard and oppressive. Within the view of your vision and limited intellect, you may often feel that all does not go right, that liberty does not flow out equally to all. We have these doubts, we have these misgivings; sometimes we harbor these unjust suspicions. Women and men, ladies and gentlemen, friends and countrymen, shake off all such thoughts, and dismiss all this ideal stuff from your minds; let it waft away, this futile and senseless trash. Come back within the scope of your own individuality; come back within the range of the powers of thought and reasoning with which God endowed you; throw away these false philosophies, and resolve, as I have done, to be true to the God in Heaven, true to the moral lessons of life, true to honesty, true to virtue and true to the flag of a Republic that waves forever a protection above our heads.

Lincoln and Garfield were alike in many respects: both

were of humble and obscure origin; both lived and died poor; both were humane and tender by nature; both were soldiers; neither rose to great distinction as such, but in what all soldiers love and hold in the highest estimation, both earned the respect and good opinion of all citizens and patriots; both were highly gifted intellectually; both endowed with the purest and loftiest morality; both were intensely devoted to the union and universal liberty; both met the same untimely end; both fell from the same high pinnacle of fame, doomed to the same sad fate by the bullets of dark and bloody, minded men; and both honored and loved, will be forever treasured in the hearts of a grateful people, ever mindful of the lives of martyrs to freedom, resting forever in the affection and love of all the people of the Republic and of all lovers of liberty throughout the world.

Here I might well afford to stay my remarks. I feel that I can add nothing to relieve the deep feeling that penetrates and permeates the hearts of all who have so patiently listened to me. Death has done its work; all these days of mournful solemnities throughout the entire Nation and the world, will close the career of the life of James A. Garfield.

Fellow citizens of Leadville, it is due to you, it is due to your community, it is due to these people, to whom I am not so much a stranger as I was a year ago, yet comparatively a stranger in your midst, that I should render and return to you, to your committee, to your mayor and councilmen, to the army, to the representatives of the State, to the militia, to the soldiers present, my thanks for this undeserved honor, for this great compliment unexpectedly bestowed upon me of officiating here upon this occasion. I live in another State; my home is in Illinois, where it has been for forty-five years, but in another and a broader and a higher sense, under the benign influence of our expansive and generous constitution, I, like you all, like every one of you present, am a citizen not only of the State wherein I reside, but am also a citizen of each State and Territory of this Union. And wherever you plant your feet, or I shall plant my foot, within the reach and surroundings of our constitution, both you and I, and all of us, are at home and secure. All of you in Colorado, in Lake county and in Leadville, you and I and all of us, are equally and securely at home and at rest to-day. But there is something further I ought to say. As I said to my old friend, Judge Ward, to-day, not only here, but wherever I shall hereafter go, it will, it shall, be most pleasant and agreeable to me to bear testimony to, the state of society that I have met with in these mountainous regions. In this State of Colorado, and in this city of Leadville, I uniformly encounter nothing but decorum, nothing but propriety, nothing but respect, nothing but cordiality, nothing but sympathy and the highest and the best of American brotherhood. I know it is too freely written, too often said that here, life, property and peace are not secure. It is wrong, it is an unjust reflection, upon the state of society that I behold before me to-day. Witness this demonstration of sympathy and sorrow. How it must affect the heart of that pure, noble, simple American woman, the bosom companion, the better part and relict of James A. Garfield, when she shall learn of these mountaineers, these miners that wield the pick and shovel, these men that dare to dive deep into the hidden riches, and mysteries of the earth, cut off for a time from the tender relations of society, by raising up men, women and children, to-day, in beautiful, majestic array, to testify in mourning and sorrow, under the influence of sweet, touching and fruitful music, their profound sympathy for the loss the mother and the children have sustained, and for the loss the nation has sustained.

I see here wherever I go, and I see here wherever I stroll, the sweet and gentle influence of women;—God bless their gentle and mild influence upon men here in Leadville! I have met them, pure, refined, delicate, elegant, casting the influence of their modest presence upon the rougher tone of society; it is felt, and humanity is lifted up. God bless the women of America!

Fellow-citizens, brother soldiers, soon I leave you, perhaps to return no more. Though not blessed with success myself, I can bear testimony to the success of others, and above that and better than that, I can and shall bear testimony to the high state of society, to the morality and to the Christian influence that pervades this entire atmosphere.

GARFIELD, THE CHRISTIAN.

By Rev. J. W. Ingram.

Delivered at the Memorial Services in Omaha, Neb., Sept. 26, 1881.

My weeping brethren and sorrowing countrymen, I am not willing that one word of mine should go to encourage anything like a man-worshiping spirit. But while the tongue of evil is ever busy painting in darkest colors, in all places, the faults and follies of our fallen race, it seems no less a duty than a pleasure to point the whole world to the brilliant life and beautiful Christian virtues of our deceased President.

The influence of this life, and the reflections of these virtues can be confined to no class, people, or nation. In every land where the torch of civilization has **driven** back the darkness of barbarism, their influence has been felt, and all national life has been made more beautiful by their embellishments.

The Christianity of James A. Garfield is so closely interwoven with his private and public life, that it is difficult to speak of one and not the other; it is the one thread of gold that runs through every upward step of his sublime life, from the dark shadows of poverty and obscurity, to the fullness of the glory and honor of the greatest of all nations.

The religion of this Christian statesman was not that of a mere outward profession, nor yet of a mere inward sentiment or feeling. Prayers, songs and public services, did not exhaust his idea of Christianity. With him religion was a life, not a creed, not a dogma, not a system of metaphysics; but a daily cross-bearing, sacrificing, charity bestowing life.

As evidence of his princely faith in an All-wise Creator, a divine Redeemer, and an inspired Bible, it might be sufficient to direct the attention of the world to his righteous life, and triumphant death, but along the pathway of his earthy pilgrimage are repeated flashes of religious light, that more clearly reveal to us his confidence in, and reliance upon a divine revelation. At the age of nineteen he made for the first time a public avowal of his belief in the gospel of God's grace. Doubtless this act was the result of his overpowering faith in God, and his deep sense of duty. No love of fame, no thirst for earthly glory, no lust for worldly wealth, could have impelled him to bow his loyal neck to the yoke of the Master; for the people with whom he made his spiritual home were an humble, and at that time a despised people, clinging to the cross, and building quietly on the rock. They could be of no possible service to him in any worldly sense whatever.

Later on in life, in October, 1876, he stood with uncovered head, face to face with death. At his feet lay the pale, lifeless form of his own darling boy. His grief was as deep and sincere as his paternal love. He took a pen in his hand, and under the direction of his great heart, wrote a note to his Christian brethren, asking that a few of them be with him in his great trial, and ended the note by subscribing himself: "In the hope of the gospel, so precious in this affliction." These are words of faith springing from a sorrowing heart, and penned by a trembling hand.

Could we have gone on some bright Sunday morning a few months ago, and opened the door of the small, unpretentious frame church in the village of Mentor, Ohio, and seen the manly form of our gifted brother, with his wife and children by his side, surrounded by a group of poor, humble country worshipers; and could we have heard his deep bass voice mingling with theirs in song, and witnessed his humble reverence as he bowed in solemn prayer with them around the same altar, our confidence in the majesty of his faith, the humility of his heart, and the purity of his life, must forever remain unspoken.

But never, since the days the Man of Sorrows expired on the cross, did the Christian faith shine forth with more heavenly lustre than during the eighty long, dreary days of the President's suffering. When the fatal shot was fired that cut him down, he was in the meridian of his manhood, the halo of a nation's glory was upon him, and the sun of his fame was high in the heavens.

That morning when he stood in the fated depot, conversing with Secretary Blaine, his body was full of health, his heart was full of hope, and his mouth was full of words of promise.

In a moment, in the twinkling of an eye, the body was smitten with the arrows of death; the hopes of his heart were blasted forever; the world of promise and cheer were changed into cries of pain and anguish; the feet so lightly started in the path of recreation and pleasure, were rudely turned into the gloomy highway leading to the shadows of death; but all this combined with great physical suffering, could not extort from the patient Christian sufferer a single murmur of complaint. Did ever mortal bear so much, with such manly courage and Christian fortitude? And how free were those days of trial from everything like fear of death, or dread of dying.

With him there was no constant demand for the presence and prayers of a minister to aid him in a preparation for the approach of death. During life he had prepared for death. He relied not so much on the power of prayer as the purity of life for happiness in the far-off forever. Some have supposed the almost constant absence from the sick-chamber of the ministers of the gospel, was evidence of a lack of faith upon the part of the nation's ruler; but to my mind, it only shows that his trust was not in feeble clay, or the prayers of erring men, but rather in a holy life and forgiving Christ.

It is the coward who has made no preparation for dying while living, who cries for preachers and prayers when the shadows of death lengthen and deepen around him.

With marvelous faith and confidence, this great man resigned all to the will of the Lord. My Christian brethren and fellow countrymen, let us embalm in our memories forever the industrious lad, the dutiful boy, the loving son, the studious youth, the faithful husband, the devoted father, the generous neighbor, the gifted teacher, the brave soldier, the eloquent preacher, the brilliant statesman, the **wise ruler**, the patient sufferer, the **pure** Christian, and—our fallen chieftain.

> "Fallen on Zion's battle-field,
> A soldier of renown.
>   Armed in the panoply of God,
> In conflict cloven down;
>   His helmet on, his armor bright,
> His cheek unblanched with fear,
>   While round his head there gleamed a light,
> His dying hour to cheer.
>
> "Fallen—a holy man of God,
> An Israelite indeed,
>   A standard-bearer of the cross,
> Mighty in word and deed;
>   A master spirit of the age,
> A bright and burning light,
>   Whose beams across the firmament
> Scattered the clouds of night.
>
> "Fallen, as sets the sun at eve,
> To rise in splendor, where
>   His kindred luminaries shine,
> Their heaven of bliss to share;
>   Beyond the strong battle-field,
> He reigns in triumph now,
>   Sweeping a harp of wondrous song,
> With glory on his brow!"

THE FUNCTIONS OF GREAT MEN.

By Rev. Dr. Rankin.

Delivered in the First Congregational Church, Washington, D. C., Sept. 25, 1881.

Is. iii., 1-3—"For, behold the Lord, the Lord of Hosts, doth take away from Jerusalem and from Judea the mighty man, the man of war, the honorable man, the counselor, and the eloquent orator."

THERE is no function of society, said the reverend speaker, more vital than the choice of rulers. In this country it is an anointing holier than that of a king. It is the utterance of a voice which is the voice of God. What foreigner or citizen thinks of this Nation without thinking of her great men? And we are largely what these great men have helped to make us. Disorganizers of society look upon great men as in some sense usurpers, as having crowded their way to stations of prominence by jostling aside their betters. Thus the Nihilist prepares his hand-grenade, and the assassin his revolver. They do not reflect that preparation for such positions is of God—that they are God's gifts. "Brutus and Cæsar! What should be in that Cæsar?" They talk as Cassius talked to Brutus.

Irreverence for rulers is one of the perils of a republic. It is all true, as Goldsmith says, that a breath can give dignity and station. But the breath that calls men to such places cannot make them fit to occupy them. How peaceful was the heart of this great Nation to feel that at last there was a genuine, typical American in the presidential chair! "Upon this arm can I lean; this head, this heart can I trust." This is what she said.

But there is something grander than the place to which James Abram Garfield was called, in the fact that he was the product of our free institutions. The American people did not make him great. Had they never selected him to occupy the presidential chair the man had been the same. And we may well ask if God did not give him the place, and his brief career in it, only that the people might love him better, and take his name and his memory more into their hearts forever. The highest product of American national life is neither patrician nor plebeian. It blends and unites them both. It has the patrician culture with the plebeian heart. Washington stands at the head of one type, Lincoln at the head of the other. Do we err when we intimate that Garfield illustrates them both? A plebeian, a common man in all his sympathies; a patrician in the quality of his mind and the extent of his culture. President Garfield's honors came to him unsought. They came so fast he could not keep up with them.

The greatness which he achieved he did not struggle for, but grew into. Life laid her honors at his feet. Place after place cried out for him. He stood up in a great convention to advocate the claims of another. He became at once the cynosure of all eyes; he ravished all ears. He could not be true to another without being his own best self. It was nothing new; it had been so all his life long. There he stood; how could the people help taking him? His nomination was an inspiration. It was foreordained, like the consummate bloom of the flower.

This man's power never degenerated. He was reverent of good things by nature, and to him all good things were great. He had no flippant flings for the religion of his mother. He revered the great New England teacher; and when the assassin first sought him it was in the sanctuary of God. He finished his education in New England. It was fitting that New England hands should place the capital on this column, which was to go into the temple of freedom side by side with Washington and Lincoln; that he who began his studies where he heard the language of the Great Lakes, should conclude them where he could listen to the hymn which the Pilgrims heard when they laid our first foundations.

He was the united, the consummate flower of the New England of the East and the New England of the West. Do you ask me why he was so rudely and cruelly taken? Not for his own sake, we may be very sure. He was our President—our representative. In smiting him God has smitten us. Do not our relations to God need fresh readjustment? Have we kept the covenant we made with Him when he walked with us in the furnace of fire? Have the men in our highest places kept it? We have Christian convictions as to the Indian question, as to Mormonism, as to traffic in liquors. Are we true to them? It is a great thing to feel that though the man at the wheel is striken down, the Ship of State moves majestically on; that the footsteps of God are in the seas before her.

Such a Government as this cannot die. It does not rest in any one man. The same authority which made Garfield President indicated his successor. We turn away from Garfield, dead, not to forget him. If he has made mistakes—as who of our greatest have not, and have we not forgiven them?—let us remember that his hand was scarcely familiar with the helm of state; that he was yet in the narrows of his administration, and that his greatest mistake must always have sprung from a great loving heart that feared no ill, because it meant none—a man always more sinned against than sinning. In taking one, God has given another. The man whom the people named second, God has now named first. No unlineal hand takes the sceptre; but a man of character and purpose, true and tried; a man who has walked in the shadow of one great eclipse with a pathetic discreetness which has won all hearts, and whose first official acts and utterances give assurance that with these unsought responsibilities has come to him peculiar grace from God. If he has made his mistakes we bury them in that still open grave of his predecessor.

May we not close with the lines in which the poet Tennyson finishes the poem Mort d'Arthur?

> "The old order changeth, yielding place to her,
> And God fulfills Himself in many ways,
> Lest one good custom should corrupt the world.
> * * * * * * * *
> And so to bed; where yet in sleep I seemed
> To sail with Arthur under looming shores.
> To me methought
> There came a barque that, flowing forward, bore
> King Arthur, a modern gentleman
> Of stateliest part; and all the people cried:
> Arthur is come again; he cannot die!"

When the Nation awakens from her grief, may she find the parable true. Then shall be fulfilled the prophecy: "Thou shalt be no more called Forsaken. Neither shall thy land be termed any more Desolate. But thou shalt be called Hephzibah and thy land Beulah. For the Lord delighteth in thee."

WHY WE MOURN.

By N. R. Harper, Esq.

Delivered at the opening of the Special Memorial Services, held by the Colored People of Louisville, Ky., Sept. 26, 1881.

This service was held in the opera house. On the stage chairs were arranged in a semi-circle, with three chairs in the center. Those in a semi-circle were thirty-five in number, which, with the three in the center, made a number equal to the number of States in the Union. These chairs were occupied by the girl pupils of the public schools, each one of them holding a small placard in her hand, with the name of one of the States printed in large letters across it. All the girls, except the three occupying the chairs in the center, were dressed in white; those in the center representing the three States, Ohio, New Jersey and Kentucky, were dressed in mourning. These were called the mourning States, because Garfield died in one, was buried in another, and the people of Kentucky universally lament his untimely death. Across the front of the stage were arranged chairs for those who were to take part in the exercises, the seats in the front rows of the parquet being reserved for the choir and school children. The inside of the building was draped in mourning in a very handsome manner, and each one of the girls representing the three mourning States held a large portrait of the

President, heavily draped in mourning. The meeting was presided over by N. R. Harper, Esq.

LADIES AND GENTLEMEN:—Pursuant to arrangements perfected in a recent mass-meeting of the colored citizens of Louisville, I announce to you the opening of the exercises at this hour.

The question may be asked by some why we, as colored citizens, should single ourselves out for special memorial services on our part, when the same shot that rang out in the ladies' waiting-room at the Baltimore and Potomac depot, in Washington City, on the 2d day of last July, was felt alike by all citizens throughout the length and breadth of our common country? Why should we, as a class of citizens of Louisville, where all hearts are bowed down with the sadness of this hour, when the booming of cannon, and the mournful pealing of bells utter the lamentations of our city?—why should we thus particularly address ourselves to the public at this hour? The answer to these questions may be given—that a Divine hand had so shaped the destiny of colored Americans, that we can feel and realize to the fullest extent the power and influence of a tried, true and faithful friend, or the blows of a heartless, uncharitable foe. And who is there who can more faithfully interpret the emotions of our hearts than we ourselves, who feel, as no other class of citizens in this country can feel, that a friend to American liberty has been called away? To-day, as a race, we mourn the loss of a tried, true and faithful friend. The sequel shows that every man who, in the dark years of the past, gave his time, his talent, his voice and his vote to the work of driving oppression from the land, in order that life, liberty and the pursuit of happiness might, indeed, become the star of hope for the American people; such man was the tried, true and faithful friend of the colored citizens of America. This meeting, therefore, can but faintly express the sentiment of the colored citizens of Louisville in this hour of national grief and mourning. The crowned spirit which took its flight heavenward on last Monday night, as James A. Garfield, was a tried, true and faithful friend of our race. He has left us. "After life's fitful fever he sleeps well." Assassination has done its worst. Nor malice, strife, envy, life's trials and tribulations, nothing can touch him further. But, even amid the darkness of this national gloom, hope sees a star, and from its silvery rays, flashing from the throne of light, reveals in golden lines, "America, live on; live ever!"

At the conclusion of Mr. Harper's address, the choir ranged themselves in order across the stage, and sang the opening anthem: "To Thee, O Lord, I yield my spirit."

REV. T. B. CALDWELL'S PRAYER.

"O God of Nations! Chief Arbiter of all things! King of Kings and Lord of Lords! In Thy presence we come this day, humbly acknowledging Thy power. Thou art mighty; Thou canst work and no one can hinder Thee. With Thee are the issues of life and death. Thy tender mercy and loving kindness have followed us all the days of our life, even until now, and Thine infinite love embraces us as a goodly-fitting garment. Thou art the same unchangeable God as Thou wast in the beginning, and shall be through all eternity. O Lord, we desire Thy help in this dark hour of our bereavement. We pray Thee, our Father, for Thy sustaining grace, while we bow to the stroke of Thy rod of providence. We are ignorant, but Thou art wise. As far as the heavens are above the earth, so far are Thy ways above ours. We pray Thee to look from Thy throne of glory in the heavens upon this Nation, bathed in tears, and while we mourn, be Thou our comforter.

Turn our sadness into joy, and by Thy wonderful providence, turn this calamity to the good of our country; clear away the shadows of death from the grave of our departed President. Remember, O Lord, we pray Thee, that heroic woman, who has tenderly watched by the death-bed of our dead Ruler through all these weary days—may she lean upon Thy strong arm and find support in this, the darkest hour of her widowhood and bereavement. Be unto her a husband and unto her children a father. Bless his mother, that one who, in the days of his youth, taught him to love Thee. O Lord, support her in her old age, and may consolation take hold upon her heart, when she realizes that she will soon be with her son upon the golden shore, where no assassin can come to rob her of her 'baby.' We pray Thee to bless those who were with him during his affliction and endeavored to win him back to strength, and as they mingle their tears to-day with ours, may they be comforted in the assurance that they have done their duty. Bless President Arthur. Give him the wisdom to fill the office vacant by the hand of death. May he trust in Thee and follow the example set before him. May he rule in righteousness and in Thy holy love. We pray Thee also, O Lord, to remember poor Guiteau, the assassin, shut out from the sunlight, incarcerated in his cell and hated by all men. O God, we pray Thee, Thou who art the sinner's friend, have mercy upon his guilty soul. Guide us as a nation, watch over us as a people, and at last save us, we ask, for our Redeemer's sake. Amen."

WE ALL MOURN.

By Captain Henry Jackson.

Delivered at the Memorial Service in Atlanta, Ga., Sept. 26, 1881.

FIFTY millions of people, of every shade of political opinion, of every form of religion; people from all the ends of the earth, from every section of this land, stand to-day before an open grave, with heads bowed in sorrow and humiliation; sorrow for greatness stricken of its glory, sorrow for the suffering widow and children. No such shock as this was ever before known in our country.

The president once fell by the hand of violence, but that was fresh upon the clash of contending armies. But now, in a time of profound peace, in a time of unparalleled national prosperity, when there is no bitterness between the sections or the two parties, when the national sun was shining with brilliancy, when the Goddess of Liberty was radiant—at that very moment the head of the government falls before the hand of the assassin.

The scene that is presented before us is one that the world has never before witnessed. What is it due to? It is due to the character of our institutions; to their possibility for developing the highest good or the direst evil. Under our institutions every man has an opportunity to reach a position which his superior talents entitle him to, at the same time the liberality of our institutions leaves a gate open where weak minds, or hearts black and tainted with crime, can go in and work irreparable damage.

No matter how we have differed in the past, now it seems Garfield was a great and good man.

Twenty years ago, Lincoln was regarded as a bad man, and yet to-day there is scarcely an intelligent man who does not admit that he was honest and great, and that his death was the severest blow that the South ever received.

The shot of Guiteau has demonstrated beyond all peradventure the attachment of the people of the South for the whole country. They knew not the President, and yet, when violence attacked him, the men, women, and the very children cried out with indignation. They prayed that the assassin might not prove to be from the South, and for nearly three months they waited with bated breath every bulletin.

The following resoultions by the special committee from Cœur de Leon Commandery were read at this meeting by Right Eminent W. D. Luckie:

Amidst the mourning of the whole land, the people of this city, led in a solemn service by the order of Knights Templar, of which our late heroic President was an honored member, would lament the untimely and unhappy severance of all their earthly relations with him by the abrupt thrust of rude and cruel death.

Widespread as is his own country's broad domain, hangs this day the sable cloud of popular sorrow, from which universal tears are falling. This day the States of the Union unite in a new brotherhood of grief over their common loss.

The people *en masse* are claiming that the bereavement is their own, for they were learning when he fell that he was the President of the whole country.

Society suffers the pang of separation from a genial companion, and the republic of letters losing a cultured citizen, would show its own peculiar grief.

The families of the land bewail with common sorrow the loss of an illustrious and exemplary son, husband, father.

The genius of republican government intensely resenting the manner of his death, presents mournful but exalted tributes to his patriotism, intelligence and virtue.

And religion asserts its rightful place in the general lament, but commits even with tearful eyes the child of grace unto Him who has received his redeemed spirit into glory.

Thus, also, this order came in union with all to offer its tribute to his memory, who was one of the knightliest soldiers of the cross.

Henceforth, with special pleasure, his biography from his earliest years to the close of his life, will be placed in the hands of our American youth, that they may emulate the character of one, who with proper ambition and generous endeavors, attained the highest places of honor and usefulness, while he maintained his Christian virtues and kept himself in the fear of God.

That Divine providence has in infinite wisdom already made the circumstances of the revolting assassination produce good in the land we can faithfully trust. That the sentiment which the thrilling event created and developed has pervaded the hearts of all the people of our great country, calls for universal congratulation; and that the future of our government will be happily shaped by the patriotic and pious influences this day profoundly felt everywhere, is a hope for whose realization all good people do most devoutly pray!

Thus cherishing in memory all the virtues of our lamented president, and with reverent awe submitting to the

Divine Will, we desire to express our sense of the bereavement in these declarations:

1. We declare our indignation at the revolting and iniquitous assassination of the president, deploring that in all this country one man could exist who was capable of so great a crime.

2. We revere the memory of him who was at once patriot, president and brother—who lived and died a Christian man.

3. We send to the venerable mother, to the devoted wife, to the fatherless children, every sentiment of sympathy, and would claim them, in common with the country, as a sacred trust.

4. We bow our will submissively to God, and making record of this paper, do direct that a copy be forwarded to the Grand Commandery of the State, and that another copy be transmitted to the family.

THE PERFECT MAN.

By Elder J. Z. Taylor.

Delivered at the Memorial Services in Kansas City, Mo., Sept. 26, 1881.

We have met on this sad day to pay the last tribute of respect to our departed President. Fifty million people to-day in this great country are uniting with us in this memorial, and even from foreign shores comes the assurance that the hearts of all mankind are with us in this reverent memorial. We come to express this tribute to the memory of the grandest man of all ages. The mightiest product of this or any other country, torn from us in the full bloom of his usefulness by the hand of an assassin, and while we contemplate this scene, we cannot but feel that there must be some disarrangement in the plans of Providence, some mighty revolution in the spheres, else why was not the bullet stayed in its progress? why was not the arm palsied that directed the blow, and the death of him whose untimely end we all mourn to-day averted?

Yet, even in this crisis, we are reminded of the words of the famous statesman and know that God reigns and that His mercies are infinite, although we may not be able to fathom the depths of His mysterious Providence.

> "God moves in a mysterious way
> His wonders to perform."

The grandeur and power of a great life, continued the speaker, is not weakened by its duration. One single act may influence all the ages. We measure life by what it accomplishes. The history of this man and his success lies in the fact that he was the embodiment of all that was grand, noble and pure in human life. Around his suffering bed gathered the hearts of fifty millions of people. Up from the hearts of the great American Nation arose the prayer, "Oh, if it be possible, let this cup pass from us, nevertheless, not my will, but thine be done."

His history was not a long one. He was born on the 19th of November, 1831, and left an orphan at 2 years. He supported his widowed mother by manly toil, and thus gained that strength of body and mind which carried him to the highest place in the gift of this Republic.

His progress was steady from the tow-path to the presidential chair, the highest gift in the province of any people or any nation. He was a man of great intellectual endowment and fine physique. He could take his stand in the front rank of the intellects of the age. He was a laborious man—a toiler. The industry which characterized him in his youth, when he cut 100 cords of wood for $25 and gave the money to his mother, characterized him in his public life, and as Congressman Havens remarked, "He was the most laborious man in the halls of Congress." He was a man characterized by virtues and upright habits. He carried these habits throughout his life. He was, however, a man of deep convictions. He said: "There is one with whom I must always be on good terms. I am compelled to walk with him, eat with him, sleep with him —I mean myself." He meant his conscience, and he lived up to this life-rule.

When preaching in Washington I never missed Garfield on Sunday from his seat in the house of worship. When we were about to leave Mentor, Garfield's voice could be heard above all the voices singing: "All hail the power of Jesus' name."

That was James A. Garfield's great nature. He was a Christian in the highest sense of the term. It made him a faithful and loving son, a devoted husband and father, and a true friend. He was the most perfect man physically, morally, intellectually and spiritually, that the ages have ever produced.

From this we may learn the great lesson that politics may be pure. James A. Garfield's life demonstrates the fact that a man may be a Christian and a politician and a statesman at the same time. We may learn that the American people will hold in their hearts a noble aim and an honorable life. It will teach future aspirants that if they would attain to the highest place of honor they must be men of virtue and integrity. We learn further the lesson that it is in the power of the humblest to attain positions of honor. This great country offers such hopes to every young man in the United States.

The grandest achievement of our sainted President lay in the fact that he was an humble follower of the lowly Savior. The American heart beats toward the Savior as the rightful ruler over human consciences. He could look down to the dark valley—it had no terrors for him.

Death had been robbed of its sting. Our beloved chieftain passed away in the hope guaranteed by the Lord Jesus Christ—the hope of a better life. In conclusion, the speaker volunteered other eloquent tributes to Garfield, who had been a member of his church, and whom he had known personally, and preached to in Washington.

A chorus of school children, led by Major White, sang beautifully: "Mark the tolling of the bell."

THE LAMENTED PRESIDENT.

By Hon. Roger A. Pryor.

Delivered at a meeting of Union and Confederate soldiers, in Brooklyn, Sept. 22, 1881.

Mr. Chairman:—I have a melancholy pleasure in participating in this demonstration of respect to the memory of our lamented President, and in uniting with the Nation in its expression of anguish over the bereavement that has befallen it.

Gen. Garfield was a person of such amiable and engaging virtues, and was in every way so worthy of the felicity awaiting him in his exalted station, that his sudden fall smites us with the shock of a cruel disappointment. Just chosen to the Chief Magistracy of the Republic by the acclaiming voice of his countrymen, endowed with every faculty essential to the successful discharge of its duties, and cheered and sustained by the support of the people, he would have achieved among the rulers of the earth an honorable and an imperishable fame, and would have transmitted his name to posterity in association with the illustrious men who have imparted dignity and renown to the American Union.

But, untimely though his end may seem, he had lived long enough for his own glory. He cannot be said to perish prematurely, who has already fulfilled the offices of civic and of martial life, and who has blazoned his name with the double lustre of the statesman and the soldier. And while, had he survived, the passions of party might have obscured the radiance of his character, and have eclipsed somewhat the splendor of his career, he sinks now amidst the universal lamentations of the people and in the full effulgence of an unclouded promise. The stroke that removes him from the scene consecrates him in the heart of the Nation, lends a tragic pathos to his fate, and invests his memory with the halo of a sacrificial offering. Hereafter, as often as men shall revert to the incidents of this catastrophe, and the sad story will be a theme of undying interest, they will accord to the martyr the tear of pity and the homage of veneration.

But while, as short-sighted mortals, we are confounded by the blow which shatters so many cherished hopes and affronts our imperfect sense of justice, let us not mistrust the wisdom and benevolence of the overruling Providence; but let us, rather, piously confide that from the cloud of calamity will issue a blessing to the Nation. Already, in the manifestations of mourning prevalent throughout the South, we discern the tokens of that union of hearts which is the surest safeguard of the union of States. And who will repel the fond belief that in the presence of this awful catastrophe, the clamor of sectional contention will be softened and subdued into an accordant strain of fraternal sympathy; and that around the bier of our departed President the scattered children of the household will be gathered into the embrace of a reconciled and reunited family. So may it be, and the life of the Republic be as invulnerable and immortal as the career of its chief was brief and precarious!

IN LONDON.

Minister LOWELL's Address in Exeter Hall.

[Among those present were the Spanish and Brazilian Ministers, the Belgian and Russian Charge d'Affaires, the Brazilian, Belgian and Chinese Secretaries of Legation, the military attache of the German Embassy, Mr. John Bard, Mr. Fish, late Minister to Berne, Mr. Seligman, Mr. Thomas Hughes, the Count of Montebello, the Lady Maynes and ex-Senator Miller of Georgia.]

WE meet to testify our respect for the character and services of the late President, and to offer such consolation as is possible to the noble widow, suffering as few women have ever been called upon to suffer. It seems a paradox, but the only alleviation of our grief is the sense of the greatness and costliness of the sacrifice that has caused it.

It is no exaggeration to say that the recent profoundly touching spectacle of womanly devotedness has moved the heart of mankind in a manner unprecedented. To Americans everywhere it comes home with a pang of mingled sorrow and pride, and of unspeakable tenderness that none but ourselves can feel. Yet you will all agree that the feeling of universal sympathy expressed here by all classes has made us sensible, as never before, that we are in a strange, but not in a foreign, land; that we are at least in what Hawthorne called the old home.

I should do injustice to your feelings, no less than to my own, if I did not offer here our grateful acknowledgments to the august lady who, herself not unacquainted with grief, has shown so repeatedly and touchingly how a true woman's heart can beat under the royal purple.

Rhetoric relative to President Garfield's noble end is out of the question. If we were allowed to follow the promptings of our own hearts we should sum all up in the sacred words, "Well done, good and faithful servant."

The death scene was unexampled. The whole civilized world gathered about it. Let us thank God that it was through the manliness, the patience and the religious fortitude of the noble victim that the tie of human brotherhood was thrilled.

That "touch of nature that makes the whole world kin," is the touch of heroism, our sympathy with which dignifies and ennobles.

When dying, though there were few from whom death wrenched a richer heritage, there were few who would, like Garfield, die well daily for eleven weeks. The fibre that could stand such a strain is only used in the making of heroic natures. Gen. Garfield, twenty years ago, offered his life for his country. He has now died for her as truly as if he had fallen dead then. His blood has cemented the fabric of the Union; his example is a stimulus to his countrymen forever.

Like the career of Joseph, Garfield had a similar humble beginning, and has died the tenant of an office second to none on earth.

It would be improper to discuss the character of him who is now our Chief Magistrate, but there is no indecorum in saying, what is known to all, that he is a gentleman of high intelligence and of unimpeachable character and ability.

I am not a believer that a democratic more than any other form of government will work of itself, but in common with you all, I have imperturbable faith in the honesty intelligence and good sense of the American people and in the destiny of the American Republic. Gen. Garfield once said to me: "There may be a defect in my character, but I never could hate anybody."

Resolutions deploring the great public misfortune of a death which plunged a nation in lasting sorrow, sympathizing with the late President's mother and widow, and acknowledging the affectionate solicitude of the Queen and people of England, were adopted in solemn silence, all the audience rising to their feet.

Eloquent speeches were made by ex-Collector Merritt of New York, Bishop Simpson, Rev. Mr. Channing, Junius S. Morgan, Moncure D. Conway, and others.

PERSONAL TRIBUTES TO GEN. GARFIELD.

JOHN G. WHITTIER—THE POET.//
Amesbury, Mass.

AND now, when South and North, Democrat and Republican, radical and conservative, lift their voices in one unbroken chord of lamentation; when I see how, in spite of greed of gain, lust of office, strifes and meanness of party politics, the great heart of the Nation proves sound and loyal, I feel a new hope for the Republic, I have a firmer faith in its stability. It is said that no man liveth to himself, and the pure and noble life of Garfield, and his slow, long martyrdom, so bravely borne in view of all, are, I believe, bearing for us as a people "the peaceable fruits of righteousness." We are stronger, wiser, better for them.

THE LORD BISHOP OF MONTREAL.
In St. George's Church, Montreal, Canada.

A WARNING voice strikes on the ear from the death-scene of one who filled a large space in the eye of the world. The late President of the United States, struck down by the hand of a dastardly assassin—" the dead yet speaketh." The chosen head of a great nation—the grandeur of his simple, upright character, illustrated by a life of fearless courage and a death of Christ-like patience, presses on our hearts by his premature and violent death the wisdom of considering the shortness of time, and of working while it is called "to-day." The true patriot—the ardency of his affection, adorned by filial piety and domestic faithfulness, appeals touchingly to our tenderest sympathies, exhorting to kindness, gentleness, love—"seeing that here we have no continuing city."

My object at present is further to speak a few words of the late noble President. I said just now that his was a premature death—it seems so to us; seeing that he had only numbered fifty years, and had just entered with wisdom and confidence on a course that bade fair to promote the best interests of the great nation over whose destinies he was called to preside. Yet it was not premature. We have faith in God. The President's work was done, and well done. His life measured by his active usefulness, was a long life. He had finished the work God had given him to do; and when we see by the light of eternity, we shall see that the very time and place, and way were the best for his departure from this existence. We are sure of this, for the Christian world was on its knees supplicating for the President's life; with us not only was there public prayer, but also, as I visited in various missions, in family and social prayer, there was a petition for the President, and a cry for help, and strength and comfort from God for those who waited in terrible anxiety and anguish on the issue of the struggle between life and death. His death was not premature. The senseless cruelty of the act drew the attention of the world, and the worth of the victim gave to the world a splendid lesson of all that is great in man of goodness, courage, manliness, energy, virtue, combined with trust in God—a lesson to which history will point, saying to princes and rulers, "Go and do thou likewise." I dare not draw aside the curtain that hides yet tells of the grief of that stricken home. We will each pray, and unitedly pray—" O God, of Thine infinite mercy bind up the broken heart, heal the wounded spirit, minister to the afflicted ones that strong consolation which Thine own tender and wise hand alone can bestow."

A CLASS-MATE'S REMINISCENCES.

DR. FRANKLIN NOBLE, Washington, D. C.

My words can add nothing to his fame. I am honored that I can say I knew him. I met him first when he was entering Williams College. One could see that he was poor. He began poor, and never had time to grow rich. His slender property refuted the slander of corruption. With his talents and opportunities he remained poor, only because he would not take money corruptly. He made his way independently, but if he leaves his family rich it is by the gifts of a grateful people. But he was rich in cordiality. His smile as he held out his hand in our first meeting was the same as when I saw him last, just before he was stricken down. He was hearty and princely in hospitality and cordial friendliness. In college he soon took high rank. His honorary graduating oration on "The Seen and the Unseen," suggests that he reached the heights of scholarship. He was called the best, read historian in Congress. His speeches are original and suggestive.

He entered college a Christian ; his voice was heard in prayer-meetings, and he worked with Hammond, the evangelist, in a backwoods mission Sunday school. Twenty-five years ago last 4th of July, a company of students spent the night on Mount Greylock. As they were lying down to sleep Garfield said : " Boys, I read a chapter in the Bible every night with my mother. If you please, I will read it aloud," and afterward he asked the oldest of them to lead in prayer.

One Sunday, some years ago, I preached here. He learned of it and came, bringing two classmates to hear me, and as we went away his talk was a pleasant and discriminating criticism of my sermon.

But the best witness is his pastor's—that he was regular and faithful in his own church. That was the every-day religion that was at call when he was laid low, and that did not fail him in the face of death. And by such men the country is saved; such integrity and broad statesmanship as his influencing other statesmen and elevating all. Some thought Christ's life of no avail in a wicked world: and some say, "What avails one good and wise man?" It avails much. God does not make such men in vain.

After a while men will speak of Garfield along with Lincoln and Washington. His life and character will be wrought into the Nation's life and character. They will quote his speeches—especially, I think, those of the summer of 1880—with Washington's farewell address and Lincoln's Gettysburg speech. Men who fail to admire him will be ashamed to say so. The land is to be saved by largeness and greatness like his. There are also personal lessons to us each one. They are:

First—The worth of work. Garfield worked during college vacations. I knew him to work all night. His so-called "luck" was hard, unceasing work.

Second—The worth of prayer. He was no stranger to prayer; and when he fell the Nation fell to praying without hesitation. Even Ingersoll is said to have said—"God help us." We have learned a habit of prayer.

Third—the worth of a complete character. Work and prayer make a complete man. Such was he. Such a one is useful in affairs, peaceful in the face of death, blessed in the memory of men. Such may we be.

A FELLOW STUDENT'S RECOLLECTIONS.

I. A. EDSON, D.D., Indianapolis, Ind.

THE demands of an era like this will perhaps be met most fully if each tries frankly to say that which lies nearest to his own personality. It is too early to treat the theme exhaustively or elaborately. This man belongs to history and to the race. No small clan of partisans could encircle his greatness while he lived; no sect, or party, or people has proprietorship of him now that he is dead. A student, a teacher, a clergyman, a soldier, a statesman, the President, with mother, wife and children around him, touched noble life at every point, and handled nothing which he did not dignify and adorn.

My own immediate knowledge of James A. Garfield was as a fellow student at Williams College. In the autumn of 1852, entering as sophomore, I was lodged in old West College, at the southwest corner of the second floor, with Phineas W. Hitchcock, who, having served as United States Senator from Nebraska, died suddenly last July. Across the the narrow hall, with another student from New York Mills, was Garfield's class-maté, Ferdinand, now Colonel Rockwell, one of the prominent and beautiful figures of this chamber of suffering and death. After two years, arrived the future President, entering his class as junior and accompanied from the West by an associate who walked with crutches—the complete physical contrast of his vigorous and symmetrical roommate, though intellectual sympathy furnished ample grounds for the close companionship. The two made a striking pair. For a time they sat with us at Mrs. Tyler's table.

Without delay Garfield won respect and admiration. Already he had that marvelous friendliness of manner which afterward conquered everything. He was transparent and natural. He had the habits of morality and religion. His mind possessed both breadth and symmetry. He was powerful in debate. His chosen objects he pursued with tremendous energy and enthusiasm. Long before a year had passed he was a recognized leader. There were manifold prophecies of coming eminence. And the man left College, as he was to leave Congress, without an enemy."

GEN. SIBLEY'S TRIBUTE.

St. Paul, Sept. 26, 1881.

FELLOW-CITIZENS:—We have met together this day to perform our part of a sad and solemn duty. In common with millions of our countrymen at this hour, when the lifeless body of the late president of the Republic is being entombed in the city of Cleveland, we assemble to mourn his untimely death, and to evince our profound respect for for his memory. It seems but a little time since his inauguration, when his clarion voice gave utterance to patriotic sentiments which thrilled the public heart, and inspired the conviction that he would rise above all sectional and party trammels, and administer the government with a single eye to the general welfare.

Less than four months had elapsed when the horror and consternation, not only of our citizens, but of foreign nations, and in a time of peace and general prosperity, the bullet of a base and cowardly assassin found a lodgment in the vitals of the president and closed his earthly existence, after a gallant struggle for life of nearly three months of fearful suffering. During this interval, the solicitude of our people for his recovery was universal, and alternate hope and fear agitated them with emotion as tender and touching as though manifested by a loving mother at the bedside of her sick child. But the fiat of the most high had gone forth, and the prayers of united Christendom were unavailing to save the life of the illustrious sufferer.

It does not become us to seek to penetrate the mysteries of the infinite, or to be wise above what is written. With resignation to His will who holds in His hand the destinies of nations, we are permitted to extract some consolation from the event we so much deplore. It has had the effect to bring together in the close bonds of a common grief, the North, the South, the East and the West, to soften and diminish sectional and party animosities; to quicken the national conscience; to waft us back to the faith of our fathers, and to make us realize more vividly that "The Lord God omnipotent reigneth."

While, therefore, we join in lamenting the loss the country has sustained, deeply sympathizing with the aged mother, the devoted widow and the bereaved children in their affliction, let us take comfort in the reflection that the nation moves on to accomplish its general mission, unchecked and unimpeded even by the death of its best. God save the Republic!

GARFIELD'S DEATH AND ITS LESSONS.

By REV. J. P. BODFISH, delivered in the Cathedral of the Holy Cross, Boston, Sept. 25, 1881.

It is a solemn thing to stand at any time in the presence of death. The sight of marks of mourning upon the door, our entrance into the darkened chamber, and our meeting with the sorrowful, grief-stricken family, are all intended to chasten and subdue our hearts.

These seasons of mourning should not go by unheeded. They should teach us that all things earthly are vanity, ending in death. To-day we are called upon to witness an extraordinary sight. It is not alone one family we see in mourning, not alone one circle of relatives bowed down in grief, but truly and sincerely a nation weeps. How keenly we realize that we are all members of that one nation, of one body politic, and when its head is stricken low the whole body is affected. The great and noble man who so lately presided over its destinies is gone. Noble son of a worthy mother, fighting against poverty, with a strong ambition to do good deeds—when we think of the struggle he made to educate himself, to prepare himself for public life, we recognize in him only the able, just man, who aimed at nothing but the Nation's good.

After his labors, then, to fit himself for the highest gift in the Nation, we see him cut down by an assassin's hand, and a whole country agonized throughout its length and breadth. I should be wanting in my duty to-day, if I did not, as the occasion suggests, pay my tribute to this good man, and strive to derive from his sad death some of the great lessons which Providence teaches us.

As Catholics and members of the Roman Church, not only do we join with our neighbors in the general grief, but we have a special horror at the act that has been committed. We should remember that the Catholic Church has been, throughout the world and the world's history, the bulwark of civil order, and she has at all times urged upon her children to do their part in preserving civil law and civil government. Often have prelates and priests of our church been called upon to aid in the preservation of constitutional authority, and they have always responded, though it be at the peril of their lives.

When we find socialism, communism or the spoils system culminating in the assassination of a good man, there is no heart so profoundly shocked as the Catholic heart.

And there are many lessons to be drawn from the occurrence. It shows us that we are one; that, in the presence of death we are all united; that partisan bitterness and even sectional strife is hushed beneath the sorrow of one common affliction. In the record of this man, who was so distinctively an American statesman, and so natural an outcome of our glorious American institutions, we are taught that good men and true are appreciated.

What a lesson to young men, growing up under the fostering care of American civilization! Would you be beloved by your fellow-citizens, and your death mourned by a nation? Then imitate the illustrious dead. Be a man, good and true and without reproach, and the end will surely be a glorious one. "God reigns, and the government still lives," said Garfield. And the government does live, and may all honest and intelligent citizens of every creed and race and color join to-day in a renewed act of consecration to those institutions which have done so much to develop liberty and fraternity among us.

MRS. GARFIELD.

See her, like a ministering angel, by day and by night at his side, bearing up to the last with undaunted courage. See her, with a true, womanly reserve, shrinking from all publicity; and see her, alone by his bier, still hiding her sorrow, whose depth no man can fathom, no mind contemplate, but God's.

What a lesson to Catholic women! What a lesson to every young woman, and to every wife and mother! Throughout the whole civilized world there is not a heart, however stern, but will do her the honor she so richly deserves. It is the lesson of the true wife and mother. These are the qualities the world honors; this is woman's sphere, indeed, and this the sacred duty she alone can fulfill. Ah, my dear friends, remember, in the hour of your own affliction, the wife and mother who will sit by your side and smooth your pillow. Honor, and love and cherish her, for she is truly the angel of your household through all your days. Let us, then, mourn over the Nation's dead, and pray with fervor, for we have, as our text tells us, "lost some great heart." Let us pray that the children of the dead President may grow up in usefulness and strength, following in the footsteps of their father, and by the light of their good lives cheering and sustaining their heart-broken mother. Let us, too, not forget that aged, grief-stricken woman, who, parting with the cherished son of her bosom, sees her "darling boy" brought back to her a corpse. And, in all our prayers, in all our grief, let us take to heart the lessons of the calamity that has overtaken us, and so strive to conduct ourselves that the reward to come may be ours through eternity.

A PUPIL'S TRIBUTE.

BY F. E. UDELL, one of Garfield's Students at Hiram College.

Delivered at the Memorial Services in St. Louis, Sept. 26, 1881.

For nearly thirty years I have had an intimate acquaintance with Mr. Garfield. As a member of the same household, as a fellow-student, as a pupil, in our church relations as a member of the same congregation, and later associated with him as trustees of Hiram College and a constituent and supporter is his congressional district, I have had opportunities, such as perhaps no other person present, of an intimate knowledge of his inner life, of his school days and his young manhood.

I first went to Hiram College, then the "Western Reserve Eclectic Institute," in 1853, and there first met James A. Garfield. He was at that time a student at this school, and also teaching a few classes to pay his way. I remember him as a stout, hale, well developed young man of twenty-one, plainly clad, but of striking physique and bearing. He was a hard student, burning the midnight oil for six nights in the week, and by thus applying himself to his studies, he in three years' time crowded six years of study, and thus in this short space of time fitted himself to enter the junior class, besides at the same time teaching for his support. To accomplish this he shut the whole world out from his mind, save that portion within the range of his studies, knowing little of the news of the day, reading no light literature, and engaging in no social recreations that took his time from his books.

As a student and as a scholar of great promise, he had no equals in that school, and in native ability and already acquired brilliancy he stood head and shoulders above his classmates, and was often spoken of in laudatory terms by all who knew him. But notwithstanding all this—and he was certainly conscious of his attainments—he was never susceptible to flattery, never exhibited the least arrogance, but was as humble as when a boy he supported his widowed mother by the sweat of his brow, unconscious of the latent possibilities of that great head and heart.

As a teacher he was unexcelled. How vividly can I now see that manly form, with his large, well-developed head, standing on the platform before his class, chalk in hand, his pleasant luminous face, and clear silvery voice, explaining and demonstrating the problem before him. He was *par excellence* the best teacher I ever recited to, and he was loved by all his pupils. I might also speak of his forensic powers, at this early period of his life, in the literary society of the school, and also of his occasional addresses in the church, but time forbids; suffice to say, he was then as in later life a fluent speaker and a devoted earnest Christian.

It would have been a source of gratification to me to have been at Cleveland to-day and to have dropped a tear on his casket, but it affords me a still greater satisfaction to be here in the quiet of this sympathizing brotherhood to testify to his great worth and his Christian manhood, and the love and adoration I bore him, and with you to weep over his grave. It is not so much for the dead President I mourn as the dead Garfield. Others eulogized him for his great statesmanship, his nobility of character and his well-developed manhood. I loved and reverenced him most because he had a warm, loving heart, because of his nobility of soul, and because he was a true friend. Most men, when elevated to high positions, grow away from the humble friends of their earlier days. Not so with Jas. A. Garfield.

I shall never forget the hearty greeting with which he always met an acquaintance in his school days, and to feel the grasp of that honest, sturdy hand impressed you that you had met one of God's noblemen. And all through the years since then, no matter what station he occupied, or how weighed down with the labors and responsibilities of his office, this quality of the man has ever remained the same. Any son of toil who had known him in his earlier life could approach him without the least embarrassment or trepidation, and would be met by that same warm, cordial greeting as in days of yore. In his presence you would forget he was the leader of his party in the house, that he was Senator or that he was President, and for the moment he would be to you your old, kind, big-hearted friend Garfield.

I deem it the greatest honor of my life to have had his acquaintance and friendship, and to have been his pupil, and as to-day I see the whole world moved to affectionate tears over the death of this one man, as never in the history of civilization they were moved before, it is with a thrill of justifiable pride that I can say of my own personal knowledge of the man, he was worthy of all these honors, and I thank God that such a man has lived and left the impress of this grand life upon this and all succeeding generations, and that it is my privilege, with the other fifty millions of our free America, besides the millions in other lands, to give expression to the sorrow I feel over the death of the President—the statesman, the Christian—my friend.

A WISE MAN.

By Rev. Dr. Sprole.

Delivered at the Memorial Service in the First Street Presbyterian Church, Detroit, Mich., Sept. 26, 1881.

Among those present was Solomon Davis, who now resides at 760 Jefferson avenue When but seven years of age he, with his father in Vermont, attended the funeral services of George Washington, and, wherever held, has attended those of every deceased President of the United States. This circumstance was mentioned by Dr. Pierson, and all eyes were turned to the pew where sat the venerable man whose personal recollection extend back into the eighteenth century.

The inspired record tells us that when Stephen fell by the ungodly, devout men carried him to burial and made great lamentation over his mutilated form. We are engaged to-day in these solemn services, while others, devout and undevout, are carrying to their last resting place the remains of our beloved President. He was cut off from his usefulness at a time when it was most desirable that he should live; at a time when desire for continued life was a righteous emotion. He had disappointed the hopes of his enemies and surprised his friends by the wisdom he displayed in the high office.

God directed us in the choice of our Chief Magistrate, and when his sun was shining in all its noon-tide glory, it was extinguished. Why is this? It is one of God's mysteries, and He alone can unravel it. "What I do thou knowest not now, but thou shalt know hereafter." It is no wonder that the people of our and other Christian lands mourn his taking off. But few equaled him in those elements that make man the image of his Maker. His distinguishing characteristic was his great loving heart. Though sorely tried, it never failed.

The elevation of James A. Garfield to the Presidential chair did not change his character. As a teacher of a country school; President of a College; taking up arms in defense of his country; in the halls of Congress, in the Presidential chair; while hanging upon the borders of the grave for weeks, he ever manifested the same gentle, loving spirit. How touching are the thoughtfully worded telegrams sent to his mother and wife, calming and soothing their fears. Such a man! Such a loss! I can't quite understand it. Did I not know the wisdom and goodness of God, I might question its right; but I dare not do it.

Why did God keep him hanging there so long on the brink of the grave? It might be to prepare the Nation for the great loss it was to suffer. It might be to start the tears of the Nation from the mountains to the great waters, and cement more closely the brotherhood of States. It may have been to bring the hearts of trans-Atlantic nations closer to us. It has had its practical lesson, for it has demonstrated that our Nation does not hang upon the life of a single individual.

The Rev. D. M. Cooper then read, and the choir sang the following dirge from the pen of D. Bethune Duffield:

I.

Toll,
Aye toll, ye mournful bells,
A world-wide passing knell
Toll for a hero's soul.

II.

Drape,
And sadly drop the flag

A WISE MAN.

Half-mast o'er land and sea,
   And bind each door with crape.

III.

Weep,
Ye stricken people weep,
Around the hallowed bier
   Of Garfield's silent sleep.

IV.

Great,
Sublimely great and brave
Was this our chosen chief,
   In battle or debate.

V.

Love,
Whole-souled, deep love was his,
For country, home and truth,
   Like to that love above.

VI.

Write
Amid the stars and stripes—
Write high his worthy name,
   'T will make the stars more bright.

VII.

Praise,
Yes, praise the Lord on high,
For all he was to us,
   While heavenward we gaze.

VIII.

Well,
"He doeth all things well,"
For age to distant age
   His name and fame shall tell.

IX

Fears,
No, not one fear for him,
Nor for our smitten land,
   Tho' flood-like fall our tears.

X.

Toll,
Yes, toll, ye mournful bells,
And roll, ye muffled drums,
Farewell, oh, noble soul,
           Farewell.

MEMORY.

BY JAMES A. GARFIELD.

This little poem, from the pen of the President, was written before his first term in Congress—hence some twenty years ago. At that time, possibly, the Presidency of a Christian college was the "summit where the sunbeams fell," but the last lines are all but a prophecy:

'Tis beauteous night; the stars look brightly down
Upon the earth, decked in her robe of snow.
No light gleams at the window, save my own,
Which gives its cheer to midnight and to me.
And now, with noiseless step, sweet memory comes,
And leads me gently through her twilight realms.
What poet's tuneful lyre has ever sung,
Or delicate pen e'er portrayed,
The enchanted, shadowy land where memory dwells?
It has its valleys, cheerless, lone and drear,
Dark-shaded by the mournful cypress tree;
And yet its sunlit mountain tops are bathed
In heaven's own blue. Upon its craggy cliffs,
Robed in the dreamy light of distant years,
Are clustered joys serene of other days;
Upon its gentle, sloping hillsides bend
The weeping willows o'er the sacred dust
Of dear departed ones; and yet in that land,
Where'er our footsteps fall upon the shore,
They that were sleeping rise from out the dust

Of death's long, silent years, and round us stand,
As erst they did before the prison tomb
Received their clay within its voiceless halls.
The heavens that bend above that land are hung
With clouds of various hues. Some dark and chill,
Surcharged with sorrow, cast with somber shade
Upon the sunny, joyous land below.
Others are floating through the dreamy air,
White as the falling snow, their margins tinged
With gold and crimsoned hues; their shadows fall
Upon the flowery meads and sunny slopes,
Soft as the shadow of an angel's wing.
When the rough battle of the day is done,
And evening's peace falls gently on the heart,
I bound away, across the noisy years,
Unto the utmost verge of memory's land,
Where earth and sky in dreamy distance meet,
And memory, dim with dark oblivion, joins,
Where woke the first remembered sounds that fell
Upon the ear in childhood's early morn;
And, wandering thence along the rolling years,
I see the shadow of my former self,
Gliding from childhood up to man's estate.
The path of youth winds down through many a vale
And on the brink of many a dread abyss,
From out whose darkness comes no ray of light,
Save that a phantom dances o'er the gulf
And beckons toward the verge. Again the path
Leads o'er the summit where the sunbeams fall;
And thus in light and shade, sunshine and gloom,
Sorrow and joy, the life-path leads along.

THE END.

www.ingramcontent.com/pod-product-compliance
Lightning Source LLC
Chambersburg PA
CBHW030321020526
44117CB00030B/319